T0289052

TOTAL PRAISE

Songs and Other Worship Resources
for Every Generation

GIA Publications, Inc.

Sunday School Publishing Board

G-8050

Copyright © 2011 by GIA Publications, Inc. and
Sunday School Publishing Board, administered by GIA.

GIA Publications, Inc.
7404 South Mason Avenue
Chicago, IL 60638
(800) 442-1358
www.giamusic.com

Sunday School Publishing Board
330 Charlotte Avenue
Nashville, TN 37201
(800) 359-9398
www.sspbnbc.com

International copyright secured. All rights reserved.
Printed in the United States of America.

Scriptures taken from the *Holy Bible, New International Version*® NIV®
Copyright © 1973, 1978, 1984 by Biblica, Inc.™
Used by permission. All rights reserved worldwide.

Despite extensive efforts to determine the copyright ownership of the selections included
in this hymnal, at press time the source of some material remains unknown. Believing
that hymn writers ultimately intend their creations to be sung in divine worship, we
chose to include this material with the intent that acknowledgment will be made in
future editions and appropriate royalties paid as such information becomes available.

Dr. Julius R. Scruggs, President, National Baptist Convention, USA, Inc.
Dr. Kelly M. Smith Jr., Executive Director, Sunday School Publishing Board
Mrs. Kathlyn T. Pillow, Associate Director, Sunday School Publishing Board
Rev. Debra Berry, Director of Publishing Administration, Sunday School Publishing
   Board
Dr. Sherman R. Tribble, Editor
Mrs. Tanae C. McKnight Murdic, Copy Editor

Cover design by Donn S. Jobe

Also available: G-8050K, Accompaniment Edition

ISBN: 978-1-57999-851-6
ISBN: 978-1-57999-852-3 Pulpit Edition

8 9 10 11 12 13 14 15 16 17 18 19 20

FOREWORD

In the *Baptist Standard Hymnal*, which was published in the early part of the twentieth century and subsequently reissued, Dr. Arthur M. Townsend, Executive Secretary of the Sunday School Publishing Board, shared this sentiment about that work:

> One of the most serious concerns of our churches today is to promote good wholesome singing, and it is very evident that much education is needed along this line. Together with good preaching and good praying goes good singing, and in no better way can the churches hope to promote their spiritual growth...after deliberate consideration [there is] the urgent need of such a song book.[1]

In the twenty-first century, we still need singing that is biblically based, doctrinally sound, and life-centered. And we believe that this goal is accomplished in this new publication, *Total Praise: Songs and Other Worship Resources for Every Generation*.

We congratulate Dr. Kelly M. Smith Jr., Executive Director, Dr. Sherman R. Tribble, Associate Director of Book Publishing, the Sunday School Publishing Board staff, the talented national committee, and others for bringing this resource to our churches. Such a work is long overdue and can only enhance our work in the national church and the local church, as well as promote individual piety. We not only heartily endorse this work, but also urge each church to carefully and prayerfully use this volume to assist in praising God.

Julius R. Scruggs, President
National Baptist Convention, USA, Inc.
June 2011

---

[1] Publisher's Note, *Baptist Standard Hymnal with Responsive Readings*, Townsend Press: Nashville, TN, 1985, p. 4.

A NOTE FROM THE PUBLISHER

Praise God from whom all blessings flow!

It is a tremendous blessing for the Sunday School Publishing Board to present to you *Total Praise: Songs and Other Worship Resources for Every Generation*. This is a work that is long overdue, in regards to the products we have produced over the last several years. There have been efforts over the years to try to bring a hymnal project to fruition, but for one reason or another it never completely materialized. But we have never lost sight of how music and hymnody have played important roles in and impacted the lives of all of our religious experiences. That richness of music has been intertwined with our faith journey, even from the native lands of our foreparents.

Music has become a sincere expression of our faith. Even when we are not able to always give a clear, verbal articulation of our faith, there seems to always be a song that fits the times, the mood, and the circumstance. From a new birth in Christ to a continuing journey in Christ, there is a hymn for it. From experiences of victory to seasons of struggle, there is a spiritual melody for it. From an attitude of praise to postures of prayer, there is a sacred song for it. From stances of patriotism to positions of protest, there is a musical expression for it. From the cradle to the grave, there is a spiritual song for it.

The people of Israel understood this, thus giving us such a wealth in their own songbook—the book of Psalms. It is hoped that as treasured as that book was to them (and even to us now) you will find our hymnal, *Total Praise*, to be as rich and rewarding. Our intent for this hymnal is not simply to give you songs to sing, but to provide for you a resource for worship that we know will aid you in various aspects of worship.

We believe this is Christ speaking to us. It is to nurture, aid, and guide us as we face the many facets of life and seek to address them through worship. The apostle Paul reminded us of the importance of such a resource in the book of Colossians, where he stated, "Let the word of Christ dwell in you richly as you teach and admonish one another with all wisdom, and as you sing psalms, hymns and spiritual songs with gratitude in your hearts to God" (Colossians 3:16, NIV).

We thank Dr. Sherman R. Tribble, Associate Director of Book Publishing, others who are resident staff of the Sunday School Publishing Board, and the hymnal committee for the hard and diligent work they put into the marvelous work. We thank those who are a part of GIA Publications for their facilitation of the project. We thank the National Baptist Convention, USA, Inc.—Dr. Julius R. Scruggs, President—for their support of the project. We give "total praise" to God for His grace and mercy over all that we do.

May we be blessed by what God has made available to us through this hymnal.

Kelly M. Smith Jr.
Executive Director
Sunday School Publishing Board
In the year of our Lord 2011

PREFACE

The psalmist raised a timeless rhetorical query: "How shall we sing the Lord's song in a strange land?" Whereas there was no answer directly given in this passage, believers of biblical times and in subsequent ages have provided their own responses: they raised their voices in total praise to God, believing that praise was a reflection of their redemption. This is the stream out of which this work springs. *Total Praise: Songs and Other Worship Resources for Every Generation* seeks to offer believers resources through which they can express their adoration to God.

Why publish another hymnal? There are many good books in print for the modern age. We believe that *Total Praise* will not only be an excellent tool for singing congregations in a classic sense of hymnody, but that also it will assist in the planning of worship, as well as provide print resources for choir directors and praise-team leaders. Thus, we have included songs of a number of genres. There are classic and majestic hymns, there are historic gospel songs, and there are modern praise choruses. We can literally claim that our work spans from Beethoven to Watts to Crosby to Dorsey to Smallwood to Kurt Carr. While we have sought to be comprehensive, the work is not exhaustive. Yet we consider this a seminal work that should be used by congregations in the National Baptist Convention, USA, Inc., sister congregations of other denominations, as well as individuals for their own devotion and spiritual development.

Such a work would not have come to fruition without the vision of our leadership, the work of many very hardworking persons, the support of our Corporate Board, the partnership of GIA Publications, and the interest of the member churches of the National Baptist Convention, USA, Inc. We certainly thank former President William J. Shaw and our current chieftain, Dr. Julius R. Scruggs, for their unstinting support. We are grateful for the leadership and vision of our esteemed Executive Director, Dr. Kelly M. Smith Jr., a Morehouse-trained musician who loves worship and empowering the people of God, as well as Mrs. Kathlyn T. Pillow, Associate Director, a consummate lover of God's work who ensured that the committee had resources to accomplish the work. We thank the late Dr. John H. Rouse and the Corporate Board for giving us rein to accomplish this project. Our undying gratitude goes to the members of our committee who are listed on the next page. Their sagacious efforts and expertise in leading the worship was needed to ably shepherd this effort. Our partner in publishing this volume has been GIA Publications, Alec Harris (President), Robert J. Batastini (project director), Jeff Mickus (project coordinator and layout), and others. They have proven to be invaluable in developing this work. O for a thousand tongues to thank all of the talented persons who submitted original music and litanies to us. We appreciate your dedication to the craft, inspiration from God, and submission to our work. We also thank the people and pastors of New Visions Baptist Church of Nashville, Tennessee, pastored by the author of this statement, and Pilgrim Rest Baptist Church of Memphis, Tennessee, pastored by Dr. A. McKinley Royal, for making their facilities available for committee work. We also gratefully acknowledge the visionary work done by the Reverend Dr. Delores Carpenter and the Reverend Nolan E. Williams Jr., principal editors of the *African American Heritage Hymnal*, et al.—for *Total Praise* owes much to this earlier volume. Without the labor of all these persons, *Total Praise* would not have been possible.

As you use this book, may it be a blessing to you and those to whom you minister as you give total praise to God!

Sherman R. Tribble, Ph.D.
Associate Director of Book Publishing
Sunday School Publishing Board
National Baptist Convention, USA, Inc.

Committee Members
Dr. W. James Abbington
Rev. Stephanie Cunningham
Dr. Joyce Marie Davis
Dr. Christopher Duke
Dr. Nathan Johnson
Rev. Glenn L. Jones
Mrs. Diana Kittrell Poe
Professor James A. Scandrick Jr.

Chair and General Editor
Dr. Sherman Roosevelt Tribble

Associate Editors
Rev. Dr. Delores Carpenter
Rev. Nolan E. Williams Jr.

Project Director
Mr. Robert J. Batastini

Administrative Support Person
Ms. Sharanda N. Smith

Intern
Mr. Brandon Boyd

Ex-Officio Members
Rev. Debra Berry
Mrs. Kathlyn T. Pillow
*Dr. John H. Rouse
Dr. Julius R. Scruggs
Dr. William J. Shaw
Dr. Kelly M. Smith Jr.

Litany Writers
Dr. Jacquelyn Bragg
The Honorable Wendell Griffen
Dr. Nathan Johnson
Rev. Glenn L. Jones
Professor James A. Scandrick Jr.
Dr. Sherman R. Tribble
Rev. Vanessa M. Upshire-Tribble
Dr. Edith Winters-Kimbrough

*Deceased

ENDORSERS

The following persons, churches, and organizations are entities that enthusiastically encourage the use of *Total Praise: Songs and Other Worship Resources for Every Generation*. As members of the Christian community and the National Baptist Convention, USA, Inc. in particular, we realize the importance of having biblically and musically sound resources to assist in public worship and private devotion. Our participating in advance sales of this volume or offering other assistance is our tangible endorsement of the merits of this work. We earnestly urge churches, pastors, and individuals to purchase and use this book.

National Baptist Convention, USA, Inc.
First Missionary Baptist Church
Huntsville, Alabama
Dr. Julius R. Scruggs, Pastor
President, NBC, USA, Inc.

New Hope Baptist Church
Jackson, Mississippi
Dr. Jerry Young, Pastor
Vice President at Large

Evening Star Baptist Church
Brooklyn, New York
Dr. Washington L. Lundy, Pastor
Vice President—Northeast

Mount Calvary Baptist Church
Fairfield, California
Dr. Claybon Lea Jr., Pastor
Vice President—West

Mount Canaan Baptist Church
Shreveport, Louisiana
Dr. Harry Blake, Pastor
Vice President—Southwest

St. Luke Memorial Missionary Baptist Church
St. Louis, Missouri
Dr. Jimmy L. Brown, Pastor
Vice President—Midwest

Calvary Baptist Church
Garfield, New Jersey
Dr. Calvin McKinney, Pastor
General Secretary

New Mount Olive Baptist Church
Fort Lauderdale, Florida
Rev. Marcus D. Davidson, Pastor
Assistant Treasurer

Dr. Robert Scott Jones
Downingtown, Pennsylvania
Executive Assistant to the President

Zion Hill Baptist Church
Chicago, Illinois
Dr. George Waddles Sr., Pastor
President, Congress of Christian Education

Dr. Forrest E. Harris Sr.
Nashville, Tennessee
President, American Baptist College

Dr. Hugh Dell Gatewood
Houston, Texas
President, Woman's Auxiliary

Board of Directors
Sunday School Publishing Board
Mt. Zion Baptist Church
East St. Louis, Illinois
Dr. John H. Rouse, Pastor (Deceased)
Chairman, SSPB

St. John Baptist Church
Little Rock, Arkansas
Rev. C. Dennis Edwards, Pastor
Vice Chairman, SSPB

Baptist General Convention of Virginia
Richmond, Virginia
Rev. Cessar Scott, Executive Minister
Secretary, SSPB

First Baptist Church, Capitol Hill
Nashville, Tennessee
Dr. Kelly M. Smith Jr., Pastor
Executive Director, SSPB

Cherry Hill Missionary Baptist Church
Conway, South Carolina
Dr. James H. Cokley, Pastor

Fifteenth Avenue Baptist Church
Nashville, Tennessee
Dr. William F. Buchanan, Pastor

Mt. Pilgrim Baptist Church
Compton, California
Bishop Richard Sanders, Pastor

Mt. Zion Missionary Baptist Church
Kansas City, Kansas
Rev. C. L. Bachus, Pastor

Third New Hope Baptist Church
Detroit, Michigan
Dr. Edward L. Branch, Pastor

New Era Baptist State Convention of Nebraska
Omaha, Nebraska
Ms. Gloria J. Epps, State Director, Christian
  Education

Churches and Organizations
Emmanuel Missionary Baptist Church
Jackson, Mississippi
Dr. Jesse Horton Sr., Pastor

First Baptist Church
Gallatin, Tennessee
Rev. Derrick L. Jackson, Pastor

First Street Baptist Church
Hopkinsville, Kentucky
Rev. C. E. Timberlake, Pastor

Friendship West Baptist Church
Dallas, Texas
Dr. Freddie Haynes III, Pastor

Greater Hope Baptist Church
Buffalo, New York
Dr. James C. Blackburn, Pastor

Greater Pleasant View Baptist Church
Brentwood, Tennessee
Rev. Eric Williams, Pastor

Mt. Olive Baptist Church
Knoxville, Tennessee

Mount Pilgrim Baptist Church
Baton Rouge, Louisiana
Dr. Jesse B. Bilberry Jr., Pastor

New Visions Baptist Church
Nashville, Tennessee
Dr. Sherman R. Tribble, Pastor

Pilgrim Rest Baptist Church
Memphis, Tennessee
Dr. A. McKinley Royal, Pastor

Second Baptist Church
Elyria, Ohio
Rev. Carl P. Small, Pastor

Spruce Street Baptist Church
Nashville, Tennessee
Rev. Raymond Bowman, Pastor

St. Paul Missionary Baptist Church
Pine Bluff, Arkansas
Rev. Stephen King, Pastor

Star of Bethlehem Missionary Baptist Church
Ossining, New York
Dr. Arthur L. Lewter, Pastor

Tabernacle Missionary Baptist Church
Detroit, Michigan
Dr. Nathan Johnson, Senior Pastor

Tabernacle Community Baptist Church
Milwaukee, Wisconsin
Rev. Don Darius Butler, Pastor

Zion Baptist Church
Omaha, Nebraska
Dr. Kenneth A. Allen, Pastor

Institute on Black Sacred Music
American Baptist College
Nashville, Tennessee
Mr. James A. Scandrick Jr., Director

Tennessee Baptist Missionary and Educational
  Convention
Nashville, Tennessee
Dr. Marvin Mercer, President

Women's Auxiliary
Missionary Baptist State Convention of Missouri
St. Louis, Missouri

CONTENTS

HYMNS AND SONGS

God, Our Father

Jesus Christ

The Holy Spirit

God and the Church

Life in Christ

1. *Church Covenant*

Having been led, as we believe, by the Spirit of God to receive the Lord Jesus Christ as our Savior; and on the profession of our faith, having been baptized in the name of the Father, and of the Son, and of the Holy Spirit, we do now in the presence of God, angels and this assembly, most solemnly and joyfully enter into covenant with one another, as one body in Christ.

We engage, therefore, by the aid of the Holy Spirit, to walk together in Christian love; to strive for the advancement of this church in knowledge and holiness; to give it a place in our affections, prayers and services above every organization of human origin; to sustain its worship, ordinances, discipline and doctrine; to contribute cheerfully and regularly, as God has prospered us, toward its expenses, for the support of a faithful and evangelical ministry among us, the relief of the poor and the spread of the Gospel throughout the world. In case of difference of opinion in the church, we will strive to avoid a contentious spirit, and if we cannot unanimously agree, we will cheerfully recognize the right of the majority to govern.

We also engage to maintain family and secret devotion; to study diligently the word of God; to religiously educate our children; to seek the salvation of our kindred and acquaintance; to walk circumspectly in the world; to be kind and just to those in our employ, and faithful in the service we promise others; endeavoring in the purity of heart and good will towards all to exemplify and commend our holy faith.

We further engage to watch over, to pray for, to exhort and stir up each other unto every good word and work; to guard each other's reputation, not needlessly exposing the infirmities of others; to participate in each other's joys, and with tender sympathy bear one another's burdens and sorrows; to cultivate Christian courtesy; to be slow to give or take offense, but always ready for reconciliation, being mindful of the rules of the Savior in the eighteenth chapter of Matthew, to secure it without delay; and through life, amid evil report, and good report, to seek to live to the glory of God, who hath called us out of darkness into his marvelous light.

When we remove from this place, we engage as soon as possible to unite with some other church where we can carry out the spirit of this covenant and the principles of God's word.

2. Articles of Faith

I. The Scripture.
We believe that the Holy Bible was written by divinely inspired persons, and is a perfect treasure of heavenly instruction; that it has God for its author, salvation for its end, and truth without any mixture of error for its matter; that it reveals the principles by which God will judge us, and therefore is, and shall remain to the end of the world, the true center of Christian union, and the supreme standard by which all human conduct, creeds, and opinions shall be tried.

II. The True God.
We believe the Scriptures teach that there is one, and only one, living and true God, an infinite, intelligent Spirit, whose name is Jehovah, the Maker and Supreme Ruler of heaven and earth; inexpressibly glorious in holiness, and worthy of all possible honor, confidence and love; that in the unity of the Godhead there are three persons, the Father, the Son, and the Holy Ghost; equal in every divine perfection, and executing distinct but harmonious offices in the great work of redemption.

III. The Fall of Humanity.
We believe the Scriptures teach that Humanity was created in holiness, under the law of the Maker; but by voluntary transgressions fell from that holy and happy state; in consequence of which all humankind are now sinners, not by constraint but choice; being by nature utterly void of that holiness required by the law of God, positively inclined to evil; and therefore under just condemnation to eternal ruin, without defense or excuse.

IV. The Way of Salvation.
We believe that the Scriptures teach that the salvation of sinners is wholly of grace; through the mediatorial offices of the Son of God; who by the appointment of the Father, freely took upon him our nature, yet without sin; honored the divine law by his personal obedience, and by his death made a full atonement for our sins; that having risen from the dead, he is now enthroned in heaven; and uniting in his wonderful person the most tender of sympathies with divine perfections, he is in every way qualified to be a suitable, a compassionate, and an all-sufficient Savior.

V. Justification.
We believe the Scriptures teach that the great Gospel blessing which Christ secures to such as believe in him is justification; that justification includes the pardon of sin, and the promise of eternal life on principles of righteousness; that it is bestowed, not in consideration of any works of righteousness which we have done, but solely through faith in the Redeemer's blood; by virtue of which faith

his perfect righteousness is freely imputed to us of God; that it brings us into a state of most blessed peace and favor with God, and secures every other blessing needful for time and eternity.

VI. The Freeness of Salvation.

We believe that the Scriptures teach that the blessings of salvation are made free to all by the Gospel; that it is the immediate duty of all to accept them by cordial, penitent and obedient faith; and that nothing prevents the salvation of the greatest sinner on earth, but this person's own determined depravity and voluntary rejection of the Gospel; which rejection involves him or her in an aggravated condemnation.

VII. Regeneration.

We believe that the Scriptures teach that in order to be saved, sinners must be regenerated, or born again; that regeneration consists in giving a holy disposition to the mind that it is effected in a manner above our comprehension by the power of the Holy Spirit in connection with divine truth, so as to secure our voluntary obedience to the Gospel; and that its proper evidence appears in the holy fruits of repentance and faith, and newness of life.

VIII. Repentance and Faith.

We believe the Scriptures teach that repentance and faith are sacred duties, and also inseparable graces, wrought in our souls by the regenerating Spirit of God; whereby being deeply convinced of our guilt, danger and helplessness and of the way of salvation by Christ, we turn to God with unfeigned contrition, confession, and supplication for mercy; at the same time heartily receiving the Lord Jesus Christ as our prophet, priest and king, and relying on him alone as the only and all-sufficient Savior.

IX. God's Purpose of Grace.

We believe the Scriptures teach that election is the eternal purpose of God, according to which he graciously regenerates, sanctifies and saves sinners; that being perfectly consistent with the free agency of humankind, it comprehends all the means in connection with the end; that it is a most glorious display of God's sovereign goodness, being infinitely free, wise, holy and unchangeable; that it utterly excludes boasting and promotes humility, love, prayer, praise, trust in God, and active imitation of his free mercy; that it encourages the use of means in the highest degree; that it may be ascertained by its effects in all who truly believe the Gospel; that it is the foundation of Christian assurance; and that to ascertain it with regard to ourselves demands and deserves the utmost diligence.

X. Sanctification.

We believe the Scriptures teach that Sanctification is the process by which, according to the will of God, we are made partakers of his holiness; that it is a progressive work; that it is begun in regeneration; and that it is carried on in the hearts of believers by the presence and power of the Holy Spirit, the Sealer and Comforter, in the continual use of the appointed means especially the word of God, self-examination, self-denial, watchfulness, and prayer.

XI. Perseverance of Saints.

We believe the Scriptures teach that such only are real believers as endure to the end; that their persevering attachment to Christ is the grand mark which distinguishes them from superficial professors; that a special Providence watches over their welfare; and they are kept by the power of God through faith unto salvation.

XII. The Law and Gospel.

We believe the Scriptures teach that the Law of God is the eternal and unchangeable rule of God's moral government; that it is holy, just and good; and that the inability which the Scriptures ascribe to fallen humanity to fulfill its precepts, arise entirely from their love of sin; to deliver them from which, and to restore them through a Mediator to unfeigned obedience to the holy Law, is one great end of the Gospel, and of the Means of Grace connected with the establishment of the visible church.

XIII. A Gospel Church.

We believe the Scriptures teach that a visible church of Christ is a congregation of baptized believers, associated by covenant in the faith and fellowship of the Gospel; observing the ordinances of Christ; governed by his laws; and exercising the gifts, rights, and privileges invested in them by His Word; that its only scriptural officers are Bishops or Pastors, and Deacons whose Qualifications, claims and duties are defined in the Epistles to Timothy and Titus.

XIV. Baptism and the Lord's Supper.

We believe the Scriptures teach that Christian baptism is the immersion in water of a believer, into the name of the Father, and Son, and Holy Ghost; to show forth in a solemn and beautiful emblem, our faith in the crucified, buried, and risen Savior, with its effect, in our death to sin and resurrection to a new life; that it is prerequisite to the privileges of a church relation; and to the Lord's Supper, in which the members of the church, by the sacred use of bread and wine, are to commemorate together the dying love of Christ; preceded always by solemn self-examination.

XV. The Christian Sabbath.

We believe the Scriptures teach that the first day of the week is the Lord's Day, or Christian Sabbath, and is to be kept sacred to religious purposes, by abstaining from all secular labor and sinful recreations, by the devout observance of all the means of grace, both private and public, and by preparation for that rest that remains for the people of God.

XVI. Civil Government.

We believe the Scriptures teach that civil government is of divine appointment, for the interest and good order of human society; and that magistrates are to be prayed for, conscientiously honored and obeyed; except only in things opposed to the will of our Lord Jesus Christ, who is the only Lord of the conscience, and the Prince of the Kings of the earth.

XVII. Righteous and Wicked.

We believe the Scriptures teach that there is a radical and essential difference between the righteous and the wicked; that such only as through faith are justified in the name of the Lord Jesus, and sanctified by the Spirit of our God, are truly righteous in his esteem; while all such as continue in impenitence and unbelief are in his sight wicked, and under the curse; and this distinction holds among all persons both in and after death.

XVIII. The World to Come.

We believe the Scriptures teach that the end of the world is approaching; that at the last day, Christ will descend from heaven, and raise the dead from the grave for final retribution; that a solemn separation will then take place; that the wicked will be adjudged to endless punishment, and the righteous to endless joy; and that this judgment will fix forever the final state of humankind in heaven or hell, on principles of righteousness.

3. ANOINTING

Old Testament: Isa. 61:1–3; Ps. 23:5–6; 20:6; 1 Chr. 16:19–22; 2 Sam. 22:51

New Testament: Acts 10:36–38; 2 Cor. 1:20–22; 1 Jn. 2:27–28; Heb. 1:8–9

The Spirit of the Sovereign LORD is on me, because the LORD has anointed me to preach good news to the poor.

He has sent me to bind up the broken-hearted, to proclaim freedom for the captives and release from darkness for the prisoners,

To proclaim the year of the LORD's favor and the day of vengeance of our God,

To comfort all who mourn, and provide for those who grieve in Zion—

To bestow on them a crown of beauty instead of ashes,

The oil of gladness instead of mourning,

And a garment of praise instead of a spirit of despair.

You anoint my head with oil; my cup overflows.

Surely goodness and love will follow me all the days of my life,

And I will dwell in the house of the LORD forever.

Now I know that the LORD saves his anointed; he answers him from his holy heaven with the saving power of his right hand.

When they were but few in number, few indeed, and strangers in it, they wandered from nation to nation, from one kingdom to another.

He allowed no man to oppress them; for their sake he rebuked kings: "Do not touch my anointed ones; do my prophets no harm."

He gives his king great victories; he shows unfailing kindness to his anointed, to David and his descendants forever.

You know the message God sent to the people of Israel, telling the good news of peace through Jesus Christ, who is Lord of all. You know what has happened throughout Judea, beginning in Galilee after the baptism that John preached—

How God anointed Jesus of Nazareth with the Holy Spirit and power,

And how he went around doing good and healing all who were under the power of the devil, because God was with him.

For no matter how many promises God has made, they are "Yes" in Christ. And so through him the "Amen" is spoken by us to the glory of God.

Now it is God who makes both us and you stand firm in Christ. He anointed us, set his seal of ownership on us, and put his Spirit in our hearts as a deposit, guaranteeing what is to come.

As for you, the anointing you received from him remains in you, and you do not need anyone to teach you.

But as his anointing teaches you about all things and as that anointing is real, not counterfeit—just as it has taught you, remain in him.

And now, dear children, continue in him, so that when he appears we may be confident and unashamed before him at his coming.

But about the Son he says, "Your throne, O God, will last for ever and ever, and righteousness will be the scepter of your kingdom.

You have loved righteousness and hated wickedness; therefore God, your God, has set you above your companions by anointing you with the oil of joy."

4. BLESSINGS

Old Testament: Deut. 30:15–20; Mal. 3:10; Gen. 12:2–3

New Testament: Eph. 1:3–6; 2 Cor. 9:7–8; Rom. 15:25–26; 1 Pet. 3:8–9

See, I set before you today life and prosperity, death and destruction.

For I command you today to love the LORD your God, to walk in his ways, and to keep his commands, decrees and laws; then you will live and increase,

And the LORD your God will bless you in the land you are entering to possess. But if your heart turns away and you are not obedient, and if you are drawn away to bow down to other gods and worship them,

I declare to you this day that you will certainly be destroyed. You will not live long in the land you are crossing the Jordan to enter and possess.

This day I call heaven and earth as witnesses against you that I have set before you life and death, blessings and curses.

Now choose life, so that you and your children may live and that you may love the LORD your God, listen to his voice, and hold fast to him. For the LORD is your life,

And he will give you many years in the land he swore to give to your fathers, Abraham, Isaac and Jacob.

"Bring the whole tithe into the storehouse, that there may be food in my house. Test me in this," says the LORD Almighty, "and see if I will not throw open the floodgates of heaven and pour out so much blessing that you will not have room enough for it."

"I will make you into a great nation and I will bless you; I will make your name great, and you will be a blessing.

I will bless those who bless you, and whoever curses you I will curse; and all peoples on earth will be blessed through you."

Praise be to the God and Father of our Lord Jesus Christ, who has blessed us in the heavenly realms with every spiritual blessing in Christ.

For he chose us in him before the creation of the world to be holy and blameless in his sight.

In love he predestined us to be adopted as his sons through Jesus Christ, in accordance with his pleasure and will— to the praise of his glorious grace, which he has freely given us in the One he loves.

Each man should give what he has decided in his heart to give, not reluctantly or under compulsion, for God loves a cheerful giver.

And God is able to make all grace abound to you, so that in all things at all times, having all that you need, you will abound in every good work.

Now, however, I am on my way to Jerusalem in the service of the saints there. For Macedonia and Achaia were pleased to make a contribution for the poor among the saints in Jerusalem.

Finally, all of you, live in harmony with one another; be sympathetic, love as brothers, be compassionate and humble.

Do not repay evil with evil or insult with insult, but with blessing, because to this you were called so that you may inherit a blessing.

5. CHILDREN

Old Testament: Deut. 6:4–9; Prov. 20:11; 22:6; Eccl. 12:1; Ps. 78:5–8; Isa. 11:6

New Testament: Matt. 18:2–5; Lk. 2:41–43, 46–49, 52; Mk. 10:13–15

Hear, O Israel: The LORD our God, the LORD is one.

Love the LORD your God with all your heart and with all your soul and with all your strength. These commandments that I give you today are to be upon your hearts.

Impress them on your children. Talk about them when you sit at home and when you walk along the road, when you lie down and when you get up.

Tie them as symbols on your hands and bind them on your foreheads. Write them on the doorframes of your houses and on your gates.

Even a child is known by his actions, by whether his conduct is pure and right. Train a child in the way he should go, and when he is old he will not turn from it.

Remember your Creator in the days of your youth, before the days of trouble come and the years approach when you will say, "I find no pleasure in them."

He decreed statutes for Jacob and established the law in Israel, which he commanded our forefathers to teach their children,

So the next generation would know them, even the children yet to be born, and they in turn would tell their children.

Then they would put their trust in God and would not forget his deeds but would keep his commands. They would not be like their forefathers— a stubborn and rebellious generation.

The wolf will live with the lamb, the leopard will lie down with the goat, the calf and the lion and the yearling together; and a little child will lead them.

Every year his parents went to Jerusalem for the Feast of the Passover. When he was twelve years old, they went up to the Feast, according to the custom.

After the Feast was over, while his parents were returning home, the boy Jesus stayed behind in Jerusalem... After three days they found him in the temple courts, sitting among the teachers, listening to them and asking them questions. Everyone who heard him was amazed at his understanding and his answers.

When his parents saw him, they were astonished. His mother said to him, "... Your father and I have been anxiously searching for you."

"Why were you searching for me?" he asked. "Didn't you know I had to be in my Father's house?" And Jesus grew in wisdom and stature, and in favor with God and men.

People were bringing little children to Jesus to have him touch them, but the disciples rebuked them. When Jesus saw this, he was indignant. He said to them,

"Let the little children come to me, and do not hinder them, for the kingdom of God belongs to such as these. I tell you the truth, anyone who will not receive the kingdom of God like a little child will never enter it."

6. THE CHURCH

Old Testament: Ps. 15; 27:4–6; 1 Kgs. 7:51; 8:1; 2 Chr. 5:1–2; 6:20

LORD, who may dwell in your sanctuary? Who may live on your holy hill?

He whose walk is blameless and who does what is righteous, who speaks the truth from his heart and has no slander on his tongue,

Who does his neighbor no wrong and casts no slur on his fellowman, who despises a vile man but honors those who fear the LORD, who keeps his oath even when it hurts,

Who lends his money without usury and does not accept a bribe against the innocent. He who does these things will never be shaken.

One thing I ask of the LORD, this is what I seek: that I may dwell in the house of the LORD all the days of my life, to gaze upon the beauty of the LORD and to seek him in his temple.

For in the day of trouble he will keep me safe in his dwelling; he will hide me in the shelter of his tabernacle and set me high upon a rock.

Then my head will be exalted above the enemies who surround me; at his tabernacle will I sacrifice with shouts of joy; I will sing and make music to the LORD.

When all the work King Solomon had done for the temple of the LORD was finished, he brought in the things his father David had dedicated—the silver and gold and the furnishings—and he placed them in the treasuries of the LORD's temple.

Then King Solomon summoned into his presence at Jerusalem the elders of Israel, all the heads of the tribes and the chiefs of the Israelite families, to bring up the ark of the LORD's covenant from Zion, the City of David.

May your eyes be open toward this temple day and night, this place of which you said you would put your Name there. May you hear the prayer your servant prays toward this place.

New Testament: 1 Cor. 12:12–14, 20, 26–27; Eph. 4:4–6; 1 Cor. 3:10–11; Eph. 2:19–22

The body is a unit, though it is made up of many parts; and though all its parts are many, they form one body. So it is with Christ.

For we were all baptized by one Spirit into one body—whether Jews or Greeks, slave or free—and we were all given the one Spirit to drink. Now the body is not made up of one part but of many.

As it is, there are many parts, but one body. If one part suffers, every part suffers with it; if one part is honored, every part rejoices with it.

Now you are the body of Christ, and each one of you is a part of it.

There is one body and one Spirit—just as you were called to one hope when you were called— one Lord, one faith, one baptism; one God and Father of all, who is over all and through all and in all.

By the grace God has given me, I laid a foundation as an expert builder, and someone else is building on it. But each one should be careful how he builds. For no one can lay any foundation other than the one already laid, which is Jesus Christ.

Consequently, you are no longer foreigners and aliens, but fellow citizens with God's people and members of God's household, built on the foundation of the apostles and prophets, with Christ Jesus himself as the chief cornerstone.

In him the whole building is joined together and rises to become a holy temple in the Lord. And in him you too are being built together to become a dwelling in which God lives by his Spirit.

7. COMFORT

Old Testament: Eccl. 4:1; Isa. 40:1–2; Ps. 119:50, 52, 76–77; Isa. 51:3; 66:10, 13–14; 51:16

New Testament: Mt. 2:17–18; 5:4; Phil. 2:1–5; Rev. 7:16–17; 2 Thess. 2:16–17; 2 Cor. 1:3–4

Again I looked and saw all the oppression that was taking place under the sun: I saw the tears of the oppressed— and they have no comforter; power was on the side of their oppressors— and they have no comforter.

Comfort, comfort my people, says your God. Speak tenderly to Jerusalem, and proclaim to her that her hard service has been completed, that her sin has been paid for, that she has received from the LORD's hand double for all her sins.

My comfort in my suffering is this: Your promise preserves my life. I remember your ancient laws, O LORD, and I find comfort in them.

May your unfailing love be my comfort, according to your promise to your servant. Let your compassion come to me that I may live, for your law is my delight.

The LORD will surely comfort Zion and will look with compassion on all her ruins; he will make her deserts like Eden, her wastelands like the garden of the LORD. Joy and gladness will be found in her, thanksgiving and the sound of singing.

"Rejoice with Jerusalem and be glad for her, all you who love her; rejoice greatly with her, all you who mourn over her. As a mother comforts her child, so will I comfort you; and you will be comforted over Jerusalem."

When you see this, your heart will rejoice and you will flourish like grass; the hand of the LORD will be made known to his servants, but his fury will be shown to his foes.

"I have put my words in your mouth and covered you with the shadow of my hand— I who set the heavens in place, who laid the foundations of the earth, and who say to Zion, 'You are my people.'"

Then what was said through the prophet Jeremiah was fulfilled: "A voice is heard in Ramah, weeping and great mourning, Rachel weeping for her children and refusing to be comforted, because they are no more."

Blessed are those who mourn, for they will be comforted.

If you have any encouragement from being united with Christ, if any comfort from his love, if any fellowship with the Spirit, if any tenderness and compassion,

Then make my joy complete by being like-minded, having the same love, being one in spirit and purpose.

Do nothing out of selfish ambition or vain conceit, but in humility consider others better than yourselves. Each of you should look not only to your own interests, but also to the interests of others. Your attitude should be the same as that of Christ Jesus:

Never again will they hunger; never again will they thirst. The sun will not beat upon them, nor any scorching heat. For the Lamb at the center of the throne will be their shepherd;

He will lead them to springs of living water. And God will wipe away every tear from their eyes.

May our Lord Jesus Christ himself and God our Father, who loved us and by his grace gave us eternal encouragement and good hope, encourage your hearts and strengthen you in every good deed and word.

Praise be to the God and Father of our Lord Jesus Christ, the Father of compassion and the God of all comfort, who comforts us in all our troubles,

So that we can comfort those in any trouble with the comfort we ourselves have received from God.

8. COMMITMENT

Old Testament: Ruth 1:6, 16–17, 22; 1 Kings 18:20–21, 38–39; Ps. 37:3–6

New Testament: Jn. 17:4–6; Rom. 12:1–2; Col. 4:2; Eph. 6:10–13; 2 Tim. 4:7–8

When she heard in Moab that the LORD had come to the aid of his people by providing food for them, Naomi and her daughters-in-law prepared to return home from there.

But Ruth replied, "Don't urge me to leave you or to turn back from you. Where you go I will go, and where you stay I will stay. Your people will be my people and your God my God.

Where you die I will die, and there I will be buried. May the LORD deal with me, be it ever so severely, if anything but death separates you and me."

So Naomi returned from Moab accompanied by Ruth the Moabitess, her daughter-in-law, arriving in Bethlehem as the barley harvest was beginning.

So Ahab sent word throughout all Israel and assembled the prophets on Mount Carmel. Elijah went before the people and said, "How long will you waver between two opinions? If the LORD is God, follow him; but if Baal is God, follow him." But the people said nothing.

Then the fire of the LORD fell and burned up the sacrifice, the wood, the stones and the soil, and also licked up the water in the trench. When all the people saw this, they fell prostrate and cried, "The LORD—he is God! The LORD—he is God!"

Trust in the LORD and do good; dwell in the land and enjoy safe pasture. Delight yourself in the LORD and he will give you the desires of your heart.

Commit your way to the LORD; trust in him and he will do this: He will make your righteousness shine like the dawn, the justice of your cause like the noonday sun.

I have brought you glory on earth by completing the work you gave me to do. And now, Father, glorify me in your presence with the glory I had with you before the world began.

"I have revealed you to those whom you gave me out of the world. They were yours; you gave them to me and they have obeyed your word.

Therefore, I urge you, brothers, in view of God's mercy, to offer your bodies as living sacrifices, holy and pleasing to God—this is your spiritual act of worship.

Do not conform any longer to the pattern of this world, but be transformed by the renewing of your mind. Then you will be able to test and approve what God's will is—his good, pleasing and perfect will.

Devote yourselves to prayer, being watchful and thankful.

Finally, be strong in the Lord and in his mighty power.

Put on the full armor of God so that you can take your stand against the devil's schemes.

For our struggle is not against flesh and blood, but against the rulers, against the authorities, against the powers of this dark world and against the spiritual forces of evil in the heavenly realms.

Therefore put on the full armor of God, so that when the day of evil comes, you may be able to stand your ground, and after you have done everything, to stand. I have fought the good fight, I have finished the race, I have kept the faith.

Now there is in store for me the crown of righteousness, which the Lord, the righteous Judge, will award to me on that day—and not only to me, but also to all who have longed for his appearing.

9. COVENANT

Old Testament: Gen. 9:8, 11; 17:1–2; Ex. 19:5–6; Ps. 105:7–11; Jer. 31:33–34

New Testament: Lk. 1:67–75; 2 Cor. 1:20; Mt. 26:27–28; Heb. 13:20–21

Then God said to Noah and to his sons with him: "I establish my covenant with you: Never again will all life be cut off by the waters of a flood; never again will there be a flood to destroy the earth."

When Abram was ninety-nine years old, the LORD appeared to him and said, "I am God Almighty; walk before me and be blameless. I will confirm my covenant between me and you and will greatly increase your numbers."

Now if you obey me fully and keep my covenant, then out of all nations you will be my treasured possession. Although the whole earth is mine, you will be for me a kingdom of priests and a holy nation.

He is the LORD our God; his judgments are in all the earth. He remembers his covenant forever, the word he commanded, for a thousand generations, the covenant he made with Abraham, the oath he swore to Isaac.

He confirmed it to Jacob as a decree, to Israel as an everlasting covenant: "To you I will give the land of Canaan as the portion you will inherit."

"This is the covenant I will make with the house of Israel after that time," declares the LORD. "I will put my law in their minds and write it on their hearts. I will be their God, and they will be my people.

No longer will a man teach his neighbor, or a man his brother, saying, 'Know the LORD,' because they will all know me, from the least of them to the greatest," declares the LORD.

"For I will forgive their wickedness and will remember their sins no more."

His father Zechariah was filled with the Holy Spirit and prophesied: "Praise be to the Lord, the God of Israel, because he has come and has redeemed his people.

He has raised up a horn of salvation for us in the house of his servant David (as he said through his holy prophets of long ago),

Salvation from our enemies and from the hand of all who hate us— to show mercy to our fathers and to remember his holy covenant, the oath he swore to our father Abraham:

To rescue us from the hand of our enemies, and to enable us to serve him without fear in holiness and righteousness before him all our days."

For no matter how many promises God has made, they are "Yes" in Christ. And so through him the "Amen" is spoken by us to the glory of God.

Then he took the cup, gave thanks and offered it to them, saying, "Drink from it, all of you. This is my blood of the covenant, which is poured out for many for the forgiveness of sins."

May the God of peace, who through the blood of the eternal covenant brought back from the dead our Lord Jesus, that great Shepherd of the sheep, equip you with everything good for doing his will,

And may he work in us what is pleasing to him, through Jesus Christ, to whom be glory for ever and ever. Amen.

10. THE CROSS

Old Testament: Isa. 50:6–7; 53:3–5, 7; Jer. 31:34; Zech. 9:11

I offered my back to those who beat me, my cheeks to those who pulled out my beard; I did not hide my face from mocking and spitting.

Because the Sovereign LORD helps me, I will not be disgraced. Therefore have I set my face like flint, and I know I will not be put to shame.

He was despised and rejected by men, a man of sorrows, and familiar with suffering. Like one from whom men hide their faces he was despised, and we esteemed him not.

Surely he took up our infirmities and carried our sorrows, yet we considered him stricken by God, smitten by him, and afflicted.

But he was pierced for our transgressions, he was crushed for our iniquities; the punishment that brought us peace was upon him, and by his wounds we are healed.

He was oppressed and afflicted, yet he did not open his mouth; he was led like a lamb to the slaughter, and as a sheep before her shearers is silent, so he did not open his mouth.

"For I will forgive their wickedness and will remember their sins no more."

As for you, because of the blood of my covenant with you, I will free your prisoners from the waterless pit.

New Testament: Lk. 23:33–34, 42–46; Jn. 19:26–30; Mt. 27:46, 54

When they came to the place called the Skull, there they crucified him, along with the criminals—one on his right, the other on his left.

Jesus said, "Father, forgive them, for they do not know what they are doing." And they divided up his clothes by casting lots.

Then [the criminal] said, "Jesus, remember me when you come into your kingdom." Jesus answered him, "I tell you the truth, today you will be with me in paradise."

It was now about the sixth hour, and darkness came over the whole land until the ninth hour, for the sun stopped shining. And the curtain of the temple was torn in two.

Jesus called out with a loud voice, "Father, into your hands I commit my spirit." When he had said this, he breathed his last.

When Jesus saw his mother there, and the disciple whom he loved standing nearby, he said to his mother, "Dear woman, here is your son," and to the disciple, "Here is your mother." From that time on, this disciple took her into his home.

Later, knowing that all was now completed, and so that the Scripture would be fulfilled, Jesus said, "I am thirsty." A jar of wine vinegar was there, so they soaked a sponge in it, put the sponge on a stalk of the hyssop plant, and lifted it to Jesus' lips.

When he had received the drink, Jesus said, "It is finished." With that, he bowed his head and gave up his spirit.

About the ninth hour Jesus cried out in a loud voice, "Eloi, Eloi, lama sabachthani?"—which means, "My God, my God, why have you forsaken me?"

When the centurion and those with him who were guarding Jesus saw the earthquake and all that had happened, they were terrified, and exclaimed, "Surely he was the Son of God!"

11. DISCIPLESHIP

Old Testament: Ex. 20:3–5, 7–8, 12–17; 1 Kings 19:19, 21

New Testament: Mk. 6:7–13; 10:28–30; Lk. 14:26–27; Jn. 13:34–35

"You shall have no other gods before me. You shall not make for yourself an idol in the form of anything in heaven above or on the earth beneath or in the waters below.

You shall not bow down to them or worship them; for I, the LORD your God, am a jealous God.

You shall not misuse the name of the LORD your God, for the LORD will not hold anyone guiltless who misuses his name.

Remember the Sabbath day by keeping it holy. Honor your father and your mother, so that you may live long in the land the LORD your God is giving you.

You shall not murder. You shall not commit adultery. You shall not steal. You shall not give false testimony against your neighbor.

You shall not covet your neighbor's house. You shall not covet your neighbor's wife, or his manservant or maidservant, his ox or donkey, or anything that belongs to your neighbor."

So Elijah went from there and found Elisha son of Shaphat. He was plowing with twelve yoke of oxen, and he himself was driving the twelfth pair. Elijah went up to him and threw his cloak around him.

Then he set out to follow Elijah and became his attendant.

Calling the Twelve to him, he sent them out two by two and gave them authority over evil spirits.

These were his instructions: "Take nothing for the journey except a staff—no bread, no bag, no money in your belts. Wear sandals but not an extra tunic.

Whenever you enter a house, stay there until you leave that town. And if any place will not welcome you or listen to you, shake the dust off your feet when you leave, as a testimony against them."

They went out and preached that people should repent. They drove out many demons and anointed many sick people with oil and healed them.

Peter said to him, "We have left everything to follow you!" "I tell you the truth," Jesus replied, "no one who has left home or brothers or sisters or mother or father or children or fields

For me and the gospel will fail to receive a hundred times as much in this present age (homes, brothers, sisters, mothers, children and fields—and with them, persecutions) and in the age to come, eternal life.

"If anyone comes to me and does not hate his father and mother, his wife and children, his brothers and sisters—yes, even his own life—he cannot be my disciple.

And anyone who does not carry his cross and follow me cannot be my disciple. "A new command I give you: Love one another. As I have loved you, so you must love one another. By this all men will know that you are my disciples, if you love one another."

12. FAITHFULNESS

Old Testament: Ps. 36:5–6; 40:10; 89:1–2, 5–8; Lam. 3:22–23

New Testament: 1 Cor. 10:13; 1:9; 2 Thess. 3:1–3; 2 Tim. 2:11–13; 1 Jn. 1:8–9; Heb. 10:23; Rev. 2:10

Your love, O LORD, reaches to the heavens, your faithfulness to the skies.

Your righteousness is like the mighty mountains, your justice like the great deep. O LORD, you preserve both man and beast.

I do not hide your righteousness in my heart; I speak of your faithfulness and salvation. I do not conceal your love and your truth from the great assembly.

I will sing of the LORD's great love forever; with my mouth I will make your faithfulness known through all generations. I will declare that your love stands firm forever,

That you established your faithfulness in heaven itself. The heavens praise your wonders, O LORD, your faithfulness too, in the assembly of the holy ones. For who in the skies above can compare with the LORD?

Who is like the LORD among the heavenly beings? In the council of the holy ones God is greatly feared; he is more awesome than all who surround him. O LORD God Almighty, who is like you?

You are mighty, O LORD, and your faithfulness surrounds you.

Because of the LORD's great love we are not consumed, for his compassions never fail. They are new every morning; great is your faithfulness.

No temptation has seized you except what is common to man. And God is faithful; he will not let you be tempted beyond what you can bear. But when you are tempted, he will also provide a way out so that you can stand up under it.

God, who has called you into fellowship with his Son Jesus Christ our Lord, is faithful.

Finally, brothers, pray for us that the message of the Lord may spread rapidly and be honored, just as it was with you. And pray that we may be delivered from wicked and evil men, for not everyone has faith.

But the Lord is faithful, and he will strengthen and protect you from the evil one.

Here is a trustworthy saying: If we died with him, we will also live with him; if we endure, we will also reign with him. If we disown him, he will also disown us;

If we are faithless, he will remain faithful, for he cannot disown himself.

If we claim to be without sin, we deceive ourselves and the truth is not in us.

If we confess our sins, he is faithful and just and will forgive us our sins and purify us from all unrighteousness.

Let us hold unswervingly to the hope we profess, for he who promised is faithful.

Be faithful, even to the point of death, and I will give you the crown of life.

13. FAMILY

Old Testament: Deut. 6:4–7; Prov. 23:12–13, 15; 22:6; Isa. 54:4–8

New Testament: Mk. 3:31–35; Lk. 11:11–13; Jn. 19:26–27; Col. 3:14–15, 18–21

Hear, O Israel: The LORD our God, the LORD is one. Love the LORD your God with all your heart and with all your soul and with all your strength.

These commandments that I give you today are to be upon your hearts.

Impress them on your children. Talk about them when you sit at home and when you walk along the road, when you lie down and when you get up.

Apply your heart to instruction and your ears to words of knowledge. Do not withhold discipline from a child.

My son, if your heart is wise, then my heart will be glad;

Train a child in the way he should go, and when he is old he will not turn from it.

"Do not be afraid; you will not suffer shame. Do not fear disgrace; you will not be humiliated.

You will forget the shame of your youth and remember no more the reproach of your widowhood.

For your Maker is your husband— the LORD Almighty is his name— the Holy One of Israel is your Redeemer; he is called the God of all the earth.

The LORD will call you back as if you were a wife deserted and distressed in spirit— a wife who married young, only to be rejected," says your God.

"For a brief moment I abandoned you, but with deep compassion I will bring you back.

In a surge of anger I hid my face from you for a moment, but with everlasting kindness I will have compassion on you," says the LORD your Redeemer.

Then Jesus' mother and brothers arrived. Standing outside, they sent someone in to call him. A crowd was sitting around him, and they told him, "Your mother and brothers are outside looking for you."

"Who are my mother and my brothers?" he asked.

Then he looked at those seated in a circle around him and said, "Here are my mother and my brothers! Whoever does God's will is my brother and sister and mother."

"Which of you fathers, if your son asks for a fish, will give him a snake instead? Or if he asks for an egg, will give him a scorpion?

If you then, though you are evil, know how to give good gifts to your children, how much more will your Father in heaven give the Holy Spirit to those who ask him!"

When Jesus saw his mother there, and the disciple whom he loved standing nearby, he said to his mother, "Dear woman, here is your son,"

And to the disciple, "Here is your mother." From that time on, this disciple took her into his home.

And over all these virtues put on love, which binds them all together in perfect unity. Let the peace of Christ rule in your hearts, since as members of one body you were called to peace. And be thankful.

Wives, submit to your husbands, as is fitting in the Lord. Husbands, love your wives and do not be harsh with them.

Children, obey your parents in everything, for this pleases the Lord. Fathers, do not embitter your children, or they will become discouraged.

14. FORGIVENESS

Old Testament: Gen. 45:4–7, 11; Ps. 103:2–3; 2 Chr. 6:21; Neh. 9:17

New Testament: Mt. 5:3–12; Col. 3:12–13; Mt. 26:27–28

Then Joseph said to his brothers, "Come close to me." When they had done so, he said, "I am your brother Joseph, the one you sold into Egypt!

And now, do not be distressed and do not be angry with yourselves for selling me here, because it was to save lives that God sent me ahead of you.

For two years now there has been famine in the land, and for the next five years there will not be plowing and reaping.

But God sent me ahead of you to preserve for you a remnant on earth and to save your lives by a great deliverance.

I will provide for you there, because five years of famine are still to come. Otherwise you and your household and all who belong to you will become destitute.'

Praise the LORD, O my soul, and forget not all his benefits—who forgives all your sins and heals all your diseases,

Hear the supplications of your servant and of your people Israel when they pray toward this place. Hear from heaven, your dwelling place; and when you hear, forgive.

They refused to listen and failed to remember the miracles you performed among them.

They became stiff-necked and in their rebellion appointed a leader in order to return to their slavery.

But you are a forgiving God, gracious and compassionate, slow to anger and abounding in love. Therefore you did not desert them.

Blessed are the poor in spirit, for theirs is the kingdom of heaven. Blessed are those who mourn, for they will be comforted.

Blessed are the meek, for they will inherit the earth. Blessed are those who hunger and thirst for righteousness, for they will be filled.

Blessed are the merciful, for they will be shown mercy. Blessed are the pure in heart, for they will see God.

Blessed are the peacemakers, for they will be called sons of God. Blessed are those who are persecuted because of righteousness, for theirs is the kingdom of heaven.

Blessed are you when people insult you, persecute you and falsely say all kinds of evil against you because of me.

Rejoice and be glad, because great is your reward in heaven, for in the same way they persecuted the prophets who were before you.

Therefore, as God's chosen people, holy and dearly loved, clothe yourselves with compassion, kindness, humility, gentleness and patience.

Bear with each other and forgive whatever grievances you may have against one another. Forgive as the Lord forgave you.

Then he took the cup, gave thanks and offered it to them, saying, "Drink from it, all of you.

This is my blood of the covenant, which is poured out for many for the forgiveness of sins."

15. THE COMING OF THE LORD

Old Testament: Isa. 13:9; Am. 5:18; Mal. 4:1–3;
Zeph. 1:17–18; Dan. 12:1–2

New Testament: Heb. 13:14; 2 Cor. 5:10; 1 Cor.
15:51–52, 54–55; 1 Thess. 4:16–17; 2 Thess. 2:3–4;
Rev. 22:20

See, the day of the LORD is coming —a cruel day, with wrath and fierce anger— to make the land desolate and destroy the sinners within it.

Woe to you who long for the day of the LORD! Why do you long for the day of the LORD? That day will be darkness, not light.

"Surely the day is coming; it will burn like a furnace. All the arrogant and every evildoer will be stubble, and the day that is coming will set them on fire," says the LORD Almighty. "Not a root or a branch will be left to them.

But for you who revere my name, the sun of righteousness will rise with healing in its wings. And you will go out and leap like calves released from the stall.

Then you will trample down the wicked; they will be ashes under the soles of your feet on the day when I do these things," says the LORD Almighty.

I will bring distress on the people and they will walk like blind men, because they have sinned against the LORD.

Their blood will be poured out like dust and their entrails like filth. Neither their silver nor their gold will be able to save them on the day of the LORD's wrath. In the fire of his jealousy the whole world will be consumed,

For he will make a sudden end of all who live in the earth.

There will be a time of distress such as has not happened from the beginning of nations until then. But at that time your people— everyone whose name is found written in the book—will be delivered.

Multitudes who sleep in the dust of the earth will awake: some to everlasting life, others to shame and everlasting contempt.

For here we do not have an enduring city, but we are looking for the city that is to come.

For we must all appear before the judgment seat of Christ, that each one may receive what is due him for the things done while in the body, whether good or bad.

Listen, I tell you a mystery: We will not all sleep, but we will all be changed— in a flash, in the twinkling of an eye, at the last trumpet.

For the trumpet will sound, the dead will be raised imperishable, and we will be changed.

When the perishable has been clothed with the imperishable, and the mortal with immortality, then the saying that is written will come true: "Death has been swallowed up in victory." "Where, O death, is your victory? Where, O death, is your sting?"

For the Lord himself will come down from heaven, with a loud command, with the voice of the archangel and with the trumpet call of God, and the dead in Christ will rise first.

After that, we who are still alive and are left will be caught up together with them in the clouds to meet the Lord in the air. And so we will be with the Lord forever.

Don't let anyone deceive you in any way, for (that day will not come) until the rebellion occurs and the man of lawlessness is revealed, the man doomed to destruction.

He will oppose and will exalt himself over everything that is called God or is worshiped, so that he sets himself up in God's temple, proclaiming himself to be God.

He who testifies to these things says, "Yes, I am coming soon." Amen. Come, Lord Jesus.

16. FRUIT OF THE HOLY SPIRIT

Old Testament: Ps. 143:10; Isa. 32:14–15; 42:1; 44:3–4; 61:1; Ezek. 36:25–27

New Testament: Gal. 5:16–23, 24–26; 6:7–10

Teach me to do your will, for you are my God; may your good Spirit lead me on level ground.

The fortress will be abandoned, the noisy city deserted; citadel and watchtower will become a wasteland forever, the delight of donkeys, a pasture for flocks,

Till the Spirit is poured upon us from on high, and the desert becomes a fertile field, and the fertile field seems like a forest.

Here is my servant, whom I uphold, my chosen one in whom I delight; I will put my Spirit on him and he will bring justice to the nations.

For I will pour water on the thirsty land, and streams on the dry ground; I will pour out my Spirit on your offspring, and my blessing on your descendants.

They will spring up like grass in a meadow, like poplar trees by flowing streams.

The Spirit of the Sovereign LORD is on me, because the LORD has anointed me to preach good news to the poor. He has sent me to bind up the brokenhearted, to proclaim freedom for the captives and release from darkness for the prisoners.

I will sprinkle clean water on you, and you will be clean; I will cleanse you from all your impurities and from all your idols.

I will give you a new heart and put a new spirit in you; I will remove from you your heart of stone and give you a heart of flesh.

And I will put my Spirit in you and move you to follow my decrees and be careful to keep my laws.

So I say, live by the Spirit, and you will not gratify the desires of the sinful nature. For the sinful nature desires what is contrary to the Spirit, and the Spirit what is contrary to the sinful nature.

They are in conflict with each other, so that you do not do what you want. But if you are led by the Spirit, you are not under law.

The acts of the sinful nature are obvious: sexual immorality, impurity and debauchery; idolatry and witchcraft; hatred, discord, jealousy, fits of rage, selfish ambition, dissensions, factions and envy; drunkenness, orgies, and the like.

I warn you, as I did before, that those who live like this will not inherit the kingdom of God.

But the fruit of the Spirit is love, joy, peace, patience, kindness, goodness, faithfulness, gentleness and self-control.

Those who belong to Christ Jesus have crucified the sinful nature with its passions and desires.

Since we live by the Spirit, let us keep in step with the Spirit. Let us not become conceited, provoking and envying each other.

Do not be deceived: God cannot be mocked. A man reaps what he sows. The one who sows to please his sinful nature, from that nature will reap destruction;

The one who sows to please the Spirit, from the Spirit will reap eternal life. Let us not become weary in doing good, for at the proper time we will reap a harvest if we do not give up.

Therefore, as we have opportunity, let us do good to all people, especially to those who belong to the family of believers.

17. GIFTS OF THE HOLY SPIRIT

Old Testament: Ex. 35:30–33, 35; Isa. 11:1–3; Ezek. 37:1, 3, 7, 10

New Testament: 1 Cor. 12:4–10; Rom. 12:6–8; 1 Cor. 12:28; Eph. 4:11–13

Then Moses said to the Israelites, "See, the LORD has chosen Bezalel son of Uri, the son of Hur, of the tribe of Judah,

And he has filled him with the Spirit of God, with skill, ability and knowledge in all kinds of crafts-

To make artistic designs for work in gold, silver and bronze, to cut and set stones, to work in wood and to engage in all kinds of artistic craftsmanship.

He has filled them with skill to do all kinds of work as craftsmen, designers, embroiderers in blue, purple and scarlet yarn and fine linen, and weavers—all of them master craftsmen and designers."

A shoot will come up from the stump of Jesse; from his roots a Branch will bear fruit. The Spirit of the LORD will rest on him— the Spirit of wisdom and of understanding, the Spirit of counsel and of power, the Spirit of knowledge and of the fear of the LORD—

And he will delight in the fear of the LORD.

The hand of the LORD was upon me, and he brought me out by the Spirit of the LORD and set me in the middle of a valley; it was full of bones.

He asked me, "Son of man, can these bones live?" I said, "O Sovereign LORD, you alone know."

So I prophesied as I was commanded. And as I was prophesying, there was a noise, a rattling sound, and the bones came together, bone to bone.

So I prophesied as he commanded me, and breath entered them; they came to life and stood up on their feet—a vast army.

There are different kinds of gifts, but the same Spirit. There are different kinds of service, but the same Lord. There are different kinds of working, but the same God works all of them in all men.

Now to each one the manifestation of the Spirit is given for the common good.

To one there is given through the Spirit the message of wisdom, to another the message of knowledge by means of the same Spirit, to another faith by the same Spirit, to another gifts of healing by that one Spirit,

To another miraculous powers, to another prophecy, to another distinguishing between spirits, to another speaking in different kinds of tongues, and to still another the interpretation of tongues.

We have different gifts, according to the grace given us. If a man's gift is prophesying, let him use it in proportion to his faith. If it is serving, let him serve; if it is teaching, let him teach; if it is encouraging, let him encourage;

If it is contributing to the needs of others, let him give generously; if it is leadership, let him govern diligently; if it is showing mercy, let him do it cheerfully.

And in the church God has appointed first of all apostles, second prophets, third teachers,

Then workers of miracles, also those having gifts of healing, those able to help others, those with gifts of administration, and those speaking in different kinds of tongues.

It was he who gave some to be apostles, some to be prophets, some to be evangelists, and some to be pastors and teachers, to prepare God's people for works of service, so that the body of Christ may be built up

Until we all reach unity in the faith and in the knowledge of the Son of God and become mature, attaining to the whole measure of the fullness of Christ.

18. GLORY

Old Testament: Ps. 24:9–10; 96:3, 8–9; Hag. 2:9; Isa. 60:1; Ps. 64:10; 57:5; Isa. 42:8; Ps. 72:19

New Testament: Lk. 2:9–11, 14; Jn. 1:14; 2 Cor. 3:18; Rom. 2:7; Jn. 7:18; 1 Cor. 10:31; Mt. 25:31; Rev. 19:1, 7

Lift up your heads, O you gates; lift them up, you ancient doors, that the King of glory may come in.

Who is he, this King of glory? The LORD Almighty— he is the King of glory.

Declare his glory among the nations, his marvelous deeds among all peoples.

Ascribe to the LORD the glory due his name; bring an offering and come into his courts.

Worship the LORD in the splendor of his holiness; tremble before him, all the earth.

The glory of this present house will be greater than the glory of the former house,' says the LORD Almighty. 'And in this place I will grant peace,' declares the LORD Almighty.

Arise, shine, for your light has come,

And the glory of the LORD rises upon you.

Let the righteous rejoice in the LORD and take refuge in him; let all the upright in heart praise him!

Be exalted, O God, above the heavens; let your glory be over all the earth.

"I am the LORD; that is my name! I will not give my glory to another or my praise to idols."

Praise be to his glorious name forever; may the whole earth be filled with his glory.

An angel of the Lord appeared to them, and the glory of the Lord shone around them, and they were terrified.

But the angel said to them, "Do not be afraid. I bring you good news of great joy that will be for all the people.

Today in the town of David a Savior has been born to you; he is Christ the Lord."

Glory to God in the highest, and on earth peace to men on whom his favor rests.

The Word became flesh and made his dwelling among us. We have seen his glory, the glory of the One and Only, who came from the Father, full of grace and truth.

And we, who with unveiled faces all reflect the Lord's glory,

Are being transformed into his likeness with ever-increasing glory, which comes from the Lord, who is the Spirit.

To those who by persistence in doing good seek glory, honor and immortality, he will give eternal life.

He who speaks on his own does so to gain honor for himself, but he who works for the honor of the one who sent him is a man of truth; there is nothing false about him.

So whether you eat or drink or whatever you do, do it all for the glory of God.

When the Son of Man comes in his glory, and all the angels with him, he will sit on his throne in heavenly glory.

Hallelujah! Salvation and glory and power belong to our God. Let us rejoice and be glad and give him glory!

19. GOOD SHEPHERD

Old Testament: Ps. 23; Jer. 23:1–2; Ps. 80:1; Ezek. 34:11, 15–16

New Testament: Jn. 10:11–16; Lk. 15:3–6; Acts 20:28; 1 Pet. 5:4

The LORD is my shepherd, I shall not be in want. He makes me lie down in green pastures,

He leads me beside quiet waters, he restores my soul. He guides me in paths of righteousness for his name's sake.

Even though I walk through the valley of the shadow of death, I will fear no evil, for you are with me; your rod and your staff, they comfort me.

You prepare a table before me in the presence of my enemies. You anoint my head with oil; my cup overflows.

Surely goodness and love will follow me all the days of my life, and I will dwell in the house of the LORD forever.

"Woe to the shepherds who are destroying and scattering the sheep of my pasture!" declares the LORD. Therefore this is what the LORD, the God of Israel, says to the shepherds who tend my people:

"Because you have scattered my flock and driven them away and have not bestowed care on them, I will bestow punishment on you for the evil you have done," declares the LORD.

Hear us, O Shepherd of Israel, you who lead Joseph like a flock! For this is what the Sovereign LORD says: I myself will search for my sheep and look after them.

I myself will tend my sheep and have them lie down, declares the Sovereign LORD. I will search for the lost and bring back the strays.

I will bind up the injured and strengthen the weak, but the sleek and the strong I will destroy. I will shepherd the flock with justice.

"I am the good shepherd. The good shepherd lays down his life for the sheep. The hired hand is not the shepherd who owns the sheep. So when he sees the wolf coming, he abandons the sheep and runs away. Then the wolf attacks the flock and scatters it.

The man runs away because he is a hired hand and cares nothing for the sheep. I am the good shepherd; I know my sheep and my sheep know me—

Just as the Father knows me and I know the Father—and I lay down my life for the sheep. I have other sheep that are not of this sheep pen.

I must bring them also. They too will listen to my voice, and there shall be one flock and one shepherd."

Then Jesus told them this parable: "Suppose one of you has a hundred sheep and loses one of them. Does he not leave the ninety-nine in the open country and go after the lost sheep until he finds it?

And when he finds it, he joyfully puts it on his shoulders and goes home. Then he calls his friends and neighbors together and says, 'Rejoice with me; I have found my lost sheep.' "

Keep watch over yourselves and all the flock of which the Holy Spirit has made you overseers. Be shepherds of the church of God, which he bought with his own blood.

And when the Chief Shepherd appears, you will receive the crown of glory that will never fade away.

20. GOODNESS OF GOD

Old Testament: Ps. 106:1; 34:8; 73:1; 37:3; 84:11; Neh. 9:20; Deut. 6:18; Ps. 143:10; 1 Chr. 16:34

New Testament: 3 Jn. 11; 1 Tim. 4:4; Lk. 11:10–13; 2 Cor. 9:8; Lk. 6:38; 2 Pet. 3:9; Rom. 12:2; Phil. 2:13

Praise the LORD. Give thanks to the LORD, for he is good; his love endures forever.

Taste and see that the LORD is good; blessed is the man who takes refuge in him.

Surely God is good to Israel, to those who are pure in heart.

Trust in the LORD and do good; dwell in the land and enjoy safe pasture.

For the LORD God is a sun and shield; the LORD bestows favor and honor; no good thing does he withhold from those whose walk is blameless.

You gave your good Spirit to instruct them. You did not withhold your manna from their mouths, and you gave them water for their thirst.

Do what is right and good in the LORD's sight, so that it may go well with you

And you may go in and take over the good land that the LORD promised on oath to your forefathers,

Teach me to do your will, for you are my God; may your good Spirit lead me on level ground.

Give thanks to the LORD, for he is good; his love endures forever.

Dear friend, do not imitate what is evil but what is good. Anyone who does what is good is from God. Anyone who does what is evil has not seen God.

For everything God created is good, and nothing is to be rejected if it is received with thanksgiving,

For everyone who asks receives; he who seeks finds; and to him who knocks, the door will be opened.

"Which of you fathers, if your son asks for a fish, will give him a snake instead? Or if he asks for an egg, will give him a scorpion?

If you then, though you are evil, know how to give good gifts to your children, how much more will your Father in heaven give the Holy Spirit to those who ask him!"

And God is able to make all grace abound to you, so that in all things at all times, having all that you need, you will abound in every good work.

"Give, and it will be given to you. A good measure, pressed down, shaken together and running over, will be poured into your lap. For with the measure you use, it will be measured to you."

The Lord is not slow in keeping his promise, as some understand slowness. He is patient with you, not wanting anyone to perish, but everyone to come to repentance.

Do not conform any longer to the pattern of this world, but be transformed by the renewing of your mind. Then you will be able to test and approve what God's will is—his good, pleasing and perfect will.

For it is God who works in you to will and to act according to his good purpose.

21. THE POOR

Old Testament: Ex. 20:1–3; 22:21–23, 25–27; Isa. 3:15; Ps. 72:2, 12–13; Prov. 14:21; 17:5; 19:17

New Testament: Jas. 2:1–7; Lk. 14:1, 12–14

And God spoke all these words: "I am the LORD your God, who brought you out of Egypt, out of the land of slavery. You shall have no other gods before me."

Do not mistreat an alien or oppress him, for you were aliens in Egypt. Do not take advantage of a widow or an orphan.

If you do and they cry out to me, I will certainly hear their cry.

If you lend money to one of my people among you who is needy, do not be like a moneylender; charge him no interest.

If you take your neighbor's cloak as a pledge, return it to him by sunset, because his cloak is the only covering he has for his body. What else will he sleep in?

When he cries out to me, I will hear, for I am compassionate.

"What do you mean by crushing my people and grinding the faces of the poor?" declares the Lord, the LORD Almighty.

He will judge your people in righteousness, your afflicted ones with justice.

For he will deliver the needy who cry out, the afflicted who have no one to help. He will take pity on the weak and the needy and save the needy from death.

He who despises his neighbor sins, but blessed is he who is kind to the needy.

He who mocks the poor shows contempt for their Maker; whoever gloats over disaster will not go unpunished.

He who is kind to the poor lends to the LORD, and he will reward him for what he has done.

My brothers, as believers in our glorious Lord Jesus Christ, don't show favoritism.

Suppose a man comes into your meeting wearing a gold ring and fine clothes, and a poor man in shabby clothes also comes in.

If you show special attention to the man wearing fine clothes and say, "Here's a good seat for you," but say to the poor man, "You stand there" or "Sit on the floor by my feet,"

Have you not discriminated among yourselves and become judges with evil thoughts?

Listen, my dear brothers: Has not God chosen those who are poor in the eyes of the world to be rich in faith and to inherit the kingdom he promised those who love him?

But you have insulted the poor. Is it not the rich who are exploiting you?

Are they not the ones who are dragging you into court? Are they not the ones who are slandering the noble name of him to whom you belong?

One Sabbath, when Jesus went to eat in the house of a prominent Pharisee, he was being carefully watched.

Then Jesus said to his host, "When you give a luncheon or dinner, do not invite your friends, your brothers or relatives, or your rich neighbors; if you do, they may invite you back and so you will be repaid.

But when you give a banquet, invite the poor, the crippled, the lame, the blind, and you will be blessed."

22. GRACE

Old Testament: Gen. 6:5–8; Jer. 31:2–3; 23:4; Isa. 10:20–21, 27

New Testament: Jn. 1:1–2, 14, 16–17; Eph. 3:5–8; Rom. 3:23–25; 8:1

The LORD saw how great man's wickedness on the earth had become, and that every inclination of the thoughts of his heart was only evil all the time.

The LORD was grieved that he had made man on the earth, and his heart was filled with pain.

So the LORD said, "I will wipe mankind, whom I have created, from the face of the earth—men and animals, and creatures that move along the ground, and birds of the air—for I am grieved that I have made them." But Noah found favor in the eyes of the LORD.

This is what the LORD says: "The people who survive the sword will find favor in the desert; I will come to give rest to Israel."

The LORD appeared to us in the past, saying: "I have loved you with an everlasting love; I have drawn you with loving-kindness.

I will place shepherds over them who will tend them, and they will no longer be afraid or terrified, nor will any be missing," declares the LORD.

In that day the remnant of Israel, the survivors of the house of Jacob, will no longer rely on him who struck them down but will truly rely on the LORD, the Holy One of Israel.

A remnant will return, a remnant of Jacob will return to the Mighty God. In that day their burden will be lifted from your shoulders, their yoke from your neck.

In the beginning was the Word, and the Word was with God, and the Word was God. He was with God in the beginning.

The Word became flesh and made his dwelling among us. We have seen his glory, the glory of the One and Only, who came from the Father, full of grace and truth.

From the fullness of his grace we have all received one blessing after another. For the law was given through Moses; grace and truth came through Jesus Christ,

Which was not made known to men in other generations as it has now been revealed by the Spirit to God's holy apostles and prophets.

This mystery is that through the gospel the Gentiles are heirs together with Israel, members together of one body, and sharers together in the promise in Christ Jesus.

I became a servant of this gospel by the gift of God's grace given me through the working of his power.

Although I am less than the least of all God's people, this grace was given me: to preach to the Gentiles the unsearchable riches of Christ,

For all have sinned and fall short of the glory of God, and are justified freely by his grace through the redemption that came by Christ Jesus.

God presented him as a sacrifice of atonement, through faith in his blood. He did this to demonstrate his justice, because in his forbearance he had left the sins committed beforehand unpunished—

Therefore, there is now no condemnation for those who are in Christ Jesus.

23. CHRISTIAN MATURITY

Old Testament: Ps. 1:1–3; 92:12–15; 144:12; Job 17:9, Isa. 40:28–29

New Testament: Lk. 2:51–52; Col. 1:9–10; 2:6–7, 9–10; 2 Tim. 3:14–17; Eph. 4:12–13

Blessed is the man who does not walk in the counsel of the wicked or stand in the way of sinners or sit in the seat of mockers. But his delight is in the law of the LORD, and on his law he meditates day and night.

He is like a tree planted by streams of water, which yields its fruit in season and whose leaf does not wither. Whatever he does prospers.

The righteous will flourish like a palm tree, they will grow like a cedar of Lebanon; planted in the house of the LORD, they will flourish in the courts of our God.

They will still bear fruit in old age, they will stay fresh and green, proclaiming, "The LORD is upright; he is my Rock, and there is no wickedness in him."

Then our sons in their youth will be like well-nurtured plants, and our daughters will be like pillars carved to adorn a palace.

Nevertheless, the righteous will hold to their ways, and those with clean hands will grow stronger.

Do you not know? Have you not heard? The LORD is the everlasting God, the Creator of the ends of the earth.

He will not grow tired or weary, and his understanding no one can fathom. He gives strength to the weary and increases the power of the weak.

Then he went down to Nazareth with them and was obedient to them. But his mother treasured all these things in her heart. And Jesus grew in wisdom and stature, and in favor with God and men.

For this reason, since the day we heard about you, we have not stopped praying for you and asking God to fill you with the knowledge of his will through all spiritual wisdom and understanding.

And we pray this in order that you may live a life worthy of the Lord and may please him in every way: bearing fruit in every good work, growing in the knowledge of God.

So then, just as you received Christ Jesus as Lord, continue to live in him, rooted and built up in him, strengthened in the faith as you were taught, and overflowing with thankfulness.

For in Christ all the fullness of the Deity lives in bodily form, and you have been given fullness in Christ, who is the head over every power and authority.

But as for you, continue in what you have learned and have become convinced of, because you know those from whom you learned it, and how from infancy you have known the holy Scriptures, which are able to make you wise for salvation through faith in Christ Jesus.

All Scripture is God-breathed and is useful for teaching, rebuking, correcting and training in righteousness, so that the man of God may be thoroughly equipped for every good work.

To prepare God's people for works of service, so that the body of Christ may be built up until we all reach unity in the faith and in the knowledge of the Son of God and become mature, attaining to the whole measure of the fullness of Christ.

24. HEALING

Old Testament: Ex. 15:26; Jer. 17:14; Ex. 23:24–25; Ps. 103:2–4; Jer. 8:22; Ps. 41:1–3

He said, "If you listen carefully to the voice of the LORD your God and do what is right in his eyes, if you pay attention to his commands and keep all his decrees, I will not bring on you any of the diseases I brought on the Egyptians, for I am the LORD, who heals you."

Heal me, O LORD, and I will be healed; save me and I will be saved, for you are the one I praise.

Do not bow down before their gods or worship them or follow their practices. You must demolish them and break their sacred stones to pieces.

Worship the LORD your God, and his blessing will be on your food and water. I will take away sickness from among you.

Praise the LORD, O my soul, and forget not all his benefits—who forgives all your sins and heals all your diseases,

Who redeems your life from the pit and crowns you with love and compassion.

Is there no balm in Gilead? Is there no physician there? Why then is there no healing for the wound of my people?

Blessed is he who has regard for the weak; the LORD delivers him in times of trouble.

The LORD will protect him and preserve his life; he will bless him in the land and not surrender him to the desire of his foes.

The LORD will sustain him on his sickbed and restore him from his bed of illness.

New Testament: 3 Jn. 2; Mt. 9:35; Mk. 5:25–29; Mt. 14:35–36; Acts 3:4–7; Jas. 5:14–16

Dear friend, I pray that you may enjoy good health and that all may go well with you, even as your soul is getting along well.

Jesus went through all the towns and villages, teaching in their synagogues, preaching the good news of the kingdom and healing every disease and sickness.

And a woman was there who had been subject to bleeding for twelve years. She had suffered a great deal under the care of many doctors and had spent all she had, yet instead of getting better she grew worse.

When she heard about Jesus, she came up behind him in the crowd and touched his cloak, because she thought,

"If I just touch his clothes, I will be healed." Immediately her bleeding stopped and she felt in her body that she was freed from her suffering.

And when the men of that place recognized Jesus, they sent word to all the surrounding country. People brought all their sick to him and begged him to let the sick just touch the edge of his cloak, and all who touched him were healed.

Peter looked straight at him, as did John. Then Peter said, "Look at us!" So the man gave them his attention, expecting to get something from them. Then Peter said, "Silver or gold I do not have, but what I have I give you. In the name of Jesus Christ of Nazareth, walk."

Taking him by the right hand, he helped him up, and instantly the man's feet and ankles became strong.

Is any one of you sick? He should call the elders of the church to pray over him and anoint him with oil in the name of the Lord.

And the prayer offered in faith will make the sick person well; the Lord will raise him up. If he has sinned, he will be forgiven. Therefore confess your sins to each other and pray for each other so that you may be healed. The prayer of a righteous man is powerful and effective.

25. THE HOLY SPIRIT

Old Testament: Num. 11:24–29; 1 Kings 18:36, 38; Joel 2:28

New Testament: Lk. 1:12–13, 15; Acts 2:38; 10:44–47; 19:1–2, 4–6

So Moses went out and told the people what the LORD had said. He brought together seventy of their elders and had them stand around the Tent.

Then the LORD came down in the cloud and spoke with him, and he took of the Spirit that was on him and put the Spirit on the seventy elders. When the Spirit rested on them, they prophesied, but they did not do so again.

However, two men, whose names were Eldad and Medad, had remained in the camp. They were listed among the elders, but did not go out to the Tent. Yet the Spirit also rested on them, and they prophesied in the camp.

A young man ran and told Moses, "Eldad and Medad are prophesying in the camp." Joshua son of Nun, who had been Moses' aide since youth, spoke up and said, "Moses, my lord, stop them!"

But Moses replied, "Are you jealous for my sake? I wish that all the LORD's people were prophets and that the LORD would put his Spirit on them!"

At the time of sacrifice, the prophet Elijah stepped forward and prayed: "O LORD, God of Abraham, Isaac and Israel,

Let it be known today that you are God in Israel and that I am your servant and have done all these things at your command."

Then the fire of the LORD fell and burned up the sacrifice, the wood, the stones and the soil, and also licked up the water in the trench.

And afterward, I will pour out my Spirit on all people. Your sons and daughters will prophesy,

Your old men will dream dreams, your young men will see visions.

When Zechariah saw him, he was startled and was gripped with fear. But the angel said to him: "Do not be afraid, Zechariah; your prayer has been heard. Your wife Elizabeth will bear you a son, and you are to give him the name John.

For he will be great in the sight of the Lord. He is never to take wine or other fermented drink, and he will be filled with the Holy Spirit even from birth.

Peter replied, "Repent and be baptized, every one of you, in the name of Jesus Christ for the forgiveness of your sins. And you will receive the gift of the Holy Spirit."

While Peter was still speaking these words, the Holy Spirit came on all who heard the message.

The circumcised believers who had come with Peter were astonished that the gift of the Holy Spirit had been poured out even on the Gentiles.

For they heard them speaking in tongues and praising God.

Then Peter said, "Can anyone keep these people from being baptized with water? They have received the Holy Spirit just as we have."

Paul took the road through the interior and arrived at Ephesus. There he found some disciples and asked them, "Did you receive the Holy Spirit when you believed?"

They answered, "No, we have not even heard that there is a Holy Spirit." Paul said, "John's baptism was a baptism of repentance. He told the people to believe in the one coming after him, that is, in Jesus."

On hearing this, they were baptized into the name of the Lord Jesus. When Paul placed his hands on them, the Holy Spirit came on them, and they spoke in tongues and prophesied.

26. HOPE

Old Testament: Ps. 71:4–6; 146:5–9; Lam. 3:19–24

New Testament: 1 Pet. 1:3; Heb. 6:11–12, 19–20; Col. 1:26–27; Eph. 1:17–19; Rom. 15:13

Deliver me, O my God, from the hand of the wicked, from the grasp of evil and cruel men.

For you have been my hope, O Sovereign LORD, my confidence since my youth.

From birth I have relied on you; you brought me forth from my mother's womb. I will ever praise you.

Blessed is he whose help is the God of Jacob, whose hope is in the LORD his God, the Maker of heaven and earth, the sea, and everything in them— the LORD, who remains faithful forever.

He upholds the cause of the oppressed and gives food to the hungry.

The LORD sets prisoners free, the LORD gives sight to the blind.

The LORD lifts up those who are bowed down, the LORD loves the righteous.

The LORD watches over the alien and sustains the fatherless and the widow, but he frustrates the ways of the wicked.

I remember my affliction and my wandering, the bitterness and the gall.

I well remember them, and my soul is downcast within me. Yet this I call to mind and therefore I have hope:

Because of the LORD's great love we are not consumed, for his compassions never fail. They are new every morning; great is your faithfulness.

I say to myself, "The LORD is my portion; therefore I will wait for him."

Praise be to the God and Father of our Lord Jesus Christ! In his great mercy he has given us new birth into a living hope through the resurrection of Jesus Christ from the dead.

We want each of you to show this same diligence to the very end, in order to make your hope sure. We do not want you to become lazy, but to imitate those who through faith and patience inherit what has been promised.

We have this hope as an anchor for the soul, firm and secure. It enters the inner sanctuary behind the curtain, where Jesus, who went before us, has entered on our behalf. He has become a high priest forever, in the order of Melchizedek.

The mystery that has been kept hidden for ages and generations, but is now disclosed to the saints. To them God has chosen to make known among the Gentiles the glorious riches of this mystery, which is Christ in you, the hope of glory.

I keep asking that the God of our Lord Jesus Christ, the glorious Father, may give you the Spirit of wisdom and revelation, so that you may know him better. I pray also that the eyes of your heart may be enlightened in order that you may know the hope to which he has called you,

The riches of his glorious inheritance in the saints, and his incomparably great power for us who believe. That power is like the working of his mighty strength. May the God of hope fill you with all joy and peace as you trust in him, so that you may overflow with hope by the power of the Holy Spirit.

27. HUMILITY

Old Testament: 2 Chr. 7:14; Prov. 15:32–33; Ps. 34:2; Prov. 16:25; 20:24; 18:12; 22:3–4; Mic. 6:8; Zeph. 2:;

New Testament: Jas. 4:6–7; Lk. 14:11; Jas. 4:10; Phil. 2:3, 5–8; 2 Cor. 12:10; Mt. 18:4; 1 Pet. 5:6

If my people, who are called by my name, will humble themselves and pray and seek my face and turn from their wicked ways, then will I hear from heaven and will forgive their sin and will heal their land.

He who ignores discipline despises himself, but whoever heeds correction gains understanding.

The fear of the LORD teaches a man wisdom, and humility comes before honor.

My soul will boast in the LORD; let the afflicted hear and rejoice.

There is a way that seems right to a man, but in the end it leads to death.

A man's steps are directed by the LORD. How then can anyone understand his own way?

Before his downfall a man's heart is proud, but humility comes before honor.

A prudent man sees danger and takes refuge, but the simple keep going and suffer for it. Humility and the fear of the LORD bring wealth and honor and life.

He has showed you, O man, what is good. And what does the LORD require of you? To act justly and to love mercy and to walk humbly with your God.

Seek the LORD, all you humble of the land, you who do what he commands. Seek righteousness, seek humility; perhaps you will be sheltered on the day of the LORD's anger.

God opposes the proud but gives grace to the humble.

Submit yourselves, then, to God. Resist the devil, and he will flee from you.

For everyone who exalts himself will be humbled, and he who humbles himself will be exalted. Humble yourselves before the Lord, and he will lift you up.

Do nothing out of selfish ambition or vain conceit, but in humility consider others better than yourselves.

Your attitude should be the same as that of Christ Jesus: Who, being in very nature God, did not consider equality with God something to be grasped,

But made himself nothing, taking the very nature of a servant, being made in human likeness.

And being found in appearance as a man, he humbled himself and became obedient to death— even death on a cross!

That is why, for Christ's sake, I delight in weaknesses, in insults, in hardships, in persecutions, in difficulties. For when I am weak, then I am strong.

Therefore, whoever humbles himself like this child is the greatest in the kingdom of heaven.

Humble yourselves, therefore, under God's mighty hand, that he may lift you up in due time.

28. JOY

Old Testament: Ps. 98:4–9; 16:11; Isa. 35:10; Jer. 31:12; Ps. 30:4–5

New Testament: Mt. 2:9–10; 13:44; Lk. 15:7; Rom. 14:17; Jn. 15:9–11; Jas. 1:2–4; Heb. 12:2

Shout for joy to the LORD, all the earth, burst into jubilant song with music; make music to the LORD with the harp, with the harp and the sound of singing,

With trumpets and the blast of the ram's horn— shout for joy before the LORD, the King.

Let the sea resound, and everything in it, the world, and all who live in it. Let the rivers clap their hands,

Let the mountains sing together for joy; let them sing before the LORD, for he comes to judge the earth.

He will judge the world in righteousness and the peoples with equity.

You have made known to me the path of life; you will fill me with joy in your presence, with eternal pleasures at your right hand.

And the ransomed of the LORD will return. They will enter Zion with singing; everlasting joy will crown their heads.

Gladness and joy will overtake them, and sorrow and sighing will flee away.

They will come and shout for joy on the heights of Zion; they will rejoice in the bounty of the LORD— the grain, the new wine and the oil, the young of the flocks and herds.

They will be like a well-watered garden, and they will sorrow no more.

Sing to the LORD, you saints of his; praise his holy name. For his anger lasts only a moment, but his favor lasts a lifetime;

Weeping may remain for a night, but rejoicing comes in the morning.

After they had heard the king, they went on their way, and the star they had seen in the east went ahead of them until it stopped over the place where the child was.

When they saw the star, they were over-joyed.

The kingdom of heaven is like treasure hidden in a field. When a man found it, he hid it again, and then in his joy went and sold all he had and bought that field.

I tell you that in the same way there will be more rejoicing in heaven over one sinner who repents than over ninety-nine righteous persons who do not need to repent.

For the kingdom of God is not a matter of eating and drinking, but of righteousness, peace and joy in the Holy Spirit.

As the Father has loved me, so have I loved you. Now remain in my love.

If you obey my commands, you will remain in my love, just as I have obeyed my Father's commands and remain in his love.

I have told you this so that my joy may be in you and that your joy may be complete.

Consider it pure joy, my brothers, whenever you face trials of many kinds, because you know that the testing of your faith develops perseverance.

Perseverance must finish its work so that you may be mature and complete, not lacking anything.

Let us fix our eyes on Jesus, the author and perfecter of our faith, who for the joy set before him endured the cross,

Scorning its shame, and sat down at the right hand of the throne of God.

29. JESUS CHRIST

Old Testament: Isa. 9:6–7; 11:1–3; 53:4–7

New Testament: Jn. 1:29; 13:34–35; 8:12; 11:25–26; 1 Jn. 2:1–2; Phil. 2:9–11

For to us a child is born, to us a son is given, and the government will be on his shoulders. And he will be called Wonderful Counselor, Mighty God, Everlasting Father, Prince of Peace.

John saw Jesus coming toward him and said, "Look, the Lamb of God, who takes away the sin of the world!"

Of the increase of his government and peace there will be no end. He will reign on David's throne and over his kingdom,

A new command I give you: Love one another. As I have loved you, so you must love one another.

Establishing and upholding it with justice and righteousness from that time on and forever. The zeal of the LORD Almighty will accomplish this.

By this all men will know that you are my disciples, if you love one another.

A shoot will come up from the stump of Jesse; from his roots a Branch will bear fruit.

When Jesus spoke again to the people, he said, "I am the light of the world. Whoever follows me will never walk in darkness, but will have the light of life."

The Spirit of the LORD will rest on him— the Spirit of wisdom and of understanding, the Spirit of counsel and of power, the Spirit of knowledge and of the fear of the LORD—

Jesus said to her, "I am the resurrection and the life. He who believes in me will live, even though he dies; and whoever lives and believes in me will never die. Do you believe this?"

And he will delight in the fear of the LORD.

My dear children, I write this to you so that you will not sin. But if anybody does sin, we have one who speaks to the Father in our defense—Jesus Christ, the Righteous One.

Surely he took up our infirmities and carried our sorrows, yet we considered him stricken by God, smitten by him, and afflicted.

He is the atoning sacrifice for our sins, and not only for ours but also for the sins of the whole world.

But he was pierced for our transgressions, he was crushed for our iniquities; the punishment that brought us peace was upon him, and by his wounds we are healed.

Therefore God exalted him to the highest place and gave him the name that is above every name,

We all, like sheep, have gone astray, each of us has turned to his own way; and the LORD has laid on him the iniquity of us all.

That at the name of Jesus every knee should bow, in heaven and on earth and under the earth, and every tongue confess that Jesus Christ is Lord,

He was oppressed and afflicted, yet he did not open his mouth; he was led like a lamb to the slaughter, and as a sheep before her shearers is silent, so he did not open his mouth.

To the glory of God the Father.

30. JUSTICE

Old Testament: Ps. 89:14; 140:12; 146:5–7; Isa. 56:1; 59:14; 61:8; Am. 5:21–24; Mic. 6:8

New Testament: Lk. 18:7–8; 11:42; Mt. 12:18–21; Rom. 1:16–17; 8:31–33

Righteousness and justice are the foundation of your throne; love and faithfulness go before you. I know that the LORD secures justice for the poor and upholds the cause of the needy.

Blessed is he whose help is the God of Jacob, whose hope is in the LORD his God, the Maker of heaven and earth, the sea, and everything in them—

The LORD, who remains faithful forever. He upholds the cause of the oppressed and gives food to the hungry.

This is what the LORD says: "Maintain justice and do what is right, for my salvation is close at hand and my righteousness will soon be revealed."

So justice is driven back, and righteousness stands at a distance; truth has stumbled in the streets, honesty cannot enter.

For I, the LORD, love justice; I hate robbery and iniquity. In my faithfulness I will reward them and make an everlasting covenant with them.

I hate, I despise your religious feasts; I cannot stand your assemblies. Even though you bring me burnt offerings and grain offerings,

I will not accept them. Though you bring choice fellowship offerings, I will have no regard for them.

Away with the noise of your songs! I will not listen to the music of your harps. But let justice roll on like a river, righteousness like a never-failing stream!

He has showed you, O man, what is good. And what does the LORD require of you? To act justly and to love mercy and to walk humbly with your God.

And will not God bring about justice for his chosen ones, who cry out to him day and night? Will he keep putting them off? I tell you, he will see that they get justice, and quickly.

However, when the Son of Man comes, will he find faith on the earth?

Woe to you Pharisees, because you give God a tenth of your mint, rue and all other kinds of garden herbs, but you neglect justice and the love of God. You should have practiced the latter without leaving the former undone.

Here is my servant whom I have chosen, the one I love, in whom I delight; I will put my Spirit on him, and he will proclaim justice to the nations.

He will not quarrel or cry out; no one will hear his voice in the streets.

A bruised reed he will not break, and a smoldering wick he will not snuff out, till he leads justice to victory. In his name the nations will put their hope.

I am not ashamed of the gospel, because it is the power of God for the salvation of everyone who believes: first for the Jew, then for the Gentile.

For in the gospel a righteousness from God is revealed, a righteousness that is by faith from first to last, just as it is written: "The righteous will live by faith."

What, then, shall we say in response to this? If God is for us, who can be against us? He who did not spare his own Son, but gave him up for us all—how will he not also, along with him, graciously give us all things?

Who will bring any charge against those whom God has chosen? It is God who justifies.

31. KINGDOM OF GOD

Old Testament: Isa. 29:18–21; 35:10; Ps. 93:1–2; 99:4–5; 145:11–13

New Testament: Mt. 7:21–23; 13:44–50; 18:1–5; Rom. 14:17

In that day the deaf will hear the words of the scroll, and out of gloom and darkness the eyes of the blind will see.

Once more the humble will rejoice in the LORD; the needy will rejoice in the Holy One of Israel.

The ruthless will vanish, the mockers will disappear, and all who have an eye for evil will be cut down —

Those who with a word make a man out to be guilty, who ensnare the defender in court and with false testimony deprive the innocent of justice.

And the ransomed of the LORD will return. They will enter Zion with singing; everlasting joy will crown their heads.

Gladness and joy will overtake them, and sorrow and sighing will flee away.

The LORD reigns, he is robed in majesty; the LORD is robed in majesty and is armed with strength.

The world is firmly established; it cannot be moved. Your throne was established long ago; you are from all eternity.

The King is mighty, he loves justice— you have established equity; in Jacob you have done what is just and right.

Exalt the LORD our God and worship at his footstool; he is holy.

They will tell of the glory of your kingdom and speak of your might, so that all men may know of your mighty acts and the glorious splendor of your kingdom.

Your kingdom is an everlasting kingdom, and your dominion endures through all generations.

Not everyone who says to me, 'Lord, Lord,' will enter the kingdom of heaven, but only he who does the will of my Father who is in heaven. Many will say to me on that day, 'Lord, Lord, did we not prophesy in your name, and in your name drive out demons and perform many miracles?'

Then I will tell them plainly, 'I never knew you. Away from me, you evildoers!'

The kingdom of heaven is like treasure hidden in a field. When a man found it, he hid it again, and then in his joy went and sold all he had and bought that field.

Again, the kingdom of heaven is like a merchant looking for fine pearls. When he found one of great value, he went away and sold everything he had and bought it.

Once again, the kingdom of heaven is like a net that was let down into the lake and caught all kinds of fish. When it was full, the fishermen pulled it up on the shore. Then they sat down and collected the good fish in baskets, but threw the bad away.

This is how it will be at the end of the age. The angels will come and separate the wicked from the righteous and throw them into the fiery furnace, where there will be weeping and gnashing of teeth.

At that time the disciples came to Jesus and asked, "Who is the greatest in the kingdom of heaven?"

He called a little child and had him stand among them. And he said: "I tell you the truth, unless you change and become like little children, you will never enter the kingdom of heaven.

Therefore, whoever humbles himself like this child is the greatest in the kingdom of heaven. And whoever welcomes a little child like this in my name welcomes me."

For the kingdom of God is not a matter of eating and drinking, but of righteousness, peace and joy in the Holy Spirit.

32. LIBERATION

Old Testament: Ex. 3:7–10; Lev. 25:13, 18; Isa. 61:1–3; Ps. 18:2

New Testament: Jn. 8:31–32, 36; Rom. 6:17–18; 2 Cor. 3:17; Gal. 5:1, 13; Titus 3:3–5

The LORD said, "I have indeed seen the misery of my people in Egypt. I have heard them crying out because of their slave drivers,

And I am concerned about their suffering. So I have come down to rescue them from the hand of the Egyptians and to bring them up out of that land into a good and spacious land, a land flowing with milk and honey...

And now the cry of the Israelites has reached me, and I have seen the way the Egyptians are oppressing them.

So now, go. I am sending you to Pharaoh to bring my people the Israelites out of Egypt."

In this Year of Jubilee everyone is to return to his own property. Follow my decrees and be careful to obey my laws, and you will live safely in the land.

The Spirit of the Sovereign LORD is on me, because the LORD has anointed me to preach good news to the poor.

He has sent me to bind up the brokenhearted, to proclaim freedom for the captives and release from darkness for the prisoners,

To proclaim the year of the LORD's favor and the day of vengeance of our God, to comfort all who mourn,

And provide for those who grieve in Zion— to bestow on them a crown of beauty instead of ashes, the oil of gladness instead of mourning, and a garment of praise instead of a spirit of despair.

The LORD is my rock, my fortress and my deliverer; my God is my rock, in whom I take refuge. He is my shield and the horn of my salvation, my stronghold.

To the Jews who had believed him, Jesus said, "If you hold to my teaching, you are really my disciples. Then you will know the truth, and the truth will set you free."

So if the Son sets you free, you will be free indeed.

But thanks be to God that, though you used to be slaves to sin, you wholeheartedly obeyed the form of teaching to which you were entrusted. You have been set free from sin and have become slaves to righteousness.

Now the Lord is the Spirit, and where the Spirit of the Lord is, there is freedom.

It is for freedom that Christ has set us free. Stand firm, then, and do not let yourselves be burdened again by a yoke of slavery.

You, my brothers, were called to be free. But do not use your freedom to indulge the sinful nature; rather, serve one another in love.

At one time we too were foolish, disobedient, deceived and enslaved by all kinds of passions and pleasures. We lived in malice and envy, being hated and hating one another.

But when the kindness and love of God our Savior appeared, he saved us, not because of righteous things we had done, but because of his mercy. He saved us through the washing of rebirth and renewal by the Holy Spirit.

33. LOVE

Old Testament: Deut. 6:5–7; Ps. 136:1; 116:1–2; 100:4–5; Song 4:1; 8:6–7

New Testament: Jn. 3:16; 15:12–13; Col. 3:13–14; 1 Cor. 13:1–8, 13

Love the LORD your God with all your heart and with all your soul and with all your strength.

For God so loved the world that he gave his one and only Son, that whoever believes in him shall not perish but have eternal life.

These commandments that I give you today are to be upon your hearts.

My command is this: Love each other as I have loved you. Greater love has no one than this, that he lay down his life for his friends.

Impress them on your children. Talk about them when you sit at home and when you walk along the road, when you lie down and when you get up.

Bear with each other and forgive whatever grievances you may have against one another. Forgive as the Lord forgave you.

Give thanks to the LORD, for he is good. His love endures forever.

And over all these virtues put on love, which binds them all together in perfect unity.

I love the LORD, for he heard my voice; he heard my cry for mercy. Because he turned his ear to me, I will call on him as long as I live.

If I speak in the tongues of men and of angels, but have not love, I am only a resounding gong or a clanging cymbal.

Enter his gates with thanksgiving and his courts with praise; give thanks to him and praise his name.

If I have the gift of prophecy and can fathom all mysteries and all knowledge, and if I have a faith that can move mountains, but have not love, I am nothing.

For the LORD is good and his love endures forever; his faithfulness continues through all generations.

If I give all I possess to the poor and surrender my body to the flames, but have not love, I gain nothing.

How beautiful you are, my darling! Oh, how beautiful!

Love is patient, love is kind. It does not envy, it does not boast, it is not proud. It is not rude, it is not self-seeking, it is not easily angered, it keeps no record of wrongs.

Your eyes behind your veil are doves. Your hair is like a flock of goats descending from Mount Gilead.

Love does not delight in evil but rejoices with the truth. It always protects, always trusts, always hopes, always perseveres.

Place me like a seal over your heart, like a seal on your arm;

Love never fails. And now these three remain: faith, hope and love. But the greatest of these is love.

For love is as strong as death, its jealousy unyielding as the grave. It burns like blazing fire, like a mighty flame.

Many waters cannot quench love; rivers cannot wash it away.

34. MARRIAGE

Old Testament: Gen. 2:18, 23–24; 24:64–67; 25:20–21; 29:18–20

New Testament: Mt. 19:7–9; Heb. 13:1, 4; Eph. 5:22, 25–33

The LORD God said, "It is not good for the man to be alone. I will make a helper suitable for him." The man said, "This is now bone of my bones and flesh of my flesh."

She shall be called 'woman,' for she was taken out of man. "For this reason a man will leave his father and mother and be united to his wife, and they will become one flesh.

Rebekah also looked up and saw Isaac. She got down from her camel and asked the servant, "Who is that man in the field coming to meet us?" "He is my master," the servant answered.

So she took her veil and covered herself. Then the servant told Isaac all he had done.

Isaac brought her into the tent of his mother Sarah, and he married Rebekah. So she became his wife, and he loved her; and Isaac was comforted after his mother's death. And Isaac was forty years old when he married Rebekah.

Isaac prayed to the LORD on behalf of his wife, because she was barren. The LORD answered his prayer, and his wife Rebekah became pregnant.

Jacob was in love with Rachel and said, "I'll work for you seven years in return for your younger daughter Rachel." Laban said, "It's better that I give her to you than to some other man. Stay here with me."

So Jacob served seven years to get Rachel, but they seemed like only a few days to him because of his love for her.

"Why then," they asked, "did Moses command that a man give his wife a certificate of divorce and send her away?"

Jesus replied, "Moses permitted you to divorce your wives because your hearts were hard. But it was not this way from the beginning.

I tell you that anyone who divorces his wife, except for marital unfaithfulness, and marries another woman commits adultery."

Keep on loving each other as brothers. Marriage should be honored by all, and the marriage bed kept pure, for God will judge the adulterer and all the sexually immoral.

Wives, submit to your husbands as to the Lord. Husbands, love your wives, just as Christ loved the church and gave himself up for her

To make her holy, cleansing her by the washing with water through the word,

And to present her to himself as a radiant church, without stain or wrinkle or any other blemish, but holy and blameless.

In this same way, husbands ought to love their wives as their own bodies. He who loves his wife loves himself.

After all, no one ever hated his own body, but he feeds and cares for it, just as Christ does the church— for we are members of his body.

For this reason a man will leave his father and mother and be united to his wife, and the two will become one flesh.

This is a profound mystery—but I am talking about Christ and the church.

However, each one of you also must love his wife as he loves himself, and the wife must respect her husband.

35. MERCY

Old Testament: Lam. 3:22–23; Ps. 145:8–9; 85:10; Prov. 3:3–4; Ps 103:8; Mic. 6:8; Ps. 100:5

New Testament: Mt. 5:7; Eph. 2:4–6; Titus 3:5; Rom. 9:16–18; Lk. 1:50; 1 Pet. 2:10; Jude 21–23; Lk. 6:36

Because of the LORD's great love we are not consumed, for his compassions never fail. They are new every morning; great is your faithfulness.

Blessed are the merciful, for they will be shown mercy.

The LORD is gracious and compassionate, slow to anger and rich in love. The LORD is good to all; he has compassion on all he has made.

But because of his great love for us, God, who is rich in mercy, made us alive with Christ even when we were dead in transgressions—

Love and faithfulness meet together; righteousness and peace kiss each other.

It is by grace you have been saved. And God raised us up with Christ and seated us with him in the heavenly realms in Christ Jesus.

Let love and faithfulness never leave you; bind them around your neck, write them on the tablet of your heart.

He saved us, not because of righteous things we had done, but because of his mercy. He saved us through the washing of rebirth and renewal by the Holy Spirit,

Then you will win favor and a good name in the sight of God and man.

It does not, therefore, depend on man's desire or effort, but on God's mercy.

The LORD is compassionate and gracious, slow to anger, abounding in love.

For the Scripture says to Pharaoh: "I raised you up for this very purpose, that I might display my power in you and that my name might be proclaimed in all the earth."

He has showed you, O man, what is good. And what does the LORD require of you? To act justly and to love mercy and to walk humbly with your God.

Therefore God has mercy on whom he wants to have mercy, and he hardens whom he wants to harden.

For the LORD is good and his love endures forever; his faithfulness continues through all generations.

His mercy extends to those who fear him, from generation to generation.

Once you were not a people, but now you are the people of God; once you had not received mercy, but now you have received mercy.

Keep yourselves in God's love as you wait for the mercy of our Lord Jesus Christ to bring you to eternal life.

Be merciful to those who doubt; snatch others from the fire and save them; to others show mercy, mixed with fear—hating even the clothing stained by corrupted flesh.

Be merciful, just as your Father is merciful.

36. MISSION

Old Testament: Gen. 12:1–3; Isa. 60:1–5; 58:7–9

New Testament: 1 Pet. 2:9; Lk. 9:1–2, 6; 10:17–20; Titus 2:11–12; Mt. 28:19–20

The LORD had said to Abram, "Leave your country, your people and your father's household and go to the land I will show you. I will make you into a great nation and I will bless you; I will make your name great, and you will be a blessing.

I will bless those who bless you, and whoever curses you I will curse; and all peoples on earth will be blessed through you."

Arise, shine, for your light has come, and the glory of the LORD rises upon you.

See, darkness covers the earth and thick darkness is over the peoples, but the LORD rises upon you and his glory appears over you.

Nations will come to your light, and kings to the brightness of your dawn.

Lift up your eyes and look about you: All assemble and come to you; your sons come from afar, and your daughters are carried on the arm.

Then you will look and be radiant, your heart will throb and swell with joy; the wealth on the seas will be brought to you, to you the riches of the nations will come.

Is it not to share your food with the hungry and to provide the poor wanderer with shelter— when you see the naked, to clothe him, and not to turn away from your own flesh and blood?

Then your light will break forth like the dawn, and your healing will quickly appear; then your righteousness will go before you, and the glory of the LORD will be your rear guard.

Then you will call, and the LORD will answer; you will cry for help, and he will say: Here am I.

But you are a chosen people, a royal priesthood, a holy nation, a people belonging to God, that you may declare the praises of him who called you out of darkness into his wonderful light.

When Jesus had called the Twelve together, he gave them power and authority to drive out all demons and to cure diseases, and he sent them out to preach the kingdom of God and to heal the sick.

So they set out and went from village to village, preaching the gospel and healing people everywhere.

The seventy-two returned with joy and said, "Lord, even the demons submit to us in your name." He replied, "I saw Satan fall like lightning from heaven. I have given you authority to trample on snakes and scorpions and to overcome all the power of the enemy; nothing will harm you.

However, do not rejoice that the spirits submit to you, but rejoice that your names are written in heaven."

For the grace of God that brings salvation has appeared to all men. It teaches us to say "No" to ungodliness and worldly passions, and to live self-controlled, upright and godly lives in this present age.

"Therefore go and make disciples of all nations, baptizing them in the name of the Father and of the Son and of the Holy Spirit,

And teaching them to obey everything I have commanded you. And surely I am with you always, to the very end of the age."

37. OBEDIENCE

Old Testament: Deut. 11:1, 26–28; Josh. 24:24; 1 Sam. 15:22–23; Isa. 1:18–20; Jer. 38:20

New Testament: Heb. 5:7–9; Acts 5:29–32; Jn. 3:36; 1 Pet. 1:14–15; Phil. 2:8–11

Love the LORD your God and keep his requirements, his decrees, his laws and his commands always.

See, I am setting before you today a blessing and a curse: the blessing if you obey the commands of the LORD your God that I am giving you today;

The curse if you disobey the commands of the LORD your God.

And the people said to Joshua, "We will serve the LORD our God and obey him."

But Samuel replied: "Does the LORD delight in burnt offerings and sacrifices as much as in obeying the voice of the LORD? To obey is better than sacrifice, and to heed is better than the fat of rams.

For rebellion is like the sin of divination, and arrogance like the evil of idolatry.

Because you have rejected the word of the LORD, he has rejected you as king."

"Come now, let us reason together," says the LORD. "Though your sins are like scarlet, they shall be as white as snow; though they are red as crimson, they shall be like wool.

If you are willing and obedient, you will eat the best from the land; but if you resist and rebel, you will be devoured by the sword."

Obey the LORD by doing what I tell you. Then it will go well with you, and your life will be spared.

During the days of Jesus' life on earth, he offered up prayers and petitions with loud cries and tears to the one who could save him from death, and he was heard because of his reverent submission.

Although he was a son, he learned obedience from what he suffered and, once made perfect, he became the source of eternal salvation for all who obey him.

Peter and the other apostles replied: "We must obey God rather than men! The God of our fathers raised Jesus from the dead — whom you had killed by hanging him on a tree.

God exalted him to his own right hand as Prince and Savior that he might give repentance and forgiveness of sins to Israel. We are witnesses of these things, and so is the Holy Spirit, whom God has given to those who obey him."

Whoever believes in the Son has eternal life, but whoever rejects the Son will not see life, for God's wrath remains on him.

As obedient children, do not conform to the evil desires you had when you lived in ignorance. But just as he who called you is holy, so be holy in all you do.

And being found in appearance as a man, he humbled himself and became obedient to death — even death on a cross!

Therefore God exalted him to the highest place and gave him the name that is above every name,

That at the name of Jesus every knee should bow, in heaven and on earth and under the earth, and every tongue confess that Jesus Christ is Lord,

To the glory of God the Father.

38. PATICENCE

Old Testament: Ps. 62:1–2; Eccl. 7:8–9; Ps. 37:7–9; 40:1–3; 27:13–14

New Testament: Gal. 5:22–23; Rom. 5:3–5; 1 Thess. 5:14; Jas. 5:7–11

My soul finds rest in God alone; my salvation comes from him.

He alone is my rock and my salvation; he is my fortress, I will never be shaken.

The end of a matter is better than its beginning, and patience is better than pride.

Do not be quickly provoked in your spirit, for anger resides in the lap of fools.

Be still before the LORD and wait patiently for him; do not fret when men succeed in their ways, when they carry out their wicked schemes.

Refrain from anger and turn from wrath; do not fret—it leads only to evil.

For evil men will be cut off,

But those who hope in the LORD will inherit the land.

I waited patiently for the LORD; he turned to me and heard my cry. He lifted me out of the slimy pit, out of the mud and mire; he set my feet on a rock and gave me a firm place to stand.

He put a new song in my mouth, a hymn of praise to our God. Many will see and fear and put their trust in the LORD.

I am still confident of this: I will see the goodness of the LORD in the land of the living.

Wait for the LORD; be strong and take heart and wait for the LORD.

The fruit of the Spirit is love, joy, peace, patience, kindness, goodness, faithfulness, gentleness and self-control.

Not only so, but we also rejoice in our sufferings, because we know that suffering produces perseverance; perseverance, character; and character, hope.

And hope does not disappoint us, because God has poured out his love into our hearts by the Holy Spirit, whom he has given us.

And we urge you, brothers, warn those who are idle, encourage the timid, help the weak, be patient with everyone.

Be patient, then, brothers, until the Lord's coming.

See how the farmer waits for the land to yield its valuable crop and how patient he is for the autumn and spring rains.

You too, be patient and stand firm, because the Lord's coming is near.

Don't grumble against each other, brothers, or you will be judged. The Judge is standing at the door!

Brothers, as an example of patience in the face of suffering, take the prophets who spoke in the name of the Lord. As you know, we consider blessed those who have persevered.

You have heard of Job's perseverance and have seen what the Lord finally brought about. The Lord is full of compassion and mercy.

39. PEACE

Old Testament: Ps. 85:8–10; Isa. 52:7; Ps. 119:164–165; Prov. 16:7–9; 1 Kings 5:4–5; Isa. 32:18

New Testament: Jn. 14:27; Mt. 5:9; Eph. 2:13–15; Col. 3:15; Heb. 12:14–15; 2 Thess. 3:16

I will listen to what God the LORD will say; he promises peace to his people, his saints— but let them not return to folly.

Surely his salvation is near those who fear him, that his glory may dwell in our land.

Love and faithfulness meet together; righteousness and peace kiss each other.

How beautiful on the mountains are the feet of those who bring good news, who proclaim peace, who bring good tidings, who proclaim salvation, who say to Zion, "Your God reigns!"

Seven times a day I praise you for your righteous laws.

Great peace have they who love your law, and nothing can make them stumble.

When a man's ways are pleasing to the LORD, he makes even his enemies live at peace with him.

Better a little with righteousness than much gain with injustice.

In his heart a man plans his course, but the LORD determines his steps.

But now the LORD my God has given me rest on every side, and there is no adversary or disaster.

I intend, therefore, to build a temple for the Name of the LORD my God.

My people will live in peaceful dwelling places, in secure homes, in undisturbed places of rest.

Peace I leave with you; my peace I give you. I do not give to you as the world gives. Do not let your hearts be troubled and do not be afraid.

Blessed are the peacemakers, for they will be called sons of God.

But now in Christ Jesus you who once were far away have been brought near through the blood of Christ.

For he himself is our peace, who has made the two one and has destroyed the barrier, the dividing wall of hostility,

By abolishing in his flesh the law with its commandments and regulations. His purpose was to create in himself one new man out of the two, thus making peace.

Let the peace of Christ rule in your hearts, since as members of one body you were called to peace. And be thankful.

Make every effort to live in peace with all men and to be holy; without holiness no one will see the Lord.

See to it that no one misses the grace of God and that no bitter root grows up to cause trouble and defile many.

Now may the Lord of peace himself give you peace at all times and in every way.

The Lord be with all of you.

40. POWER

Old Testament: Ex. 15:2, 11, 17–18; Deut. 8:18; Jer. 10:12–13; Isa. 40:12, 29

New Testament: 1 Cor. 1:18, 22–25; Rom. 1:20; Col. 1:15–18; Acts 1:8

The LORD is my strength and my song; he has become my salvation. He is my God, and I will praise him, my father's God, and I will exalt him.

Who among the gods is like you, O LORD? Who is like you— majestic in holiness, awesome in glory, working wonders?

You will bring them in and plant them on the mountain of your inheritance—

The place, O LORD, you made for your dwelling, the sanctuary, O Lord, your hands established.

The LORD will reign for ever and ever.

But remember the LORD your God, for it is he who gives you the ability to produce wealth, and so confirms his covenant, which he swore to your forefathers, as it is today.

But God made the earth by his power; he founded the world by his wisdom and stretched out the heavens by his understanding.

When he thunders, the waters in the heavens roar; he makes clouds rise from the ends of the earth.

He sends lightning with the rain and brings out the wind from his storehouses.

Who has measured the waters in the hollow of his hand, or with the breadth of his hand marked off the heavens? Who has held the dust of the earth in a basket,

Or weighed the mountains on the scales and the hills in a balance?

He gives strength to the weary and increases the power of the weak.

For the message of the cross is foolishness to those who are perishing, but to us who are being saved it is the power of God.

Jews demand miraculous signs and Greeks look for wisdom, but we preach Christ crucified: a stumbling block to Jews and foolishness to Gentiles,

But to those whom God has called, both Jews and Greeks, Christ the power of God and the wisdom of God. For the foolishness of God is wiser than man's wisdom, and the weakness of God is stronger than man's strength.

For since the creation of the world God's invisible qualities—his eternal power and divine nature—have been clearly seen, being understood from what has been made.

He is the image of the invisible God, the firstborn over all creation. For by him all things were created: things in heaven and on earth,

Visible and invisible, whether thrones or powers or rulers or authorities; all things were created by him and for him.

He is before all things, and in him all things hold together. And he is the head of the body, the church; he is the beginning and the firstborn from among the dead, so that in everything he might have the supremacy.

But you will receive power when the Holy Spirit comes on you; and you will be my witnesses in Jerusalem, and in all Judea and Samaria, and to the ends of the earth.

41. PRAISE

Old Testament: Ps. 146:1–2; 2 Chr. 5:13–14; Ps. 34:1–3; 150

New Testament: Phil. 4:4–7; Rom. 15:8–11; Heb. 13:15–16; Rev. 19:1, 6

Praise the LORD. Praise the LORD, O my soul. I will praise the LORD all my life;

I will sing praise to my God as long as I live.

The trumpeters and singers joined in unison, as with one voice, to give praise and thanks to the LORD.

Accompanied by trumpets, cymbals and other instruments, they raised their voices in praise to the LORD and sang: "He is good; his love endures forever."

Then the temple of the LORD was filled with a cloud, and the priests could not perform their service because of the cloud, for the glory of the LORD filled the temple of God.

I will extol the LORD at all times; his praise will always be on my lips.

My soul will boast in the LORD; let the afflicted hear and rejoice.

Glorify the LORD with me; let us exalt his name together.

Praise the LORD. Praise God in his sanctuary; praise him in his mighty heavens.

Praise him for his acts of power; praise him for his surpassing greatness.

Praise him with the sounding of the trumpet, praise him with the harp and lyre,

Praise him with tambourine and dancing, praise him with the strings and flute,

Praise him with the clash of cymbals, praise him with resounding cymbals.

Let everything that has breath praise the LORD. Praise the LORD.

Rejoice in the Lord always. I will say it again: Rejoice! Let your gentleness be evident to all. The Lord is near.

Do not be anxious about anything, but in everything, by prayer and petition, with thanksgiving, present your requests to God.

And the peace of God, which transcends all understanding, will guard your hearts and your minds in Christ Jesus.

For I tell you that Christ has become a servant of the Jews on behalf of God's truth, to confirm the promises made to the patriarchs

So that the Gentiles may glorify God for his mercy, as it is written:

"Therefore I will praise you among the Gentiles; I will sing hymns to your name."

Again, it says, "Rejoice, O Gentiles, with his people." And again, "Praise the Lord, all you Gentiles, and sing praises to him, all you peoples."

Through Jesus, therefore, let us continually offer to God a sacrifice of praise— the fruit of lips that confess his name.

And do not forget to do good and to share with others, for with such sacrifices God is pleased.

After this I heard what sounded like the roar of a great multitude in heaven shouting: "Hallelujah! Salvation and glory and power belong to our God."

Then I heard what sounded like a great multitude, like the roar of rushing waters and like loud peals of thunder, shouting:

"Hallelujah! For our Lord God Almighty reigns."

42. PRAYER

Old Testament: Ps. 39:12; 2 Chr. 7:14; 1 Sam. 12:19, 23; 7:9; Job 42:8–9; 1 Kings 8:22–23; Ps. 66:18–19; Prov. 15:29

Hear my prayer, O LORD, listen to my cry for help; be not deaf to my weeping.

If my people, who are called by my name, will humble themselves and pray and seek my face and turn from their wicked ways, then will I hear from heaven and will forgive their sin and will heal their land.

The people all said to Samuel, "Pray to the LORD your God for your servants so that we will not die, for we have added to all our other sins the evil of asking for a king."

And Samuel said: "As for me, far be it from me that I should sin against the LORD by failing to pray for you. And I will teach you the way that is good and right."

He cried out to the LORD on Israel's behalf, and the LORD answered him.

So now take seven bulls and seven rams and go to my servant Job and sacrifice a burnt offering for yourselves. My servant Job will pray for you, and I will accept his prayer and not deal with you according to your folly. You have not spoken of me what is right, as my servant Job has.

So Eliphaz the Temanite, Bildad the Shuhite and Zophar the Naamathite did what the LORD told them; and the LORD accepted Job's prayer.

Then Solomon stood before the altar of the LORD in front of the whole assembly of Israel, spread out his hands toward heaven and said:

"O LORD, God of Israel, there is no God like you in heaven above or on earth below— you who keep your covenant of love with your servants who continue wholeheartedly in your way."

If I had cherished sin in my heart, the Lord would not have listened;

But God has surely listened and heard my voice in prayer.

The LORD is far from the wicked but he hears the prayer of the righteous.

New Testament: 1 Thess. 5:16–18; Mt. 21:22; Jas. 5:16; Lk. 18:7–8; Mt. 6:6–13

Be joyful always; pray continually; give thanks in all circumstances, for this is God's will for you in Christ Jesus.

If you believe, you will receive whatever you ask for in prayer.

Therefore confess your sins to each other and pray for each other so that you may be healed. The prayer of a righteous man is powerful and effective.

And will not God bring about justice for his chosen ones, who cry out to him day and night? Will he keep putting them off? I tell you, he will see that they get justice, and quickly. However, when the Son of Man comes, will he find faith on the earth?

But when you pray, go into your room, close the door and pray to your Father, who is unseen. Then your Father, who sees what is done in secret, will reward you.

And when you pray, do not keep on babbling like pagans, for they think they will be heard because of their many words. Do not be like them, for your Father knows what you need before you ask him.

This, then, is how you should pray:

Our Father in heaven, hallowed be your name, your kingdom come, your will be done on earth as it is in heaven. Give us today our daily bread. Forgive us our debts, as we also have forgiven our debtors. And lead us not into temptation, but deliver us from the evil one.

43. PRESENCE OF GOD

Old Testament: Ps. 139:7–10; 51:11; Ex. 13:21–22; 19:4; Deut. 31:8; Ps. 16:11; Isa. 6:1, 5; Ps. 15:1–2

Where can I go from your Spirit? Where can I flee from your presence?

If I go up to the heavens, you are there; if I make my bed in the depths, you are there.

If I rise on the wings of the dawn, if I settle on the far side of the sea, even there your hand will guide me, your right hand will hold me fast.

Do not cast me from your presence or take your Holy Spirit from me.

By day the LORD went ahead of them in a pillar of cloud to guide them on their way and by night in a pillar of fire to give them light, so that they could travel by day or night.

Neither the pillar of cloud by day nor the pillar of fire by night left its place in front of the people.

You yourselves have seen what I did to Egypt, and how I carried you on eagles' wings and brought you to myself. The LORD himself goes before you and will be with you; he will never leave you nor forsake you. Do not be afraid; do not be discouraged.

You have made known to me the path of life; you will fill me with joy in your presence, with eternal pleasures at your right hand.

In the year that King Uzziah died, I saw the Lord seated on a throne, high and exalted, and the train of his robe filled the temple.

"Woe to me!" I cried. "I am ruined! For I am a man of unclean lips, and I live among a people of unclean lips, and my eyes have seen the King, the LORD Almighty."

LORD, who may dwell in your sanctuary? Who may live on your holy hill?

He whose walk is blameless and who does what is righteous, who speaks the truth from his heart.

New Testament: Jn. 1:1–2, 14; 8:28–29; Acts 17:26–28; Rom. 8:9; 1 Cor. 3:16; Eph. 2:21–22

In the beginning was the Word, and the Word was with God, and the Word was God. He was with God in the beginning.

The Word became flesh and made his dwelling among us. We have seen his glory, the glory of the One and Only, who came from the Father, full of grace and truth.

So Jesus said, "When you have lifted up the Son of Man, then you will know that I am the one I claim to be and that I do nothing on my own

But speak just what the Father has taught me. The one who sent me is with me; he has not left me alone, for I always do what pleases him."

From one man he made every nation of men, that they should inhabit the whole earth; and he determined the times set for them and the exact places where they should live.

God did this so that men would seek him and perhaps reach out for him and find him, though he is not far from each one of us.

For in him we live and move and have our being.

You, however, are controlled not by the sinful nature but by the Spirit, if the Spirit of God lives in you.

Don't you know that you yourselves are God's temple and that God's Spirit lives in you?

In him the whole building is joined together and rises to become a holy temple in the Lord. And in him you too are being built together to become a dwelling in which God lives by his Spirit.

44. PROMISES OF GOD

Old Testament: Gen. 28:13–15; 2 Chr. 7:14; Ps. 91:9–11; Ezek. 34:27–28; Isa. 25:7–8; Num. 23:19

There above it stood the LORD, and he said: "I am the LORD, the God of your father Abraham and the God of Isaac.

I will give you and your descendants the land on which you are lying.

Your descendants will be like the dust of the earth, and you will spread out to the west and to the east, to the north and to the south.

I am with you and will watch over you wherever you go, and I will bring you back to this land. I will not leave you until I have done what I have promised you."

If my people, who are called by my name, will humble themselves and pray and seek my face and turn from their wicked ways, then will I hear from heaven and will forgive their sin and will heal their land.

If you make the Most High your dwelling— even the LORD, who is my refuge— then no harm will befall you, no disaster will come near your tent.

For he will command his angels concerning you to guard you in all your ways;

They will know that I am the LORD, when I break the bars of their yoke

And rescue them from the hands of those who enslaved them. They will live in safety, and no one will make them afraid.

On this mountain he will destroy the shroud that enfolds all peoples, the sheet that covers all nations; he will swallow up death forever.

The Sovereign LORD will wipe away the tears from all faces; he will remove the disgrace of his people from all the earth. The LORD has spoken.

God is not a man, that he should lie, nor a son of man, that he should change his mind. Does he speak and then not act? Does he promise and not fulfill?

New Testament: Heb. 4:1, 9–10; Acts 2:15–17, 38–39; Jn. 14:1–3; Rev. 22:2

Therefore, since the promise of entering his rest still stands, let us be careful that none of you be found to have fallen short of it.

There remains, then, a Sabbath-rest for the people of God; for anyone who enters God's rest also rests from his own work, just as God did from his.

These men are not drunk, as you suppose. It's only nine in the morning! No, this is what was spoken by the prophet Joel:

"In the last days, God says, I will pour out my Spirit on all people. Your sons and daughters will prophesy, your young men will see visions, your old men will dream dreams."

Peter replied, "Repent and be baptized, every one of you, in the name of Jesus Christ for the forgiveness of your sins. And you will receive the gift of the Holy Spirit.

The promise is for you and your children and for all who are far off—for all whom the Lord our God will call."

Do not let your hearts be troubled. Trust in God; trust also in me. In my Father's house are many rooms;

If it were not so, I would have told you. I am going there to prepare a place for you.

And if I go and prepare a place for you, I will come back and take you to be with me that you also may be where I am.

On each side of the river stood the tree of life, bearing twelve crops of fruit, yielding its fruit every month. And the leaves of the tree are for the healing of the nations.

45. RECONCILIATION

Old Testament: Gen. 27:41; 28:1, 3, 5; 31:41–42; 32:3–7; 33:1, 3–4

New Testament: Mt. 18:21–22; 5:23–24; 6:14–15; Eph. 4:31–32; 2 Cor. 5:18–20; Col. 1:19–20

Esau held a grudge against Jacob because of the blessing his father had given him.

He said to himself, "...I will kill my brother Jacob."

So Isaac called for Jacob and blessed him and commanded him: "...Go at once to Paddan Aram, to the house of your mother's father Bethuel. Take a wife for yourself there, from among the daughters of Laban... May God Almighty bless you and make you fruitful and increase your numbers... May he give you and your descendants the blessing given to Abraham..."

Then Isaac sent Jacob on his way, and he went to Paddan Aram.

Jacob said to Laban, "It was like this for the twenty years I was in your household. I worked for you fourteen years for your two daughters and six years for your flocks...

But God has seen my hardship and the toil of my hands..."

Jacob sent messengers ahead of him to his brother Esau... He instructed them: "This is what you are to say to my master Esau: 'Your servant Jacob says, I have been staying with Laban and have remained there till now. I have cattle and donkeys, sheep and goats, menservants and maidservants. Now I am sending this message to my lord, that I may find favor in your eyes.'"

When the messengers returned to Jacob, they said, "We went to your brother Esau, and now he is coming to meet you, and four hundred men are with him."

In great fear and distress Jacob divided the people who were with him into two groups, and the flocks and herds and camels as well. Jacob looked up and there was Esau, coming with his four hundred men... He himself went on ahead and bowed down to the ground seven times as he approached his brother.

But Esau ran to meet Jacob and embraced him; he threw his arms around his neck and kissed him. And they wept.

Then Peter came to Jesus and asked, "Lord, how many times shall I forgive my brother when he sins against me? Up to seven times?"

Jesus answered, "I tell you, not seven times, but seventy-seven times."

Therefore, if you are offering your gift at the altar and there remember that your brother has something against you,

Leave your gift there in front of the altar. First go and be reconciled to your brother; then come and offer your gift.

For if you forgive men when they sin against you, your heavenly Father will also forgive you.

But if you do not forgive men their sins, your Father will not forgive your sins.

Get rid of all bitterness, rage and anger, brawling and slander, along with every form of malice. Be kind and compassionate to one another,

Forgiving each other, just as in Christ God forgave you.

All this is from God, who reconciled us to himself through Christ and gave us the ministry of reconciliation:

That God was reconciling the world to himself in Christ, not counting men's sins against them. And he has committed to us the message of reconciliation.

We are therefore Christ's ambassadors, as though God were making his appeal through us. We implore you on Christ's behalf: Be reconciled to God.

For God was pleased to have all his fullness dwell in him, and through him to reconcile to himself all things,.... by making peace through his blood, shed on the cross.

46. REPENTANCE

Old Testament: Ps. 51:1–4, 6, 9–13; Ezek. 18:27–28

New Testament: Mt. 3:2; Jn. 3:3; Lk. 5:30–32; 15:10; Acts 5:31–32; 2 Pet. 3:9; Lk. 24:44–48

Have mercy on me, O God, according to your unfailing love; according to your great compassion blot out my transgressions.

Repent, for the kingdom of heaven is near.

Wash away all my iniquity and cleanse me from my sin.

Jesus declared, "I tell you the truth, no one can see the kingdom of God unless he is born again."

For I know my transgressions, and my sin is always before me.

But the Pharisees and the teachers of the law who belonged to their sect complained to his disciples, "Why do you eat and drink with tax collectors and 'sinners'?"

Against you, you only, have I sinned and done what is evil in your sight, so that you are proved right when you speak and justified when you judge.

Jesus answered them, "It is not the healthy who need a doctor, but the sick. I have not come to call the righteous, but sinners to repentance."

Surely you desire truth in the inner parts; you teach me wisdom in the inmost place.

"In the same way, I tell you, there is rejoicing in the presence of the angels of God over one sinner who repents."

Hide your face from my sins and blot out all my iniquity.

God exalted him to his own right hand as Prince and Savior that he might give repentance and forgiveness of sins to Israel. We are witnesses of these things, and so is the Holy Spirit, whom God has given to those who obey him.

Create in me a pure heart, O God, and renew a steadfast spirit within me.

Do not cast me from your presence or take your Holy Spirit from me.

The Lord is not slow in keeping his promise, as some understand slowness. He is patient with you, not wanting anyone to perish, but everyone to come to repentance.

Restore to me the joy of your salvation and grant me a willing spirit, to sustain me.

Then I will teach transgressors your ways, and sinners will turn back to you.

He said to them, "This is what I told you while I was still with you: Everything must be fulfilled that is written about me in the Law of Moses, the Prophets and the Psalms."

But if a wicked man turns away from the wickedness he has committed and does what is just and right, he will save his life.

Then he opened their minds so they could understand the Scriptures. He told them, "This is what is written: The Christ will suffer and rise from the dead on the third day,

Because he considers all the offenses he has committed and turns away from them, he will surely live; he will not die.

And repentance and forgiveness of sins will be preached in his name to all nations, beginning at Jerusalem. You are witnesses of these things."

47. SALVATION

Old Testament: Ps. 27:1; 95:1; Isa. 55:1–2, 6–7; Hos. 13:4; Isa. 35:4; 2 Chr. 20:17

New Testament: Lk. 2:11; Jn. 3:16–17; Acts 4:12; Rom. 1:16; 5:10; 10:13; 1 Tim. 4:10; 2 Cor. 6:2; Jude 25

The LORD is my light and my salvation— whom shall I fear? The LORD is the stronghold of my life— of whom shall I be afraid?

Come, let us sing for joy to the LORD; let us shout aloud to the Rock of our salvation.

Come, all you who are thirsty, come to the waters; and you who have no money, come, buy and eat! Come, buy wine and milk without money and without cost.

Why spend money on what is not bread, and your labor on what does not satisfy?

Seek the LORD while he may be found; call on him while he is near. Let the wicked forsake his way and the evil man his thoughts.

Let him turn to the LORD, and he will have mercy on him, and to our God, for he will freely pardon.

But I am the LORD your God, who brought you out of Egypt. You shall acknowledge no God but me, no Savior except me.

Say to those with fearful hearts, "Be strong, do not fear; your God will come, he will come with vengeance; with divine retribution he will come to save you."

You will not have to fight this battle. Take up your positions; stand firm and see the deliverance the LORD will give you, O Judah and Jerusalem.

Do not be afraid; do not be discouraged. Go out to face them tomorrow, and the LORD will be with you.

Today in the town of David a Savior has been born to you; he is Christ the Lord.

For God so loved the world that he gave his one and only Son, that whoever believes in him shall not perish but have eternal life.

For God did not send his Son into the world to condemn the world, but to save the world through him.

Salvation is found in no one else, for there is no other name under heaven given to men by which we must be saved.

I am not ashamed of the gospel, because it is the power of God for the salvation of everyone who believes: first for the Jew, then for the Gentile.

For if, when we were God's enemies, we were reconciled to him through the death of his Son, how much more, having been reconciled, shall we be saved through his life!

For, "Everyone who calls on the name of the Lord will be saved."

And for this we labor and strive, that we have put our hope in the living God, who is the Savior of all men, and especially of those who believe.

Now is the time of God's favor, now is the day of salvation.

To the only God our Savior be glory, majesty, power and authority, through Jesus Christ our Lord, before all ages, now and forevermore! Amen.

48. SANCTIFICATION

Old Testament: Ps. 15:1–5; Ex. 19:5–6; 31:13; Ps. 24:3–4; Lev. 20:7–8

New Testament: 1 Thess. 4:3–5; 2 Thess. 2:13; 2 Cor. 6:14–18; 7:1

LORD, who may dwell in your sanctuary? Who may live on your holy hill?

He whose walk is blameless and who does what is righteous, who speaks the truth from his heart

And has no slander on his tongue, who does his neighbor no wrong

And casts no slur on his fellowman, who despises a vile man but honors those who fear the LORD,

Who keeps his oath even when it hurts, who lends his money without usury and does not accept a bribe against the innocent.

He who does these things will never be shaken.

Now if you obey me fully and keep my covenant, then out of all nations you will be my treasured possession.

Although the whole earth is mine, you will be for me a kingdom of priests and a holy nation.

You must observe my Sabbaths. This will be a sign between me and you for the generations to come, so you may know that I am the LORD, who makes you holy.

Who may ascend the hill of the LORD? Who may stand in his holy place?

He who has clean hands and a pure heart,

Who does not lift up his soul to an idol or swear by what is false.

Consecrate yourselves and be holy, because I am the LORD your God.

Keep my decrees and follow them. I am the LORD, who makes you holy.

It is God's will that you should be sanctified: that you should avoid sexual immorality;

That each of you should learn to control his own body in a way that is holy and honorable, not in passionate lust like the heathen, who do not know God;

But we ought always to thank God for you, brothers loved by the Lord, because from the beginning God chose you to be saved through the sanctifying work of the Spirit and through belief in the truth.

Do not be yoked together with unbelievers.

For what do righteousness and wickedness have in common? Or what fellowship can light have with darkness?

What harmony is there between Christ and Belial? What does a believer have in common with an unbeliever? What agreement is there between the temple of God and idols?

For we are the temple of the living God. As God has said: "I will live with them and walk among them, and I will be their God, and they will be my people."

Therefore, "come out from them and be separate, says the Lord. Touch no unclean thing, and I will receive you."

"I will be a Father to you, and you will be my sons and daughters, says the Lord Almighty."

Since we have these promises, dear friends, let us purify ourselves from everything that contaminates body and spirit, perfecting holiness out of reverence for God.

49. SUFFERING

Old Testament: Ex. 3:7–8; Ps. 55:1–2, 5–8, 16, 22; Lam. 3:16–17, 20–23; Ps. 34:19

New Testament: 1 Pet. 4:12–13, 19; Rom. 8:18; 5:3–4; Lk. 22:41–42, 44; Rev. 7:13–15, 17

The LORD said, "I have indeed seen the misery of my people in Egypt. I have heard them crying out because of their slave drivers, and I am concerned about their suffering.

So I have come down to rescue them from the hand of the Egyptians and to bring them up out of that land into a good and spacious land, a land flowing with milk and honey."

Listen to my prayer, O God, do not ignore my plea; hear me and answer me. My thoughts trouble me and I am distraught. Fear and trembling have beset me; horror has overwhelmed me.

I said, "Oh, that I had the wings of a dove! I would fly away and be at rest—I would flee far away and stay in the desert;

I would hurry to my place of shelter, far from the tempest and storm." But I call to God, and the LORD saves me.

Cast your cares on the LORD and he will sustain you; he will never let the righteous fall.

He has broken my teeth with gravel; he has trampled me in the dust. I have been deprived of peace; I have forgotten what prosperity is.

I well remember them, and my soul is downcast within me. Yet this I call to mind and therefore I have hope:

Because of the LORD's great love we are not consumed, for his compassions never fail. They are new every morning; great is your faithfulness.

A righteous man may have many troubles, but the LORD delivers him from them all.

Dear friends, do not be surprised at the painful trial you are suffering, as though something strange were happening to you.

But rejoice that you participate in the sufferings of Christ, so that you may be overjoyed when his glory is revealed.

So then, those who suffer according to God's will should commit themselves to their faithful Creator and continue to do good.

I consider that our present sufferings are not worth comparing with the glory that will be revealed in us.

Not only so, but we also rejoice in our sufferings, because we know that suffering produces perseverance; perseverance, character; and character, hope.

He withdrew about a stone's throw beyond them, knelt down and prayed, "Father, if you are willing, take this cup from me; yet not my will, but yours be done."

And being in anguish, he prayed more earnestly, and his sweat was like drops of blood falling to the ground.

These in white robes—who are they, and where did they come from? These are they who have come out of the great tribulation; they have washed their robes and made them white in the blood of the Lamb.

Therefore, "they are before the throne of God and serve him day and night in his temple;

And he who sits on the throne will spread his tent over them. And God will wipe away every tear from their eyes."

50. THANKSGIVING

Old Testament: Ps. 92:1–4; Ezra 3:10–11; 1 Chr.
29:10–13

New Testament: 1 Thess. 5:18; 1 Tim. 4:4–5; Col.
2:6–7; Phil. 4:6–7; 1 Cor. 1:4–7; 2 Cor. 2:14–15

It is good to praise the LORD and make music to your name, O Most High, to proclaim your love in the morning and your faithfulness at night, to the music of the ten-stringed lyre and the melody of the harp.

Give thanks in all circumstances, for this is God's will for you in Christ Jesus.

For you make me glad by your deeds, O LORD; I sing for joy at the works of your hands.

For everything God created is good, and nothing is to be rejected if it is received with thanksgiving, because it is consecrated by the word of God and prayer.

When the builders laid the foundation of the temple of the LORD, the priests in their vestments and with trumpets,

So then, just as you received Christ Jesus as Lord, continue to live in him,

And the Levites (the sons of Asaph) with cymbals, took their places to praise the LORD, as prescribed by David king of Israel.

Rooted and built up in him, strengthened in the faith as you were taught, and overflowing with thankfulness.

With praise and thanksgiving they sang to the LORD: "He is good; his love to Israel endures forever."

Do not be anxious about anything, but in everything, by prayer and petition, with thanksgiving, present your requests to God.

And all the people gave a great shout of praise to the LORD, because the foundation of the house of the LORD was laid.

And the peace of God, which transcends all understanding, will guard your hearts and your minds in Christ Jesus.

David praised the LORD in the presence of the whole assembly, saying, "Praise be to you, O LORD, God of our father Israel, from everlasting to everlasting.

I always thank God for you because of his grace given you in Christ Jesus. For in him you have been enriched in every way—

Yours, O LORD, is the greatness and the power and the glory and the majesty and the splendor, for everything in heaven and earth is yours.

In all your speaking and in all your knowledge— because our testimony about Christ was confirmed in you. Therefore you do not lack any spiritual gift as you eagerly wait for our Lord Jesus Christ to be revealed.

Yours, O LORD, is the kingdom; you are exalted as head over all. Wealth and honor come from you; you are the ruler of all things. In your hands are strength and power

But thanks be to God, who always leads us in triumphal procession in Christ and through us spreads everywhere the fragrance of the knowledge of him.

To exalt and give strength to all. Now, our God, we give you thanks, and praise your glorious name."

For we are to God the aroma of Christ among those who are being saved and those who are perishing.

51. UNITY

Old Testament: Gen. 2:21–24; Ruth 1:16–17; Eccl. 4:9–10; 1 Chr. 13:2–4; Ps. 133:1

New Testament: Jn. 17:11; Acts 2:1–4; 1 Cor. 12:12–13; Eph. 4:1–6; 2 Cor. 13:11

So the LORD God caused the man to fall into a deep sleep; and while he was sleeping, he took one of the man's ribs and closed up the place with flesh.

Then the LORD God made a woman from the rib he had taken out of the man, and he brought her to the man.

The man said, "This is now bone of my bones and flesh of my flesh; she shall be called 'woman,' for she was taken out of man."

For this reason a man will leave his father and mother and be united to his wife, and they will become one flesh.

But Ruth replied, "Don't urge me to leave you or to turn back from you. Where you go I will go, and where you stay I will stay.

Your people will be my people and your God my God. Where you die I will die, and there I will be buried."

Two are better than one, because they have a good return for their work: If one falls down, his friend can help him up. But pity the man who falls and has no one to help him up!

He then said to the whole assembly of Israel, "If it seems good to you and if it is the will of the LORD our God, let us send word far and wide to the rest of our brothers throughout the territories of Israel.

Let us bring the ark of our God back to us, for we did not inquire of it during the reign of Saul." The whole assembly agreed to do this, because it seemed right to all the people.

How good and pleasant it is when brothers live together in unity!

I am coming to you. Holy Father, protect them by the power of your name—the name you gave me—so that they may be one as we are one.

When the day of Pentecost came, they were all together in one place.

Suddenly a sound like the blowing of a violent wind came from heaven and filled the whole house where they were sitting.

They saw what seemed to be tongues of fire that separated and came to rest on each of them. All of them were filled with the Holy Spirit and began to speak in other tongues as the Spirit enabled them.

The body is a unit, though it is made up of many parts; and though all its parts are many, they form one body. So it is with Christ.

For we were all baptized by one Spirit into one body—whether Jews or Greeks, slave or free—and we were all given the one Spirit to drink.

As a prisoner for the Lord, then, I urge you to live a life worthy of the calling you have received. Be completely humble and gentle; be patient, bearing with one another in love.

Make every effort to keep the unity of the Spirit through the bond of peace.

There is one body and one Spirit—just as you were called to one hope when you were called—one Lord, one faith, one baptism; one God and Father of all, who is over all and through all and in all.

Finally, brothers, good-bye. Aim for perfection, listen to my appeal, be of one mind, live in peace. And the God of love and peace will be with you.

52. VICTORY

Old Testament: Ps. 98:1–3; Ex. 15:6; 1 Chr. 29:11; Ex. 15:11; Ps. 21:13; Ex. 15:1, 18

New Testament: Lk. 1:46–49, 51–52; 1 Cor. 15:55–58; Rom. 8:38–39, 37

Sing to the LORD a new song, for he has done marvelous things;

His right hand and his holy arm have worked salvation for him.

The LORD has made his salvation known and revealed his righteousness to the nations.

He has remembered his love and his faithfulness to the house of Israel;

All the ends of the earth have seen the salvation of our God.

Your right hand, O LORD, was majestic in power. Your right hand, O LORD, shattered the enemy.

Yours, O LORD, is the greatness and the power and the glory and the majesty and the splendor.

Who among the gods is like you, O LORD?

Who is like you— majestic in holiness, awesome in glory, working wonders?

Be exalted, O LORD, in your strength; we will sing and praise your might.

I will sing to the LORD, for he is highly exalted.

The LORD will reign for ever and ever.

My soul glorifies the Lord and my spirit rejoices in God my Savior,

For he has been mindful of the humble state of his servant.

For the Mighty One has done great things for me— holy is his name.

He has performed mighty deeds with his arm; he has scattered those who are proud in their inmost thoughts.

He has brought down rulers from their thrones but has lifted up the humble.

Where, O death, is your victory? Where, O death, is your sting?

The sting of death is sin, and the power of sin is the law.

But thanks be to God! He gives us the victory through our Lord Jesus Christ.

Therefore, my dear brothers, stand firm. Let nothing move you. Always give yourselves fully to the work of the Lord, because you know that your labor in the Lord is not in vain.

For I am convinced that neither death nor life, neither angels nor demons, neither the present nor the future, nor any powers,

Neither height nor depth, nor anything else in all creation, will be able to separate us from the love of God that is in Christ Jesus our Lord.

In all these things we are more than conquerors through him who loved us.

53. WILL OF GOD

Old Testament: Ps. 119:33–34; 143:10; 37:23–24; Mic. 6:8; Prov. 14:12; 3:5–6; Jer. 29:11

New Testament: Rom. 12:1–2; Col. 1:9–10; Mk. 3:31–35; 14:36

Teach me, O LORD, to follow your decrees; then I will keep them to the end.

Give me understanding, and I will keep your law and obey it with all my heart.

Teach me to do your will, for you are my God; may your good Spirit lead me on level ground.

If the LORD delights in a man's way, he makes his steps firm;

Though he stumble, he will not fall, for the LORD upholds him with his hand.

And what does the LORD require of you? To act justly and to love mercy and to walk humbly with your God.

There is a way that seems right to a man, but in the end it leads to death.

Trust in the LORD with all your heart and lean not on your own understanding;

In all your ways acknowledge him, and he will make your paths straight.

"For I know the plans I have for you," declares the LORD, "plans to prosper you and not to harm you, plans to give you hope and a future."

Therefore, I urge you, brothers, in view of God's mercy, to offer your bodies as living sacrifices, holy and pleasing to God—this is your spiritual act of worship.

Do not conform any longer to the pattern of this world, but be transformed by the renewing of your mind. Then you will be able to test and approve what God's will is—his good, pleasing and perfect will.

For this reason, since the day we heard about you, we have not stopped praying for you and asking God to fill you with the knowledge of his will through all spiritual wisdom and understanding.

And we pray this in order that you may live a life worthy of the Lord and may please him in every way: bearing fruit in every good work, growing in the knowledge of God,

Jesus' mother and brothers arrived. Standing outside, they sent someone in to call him.

A crowd was sitting around him, and they told him, "Your mother and brothers are outside looking for you."

"Who are my mother and my brothers?" he asked. Then he looked at those seated in a circle around him and said, "Here are my mother and my brothers!

Whoever does God's will is my brother and sister and mother."

"Abba, Father," he said, "everything is possible for you. Take this cup from me.

Yet not what I will, but what you will."

54. WISDOM

Old Testament: Ps. 111:10; Prov. 3:5–8; 1 Kings 4:29, 32; 10:1, 3; Dan. 2:20–21; Prov. 3:13–18

The fear of the LORD is the beginning of wisdom; all who follow his precepts have good understanding. To him belongs eternal praise.

Trust in the LORD with all your heart and lean not on your own understanding; in all your ways acknowledge him, and he will make your paths straight.

Do not be wise in your own eyes; fear the LORD and shun evil. This will bring health to your body and nourishment to your bones.

God gave Solomon wisdom and very great insight, and a breadth of understanding as measureless as the sand on the seashore. He spoke three thousand proverbs and his songs numbered a thousand and five.

When the queen of Sheba heard about the fame of Solomon and his relation to the name of the LORD, she came to test him with hard questions.

Solomon answered all her questions; nothing was too hard for the king to explain to her.

Daniel said: "Praise be to the name of God for ever and ever; wisdom and power are his. He changes times and seasons; he sets up kings and deposes them. He gives wisdom to the wise and knowledge to the discerning.

Blessed is the man who finds wisdom, the man who gains understanding, for she is more profitable than silver and yields better returns than gold.

She is more precious than rubies; nothing you desire can compare with her. Long life is in her right hand; in her left hand are riches and honor.

Her ways are pleasant ways, and all her paths are peace. She is a tree of life to those who embrace her; those who lay hold of her will be blessed.

New Testament: Col. 3:16; 1 Cor. 1:20–21, 30–31; Jas. 1:5; 3:13–14, 17; Rom. 11:33

Let the word of Christ dwell in you richly as you teach and admonish one another with all wisdom.

Where is the wise man? Where is the scholar? Where is the philosopher of this age? Has not God made foolish the wisdom of the world?

For since in the wisdom of God the world through its wisdom did not know him, God was pleased through the foolishness of what was preached to save those who believe.

It is because of him that you are in Christ Jesus, who has become for us wisdom from God—that is, our righteousness, holiness and redemption.

Therefore, as it is written: "Let him who boasts boast in the Lord."

If any of you lacks wisdom, he should ask God, who gives generously to all without finding fault, and it will be given to him.

Who is wise and understanding among you? Let him show it by his good life, by deeds done in the humility that comes from wisdom.

But if you harbor bitter envy and selfish ambition in your hearts, do not boast about it or deny the truth.

But the wisdom that comes from heaven is first of all pure; then peace-loving, considerate, submissive, full of mercy and good fruit, impartial and sincere.

Oh, the depth of the riches of the wisdom and knowledge of God! How unsearchable his judgments, and his paths beyond tracing out!

55. ADVENT

Leader   Advent has come, O God; visit us in this world of sin and darkness with the spirit of Your Son Jesus, who is the light of the world.

People   **Jesus, our Lord, Emmanuel, while we are waiting, come.**

Leader   Our hearts cry out in anguish from the suffering of masses of people—from injustice to the poor, from the inequities of medical care, from the oppression of the helpless, from the neglect and abuse of children, from the unequal distribution of wealth, from the unwillingness of governments to correct the problems, from materialism and unemployment, and from gross immorality.

People   **Jesus, our Lord, Emmanuel, while we are waiting, come.**

Leader   Only in You, O God, is there hope for this poorly governed planet. We come to listen for words of hope and joy, promise and challenge.

People   **Come, Savior, quickly come, while we are waiting.**

Leader   Show us the light again this year. Help us to see it with the eyes of those who saw the coming of Christ all those years ago. Remind us of hope and love and peace. Convert us from our dark and selfish ways into people of the kingdom, and give us a mission in the world, to make straight the ways of our Lord and to exalt the poor and unfortunate before His coming again.

All   **With power and glory, come, Jesus our Lord, Emmanuel. We come with open ears, open minds, and open hearts. We come to receive the blessings God has in store for us in this season of waiting.**

56. CHRISTMAS DAY

Leader On this day, we remember the birth of our Savior. The birthday of Jesus is the most important birthday in the history of the world! How can we pay homage to our Lord on this special day?

People **By being meek and humble, as You advised? By going the extra mile with those who ask anything of us? By loving our enemies and praying for those who spitefully use us?**

Leader Surely by all these things, O Lord Jesus.

People **But we long to do even more. We yearn to follow You with our very lives—with our dreams and hearts' desires; with our substance and all we have; and with the hours of our days, from now until we die.**

Leader Keep Him uppermost in all your thoughts. Let His words and attitudes be imprinted on your hearts.

People **When we say Your name, let our eyes light up. When we encounter the poor or the disadvantaged, let us become Christ in Your stead. O Jesus, let our lives be conformed to Yours with such eagerness and fidelity that people will see You living through us, and have their lives touched by Yours the way ours have been.**

Leader As the bells ring out on this Christmas Day, let them ring not only in announcement of a birth twenty centuries ago, but of a birth that has occurred today, in our hearts. For as Isaiah foretold, "For unto us a child is born, to us a son is given: and the government will be on his shoulders. And he will be called Wonderful Counselor, Mighty God, Everlasting Father, Prince of Peace." *(Isaiah 9:6, NIV)*

All **Let the whole world be changed because of this day. Give us peace in our time and love in all our relationships. He is the Lord of life, and we shall find our happiness in following Him. Amen.**

57. EPIPHANY

Leader   In a world where nations are always at war, O God, we pray for the coming of their *leaders* to Christ. As the wise men of old sought the birthplace of the Savior, let those who would influence our world today be guided by Your star.

People   **Jesus, the Star of Bethlehem.**

Leader   Bring them to the humility stable filled with divine love. Make them reverent toward a Child, and toward all children, who are the promise of the future.

People   **Jesus, the Star of Bethlehem, loves all the children of the world.**

Leader   Teach them to open their treasuries and give generously of their wealth to the poor of the earth. And when they have paid their homage, send them back "by a different way"—thoughtful, grateful, and reconstituted as those who have seen and followed a great Light.

People   **Jesus, the Light of the world, we render our hearts to You.**

Leader   Let our nation be recommitted to the vision of the Christ laid in a manger. Forgive the gross materialism that has overtaken our culture, and the vast, unthinking secularism that has grown like a blight on all our ideals.

People   **Rekindle in us the dream of a world where the ox and the bear feed from the same trough and the lion and lamb lie side by side in gentleness and affection.**

Leader   Grant that the highest insight of the Christmas season may still transform the deepest evidences of our unconverted spirits, and that even yet we shall learn to love and trust and follow Your way in genuine repentance and commitment.

All   **O Star of wonder, forever guide us to Thy perfect Light!**

58. LENT

Leader   As we celebrate the season that highlights the weeks and days before our Lord goes to the Cross, we say:

People   **Here am I, Lord.**

Leader   As we remember His words, way, and witness, we bemoan our own shortcomings.

People   **Here am I, Lord.**

Leader   As we fast from food, drink, media, and other things, may it help us to better focus on the faith that makes us better and stronger for You.

People   **Here am I, Lord.**

All   **As we celebrate this holy season of Lent, may we present ourselves to You that You might be the mirror that gives us the light of redemption. Amen.**

59. PASSION/PALM SUNDAY

Call to Worship

Leader   King Jesus comes, King Jesus, Son of God, Son of Man, Messiah.

People   **Hosanna! Hosanna to the King of Kings!**

Leader   Let us recall the words of the Scriptures: "A great crowd who had come to the feast heard that Jesus was coming to Jerusalem. So they took branches and went out to meet Him, shouting,"

People   **"Hosanna! Blessed is He who comes in the name of the Lord, even the King of Israel!"**

Leader   Jesus found a young donkey and sat upon it, as it is written, "Do not be afraid, O Daughter of Zion; see, your king is coming, seated on a donkey's colt."

All   **In praise we adore You, King Jesus. Enter our hearts today as You entered Jerusalem long ago, and lead us by faith in the way everlasting.**

Responsive Prayer

Leader   There is a murmur of excitement in our hearts today, O God.

People   **We are entering Holy Week, and our thoughts are upon the conquering Savior.**

Leader   We like the pomp and pageantry of Palm Sunday, and the idea of welcoming Christ into the life of our church community.

People   **There is always something upbeat about Your riding into Jerusalem, when even the little children greeted you, singing "Hosanna."**

Leader   But we know that more somber days lie ahead, and the shadowy hours of Good Friday.

All   **Let us follow the precious Lamb of God during this Holy Week, with all of its reminders of celebration, betrayed love and crucifixion, that we may worship Him in gladness of heart on Resurrection Sunday.**

Responsive Benediction

Leader   "I am the resurrection and the life," says the Lord. May Christ's rising lift your spirits and gladden your hearts.

People   **Amen.**

Leader   All those who believe in Christ will never perish. May you pass with Christ from death to life.

People   **Lord, we thank You.**

All   **Christ has gone to prepare a place for us. May His resurrection bring you all joy and peace in believing so that you may abound in hope.**

60. HOLY THURSDAY

Leader   There is a part of Judas in every one of us.

People   **We hate to admit it, but it is true.**

Leader   Even when we try to follow Jesus, we consort with the enemy.

People   **Most of us are willing to sell Him out if the price is high enough.**

Leader   It makes Him sad, but He allows us to do what we think we have to do.

People   **He lets us seek our own destruction, even though it means crucifying Him.**

Leader   Still, He forgives us and seeks our restoration.

People   **He continues to love us in spite of ourselves.**

Leader   What can we do to honor Him now, despite our natures?

People   **We can apologize and ask for forgiveness; we can renew our love and rebuild our relationship with Him.**

Leader   We can agree to put the kingdom of God first in our lives.

People   **We can live in daily awareness of our Judas nature and seek to overcome it with the help of God's Spirit.**

Leader   Then surely goodness and mercy will follow us all the days of our lives.

All   **And we shall dwell in the house of the Lord forever. Amen.**

61. GOOD FRIDAY

Leader   This is the darkest, most somber of days.

People   **It is the day when we remember our Savior's death, and the terrible pain and suffering He endured for the sins of the world.**

Leader   We identify with Him, O God, because His suffering was so real and unforgettable.

People   **The nails in His hands; the great, spiky thorns on His head; the pull of gravity on His body—what isolation and humiliation!**

Leader   We can only pray for forgiveness, O God; we feel as guilty as if we had been there.

All   **Help us to live more worthily because of Him. Show us how to truly love one another, and to share what we have with the poor. Save us from being like His enemies and help us to live as His friends.**

62. EASTER (RESURRECTION) SUNDAY

Call to Worship

Leader   This is the good news: the grave is empty.

People   **Hallelujah!**

Leader   This is the good news: the light shines in darkness, and the darkness can never put it out.

People   **Hallelujah!**

Leader   This is the good news: once we were no people; now we are God's people.

People   **Hallelujah!**

Leader   Christ is our peace, the indestructible peace. We now share with each other.

All   **Hallelujah! Christ Jesus lives today!**

Litany

Leader   The Resurrection, when we celebrate the victory of Christ over death and despair, is the highest celebration of the year.

People   **We pray that the glorious news of Christ's resurrection may permeate the world. Help Your people to live joyfully and faithfully.**

Leader   As this day changed everything about human history, dear Lord, help it to work its changes on us as well.

People   **Transform us in the image of Christ, and grant that we may see all of life from a different vantage point.**

Leader   O God, You gave Your only Son to suffer death on the cross for our redemption; by His glorious resurrection You delivered us from the power of death.

All   **Grant us so to die daily to sin that we may forever live with Him in the joy of His resurrection; through Jesus Christ our Lord, who lives and reigns with You and the Holy Spirit, one God, now and forever. Amen.**

Benediction

"I am the resurrection and the life," says the Lord.
May Christ's rising lift your spirits and gladden your hearts.
All those who believe in Christ will never perish.
May you pass with Christ from death to life.
Christ has gone to prepare a place for us.
May His resurrection bring you all joy and peace in believing
    so that you may abound in hope.
The Lord bless you and keep you now and forever. Amen.

63. ASCENSION DAY

Leader   We gather today in reverent celebration as we remember Your ascension into heaven.

People   **We praise and thank You, O Lord.**

Leader   As the eleven disciples gathered and watched You go back to the realms of glory, we, too, through eyes of faith, see You going to prepare a place for us that we might be there with You one day.

People   **We glorify Your name, O Jesus.**

Leader   Your Ascension proves that while You died for us, You overcame death and are the first fruits of the resurrected. Yet, You did not rise just to stay in this earthly realm, a dimension of death, but You point us to life everlasting. Alleluia!

People   **We magnify Your name, Mighty One.**

Leader   We look forward to our own time of being caught up to meet You in the air. We will join the Church Triumphant and sign up with the saints and heavenly beings in everlasting choruses of jubilation and praise.

People   **We celebrate You, O Lord Jesus!**

Leader   Just as the disciples had to be lifted from the lethargy of looking heavenward, we, too, remember that we must be busy with kingdom affairs. Help us to be a going church for our coming Lord.

All   **We will not stand gazing into heaven, but will work for that unending day when the sun will not be needed — for the light from the Son will ever brighten our existence. Amen.**

64. PENTECOST SUNDAY

Leader   At the first Pentecostal experience, O God, You revealed Your power to the early Christians as tongues of fire and common understanding.

People   **Spirit of the living God, visit us again on this day of Pentecost.**

Leader   Send the wind and flame of Your transforming life to lift up the church on this day. Give us wisdom and faith, that we may know the great hope to which we are called.

People   **We pray that we, too, may have a Pentecostal experience, dear God—a clear sense of Your power in us and the joy of communing with other Christians around the world.**

Leader   Let the peace and empowerment of Christ be upon us as a church, and transform our lives from those of isolated, unrepentant souls into those of loving, sharing, harmonious brothers and sisters.

People   **Come, Holy Spirit of power, make us bold witnesses of Your redeeming love.**

Leader   Let the Spirit that galvanized the early church galvanize us as well, that we may recognize the mission field around us and reach out to those who don't yet know the Gospel of our Christ or how to live in peace and joy with others. May we be channels of Your grace to the people of our time and culture.

All   **Spirit of the living God, we humbly receive afresh the gift of the Holy Spirit and pray that Christ will be glorified in our lives. Amen.**

65. BAPTISM

Leader   As baptized believers, we are happy to share in and witness the baptism of new believers in Christ Jesus.

People   **Take me to the water to be baptized.**

Leader   Baptism is not the invention of the church, but is the command of Him who was baptized of John to fulfill all righteousness.

People   **None but the righteous shall see God.**

Leader   Baptism is a gift that was demonstrated in the New Testament. As we join a great host of witnesses across the ages, we pray that the Living Water will always spring up in the lives of these new believers.

People   **Take me to the water to be baptized.**

Leader   As we thank God for our own baptism, we pray that when sons and daughters of God go down in the liquid grave, they emerge to walk in the newness of life everlasting.

People   **Take me to the water to be baptized.**

Leader   We are not only thankful for these new converts, but also we implore God to send us more new souls into the kingdom. May each convert's baptism be a badge of honor and humility, a symbol of solidarity with the Savior, an emblem of obedience to the Lover of the church.

All   **As we invoke the name of the Father, Son, and Holy Spirit, we pray not just for a troubling of the waters, but for a quickening of the minds, hearts, and bodies of these new believers. Take me to the water to be baptized. Amen.**

66. THE LORD'S SUPPER

Leader　As we make our way to this sacred table, our hearts and minds turn to thee, O Lord.

People　**We praise and worship You, O Jesus.**

Leader　We remember how Your holy body was broken so that we might experience wholeness in our minds, spirits, bodies, and community.

People　**We praise and worship You, our Jesus.**

Leader　We recall that Your blood ran freely as an atonement for the things that we do and have done that transgress Your Word, will, and way for us.

People　**We offer the sacrifice of our praise to You for Your sacrifice of self, O Jesus.**

Leader　We thank You for Your invitation to sup with You, because You could have chronicled and cataloged our sins but, instead, You invited us to the feast called Your Supper.

People　**We praise and worship You, O Jesus.**

Leader　We wish we came to this moment without things that stood between us and You. We wish we had totally clean slates. Yet our records are so spotted that we are not even worthy to partake of crumbs from under the table. But because, in Your mercy, You invited us, we come.

All　**Lord, we come. You invited us, so we come. You fed us, so we come. You give us opportunities for renewed fellowship, so we come. May our minds never be so cloudy or our hearts so greedy that we forget the obedience that is required of believers. To Your table, we come.**

67. INSTALLATION OF CHURCH LEADERS

Leader Lord, we thank You for the opportunity to serve as *leader*s in Your work: a work that involves us in something greater than ourselves, a work that transcends the mundane pursuits of this world.

People **Lord, we are grateful.**

Leader We realize that we are stewards of this privilege of *leader*ship and we must give an account for this stewardship. We understand that You look for faithfulness in stewards, and may that faithfulness be evident in the *leader*ship we give.

People **Lord, help us to be faithful.**

Leader Let us not use these entrustments of *leader*ship to lord over Your people. Let us not seek to rule, but to serve the church through the positions we are given privilege to hold. Let us take up the towel of serving one another and not merely wear the *leader*ship title as a badge of honor.

People **Let us be servants.**

Leader May we be eager to use the gifts, talents, and resources that we have received from You, to advance Your kingdom through the *leader*ship opportunity given to us. May we not be guilty of burying our God-given assets in the earth of our excuses.

People **Let us be eager.**

Leader Help us not grow weary in well-doing, even when the task of *leader*ship becomes difficult and fails to produce immediate results. Help us to know that we will reap the harvest of faithful *leader*ship, if we faint not.

People **Let us never give up.**

Leader May we rely on the Holy Spirit both to enable us to lead and empower those we lead to advance Your kingdom. Let us never depend upon worldly tactics and means to accomplish Your work—for You have left on record, "not by power, not by might, but by my Spirit."

All **Let Your Spirit lead us.**

68. PASTOR'S APPRECIATION

Leader Holy God, we praise You for Your wisdom in gifting the church with pastors. We thank You for giving us a pastor after Your own heart.

People **Thank You for our pastor.**

Leader You knew that in order for Your people to grow, they must be fed with knowledge and understanding.

People **Thank You for our pastor, who feeds us.**

Leader You gifted the church with a pastor/teachers to make us ready to do the work of the ministry, that the church would know the truth concerning our faith in Jesus Christ and that we might no longer be gullible concerning the strange teachings of this world.

People **Thank You for our pastor.**

Leader We thank You for our pastor, who labors in the Word of God to preach and teach—rightly dividing the Word of truth. Thank You for our pastor's diligence in preaching and teaching the Word in season and out of season.

People **Thank You for our pastor's faithfulness to Your Word.**

Leader We thank You for the time our pastor spends in prayer, seeking You for directions in guiding this flock.

People **Thank You for a praying pastor.**

Leader Lord, we thank You for our pastor, who possesses a pastor's heart, a pastor with a heart that is willing to comfort and willing to correct—a heart that is full of compassion.

People **Thank You for a caring pastor.**

Leader Truly the pastor's work is great and many times is beyond our understanding, but You have told us in Your Word to honor those who work hard for You, giving spiritual guidance to Your people. Help us to acknowledge, appreciate, respect, and overwhelm our pastor with love for the work's sake.

All **Thank You for the privilege of loving our pastor.**

69. WORKER'S APPRECIATION

Leader O Lord God, we thank You for sending Your Son, Jesus Christ, in the form of a servant. He said in the Holy Word that He came to serve. Thank You for those who imitate His spirit of serving.

People **Lord, we thank You for those who have serving spirits.**

Leader We thank You, Lord, for those who have girded themselves with the towel of service, whether they possess a title or not.

People **Lord, we thank You.**

Leader We thank You for those who serve behind the scenes, doing the things that are necessary for the advancement of this church.

People **We thank You, Lord.**

Leader Lord, we thank You for those who are always willing to give of their talents and skills for the cause of Christ.

People **Thank You, Lord.**

Leader We are grateful for those who never say no when asked to serve, but are always willing to go the extra mile for Your kingdom.

People **Lord, we are grateful.**

Leader Lord, we thank You for those who serve untiringly with glad hearts, because they render their service unto You and not unto people.

People **We thank You, Lord.**

Leader Because they render their service unto you and not unto humanity, we give You glory for the level of excellence that they bring to ministry.

People **Lord, we thank You.**

Leader Knowing that You will reward everyone according to his or her works, we bless Your name for their future rewards. Lord, please enable us to speak words of encouragement and appreciation and bless them with acts of kindness in the meantime.

All **Lord, we thank You for those who serve among us.**

70. MINISTRY OF WORSHIP ARTS APPRECIATION

Leader   O Lord, our God, the creator of heaven and earth, we celebrate You for the ministry of worship arts. We praise You for visual arts, drama, music, and dance.

People   **We thank You for the ministry of worship arts.**

Leader   We thank You for those who, via the visual arts, inspire us through paintings, architectural design, and sculpture to get a glimpse of Your glory.

People   **Thank You for those who minister through the visual arts.**

Leader   We thank You for those who, through the dramatic arts, retell the narratives of Scripture and tell the stories of those who believe.

People   **Thank You for those who minister through the dramatic arts.**

Leader   We thank You for those who, through music, lead us to worship You through the sounds of the instruments, the blending of their voices, and the lifting of our voices in songs to You.

People   **Thank You for those who minister through music.**

Leader   We thank You for those who, via the ministry of dance, express praise through movement expressions that enhance our experience of worship.

People   **We thank You for the ministry of dance.**

Leader   Thank You for the individuals who give of their time and talents to enable us to worship with the whole person. Thank You for creating us with the ability to worship You through the worship arts.

All   **Lord, we thank You.**

71. WOMEN OF FAITH

Leader   Most holy and gracious Lord, we come before You today with grateful hearts for the women of faith among us. Your Word is replete with their presence.

People   **Thank You for women of faith.**

Leader   We thank You for women whose faith is evident in their daily walks and work for You.

People   **Thank You for women of faith.**

Leader   We are grateful for women who serve You with great dedication in various capacities throughout the church and the world. They speak for You; they sing for You; they serve You with undaunted trust.

People   **Lord, we thank You for women of faith.**

Leader   We are inspired by their faith, especially when they stand alone, whether in the rearing of their children, or ministering in Your name in some foreign land.

People   **Lord, we thank You for women of faith.**

Leader   Thank You for the women who trusted You against the odds to be the impetus for the building of churches, hospitals, schools, and colleges.

People   **Lord, we thank You for women of faith.**

Leader   Thank You for women of faith who taught us by example how to live with plenty or with little, all the while trusting You and giving You the glory.

People   **Thank You for women of faith.**

Leader   We are thankful for women whose faith never shrinks, even in times of sickness or in the valley of the shadow of death.

People   **Lord, thank You for women of faith.**

Leader   We thank You for women of faith who rejoice in the hope of Your glory, knowing that they will spend eternity with You.

All   **We give You glory for women of faith.**

72. MEN OF FAITH

Leader Dear God, the father of our Savior, Jesus Christ, we come before You this day thanking You for men of faith, men who believe upon the name of Jesus.

People **Oh God, we thank You.**

Leader We thank You for men whose faith in You has caused them to be the men they are today and will make them the men they need to be on tomorrow.

People **We thank You for men of confidence.**

Leader We thank You for men who, like Abraham, take You at Your Word and trust You enough to follow Your lead. We thank You for men who, like Joshua and Caleb, will trust You even when they find themselves in the minority.

People **We thank You for men who trust You.**

Leader We praise You for men who, like Martin King and Medgar Evers, speak truth to power and trust You for the outcome. We praise You for men who, like Nelson Mandela, fought a good fight, finished their course, and kept the faith.

People **We thank You for men who never gave up on You.**

Leader Thank You for men who, despite trials and tribulations, never wavered in their confidence in Your name, never take matters into their own hands—men who trust You against the odds.

People **Thank You for men who don't waver in their faith.**

Leader Lord, we thank You for men who unashamedly call upon Your name in private and public, knowing that You alone are worthy of their complete trust. We thank You for men who never claim credit for what You have done, but always give You the glory.

All **Thank You for men who give You the glory.**

73. MOTHERS

Leader   Most holy and gracious God, we give You glory this day for mothers—mothers who have carried us under their hearts, and mothers who carry us on their hearts from the cradle through adulthood.

People   **For mothers, we give You glory.**

Leader   We give thanks for the saintly women, great-grandmothers, grandmothers, aunts, sisters, neighbors, and others who did not bear us in their bodies but bore us on their hearts, and held us by our hands by choosing to mother us.

People   **For mothers, we give You thanks.**

Leader   We acknowledge the great, personal sacrifices that mothers make and have made physically, materially, and emotionally to freely provide for us the care that only a mother could give.

People   **For mothers, we give You glory.**

Leader   We are grateful for the mothers who reared us in the nurture and admonition of You, our God. We are grateful for mothers who showed us what it means to live a godly life by living godly lives before us.

People   **For mothers, we are grateful.**

Leader   We thank You for the unconditional love of mothers and the needed discipline they have given. We thank You for the life lessons they taught us: lessons about sharing, helping, forgiving, loving one another, and recovery from failures.

People   **For mothers, we thank You.**

Leader   We thank You for the unceasing prayers of our mothers. We thank You for the prayers of our mothers that were silent and those that we heard with our ears. We thank You for mothers whose faith in You and hope for us caused them to pray.

People   **Thank You for praying mothers.**

Leader   We praise You for mothers who led us to know that the only hope we have in this world and the world to come is in You, through our Lord, Jesus Christ.

All   **Lord, we praise You for our mothers.**

74. FATHERS

Leader   Almighty God, we celebrate You this day for the fathers, men who seek to follow Your pattern of fatherhood.

People   **We celebrate You for fathers.**

Leader   We honor You for fathers who have labored hard to provide for their families. We thank You for their willingness to work for the benefit of someone other than themselves.

People   **We honor You for fathers.**

Leader   We are grateful for the love of fathers that translates itself into protection and discipline. We thank You for fathers who have created for their families an environment of physical, emotional, and spiritual security.

People   **We are grateful for our fathers.**

Leader   We are thankful for fathers who never abandon their responsibilities, regardless of the circumstances in which they find themselves. We thank You for fathers whose strength is not merely in their hands but in their hearts, because their strength comes from You.

People   **We are thankful for our fathers.**

Leader   We bless Your name for fathers who pray to You for guidance as to how they should lead their families. We bless Your name for fathers who do not lean to their own understanding, but in all their ways acknowledge You.

People   **We bless Your name for our fathers.**

Leader   We give You glory for fathers who have taught us invaluable truths about life with patience, given us a balanced model of what it means to be both tough and tender, and instilled reverence and love in our hearts for You.

People   **We give You glory for our fathers.**

Leader   We praise You for fathers who unashamedly live their lives for You through Jesus Christ. We praise You for fathers who have led us to live in You, our heavenly Father, by placing our faith in Jesus Christ our Lord, Your only begotten Son. And for those of us who may not know our fathers or who had absentee dads, we thank You for being our Father and for sending us father figures to guide us and love us.

All   **We praise You for our fathers. Amen.**

75. CHILDREN

Leader   Oh, wonderful God, the giver and sustainer of life, we thank You for children. In a world that seems to devalue life, we thank You for the blessing of children.

People   **We thank You for children.**

Leader   We thank You for the joy, the laughter, the challenges, and the tears of rearing children. We thank You for their infancy, their childhood, the years of adolescence, and their transition into adulthood.

People   **We thank You for children.**

Leader   You have granted us with the responsibility to rear our children in a manner that pleases You. Help us to train up our children in the way that they should go. Help us to understand the unique bent of every child.

People   **Lord, help us rear our children.**

Leader   Give to us the means to provide for our children and protect them from things that would harm them. Help us to guard their innocence and fill them with the wisdom that is only found in Your Word.

People   **Lord, give us what we need.**

Leader   Help us to model the things You would have us model before our children. Let us love, that they might know how to love. Let us be patient, that they might know how to be patient. Let us be forgiving, that they might know how to forgive. Let us live lives that are worth imitating.

People   **Lord, help us be true role models for our children.**

Leader   May our faith in Jesus Christ shine brightly in order that they may find their way to Him. May they live their lives to Your glory.

All   **May we become as little children to glorify You.**

76. SINGLES

Leader   Unto You, O Lord, do we give glory for Christian singles. Thank You the presence of singles throughout Scripture and the ultimate example of singleness in the life of our Lord and Savior Jesus Christ.

People   **Thank You for Christian singles.**

Leader   Lord, we thank You for widowed, divorced, separated, or never-been-married single men and women whose lifestyles honor You in word and deed.

People   **Thank You for Christian singles.**

Leader   We thank You, Lord, for singles who have found peace with their singleness, considering their singleness a gift from You.

People   **Thank You for Christian singles.**

Leader   We thank You, Lord, for singles who find in their singleness great opportunity to serve You and Your cause.

People   **Lord, how we thank You!**

Leader   Lord, we thank You for singles whose faith in You empowers them to stand in the midst of temptation and trials.

People   **Lord, we thank You for Christian singles.**

Leader   Lord, we give You glory for the many singles who take seriously the study of Your Word and seek to share Your Word with others, not only in the church but also in their workplaces, schools, and homes, and in their social networking.

People   **Lord, we give You glory.**

Leader   Lord, we thank You for singles whose faith and trust in You inspire others to know the joy, peace, hope, and love that can only be found in You.

All   **Lord, we thank You for Christian singles.**

77. FAMILY

Leader   Most holy and gracious God, we come to You with great adoration, as we celebrate family. Today, we lift up families of all shapes and sizes.

People   **We lift up family.**

Leader   We thank You for extended family, which includes both biological members and members of our community. We thank You for our fathers, mothers, sisters, and brothers. We thank You for aunts, uncles, cousins, grandparents, and great-grandparents.

People   **We thank You for family.**

Leader   We thank You for families that surround us with love, uplift us with encouragement, cheer us on with laughter, bless us with guidance, and cover us with mercy and grace.

People   **We thank You for families.**

Leader   Thank You for families that stand together through times of celebration and times of tribulation. Thank You for families that allow us to be ourselves, but never cease to encourage us to be our best selves.

People   **Lord, thank You for family.**

Leader   Thank You for families that are centered in You, families that acknowledge You in all they do, and families that are determined to serve You regardless of what others may do.

People   **Father, we thank You.**

Leader   Most of all, we thank You for making us a part of Your family, a family that is brought into existence through Jesus Christ, a family that crosses every barrier—a family that will live with You forever.

All   **Lord, thank You for family.**

78. ELDER SAINTS

Leader   Lord of all generations, we extol Your name for the unique blessings found in our seniors, the elder saints among us.

People   **We extol Your name.**

Leader   Thank You for the repository of wisdom You have placed in those who walk in the way of righteousness.

People   **Thank You for their wisdom.**

Leader   Thank You for the lessons they teach from their life experiences, lessons that help us to navigate the twists and turns of life, lessons about marriage, lessons about rearing children, and lessons about letting go.

People   **Thank You for the lessons they teach.**

Leader   Lord, we thank You for the lessons that they have taught us concerning the ups and downs of life, lessons that teach us how to handle the victories and survive the failures of life.

People   **Thank You for our elder saints.**

Leader   We cherish the stories of their yesterdays when their faith in You was young and untried, and the encouragement we gain from their faith of today that is tried and true. We appreciate their willingness to share their stories.

People   **We thank You for their faith stories.**

Leader   We thank You for their never-dying faith in You, that shows us how not to give up, regardless of what life brings.

People   **We thank You for their faith.**

Leader   Lord, thank You for the elder saints who credit grace for their past and know that grace is the means of their future.

All   **Lord, how we thank You for the elder saints among us!**

79. CHURCH ANNIVERSARY

Leader   We have come another year's journey as a congregation of baptized believers in Jesus Christ.

People   **We praise You, O God, as we, Your people, reflect upon our journey. We praise You for the joys and challenges of being the church.**

Leader   The Foundation upon which we build is none other than Jesus Christ, the Lord. The church is "His new creation, by water and the word."

People   **We praise You, O God, as we, Your new creations, reflect upon our journeys. We celebrate our common bond as brothers and sisters.**

Leader   Jesus gave His life for the birth of the church. He sought the church to be His holy bride.

People   **We praise You, O God, that Jesus paid the penalty for our sin. He died, was buried, and rose from the dead "to set us right with the You, to make us fit for You."**

Leader   Jesus declared, "Upon this Rock I will build My church, and the gates of Hades shall not prevail against it." We are grateful that He has kept this commitment in our local congregation.

People   **We praise You, O God, that as we have "borne our burdens in the heat of the day, we glorify You for making a way." You have kept us in Your care through many dangers, toils, and snares!**

Leader   As this congregation looks to the future, be reminded that "we are God's workmanship, created in Christ Jesus for good works, which God prepared beforehand that we should walk in them."

People   **We are committed to "redeem the time," to "occupy until the Lord comes back." We will continue to "let our lights shine before others that they may see our good works that the Father will be glorified."**

All   **We praise You, O God, for the union we have with You, Jesus Christ, and the Holy Spirit—the Three in One. We praise You for the "mystic sweet communion we have with those whose rest is won. As happy and holy ones, we pray for grace that we, like them, the meek and lowly, on high may dwell with Thee." Hallelujah! Hallelujah! Hallelujah!**

80. MARTIN LUTHER KING JR. DAY

Leader   As we celebrate the life and legacy of Dr. Martin Luther King Jr., let us rededicate ourselves to his ministry of teaching and his art of demonstrating love, peace, and understanding to the social conditions of all humankind.

People   **We will become more committed to improving the conditions of poor and oppressed people and all God's people, as he did.**

Leader   Let us remember and practice his dedication to the strategy of nonviolence and his determination to remain identified as a Christian servant of God.

People   **We will become more concerned about the plight of our country and with Christian weapons, and will fight the system at every opportunity we have—for justice among all of God's children.**

Leader   Let us continue, as Dr. King did, to plead the case for nonviolence in our world.

People   **We will pray never to be bitter or indulge in hate—but to meet hate with love, and physical weapons with the whole armor of God.**

Leader   We will work for the establishment of the beloved community for which he so eloquently preached despite hearing the ugly discord of hate.

People   **We will raise our voices in harmonies of hope, singing "We Shall Overcome."**

All   **Help us, Lord, to continue Dr. King's dream of the bells of freedom's ringing out upon our country and justice rolling down like waters; only then can love rule gently from sea to shining sea in this sweet land of liberty.**

81. BLACK HISTORY

Leader Gracious God, we have come to celebrate Black History. We acknowledge the accomplishments, contributions, and life struggles of African Americans from slave ships to championship, and to the great dream that is now American.

People **The celebration of African-American History is important for all Americans, not just blacks. Many accomplishments have been made, possible only through the combined efforts, sacrifices, and prayers of all races' working together.**

Leader The annual observation of Black History Month is an important celebration to remove barriers that have prevented all of God's children from participating fully in the pursuit of happiness—but it is only a small step in the right direction toward wholeness in our country.

People **We have come to receive the enormous resources of faith, strength, and courage of African Americans—from Carter G. Woodson to Barack Obama—as they have pressed their way to great and godly contributions.**

Leader As we celebrate Black History, we realize that there is still work to be done to bring about equality to all of God's children: equality in housing, education, employment, health care, criminal justice, and all areas of life.

All **Thank God for the sons and daughters of Africa who grace this home of the brave. Amen!**

82. MEMORIAL DAY

Leader   Thank You, Lord, for the souls of the persons whose lives were given in sacrificial love for our country—the land of the free and the home of the brave. Help us to praise You for their memories.

People   **Let us prayerfully reflect upon our nation's history, heritage, and hope, as we celebrate this Memorial Day.**

Leader   Help us to look backwards upon our history with wonder and gratitude to You, O God.

People   **Help us, God, to be grateful for our heritage; let us be reminded of where America was born and the price that was paid for her birth.**

Leader   As we celebrate this Memorial Day, let us remember that our hope as a people does not lie in our wealth, our large budgets, or our charismatic *leaders*; our hope as a people lies in a recommitment to the spiritual values of our God—upon which the country was built.

All   **We praise You, God, and ask Your wisdom in helping us to bless our past for its lessons of experience, and to cherish the memories of the men and women who made the past a glorious prediction for the future. We pledge ourselves to loyally support those causes for which they nobly died.**

83. NATION BUILDING–FOURTH OF JULY

Leader   O God, as we prayerfully acknowledge Your presence among us, we praise You that our country is celebrating another birthday in freedom under God.

People   **We praise You, God, for keeping our nation strong, not by arms but by the good deeds of Christian men and women, who have put their trust in You.**

Leader   Accept our prayer of thanksgiving, O God, and help us to understand that only with proper balance of church freedom and state freedom can we maintain the freedom of all the people of the nation.

People   **We thank You, Lord, for the founding of our country, a country which houses people of faith—faith in the providence of a great God, who could help all of humankind to reach their highest potential.**

Leader   As we celebrate this Fourth of July, let us remember our heritage as Americans—that we were founded as a nation under God.

All   **We will always remember the place of God in our lives. Let us continue to praise God, who has made and preserved us as a nation. Amen.**

84. LABOR DAY

Leader   Beloved of God, let us affirm the goodness of honest endeavor as servants of
God—as people gathered in God's name during this holiday, that affirms the
worth and work of those who labor.

People   **We rejoice that Scripture reveals God at work, creating all things, all
life, and humanity from the beginning of our memories. We live before
an active Creator as part of a creation that is purposeful, moving,
industrious, efficient, and intended to produce glorious results to the
glory of God. Lord, teach us to be agents of redemptive labor to the
praise of Your glory.**

Leader   Let us thank God for our brothers and sisters who are owners, employers,
managers, and other *leader*s in workplaces. Let us honor the value of their
work, their preparation, courage, and willingness to face the risks and
uncertainties of ownership and management.

People   **As workers together with God, we commit to nurture cooperative
relationships between workers and owners in keeping with the justice of
God. Lord, help us foster mutual respect between those who labor and
those who manage.**

Leader   Let us remember how sin affects working conditions. How will we
demonstrate the grace and truth of God in regards to the conditions that affect
how work is done?

All   **We will remember that the justice of God demands that workers receive
fair pay for their labor. The love of God demands that employers protect
workers from unsafe working conditions. The truth of God requires us
to respect those who work as children of God. The order of God obligates
those who labor to be diligent and those who lead to be fair. Lord, help
us demonstrate Your justice, love, truth, and order by working and
managing in ways that glorify You. Amen.**

85. THANKSGIVING DAY

Leader   "Praise the Lord. Give thanks to the Lord, for he is good; *His love endures forever." (Psalm 106:1, NIV)*

People   **O Lord, our God, thank You for love so wonderful that we are not able to fully describe it with words, thoughts, or deeds. Thank You for creative love, forgiving love, redeeming love, sustaining love, victorious love, and everlasting love.**

Leader   "To him who divided the Red Sea asunder *His love endures forever.* and brought Israel through the midst of it, *His love endures forever." (Psalm 136:13–14, NIV)*

People   **O Lord, our God, thank You for bringing us through many dangers, toils, and snares, through weary years and silent tears, through tragedies and triumphs, and through the various situations of grief and struggles by Your enduring love.**

Leader   "Give thanks to the Lord of lords: *His love endures forever.* to him who alone does great wonders, *His love endures forever.* [Give thanks to him] who by his understanding made the heavens, *His love endures forever.* who spread out the earth upon the waters, [for] *His love endures forever." (Psalm 136:4–6, NIV)*

People   **O Lord, our God, You are ruler over all that is. Thank You for life, light, air, water, breath, strength, and the hope we know because of Your love. Thank You for revealing Your love for us in creation.**

Leader   "[Give thanks] to the One who remembered us in our low estate *His love endures forever.* and freed us from our enemies, *His love endures forever.* and who gives food to every creature. *His love endures forever." (Psalm 136:23–25, NIV)*

People   **O Lord, our God, thank You for lifting us from low places, for freeing us from traps and bondage of every kind, and for providing for our needs according to Your wonderful love.**

All   **"Give thanks to the God of heaven. His love endures forever."** *(Psalm 136:26, NIV)*

86. CHRISTIAN MARRIAGE

Leader In the presence of God, we have come together as family and friends to celebrate the gift of marriage that God has given to this man and woman.

People **The unity between a man and a woman in marriage is more profound than any other relationship—when they are brought together by You.**

Leader The tapestry of life, through the God-given bond of marriage, has been revealed through marriage—and by means of God's grace, you become one flesh.

People **Gracious God, may the presence of Your Son, Jesus, bring joy to this marriage, just as it did in the case of the wedding at Cana in Galilee.**

Leader Just as we pray that there are wonderful, rapturous moments in which to express joy, we know that there may be times of challenge as well.

People **Help this couple to always seek Your face and favor, O Lord.**

Leader The ceremony of marriage is only a symbol. Help us to remember that the real marriage takes place daily as we work and pray together to build a home in honor of God and each other.

All **In your marriage, may God give you lifelong companionship, love, and joy—as husband and wife.**

87. RITES OF PASSAGE FOR YOUTH

Leader   O God, we thank You for our youth. We are grateful for their presence, potential, curiosity, talent, and skill.

People   **O Lord, help us to provide the proper learning environment to assist them in making a successful transition from adolescence to goal-oriented adults.**

Leader   Help us as church and community *leader*s to become more caring, understanding, and supportive in our approach to working with our youth.

People   **We will prayerfully design programs to build and strengthen their skills and competencies—socially, morally, and physically. We will provide scholastic and spiritual development for our youth.**

Leader   We will initiate transition into adulthood through the passing on of knowledge, culture, and tradition by using committed persons from church and community.

All   **O Lord, help us as we help our youth to become productive men and women in You.**

88. FUNERALS

Leader   As family and friends, we have come together in this hour of sorrow, reflection, and triumph to reaffirm our faith in God and in His Son, Jesus Christ, whom to truly know is eternal life.

People   **Eternal life is a gift from God, who is the Creator and Sustainer of all life.**

Leader   To all of us God offers eternal life; we receive it, and we never die. We live victoriously forever.

People   **Eternal life is not a distant reward for those of us who are comforted and reassured by our faith in God. It is an ever-present reality.**

Leader   It is faith in God by which we live, and it is this faith by which we are prepared to die.

All   **So whether we live or whether we die, we are forever safe with our Lord, Jesus—who is and who gives all of us, His children, eternal life.**

89. REVIVAL

Leader   O Lord, send a revival and let it begin in me. Create in me a pure heart, O God, and renew a steadfast spirit within me.

People   **Remember Your congregation, which You have purchased of old, which You have redeemed to be the tribe of Your heritage! Restore us, O God; cause Your face to shine and we shall be saved. Will You not revive us again, that Your people may rejoice in You?**

Leader   Repent, then, and turn to God, so that your sins may be wiped out, that a time of refreshing may come from the Lord, and that He may send the Christ, who has been appointed for you—even Jesus.

People   **We were dead in our trespasses and sins, following the course of this world, following the prince of the power of the air, the spirit at work in the sons of disobedience. We once lived in the passions of our flesh, carrying out the desires of the body and the mind. We were, by nature, children of wrath.**

Leader   Restore us again, O God of our salvation, and put away Your indignation toward us! Show us Your steadfast love, O Lord, and grant us Your salvation. Revive us, and we will call upon Your name.

People   **God, being rich in mercy, because of the great love with which He loved us (even when we were dead in our trespasses), made us alive together with Christ—by grace we have been saved—and raised us up with Him in the heavenly places in Christ Jesus.**

All   **When the Day of Pentecost arrived, they were all together in one place, and suddenly there came from heaven a sound like a mighty rushing wind, and it filled the entire house where they were sitting. And divided tongues as of fire appeared to them and rested on each one of them. May the Spirit of God rest on us to do God's will!**

90. CHRISTIAN EDUCATION

Leader   O Lord God, we thank You for Your Word, which is a lamp which gives illumination that we might see Your will for our lives.

People   **Thank You for letting us study Your Word, O Lord.**

Leader   We are grateful for faithful witnesses who inscribed the inspiration that came from Your storehouse of divine revelation that we might not only see the path that the believers of biblical antiquity took, but also paths of righteousness for our own lives.

People   **Thank You for the struggle of study, writing, prayer, and listening to You.**

Leader   Lord, thank You for allowing us to accept the invitation to study that we might be approved by You, that we might be better able to work for kingdom goals.

People   **Thank You for letting us study Your Word, O Lord.**

Leader   O Sovereign God, in these days when lives seem to be easily and needlessly wrecked, we are soberly reminded that the prophet Hosea said that people are destroyed for the lack of knowledge.

People   **Give us Your knowledge, O Lord.**

Leader   We thank You for teachers who diligently dig into Your Word, that people who come to learn would get sound teaching that points us in biblical directions, rather than personal perspective.

People   **Thank You for the privilege of study, writing, prayer, and listening to You.**

Leader   We implore Your anointing on those who write materials for us to study. These materials do not replace, but enhance Your Word. May they be guided by grace.

People   **Thank You for the struggle of study, writing, prayer, and listening to You.**

All   **More about Jesus I would know; more of His grace to others show; more of His saving fullness see, more of His love who died for me. Amen.**

91. EDUCATION

Leader   O Lord, how excellent are Your ways, how marvelous Your works, and how precious Your truths—by which we may be free.

People   **We thank You for the ways that You have provided means through which we may acquire knowledge as we enjoy attending schools of our choice.**

Leader   We acknowledge those before us who were not given the opportunity to learn but held on to the hope that, someday, we would overcome. And we appreciate the sacrifices and struggles of those who fought to make our education possible.

People   **Help us, dear Lord, so we hold precious to our hearts the educational advantages that we delight in and realize "to much is given, much is required." Help us also to understand that with privilege comes responsibility—and with responsibility there is accountability.**

Leader   O Lord, in a time when the occasion to acquire knowledge is plenteous, let us not be named among those "who have not because we ask not, nor act not."

People   **Forgive us, O Lord, for times when we have wasted precious resources and did not encourage others to taste and enjoy the benefits of higher education.**

Leader   We thank You, O Lord, for the many institutions of higher learning that were built on Your principles—and for those professors who gave and continue to give of their gifts of teaching, sowing into the lives of both young and old.

People   **Help us, O God, to give back to those institutions that have been a blessing to us. May we bless them with financial support and our prayers.**

Leader   We thank You for clean hearts and right spirits and minds that have been renewed by Your regenerating power.

People   **Help us not to become puffed up by our knowledge, but let us rest in the knowledge of knowing You.**

Leader   We are confident in our confession; we have put on the mind of Christ.

All   **Therefore, we will be successful in our endeavors as we pursue knowledge, truth, and liberty.**

92. URBAN MINISTRY

Leader   God has made the cities of this world and He cares for them—and so should we.

People   **Send us, Your disciples, to bear the Good News, to bind the wounds and heal the brokenness.**

Leader   Let us think of ourselves as sent by God to share the Word of truth so that Christ, through us, will enlighten the cities.

People   **Help us to use an urban missionary strategy to bring the Good News of Jesus Christ to every area of our cities.**

Leader   Thank You for allowing us to celebrate Your goodness and grace as we enjoy and experience the joy and rhythm of urban life in our churches, communities, and homes.

People   **We are grateful for safe ball courts, theaters, church family-life centers, and places that nourish the soul and help us raise a generation that is whole and in love with You.**

Leader   Let us, as Christian men and women, show love, compassion, and hope to the hurting, helpless, hopeless people of our cities.

All   **We prayerfully ask God daily, using His guidance, to use our words and deeds to bless our cities with spiritual awakening that will bring salvation to the lost and healing to the hurting.**

93. STEWARDSHIP

Leader The earth is the Lord's and all that is in it, the world and those who live in it. All things were made through Him, and without Him was not anything made that was made.

People **You made humanity in Your image, crowned us with glory and honor, and put everything under our feet that we might have dominion over all creation. You made us to rule over the works of Your hands.**

Leader We are all stewards, called to be faithful servants, honest administrators, and responsible managers of all that God has entrusted to us. It is required that those who have been given a trust must prove faithful. Ours is a sacred responsibility.

People **Divine Giver, we are grateful for the gifts of time, talents, and treasures. Our times are in Your hands. You have assigned us gifts according to our capacity for increase. You have given us the ability to get wealth for Your purposes. We are totally dependent on Your power for our strength.**

Leader You gave us a model of exemplary servanthood in Jesus, the Son of God, who came not to be served but to serve and to give His life as a ransom for many.

People **Your Holy Spirit indwells us, teaching us to seek first Your kingdom and Your righteousness. He makes our spiritual gifts known for meeting the needs of others, especially brothers and sisters in the church. He perpetuates in us a willingness to obey Your commandments in the face of suffering, even to death.**

Leader Heal our hearts, dear Lord. Grow us up as servants of Christ and wise stewards of Your mysteries. Make us eager to give with a genuineness of love that responds in generosity. Strengthen our commitment to care for our bodies, Your temples. We present ourselves to You as living sacrifices. This is our spiritual act of worship.

All **Lord, our desire is to enlarge Your kingdom and bring honor to Your name. You say, "Well done, thou good and faithful servant: thou hast been faithful over a few things, I will make thee ruler over many things: enter thou into the joy of thy Lord."** *(Matthew 25:21, KJV)*

94. GLOBAL MISSION

Leader   Sovereign and eternal God, You loved the world so much that You gave Your one and only Son to be its Savior. With His blood, He purchased men for God from every tribe and language and people and nation.

People   **As You sent Jesus into the world, by His authority, we have been sent to make disciples of all the nations, baptizing them in the name of the Father, and of the Son, and of the Holy Spirit, teaching them to observe all things that were commanded us.**

Leader   You delay the Day of Judgment and the day of Jesus' return—not willing that any should perish, but desiring all men to be saved and to come to the knowledge of the truth.

People   **As beneficiaries of the love of Christ, we are compelled to take the message of the Gospel to a lost and dying world, compelled to witness to the reconciliation offered in Christ, and compelled to continue His work.**

Leader   May all available means be employed so the hungry may be fed, the thirsty given drink, the stranger welcomed, the naked clothed, the sick and the imprisoned ministered unto.

People   **Barriers of geography, culture, and language challenge the delivery of the Gospel to the whole world. Danger and destruction are daily realities.**

Leader   The threat of violence is ever-present in corrupt governments, unjust rulers, terrorist conspiracies, war, globalization, and tribalism. Poverty holds nations hostage, while disease ravages body and soul.

People   **Whatever is born of God conquers the world—and this is the victory that conquers the world: our faith. Who will not fear You, O Lord, and bring glory to Your name?**

Leader   Thank You for the tools and the technology that is available for communication, essential for education, and necessary for modernization.

All   **And this Gospel of the kingdom will be proclaimed throughout the whole world as a testimony to all nations, and then the end will come.**

95. HEALTH AND WELLNESS

Leader   We stand in Your presence, acknowledging You as our Creator and our all-knowing God.

People   **We thank You for creating us in Your image and after Your own likeness.**

Leader   We praise You, O God, for providing deliverance for our souls and healing for our bodies.

People   **Help us to call upon You, for You are the one who blots out our sins and heals us from our diseases.**

Leader   There are seasons in our lives when we are distracted by the cares of this world and neglect to take care of ourselves by doing that which would promote health and well-being.

People   **Forgive us for not taking care of the temple where Your Spirit resides, and help us to follow the example You gave us when You gave Your Son. Then we can present our bodies (that we have been good stewards of) back for Your use.**

Leader   For the times when unknown illness attack our bodies for seemingly no apparent reason, and when we are sick as a result of our poor choices and/or family history…

People   **Help us, O God, to seek You for comfort when our bodies do not respond to the remedies that we employ. We will rest in the knowledge that, one day, we will have new bodies that are free of sickness and pain.**

Leader   O God, You loved us so much that You gave Your Son. We now have eternal life, we have Your Spirit, we have Your Word, and we can enjoy healing that comes from You.

People   **We thank You, Lord, for Your many blessings, and for those medical personnel who give of themselves in caring for the sick. Thank You for researchers who work relentlessly to find cures for illnesses that in the past were not available. Thank You for medical facilities all over the land that provide much-needed care.**

Leader   It is You who has made us, and not we. Therefore, we will look to You as our Lord, our Savior, and our Healer.

All   **We thank You, O Lord, that it is Your desire for us to enjoy good health, even as our souls prosper.**

96. HUNGER AWARENESS

Leader   Lord of the Sabbath, Bread of Life, by Your authority hungry people can be fed. When You saw them, You had compassion on them, and gave them food to eat.

People   **We are Your disciples who will also see the crowds and have compassion on them. We are Your disciples who will obey when You respond, "You give them something to eat."**

Leader   Several billion people populate the world. One-third of them are well-fed, one-third of them are underfed, and one-third of them are starving.

People   **Today, many thousands died of hunger caused by poverty, harmful economic systems, conflict, and climate.**

Leader   What good is it, my brothers and sisters, if you say you have faith but do not have works? If a brother or sister is naked and lacks daily food and one of you says to them, "Go in peace; keep warm and eat your fill," and yet you do not supply their bodily needs, what is the good of that?

People   **Children are the most visible victims of want or lack of food in the world. We need to save the children.**

Leader   Religion that is pure and undefiled before God is this: to care for orphans and widows in their distress and to keep ourselves unstained by the world. If you offer your food to the hungry, and satisfy the needs of the afflicted, then your light shall rise in the darkness, and your gloom shall be like the noonday.

People   **What does the Lord require of you, but to do justice, and to love kindness, and to walk humbly with your God?**

Leader   The world produces enough food to feed everyone. Opportunities exist to connect people with resources to overcome poverty, to develop solutions, and to reduce hunger. Just as Jesus fed the hungry, so should we.

All   **Open your hand to the poor and needy neighbor in your community.**

97. SUBSTANCE ABUSE

Leader As we come to worship, we are reminded that our bodies are the temples of God that we bring to the altar of sacrifice and service.

People **We thank You for salvation and sobriety.**

Leader We are grateful that through Your mercies we have spirits, bodies, and minds that belong to You.

People **Help us keep them safe, whole, and stayed on Your purposes for our destinies.**

Leader Some days are harder than others, but You have kept us in Your hand and plan.

People **O God, keep on being a keeper!**

Leader Some days we fail, falter, and fall into bad habits as users or enablers.

People **Forgive us, and help us to forgive ourselves and know that You remove our sins from us as far as the east is from the west.**

Leader Lord of our lives, we know we cannot be what You would have us to be if we are high, drunk, strung-out, or wasted. Order our steps, keep us in wholesome relationships, and take the cravings away from us. We beseech You to be God, our controller in everything we do.

People **Precious Lord, take our hands that we may go where You direct and do what You want us to do.**

Leader For those of us who may not be users or enablers, we offer hands of grace to encourage, whisper prayers of hope for those who still struggle, join the band who shout, "How I got over," and realize that if it were not for God's grace, we would have the same issues.

All **O God, our help in ages past, our hope for years to come, we are grateful for the space and grace to worship Thee with clear minds. Amen.**

98. RACIAL RECONCILIATION

Leader   O Lord, we thank You for the rainbow of peoples who populate our planet.

People   **Make us one in You, O Lord.**

Leader   While we are grateful for the unique history and characteristics that You have endowed us with as a people, we are thankful for siblings of parents of different hues and ethnicities.

People   **Let us seek the good of all Your children, O Lord.**

Leader   While we are dismayed because there are wars and rumors of war that tear at the peace that should unite us, we are thankful that You offer creative concord and calm that is for all.

People   **Let us be reconciled to You as well as the whole human family, and study war no more.**

Leader   Yes, some of us have pasts that have been watered with tears, and we have tasted the bitter chastening rod. Yet, we seek that Peace that surpasses understanding.

People   **May there be freedom from strife because we put our trust in our God, who liberates the minds, bodies, and spirits of all creation.**

Leader   O Lord, let there be a grand mosaic that characterizes our neighborhoods, churches, and nation. Let there be an anthem of harmony that resounds throughout all human hearts. Let there be a reaching across the breach of difference to join Your children as we walk and work together, believing that there is a great camp meeting in the Promised Land.

All   **Let there be peace in my heart, home, and community, and let it begin with me. Amen.**

99. WORLD PEACE

Leader   "God of Peace, Why do the nations rage and the peoples plot in vain?"

People   **"There is no peace," says the Lord, "for the wicked."**

Leader   In biblical times the towns from Ekron to Gath that the Philistines had captured from Israel were restored to her, and Israel delivered the neighboring territory from the power of the Philistines. And there was peace between Israel and the Amorites.

People   **We have known an international peace, if only for a moment.**

Leader   When Solomon ruled over all the kingdoms west of the River, from Tiphsah to Gaza, he had peace on all sides.

People   **We have known a national peace, if only for a moment.**

Leader   Jesus was handed over to death for our trespasses and was raised to set us right with God. We are justified by faith; we have peace with God through our Lord, Jesus Christ.

People   **We know a civil peace, but the day is coming when the Lord will judge between and settle disputes for strong nations far and wide. They will beat their swords into plowshares and their spears into pruning hooks. Nation will not take up sword against nation, nor will they train for war anymore.**

Leader   Turn from evil and do good; seek peace and pursue it. Clothe yourselves with love, which binds everything together in perfect harmony.

People   **Now in Christ Jesus, you who once were far off have been brought near by the blood of Christ. For He is our peace; through Him we all have access in one Spirit to the Father.**

All   **And let the peace of Christ rule in your hearts, to which indeed you were called in the one body. And be thankful.**

100 Total Praise

I lift up my eyes to the hills—from where will my help come?
Psalm 121:1

Lord, I will lift mine eyes to the hills

know - ing my help is com - ing from You.

Your peace You give me in time of the storm.

You are the source of my strength.

You are the strength of my life.

I lift my hands in to-tal praise to You.

2. A - men. A -

You. A - men, a - men. A - men.

A - men, a - men. A -

men, a - men. A - men, a -

A - men, a -

men, a - men. A - men.

men, a - men. A - men, a -

men. A - men.

men. A - men, a - men.

A - men, a - men.

men. A - men, a - men.

Text: Richard Smallwood, b.1948
Tune: Richard Smallwood, b.1948; arr. by Stephen Key
© 1996, arr. © 2010, T. Autumn Music; admin. by Universal Music - Z Songs

101

My Tribute

What shall I return to the LORD for all his bounty to me?
Psalm 116:12

How can I say thanks for the things You have done for me— Things so un-de-served, Yet You give to prove Your love for me? The voic - es of a mil-lion an - gels could not ex - press my grat-i - tude— All that I am and ev - er hope to be, I owe it all to Thee.

Just let me live my life— Let it be pleas-ing, Lord, to Thee; And should I gain an-y praise, Let it go to Cal - va - ry. With His

Text: Andraé Crouch, b.1942
Tune: MY TRIBUTE; Andraé Crouch, b.1942
© 1971, Bud John Songs, admin. at EMICMGPublishing.com

Holy Rest

102

There remains, then, a Sabbath-rest for the people of God...
Hebrews 4:9

We set our work a-side, We leave our cares be-hind, On this day of ho-ly rest; On this Your ho - ly day, We come to give You praise, On this day of ho-ly rest. Ho-ly

all the week the best, We have come to be blessed, On this

day of ho - ly rest. We rest. Ho-ly rest.

Text: Gale Jones Murphy, b.1954
Tune: Gale Jones Murphy, b.1954
© Gale Jones Murphy

103   We'll Praise the Lord

Let everything that breathes praise the LORD! Praise the LORD!
Psalm 150:6

1. We'll praise the Lord for He is great, And in His
2. We'll praise the Lord for He is wise; His wis-dom
3. We'll praise the Lord for He is just, And in Him
4. We'll praise the Lord for He is true; His word the
5. Oh, praise Him for His name is Love, And from His

pres - ence an - gels wait; All heav'n is swell-ing with His
shines through all the skies; The earth He meas-ures with a
we may ev - er trust; Prin - ces and kings may turn a -
same all a - ges through; Earth, sea and sky may pass a -
glo - rious throne a - bove, He bends to wel-come our weak

praise— Shall we not, too, our an - thems raise?
span, And crowns us with His im - age: man.
side, But God by right will e'er a - bide.
way, But firm, God's truth will ev - er stay.
praise, Shall we not, then, our an - them raise?

Text: T. G. Steward
Tune: NAZREY, LM with refrain; J. T. Layton

104 In the Sanctuary

I will praise you as long as I live, and in your name I will lift up my hands.
Psalm 63:4

We lift our hands in the sanc-tu-ar-y. We lift our hands to give You the glo-ry. We lift our hands to give You the praise, and we will praise You for the

com-ing Mes - si - ah, *unis.* and we will praise You for the

rest of our days. Yes, we will praise You for the

1. rest of our days. 2. *div.* rest of our days.

Text: Kurt Carr
Tune: Kurt Carr
© 2008, Kcartunes/Lilly Mack Publishing, admin. at EMICMGPublishing.com

This Is the Day

This is the day that the LORD has made; let us rejoice and be glad in it.
Psalm 118:24

This is the day, this is the day that the Lord has made, that the

Lord has made. I will re-joice, I will re-joice and be

glad in it, and be glad in it. This is the day that the

Lord has made. I will re-joice and be glad in it.

This is the day, this is the day that the Lord has made.

Text: Psalm 118:24
Tune: Les Garrett, b.1944, © 1967, 1980, Universal Music - Brentwood-Benson Publishing (ASCAP); arr. by Stephen Key

With Hands Lifted Up

106

Praise be to the LORD, the God of Israel, from everlasting to everlasting.
1 Chronicles 16:36

Verses

1. Praise, you ser-vants of the

2. High a - bove all na-tions is the

Lord, praise the name of the Lord.

Lord; a - bove the heav-ens is God's glo -

Blest be the name,

ry. Who is like the Lord, our God,

blest   be   the   name,   both   now   and for-

who is en-throned   on   high,   and looks up-on the heav-ens

D.C.

ev   -   er.

D.C.

and   the earth   be - low?

D.C.

Text: Verses, Psalm 113:1–2, 4–6; refrain by Leon C. Roberts, 1950–1999
Tune: Leon C. Roberts, 1950–1999
© 1998, OCP

107 Joyful, Joyful, We Adore You

For the kingdom of God is not food and drink but righteousness and peace and joy in the Holy Spirit.
Romans 14:17

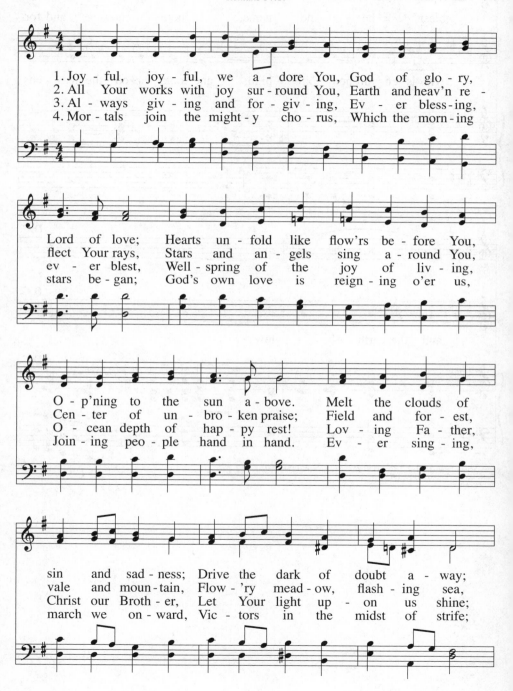

1. Joy - ful, joy - ful, we a - dore You, God of glo - ry,
2. All Your works with joy sur - round You, Earth and heav'n re -
3. Al - ways giv - ing and for - giv - ing, Ev - er bless-ing,
4. Mor - tals join the might - y cho - rus, Which the morn - ing

Lord of love; Hearts un - fold like flow'rs be - fore You,
flect Your rays, Stars and an - gels sing a - round You,
ev - er blest, Well - spring of the joy of liv - ing,
stars be - gan; God's own love is reign - ing o'er us,

O - p'ning to the sun a - bove. Melt the clouds of
Cen - ter of un - bro - ken praise; Field and for - est,
O - cean depth of hap - py rest! Lov - ing Fa - ther,
Join - ing peo - ple hand in hand. Ev - er sing - ing,

sin and sad - ness; Drive the dark of doubt a - way;
vale and moun - tain, Flow - 'ry mead - ow, flash - ing sea,
Christ our Broth - er, Let Your light up - on us shine;
march we on - ward, Vic - tors in the midst of strife;

Giv - er of im - mor - tal glad - ness, Fill us with the light of day!
Chant-ing bird and flow - ing foun - tain, Prais-ing You e - ter - nal - ly!
Teach us how to love each oth - er, Lift us to the joy di - vine.
Joy - ful mu - sic leads us sun - ward In the tri-umph song of life.

Tune: Henry van Dyke, 1852–1933, alt.
Tune: HYMN TO JOY, 8 7 8 7 D; arr. from Ludwig van Beethoven, 1770–1827, by Edward Hodges, 1796–1867

I Will Bless the Lord 108

I will bless the LORD at all times; his praise shall continually be in my mouth.
Psalm 34:1

I will bless the Lord at all times. His praise shall con-

1.
tin - u - al - ly be in my mouth.
2.
be in my mouth. In my mouth,

in my mouth, His praise shall con - tin - u - al - ly be in my mouth.

Text: Psalm 34:1
Tune: Shirley M. K. Berkeley; arr. by Valeria A. Foster, © 2000, GIA Publications, Inc.

109 Praise Him in Advance

Let everything that has breath praise the LORD. Praise the LORD.
Psalm 150:6

I've had my share of ups and downs, times when there

was no one a-round. God came and spoke these words to

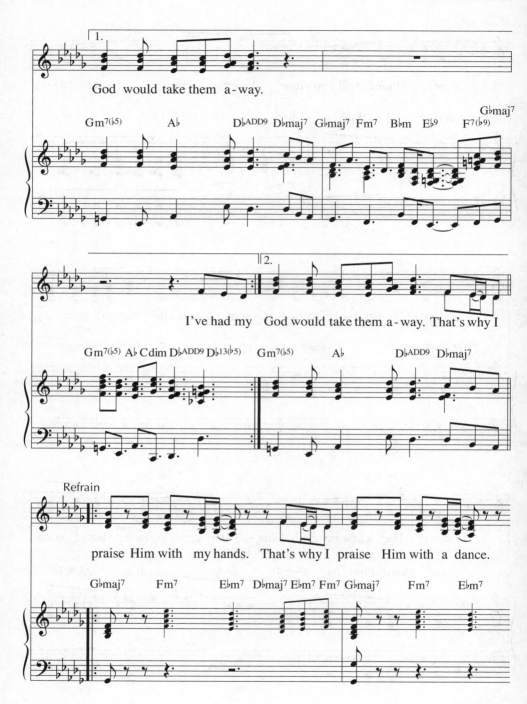

me   a   sec - ond chance.   Come on, let's

praise Him in   ad-vance. That's why I   praise Him in   ad-vance.

Text: Deon Kipping
Tune: Deon Kipping
© 2009, Meaux Hits/Gospo Music Thang/216 Music, admin. at EMICMGPublishing.com

I Will Call upon the Lord

Because he inclined his ear to me, therefore I will call on him as long as I live.
Psalm 116:2

I will call up-on the Lord, For

I will call up-on the

He is wor-thy to be praised.

Lord, For He is wor-thy to be

So shall I be saved from my en - e - mies.

praised; So shall I be

div.

The Lord liv - eth, and

saved from my en - e - mies.

bless-ed be the Rock; And let the God of my sal-va - tion be ex-

alt - ed. The Lord liv-eth, and bless-ed be the Rock;

And let the God of my sal-va - tion be ex - alt - ed.

Text : Psalm 18:2, 2 Samuel 22:47; Michael O'Shields, b.1948, © 1981, Sound III, Inc.
Tune: Michael O'Shields, b.1948, © 1981, Sound III, Inc.; arr. by Joseph Joubert, b.1958, © 2000, GIA Publications, Inc.

111 In the Beauty of Holiness

...be holy yourselves in all your conduct; for it is written, "You shall be holy, for I am holy."
1 Peter 1:15–16

Come let us wor-ship the Lord in the beau-ty of

ho-li-ness. Come let us wor-ship the Lord

in the beau-ty of ho-li-ness. Give Him the hon-

or. Give Him the praise.

Come let us wor-ship the Lord; Let's give Him the praise.

Wor-ship Him. Wor-ship Him. Give my God the glo-ry. Give my God the praise. Wor-ship Him. Wor-ship Him. Come let us wor-ship the Lord; Let's give Him the praise.

Text: Nettie L. Sawyer Lester, © 1992, Joy Publishing Co. (SESAC)
Tune: Nettie L. Sawyer Lester, © 1992, Joy Publishing Co. (SESAC); arr. by Stephen Key, © 2000, GIA Publications, Inc.

112 Welcome into This Place

I was glad when they said to me, "Let us go to the house of the LORD!"
Psalm 122:1

Wel-come in-to this place. Wel-come in-to this
bro-ken ves-sel. You de-sire to a-bide in the
prais-es of Your peo-ple, so we lift our hands and we
lift our hearts as we of-fer up this praise un-to Your name.

Text: Orlando Juarez
Tune: Orlando Juarez; arr. by James Abbington, b.1960
© 1991, CMI-HP Publishing, admin. by Word Music, LLC, Life Spring Music

Bless the Lord

113

Bless the LORD O my soul, and all that is within me, bless his holy name.
Psalm 103:1

Refrain

Bless the Lord, O my soul, and all that is with-in me, bless His ho-ly name!

Verse

He has done great things, He has done great things, He has done great things, bless His ho-ly name!

Text: Psalm 103:1
Tune: Andraé Crouch, b.1942, © 1973, Bud John Songs, admin. at EMICMGPublishing.com; arr. by Nolan Williams, Jr., b.1969

114 Thou Art Worthy

Worthy is the Lamb that was slaughtered to receive... wisdom and might and honor and glory and blessing!
Revelation 5:12

Thou art wor-thy, Thou art wor-thy,

Thou art wor-thy, O Lord.

To re-ceive glo-ry, glo-ry and hon-or,

Glo-ry and hon-or and pow'r. For

Text: Revelation 4:11, 5:9; Pauline M. Mills, 1898–1995
Tune: Pauline M. Mills, 1898–1995
© 1963, 1965, 1980, Fred Bock Music Company, Inc.

115 Amen Siakudumisa

...all the people answered, "Amen." Then they... worshipped the LORD with their faces to the ground.
Nehemiah 8:6

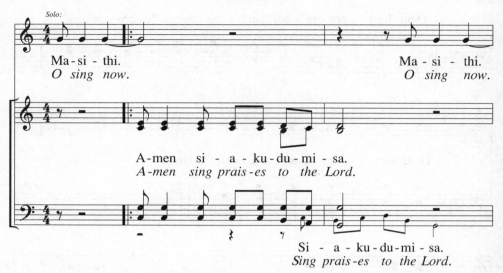

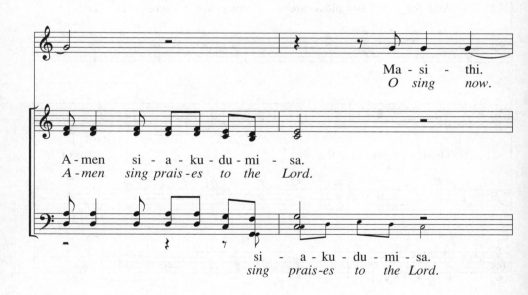

African phonetics:
Mah-see-tee
Amen see-ah-koo-doo-mee-sah

Text: *Amen. Praise the name of the Lord.* South African Traditional (Xhosa); English text, *Hymnal Version*
Tune: Attr. to Stephen C. Molefe, c.1915–1987, as taught by George Mxadana; arr. by John L. Bell, b.1949, © 1990, Iona Community,
    GIA Publications, Inc., agent

116   We've Come to Worship You

Thus says the LORD: "Let my people go, so that they may worship me."
Exodus 8:1

1. Lord, we've come to wor - ship You.
2. Lord, we've come to give You thanks.
3. Lord, we've come to give You praise.

Lord, we've come to wor - ship You, for we
Lord, we've come to give You thanks, for we
Lord, we've come to give You praise, for we

know that Your name is wor - thy, oh Lord, and we've
know that Your name is wor - thy, oh Lord, and we've
know that Your name is wor - thy, oh Lord, and we've

come to wor - ship You.
come to give You thanks.
come to give You praise.

Text: Stephen Key
Tune: Stephen Key
© 1993, StepKey Music

Praise to the Lord, the Almighty 117

Blessed be his glorious name forever; may his glory fill the whole earth. Amen and Amen.
Psalm 72:19

1. Praise to the Lord, the Al - might - y, the King of cre -
2. Praise to the Lord, who o'er all things so won - drous - ly
3. Praise to the Lord, who doth pros - per thy work and de -
4. Praise to the Lord, O let all that is in me a -

a - tion! O my soul, praise Him, for He is thy
reign - eth, Shel - ters thee un - der His wings, yea, so
fend thee; Sure - ly His good - ness and mer - cy here
dore Him! All that hath life and breath, come now with

health and sal - va - tion! All ye who hear, Now to His
gent - ly sus - tain - eth! Hast thou not seen How thy de -
dai - ly at - tend thee. Pon - der a - new What the Al -
prais - es be - fore Him. Let the A - men Sound from His

tem - ple draw near; Praise Him in glad ad - o - ra - tion.
sires e'er have been Grant - ed in what He or - dain - eth?
might - y can do, If with His love He be - friend thee.
peo - ple a - gain, For - ev - er - more we a - dore Him.

Text: German Hymn, Joachim Neander, 1650–1680; tr. by Catherine Winkworth, 1827–1878
Tune: LOBE DEN HERREN, Irregular; *Straslund Gesangbuch*, 1665; harm. by W. Sterndale Bennett, 1816–1875

118 A Child of the King

And I will be your Father and you shall be my sons and daughters, says the Lord Almighty.
2 Corinthians 6:18

1. My Fa - ther is rich in hous - es and land, He
2. My Fa - ther's own Son, the Sav - ior of men, Once
3. I once was an out - cast stran - ger on earth, A
4. A tent or a cot - tage, why should I care? They're

hold - eth the wealth of the world in His hands! Of
wan - dered on earth as the poor - est of them; But
sin - ner by choice and an a - lien by birth; But
build - ing a pal - ace for me o - ver there; Though

ru - bies and dia - monds, of sil - ver and gold, His
now He is reign - ing for ev - er on high, And will
I've been a - dopt - ed, my name's writ - ten down, An
ex - iled from home, yet still I may sing: All

cof - fers are full, He has rich - es un - told.
give me a home in heav'n by and by.
heir to a man - sion, a robe and a crown.
glo - ry to God, I'm a child of the King.

I'm a child of the King, A child of the King, With
Je - sus my Sav - ior, I'm a child of the King.

Text: Harriet E. Buell, 1834–1910
Tune: BINGHAMTON, 10 11 11 11 with refrain; John B. Sumner, 1838–1918; arr. by Valeria A. Foster, © 2000, GIA Publications, Inc.

119   A Mighty Fortress Is Our God

The LORD is my rock, my fortress, and my deliverer, my God, my rock in whom I take refuge…
Psalm 18:2

1. A might - y for - tress is our God, A
2. Did we in our own strength con - fide, Our
3. And though this world, with dev - ils filled, Should
4. That word a - bove all earth - ly pow'rs, No

bul - wark nev - er fail - ing; Our help - er He a -
striv - ing would be los - ing; Were not the right One
threat - en to un - do us, We will not fear, for
thanks to them, a - bid - eth; The Spir - it and the

mid the flood Of mor - tal ills pre - vail - ing. For
on our side, The One of God's own choos - ing. Dost
God hath willed His truth to tri - umph through us. The
gifts are ours Through Him who with us sid - eth; Let

still our an - cient foe Doth seek to work us woe; His
ask who that may be? Christ Je - sus, it is He, Lord
prince of dark - ness grim, We trem - ble not for him; His
goods and kin - dred go, This mor - tal life al - so; The

craft and pow'r are great, And, armed with cru - el
Sab - a - oth His name, From age to age the
rage we can en - dure, For lo! his doom is
bod - y they may kill, God's truth a - bid - eth

hate, On earth is not his e - qual.
same, And He must win the bat - tle.
sure, One lit - tle word shall fell him.
still, His king - dom is for - ev - er.

Text: Martin Luther, 1483–1546; tr. by Frederick H. Hedge, 1805–1890
Tune: EIN' FESTE BURG, 8 7 8 7 66 66 7; Martin Luther, 1483–1546

120 Awesome God

We give you thanks, Lord God Almighty, who are and who were,
for you have taken your great power and begun to reign.
Revelation 11:17

Text: Rich Mullins, 1955–1997, © 1988, Universal Music - MGB Songs (ASCAP)
Tune: Rich Mullins, 1955–1997, © 1988, Universal Music - MGB Songs (ASCAP); arr. by Nolan Williams, Jr., b.1969, © 2000, GIA Publications, Inc.

121   Be Still, God Will Fight Your Battles

The LORD will fight for you, and you have only to keep still.
Exodus 14:14

*Percussion is to be used throughout the piece.

Verse 2

2. *Keep a pray - in',   God will fight your bat-tles. Keep a

2. *Keep a pray - in',   God will fight your bat-tles.

pray - in',   God will fight your bat-tles. Keep a

Keep a pray - in',   God will fight your bat-tles.

pray - in',   God   will fight your bat - tles.   God

Keep a pray - in'   God   will fight your bat - tles.   God

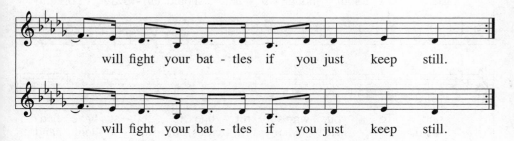

will fight your bat - tles if   you just   keep   still.

will fight your bat - tles if   you just   keep   still.

*3. Keep a waitin', God will fight your battles…
4. Keep a singin', God will fight your battles…
5. I'm a witness, God will fight your battles…

Text: African American traditional
Tune: African American traditional; arr. by Nolan Williams, Jr., b.1969, © 2000, GIA Publications, Inc.

122 How Firm a Foundation

For no one can lay any foundation other than the one that has been laid; that foundation is Jesus Christ.
1 Corinthians 3:11

1. How firm a foun - da - tion, ye saints of the
2. "Fear not, I am with thee, O be not dis -
3. "When through the deep wa - ters I call thee to
4. "When through fi - ery tri - als thy path - way shall
5. "The soul that on Je - sus hath leaned for re -

Lord, Is laid for your faith in His ex - cel - lent
mayed, For I am thy God, I will still give thee
go, The riv - ers of woe shall not thee o - ver -
lie, My grace, all suf - fi - cient, shall be thy sup -
pose, I will not, I will not de - sert to his

Word! What more can He say than to you He hath
aid; I'll strength - en thee, help thee, and cause thee to
flow; For I will be with thee, thy troub - les to
ply; The flame shall not hurt thee— I on - ly de -
foes; That soul, though all hell should en - deav - or to

said, To you, who for ref - uge to Je - sus have fled?
stand, Up - held by my gra - cious, om - nip - o - tent hand.
bless, And sanc - ti - fy to thee, thy deep - est dis - tress.
sign Thy dross to con-sume and thy gold to re - fine.
shake, I'll nev - er, no nev - er, no nev - er for - sake!"

Text: 2 Peter 1:4; "K" in Rippon's *A Selection of Hymns*, 1787
Tune: FOUNDATION, 11 11 11 11; Caldwell's *Unison Harmony*, 1837

Cast Your Cares

Cast all your anxiety on him, because he cares for you.
1 Peter 5:7

Last time

cares.   God   cares   for you!

Last time

Verse

I am learn - ing   to put

all   my trust   in   Him,   For He   knows   the

road   up   a - head.   I must not com-

plain, I must learn to trust in His name. He knows,
He cares, God real - ly cares. God
cares for you!

D.S.

Text: Carlton Burgess, © 1994
Tune: Carlton Burgess, © 1994; arr. by Nolan Williams, Jr., b.1969, © 2000 GIA Publications, Inc.
Administered by GIA Publications, Inc.

124 His Eye Is on the Sparrow

Look at the birds... they neither sow nor reap, yet your heavenly Father feeds them.
Are you not of more value than they?
Matthew 6:26

1. Why should I feel dis - cour - aged, Why should the shad - ows
2. "Let not your heart be trou - bled," His ten - der word I
3. When ev - er I am tempt - ed, When ev - er clouds a -

come, Why should my heart be lone - ly, And
hear, And rest - ing on His good - ness, I
rise, When songs give place to sigh - ing When

long for heav'n and home; When Je - sus is my
lose my doubts and fears; Though by the path He
hope with - in me dies, I draw the clos - er

por - tion? My con - stant Friend is He:
lead - eth, But one step I may see; His
to Him, From care He sets me free;

Text: Civilla D. Martin, 1860–1948
Tune: SPARROW, 7 6 7 6 7 6 7 7 7 7 with refrain; Charles H. Gabriel, 1865–1932; arr. by Horace Clarence Boyer, 1935–2009, © 1992

125 My Heavenly Father Watches over Me

The LORD watches over all who love him, but all the wicked he will destroy.
Psalm 145:20

1. I trust in God wher-ev-er I may be, Up-on the
2. He makes the rose an ob-ject of His care, He guides the
3. I trust in God, for, in the li-on's den, On bat-tle-
4. The val-ley may be dark, the shad-ows deep, But oh, the

land or on the roll-ing sea; For come what
ea - gle through the path-less air; And sure-ly
field, or in the pris-on pen; Through praise or
shep - herd guards His lone-ly sheep; And through the

may,   from day to day,   My heav'n-ly
He   re - mem-bers me,
blame,   through flood or flame,
gloom,   He'll lead me home,

Fa-ther watch-es o - ver me.

I trust in God, I know He cares for me, On moun-tain bleak or on the storm-y sea; Though bil-lows roll, He keeps my soul, My heav'n-ly Fa-ther watch-es o - ver me.

Text: W. C. Martin
Tune: HEAVENLY FATHER, 10 10 8 10 with refrain; Charles H. Gabriel, 1856–1932; arr. J. Jefferson Cleveland, 1937–1988 and Verolga Nix-Allen, b.1933

126

God Is

God is our refuge and strength, a very present help in trouble.
Psalm 46:1

Chorus

God is the joy and the strength of my life. He moves all pain, mis-er-y, and strife. He prom-ised to keep me, nev-er to leave me, He's nev-er, ev-er come short of His word. I've got to fast and pray, stay in the nar-row way. I'll keep my life clean

ev - 'ry day.   I want to go with Him when He comes back.

I've come too far   and I'll nev-er turn back.

God is,   God is,   God is,   God is.

To repeat   **D.C.**

God is my all and all.

Final ending

God is my all and all.

Text: Dr. Robert J. Fryson, 1944–1994, © 1976, Bob Jay Music Co.
Tune: Dr. Robert J. Fryson, 1944–1994, © 1976, Bob Jay Music Co.; arr. by Evelyn Simpson-Curenton, b.1953, and Nolan Williams, Jr., b.1969,
   © 2000, GIA Publications, Inc.

127 Lord, Keep Me Day by Day

...if the earthly tent we live in is destroyed, we have a building from God, ...eternal in the heavens.
2 Corinthians 5:1

1. Lord, keep me day by day
2. Lord, keep my bod - y strong
3. I'm just a stran - ger here,

in a pure and
so that I can
trav - 'ling through this

per - fect way.
do no wrong.
bar - ren land.

I want to
Lord, give me
Lord, I

live
grace just to run
know there's a build-ing some-where,

I want to live on
this Chris-tian race

Text: Eddie Williams
Tune: Eddie Williams; arr. by Valeria Foster
© 1959, (renewed), arr. © 2011, Martin and Morris, Inc., admin. by Unichappell Music, Inc.

128 God Leads Us Along

He makes me lie down in green pastures; he leads me beside still waters.
Psalm 23:2

1. In shad - y, green pas - tures, so rich and so sweet,
2. Some - times on the mount where the sun shines so bright,
3. Tho' sor - rows be - fall us and Sa - tan op - pose,
4. A - way from the mire and a - way from the clay,

God leads His dear chil - dren a - long;

Where the wa - ter's cool flow bathes the wea - ry one's feet,
Some - times in the val - ley, in dark - est of night,
Thru grace we can con - quer, de - feat all our foes,
A - way up in glo - ry, e - ter - ni - ty's day,

God leads His dear chil - dren a - long.

Some thru the wa-ters, some thru the flood,

Some thru the fire, but all thru the blood;

Some thru great sor-row, but God gives a song,

In the night sea-son, and all the day long.

Text: George A. Young, 1903–1977
Tune: GOD LEAD US, 11 8 11 8 with refrain; George A. Young, 1903–1977

129 Father, I Stretch My Hands to Thee

I stretch out my hands to you; my soul thirsts for you like a parched land.
Psalm 143:6–7

1. Fa - ther, I stretch my hands to Thee;
2. What did Thine on - ly Son en - dure,
3. Sure - ly Thou canst not let me die;
4. Au - thor of faith! to Thee I lift

No oth - er help I know.
Be - fore I drew my breath!
O speak and I shall live;
My wea - ry, long - ing eyes;

If Thou with - draw Thy - self from me,
What pain, what la - bor to se - cure
And here I will un - wea - ried lie,
O let me now re - ceive that gift!

O! whith - er shall I go?
My soul from end - less death!
Till Thou Thy Spir - it give.
My soul with - out it dies.

Text: Charles Wesley, 1707–1788
Tune: MARTYRDOM, CM; Hugh Wilson, 1766–1824; arr. by Nolan Williams, Jr., b.1969, © 2000, GIA Publications, Inc.

God Is a Wonder to My Soul

130

I came that they may have life, and have it abundantly.
John 10:10

1. God is a won - der to my soul.
2. My God's truth has set me free.
3. Now I can live a - bun-dant - ly.

God is a won - der to my soul.
My God's truth has set me free.
Now I can live a - bun-dant - ly.
Came in -

to my life one day, And took all my sins a - way.

Oh, God is a won - der to my soul.
Oh, my God's truth has set me free.
Now I can live a - bun-dant - ly.

Text: Dr. Robert J. Fryson, 1944–1994, © 1989, Bob Jay Music Co.
Tune: WONDER, 88 77 9; traditional; arr. by Valeria A. Foster, © 2000, GIA Publications, Inc.

131

Be Still, My Soul

Be still, and know that I am God! I am exalted among the nations, I am exalted in the earth.
Psalm 46:10

1. Be still, my soul— the Lord is on thy side!
2. Be still, my soul— thy God doth un - der - take
3. Be still, my soul— the hour is has - t'ning on

Bear pa - tient - ly the cross of grief or pain;
To guide the fu - ture as He has the past;
When we shall be for ev - er with the Lord,

Leave to thy God to or - der and pro - vide—
Thy hope, thy con - fi - dence let noth - ing shake—
When dis - ap - point - ment, grief, and fear are gone,

In ev - 'ry change He faith - ful will re - main.
All now mys - te - rious shall be bright at last.
Sor-row for - got, love's pur - est joys re - stored.

Be still, my soul— thy best, thy heav'n - ly Friend
Be still, my soul— the waves and winds still know
Be still, my soul— when change and tears are past,

Through thorn - y ways leads to a joy - ful end.
His voice who ruled them while He dwelt be - low.
All safe and bless - ed we shall meet at last.

Text: Katharina von Schlegel, 1697–1768; tr. by Jane L. Borthwick, 1813–1897
Tune: FINLANDIA, 10 10 10 10 10 10; Jean Sibelius, 1865–1957

132 Guide Me, O Thou Great Jehovah

The LORD will guide you continually, and satisfy your needs in parched places...
Isaiah 58:11

1. Guide me, O Thou great Je-ho-vah, Pil-grim through this bar-ren land; I am weak, but Thou art might-y; Hold me with Thy pow'r-ful hand: Bread of heav-en, Feed me till I want no more; Bread of

2. O-pen now the crys-tal foun-tain, Whence the heal-ing wa-ters flow; Let the fi-er-y, cloud-y pil-lar Lead me all my jour-ney through: Strong De-liv-erer, Be Thou still my strength and shield; Strong De-

3. When I tread the verge of Jor-dan, Bid my anx-ious fears sub-side; Bear me through the swel-ling cur-rent, Land me safe on Ca-naan's side: Songs of prais-es I will ev-er give to Thee; Songs of

heav - en,   Feed me till I want no more.
liv - erer,   Be Thou still my strength and shield.
prais - es   I will ev - er give to Thee.

Text: William Williams, 1717–1791; st. 1, tr. by Peter Williams, 1722–1796
Tune: ZION, 8 7 8 7 4 7 4 7; Thomas Hastings, 1784–1872

133 Guide Me, O Thou Great Jehovah

The LORD will guide you continually, and satisfy your needs in parched places...
Isaiah 58:11

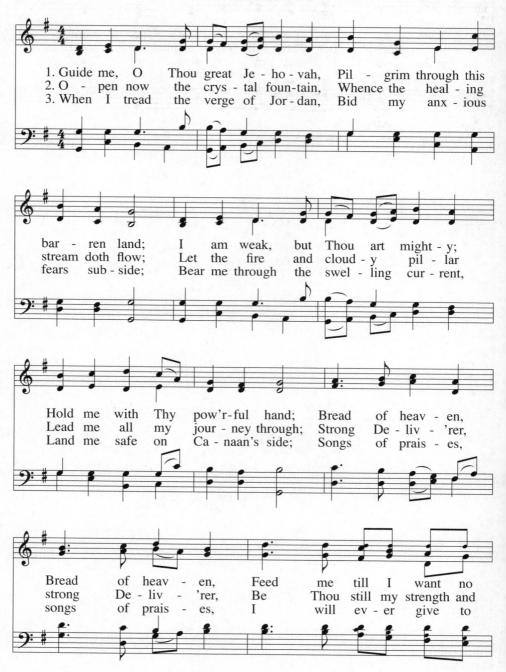

1. Guide me, O Thou great Je - ho - vah, Pil - grim through this
2. O - pen now the crys - tal foun-tain, Whence the heal - ing
3. When I tread the verge of Jor - dan, Bid my anx - ious

bar - ren land; I am weak, but Thou art might - y;
stream doth flow; Let the fire and cloud - y pil - lar
fears sub - side; Bear me through the swel - ling cur - rent,

Hold me with Thy pow'r-ful hand; Bread of heav - en,
Lead me all my jour - ney through; Strong De - liv - 'rer,
Land me safe on Ca - naan's side; Songs of prais - es,

Bread of heav - en, Feed me till I want no
strong De - liv - 'rer, Be Thou still my strength and
songs of prais - es, I will ev - er give to

more,   Feed   me   till   I   want   no   more.
shield,   Be   Thou   still   my   strength   and   shield.
Thee,   I   will   ev -   er   give   to   Thee.

Text: William Williams, 1717–1791; st. 1, tr. by Peter Williams, 1722–1796
Tune: CWM RHONDDA, 8 7 8 7 8 77; John Hughes, 1873–1932

Lead Me, Lord   134

Lead me in your truth, and teach me, for you are the God of my salvation.
Psalm 25:5

Lead me,   Lord,   lead me   in   Thy   right - eous-ness,

Make   Thy way   plain   be - fore   Thy   face.

Optional Ending

For   it   is   Thou,   Lord,   Thou,   Lord   on - ly,   that

mak - est   me   dwell   in   safe -   ty.

Text: Psalm 5:8
Tune: Samuel Sebastian Wesley, 1810–1876

135 God of Grace and God of Glory

Glory in his holy name; let the hearts of those who seek the LORD rejoice.
1 Chronicles 16:9–11

1. God of grace and God of glo - ry,
2. Lo! the hosts of e - vil round us
3. Cure Thy chil - dren's war - ring mad - ness,
4. Save us from weak res - ig - na - tion

On Thy peo - ple pour Thy pow'r;
Scorn Thy Christ, as - sail His ways!
Bend our pride to Thy con - trol;
To the e - vils we de - plore;

Crown Thine an - cient Chur - ch's sto - ry;
From the fears that long have bound us
Shame our wan - ton, self - ish glad - ness,
Let the gift of Thy sal - va - tion

Bring her bud to glo - rious flow'r.
Free our hearts to faith and praise:
Rich in things and poor in soul.
Be our glo - ry ev - er - more.

Grant us wis - dom, grant us cour - age,
Grant us wis - dom, grant us cour - age,
Grant us wis - dom, grant us cour - age,
Grant us wis - dom, grant us cour - age,

For the fac - ing of this hour,
For the liv - ing of these days,
Lest we miss Thy king - dom's goal,
Serv - ing Thee whom we a - dore,

For the fac - ing of this hour.
For the liv - ing of these days.
Lest we miss Thy king - dom's goal.
Serv - ing Thee whom we a - dore.

Text: Harry Emerson Fosdick, 1878–1969
Tune: CWM RHONDDA, 8 7 8 7 8 77; John Hughes, 1873–1932

136 The Angels Keep A-Watchin'

For he will command his angels concerning you to guard you in all your ways.
Psalm 91:11

All night, all day, the

an - gels keep a-watch-in' o-ver me, my Lord!

All night, all day, the

Last time

an-gels keep a-watch-in' o-ver me!

Last time

Text: Negro Spiritual
Tune: Negro Spiritual; arr. by Nolan Williams, Jr., b.1969, © 2000, GIA Publications, Inc.

Guide My Feet

By the tender mercy of our God, the dawn from on high will break upon us,...
to guide our feet into the way of peace.
Luke 1:78–79

1. Guide my feet
2. Hold my hand
3. Stand by me
4. I'm Your child

while I run this race,

Oh, Lord,

Guide my feet
Hold my hand
Stand by me
I'm Your child

while I run this race,

Oh, Lord,

Guide my feet
Hold my hand
Stand by me
I'm Your child

while I run this race, For I

vain.

don't want to run this race in vain, race in vain.

vain.

Text: Negro Spiritual
Tune: GUIDE MY FEET, 888 10; Negro Spiritual; harm. by Dr. Wendell P. Whalum, 1931–1987, © Estate of Wendell Whalum

138 God Will Take Care of You

Cast all your anxiety on him, because he cares for you.
1 Peter 5:7

1. Be not dis - mayed what - e'er be - tide,
2. Through days of toil when heart does fail,
3. All you may need He will pro - vide,
4. No mat - ter what may be the test,

God will take care of you; Be - neath His wings of
God will take care of you; When dan - gers fierce your
God will take care of you; Noth - ing you ask will
God will take care of you; Lean, wea - ry one, up -

love a - bide, God will take care of you.
path as - sail, God will take care of you.
be de - nied, God will take care of you.
on His breast, God will take care of you.

God will take care of you, Through ev - 'ry day,

O'er all the way; He will take care of you,
of you.

God will take care take care of you.
of you.

Text: Civilla D. Martin, 1869–1948
Tune: GOD CARES, CM with refrain; W. Stillman Martin, 1862–1935

139 He Leadeth Me

He restores my soul. He leads me in right paths for his name's sake.
Psalm 23:3

1. He lead - eth me! O bless - ed thought! O
2. Some - times 'mid scenes of deep - est gloom, Some -
3. Lord, I would clasp Thy hand in mine, Nor
4. And when my task on earth is done, When

words with heav'n - ly com - fort fraught! What -
times where E - den's bow - ers bloom, By
ev - er mur - mur nor re - pine; Con -
by Thy grace the vic - t'ry's won, E'en

e'er I do, wher - e'er I be, Still
wa - ters still, o'er trou - bled sea, Still
tent, what - ev - er lot I see, Since
death's cold wave I will not flee, Since

'tis God's hand that lead - eth me.
'tis His hand that lead - eth me!
'tis my God that lead - eth me!
God thru Jor - dan lead - eth me.

He lead-eth me, He lead-eth me, By His own hand He lead-eth me; His faith-ful fol-l'wer I would be, For by His hand He lead-eth me.

Text: Joseph H. Gilmore, 1834–1918
Tune: HE LEADETH ME, LM with refrain; William B. Bradbury, 1816–1868

140 This Is My Father's World

The earth is the LORD's and all that is in it, the world, and those who live in it.
Psalm 24:1

1. This is my Fa-ther's world, And to my list-'ning
2. This is my Fa-ther's world— The birds their car-ols
3. This is my Fa-ther's world— O let me ne'er for-

ears All na-ture sings, and round me rings The
raise; The morn-ing light, sun shin-ing bright, De-
get That tho' the wrong seems oft so strong God

mu-sic of the spheres. This is my Fa-ther's world! I
clares its Mak-er's praise. This is my Fa-ther's world! He
is the Rul-er yet. This is my Fa-ther's world! The

rest me in the thought Of rocks and trees, of
shines in all that's fair; In the rus-tling grass I
bat-tle is not done; Je - sus who died shall be

skies and seas— His hand the won - ders wrought.
hear Him pass— He speaks to me ev - 'ry - where.
sat - is - fied, And earth and heav'n be one.

Text: Maltbie D. Babcock, 1858–1901
Tune: TERRA BEATA, SMD; Franklin L. Sheppard, 1852–1930; harm. by Norman Johnson, 1928–1983, © 1984, New Spring Publishing (ASCAP)

141 All Creatures of Our God and King

Make a joyful noise to God, all the earth.
Psalm 66:1

1. All crea-tures of our God and King, Lift
2. O rush-ing wind and breez-es soft, O
3. O flow-ing wa-ters, pure and clear, Make
4. Dear moth-er earth, who day by day Un -
5. O ev-'ry one of ten-der heart, For -

up your voice and with us sing: Al - le - lu - ia! Al-le-
clouds that ride the winds a - loft: Al - le - lu - ia! Al-le-
mu - sic for your Lord to hear. Al - le - lu - ia! Al-le-
folds rich bless-ings on our way, Al - le - lu - ia! Al-le-
giv - ing oth - ers, take your part, Al - le - lu - ia! Al-le-

lu - ia! O burn - ing sun with gold - en beam And
lu - ia! O ris - ing morn, in praise re - joice, O
lu - ia! O fire so mas - ter - ful and bright, Pro -
lu - ia! The fruits and flow'rs that ver - dant grow, Let
lu - ia! All you who pain and sor - row bear, Praise

sil - ver moon with soft - er gleam:
lights of eve - ning, find a voice.
vid - ing us with warmth and light,
them God's glo - ry al - so show.
God and cast on God your care.

Al - le - lu - ia! Al-le-lu - ia! Al-le-lu - ia, al-le - lu - ia, al-le-lu - ia!

6. And you, most kind and gentle death,
Waiting to hush our final breath,
    Alleluia! Alleluia!
You lead to heav'n the child of God,
Where Christ our Lord the way has trod.
    Alleluia! Alleluia!
    Alleluia, alleluia, alleluia!

7. Let all things their Creator bless,
And worship God in humbleness,
    Alleluia! Alleluia!
Oh praise the Father, praise the Son,
And praise the Spirit, Three in One!
    Alleluia! Alleluia!
    Alleluia, alleluia, alleluia!

Text: *Laudato si, mi Signor*; Francis of Assisi, 1182–1226; tr. by William H. Draper, 1855–1933, alt.
Tune: LASST UNS ERFREUEN, LM with alleluias; *Geistliche Kirchengesänge*, 1623; harm. by Ralph Vaughan Williams, 1872–1958

142 How Great Thou Art

Great are the works of the LORD, studied by all who delight in them.
Psalm 111:2

1. O Lord my God, when I in awe - some
2. When through the woods and for - est glades I
3. And when I think that God, His Son not
4. When Christ shall come with shout of ac - cla -

won - der Con - sid - er all the works Thy hands have
wan - der And hear the birds sing sweet - ly in the
spar - ing, Sent Him to die, I scarce can take it
ma - tion And take me home, what joy shall fill my

made, I see the stars, I hear the roll - ing
trees, When I look down from loft - y moun - tain
in That on the cross, my bur - den glad - ly
heart! Then I shall bow in hum - ble ad - o -

thun - der, Thy pow'r through-out the un - i - verse dis - played!
gran-deur And hear the brook and feel the gen - tle breeze,
bear - ing, He bled and died to take a - way my sin!
ra - tion And there pro - claim, "My God, how great Thou art!"

Then sings my soul, my Sav-ior God, to Thee; How great Thou art, how great Thou art! Then sings my soul, my Sav-ior God, to Thee; How great Thou art, How great Thou art!

Text: Stuart K. Hine, 1899–1989
Tune: Traditional Swedish folk tune, 11 10 11 10 with refrain; adapt. Stuart K. Hine, 1899–1989
© 1949, 1953, The Stuart K. Hine Trust. U.S.A. print rights admin. Hope Publishing Company

143 He's Got the Whole World in His Hand

In his hand is the life of every living thing and the breath of every human being.
Job 12:10

1. He's got the whole world in His hand, He's got the whole world in His hand, He's got the whole world in His hand, He's got the whole world in His hand.
2. He's got the sun and the moon in His hand, He's got the sun and the moon in His hand, He's got the sun and the moon in His hand, He's got the whole world in His hand.
3. He's got the wind and the rain in His hand, He's got the wind and the rain in His hand, He's got the wind and the rain in His hand, He's got the whole world in His hand.
4. He's got the lit-tle bit-ty ba-by in His hand, He's got the lit-tle bit-ty ba-by in His hand, He's got the lit-tle bit-ty ba-by in His hand, He's got the whole world in His hand.
5. He's got you and me, broth-er, in His hand, He's got you and me, sis-ter, in His hand, He's got ev-'ry-bod-y here in His hand, He's got the whole world in His hand.

Text: Traditional
Tune: WHOLE WORLD, Irregular; Negro Spiritual; arr. by Hezekiah Brinson, Jr., b.1958, © 1990

Know That God Is Good/
Mungu Ni Mwema

144

Surely God is good to Israel, to those who are pure in heart.
Psalm 73:1

African phonetics: Moon-goo nee mway-mah

Text: Anonymous
Tune: Anonymous; arr. by John L. Bell, b.1949, Iona Community, GIA Publications, Inc., agent

145 Oh, What He's Done for Me

He does great things and unsearchable, marvelous things without number.
Job 5:9

1. Oh, what He's done for me.
Oh, what He's done for me.
Oh, what He's done for me. I nev-er shall for-get what He's done for me.

2. He took my feet out the miry clay, that's...
3. He feeds me when I'm hungry, that's...
4. He picked me up and turned me around, that's...
5. He gave me a home in glory, that's...

Text: Congregational Praise Song
Tune: Congregational Praise Song; arr. by James Abbington, b.1960, © 2000, GIA Publications, Inc.

For God So Loved the World

146

Believe on the Lord Jesus, and you will be saved...
Acts 16:31

Text: Lanny Wolfe, b.1942
Tune: Lanny Wolfe, b.1942; arr. by Evelyn Simpson-Curenton, b.1953
© 1982, Lanny Wolfe Music (all rights controlled by Gaither Copyright Mgmt.)

147   His Mercies Are New Every Day

...the LORD of heaven and earth, the sea, and everything in them who remains faithful forever.
Psalm 146:5

Verses 1, 2

Men:

1. Be - cause of His love we are not con - sumed, His
2. (Con-) tin - u - ous love that will nev - er fail, His

Women:

mer - cies are new ev - 'ry day;
mer - cies are new ev - 'ry day;

Men:

With -
With

out His com - pas - sion my soul is doomed,
Him in my life sin can - not pre - vail,

Women:

His
His

He is   His mer-cies are new ev-'ry day.

His mer-cies are new   ev-'ry day.

Text: Gale Jones Murphy, b.1954
Tune: Gale Jones Murphy, b.1954
© Gale Jones Murphy

God Is a Good God

148

O give thanks to the LORD, for he is good; for his steadfast love endures forever.
1 Chronicles 16:34

Text: Keith Hunter, © 1989
Tune: Keith Hunter, © 1989; arr. by Stephen Key and Nolan Williams, Jr., b.1969, © 2000, GIA Publications, Inc.
Published by Arrand Publishing Co.

149

God Has Smiled on Me

May God be gracious to us and bless us and make his face to shine upon us.
Psalm 67:1

Refrain

God has smiled on me, He has set me free.

God has smiled on me, He's been good to me.

Text: Isaiah Jones, Jr.
Tune: SMILED ON ME, 8 6 6 6 with refrain; Isaiah Jones, Jr.; arr. by Nolan Williams, Jr., b.1969
© 1973, 2000, Davike Music Co./Fricon Music Co.

150 To God Be the Glory

Grace to you and peace from God, Our Father and the Lord Jesus Christ...
to whom be the glory forever and ever.
Galatians 1:3–5

Praise the Lord, praise the Lord, let the earth hear His voice! Praise the Lord, praise the Lord, let the peo-ple re-joice! O come to the Fa-ther through Je-sus, the Son, and give Him the glo-ry— great things He hath done!

Text: Fanny J. Crosby, 1820–1915
Tune: BE THE GLORY, 11 11 11 11 with refrain; William H. Doane, 1832–1915

151 God Never Fails

Be strong and bold... because it is the LORD your God who goes with you;
he will not fail you or forsake you.
Deuteronomy 31:6–8

Text: George Jordan, 1896–1981, © 1968, Greater Detroit Music and Record Mart
Tune: George Jordan, 1896–1981, © 1968, Greater Detroit Music and Record Mart, Inc.; arr. by Jeffrey P. Radford, © 2000, GIA Publications, Inc.

152 The Lord Is My Light

The LORD is my light and my salvation; whom shall I fear?
Psalm 27:1

Verse 1

1. The Lord is my light and my sal-va-tion, the Lord is my light and my sal-va-tion, the Lord is my light and my sal-va-tion. Whom shall I fear?

Refrain

Whom shall I fear? Whom shall I fear? The Lord is the strength of my life. Whom shall I fear?

Last time to Coda

be of good cour - age, wait on the Lord and

be of good cour - age. Whom shall I fear?

Refrain

Whom shall I fear? Whom shall I fear? The

Lord is the strength of my life. Whom shall I fear?

Text: Lillian Bouknight
Tune: Lillian Bouknight; arr. by Stephen Key
© 1981, Peermusic III, Ltd. and Savgos Music, Inc.

Old Time Religion

153

I am reminded of your sincere faith... first in your grandmother... and your mother...
and now, I am sure, lives in you.
2 Timothy 1:5

Refrain: Give me that old time re - lig - ion, Give me that
1. It was good for Paul and Si - las, It was
2. It was good for the He - brew chil - dren, It was
3. It was good for our moth - ers, It was
4. Makes me love ev - 'ry - bod - y, Makes me

old time re - lig - ion, Give me that
good for Paul and Si - las, It was
good for the He - brew chil - dren, It was
good for our moth - ers, It was
love ev - 'ry - bod - y, Makes me

old time re - lig - ion,
good for Paul and Si - las,
good for the He - brew chil - dren, It's good e - nough for me.
good for our moth - ers,
love ev - 'ry - bod - y,

Text: Traditional
Tune: OLD TIME RELIGION, Irregular; traditional; arr. by Joseph Joubert, b.1958, © 2000, GIA Publications, Inc.

154   Great Is Thy Faithfulness

The steadfast love of the LORD never ceases, his mercies never come to an end... great is your faithfulness.
Lamentations 3:22–23

1. Great is Thy faith - ful-ness, O God my Fa - ther,
2. Sum - mer and win - ter, and spring-time and har - vest,
3. Par - don for sin and a peace that en - dur-eth,

There is no shad - ow of turn - ing with Thee;
Sun, moon and stars in their cours - es a - bove,
Thine own dear pres - ence to cheer and to guide;

Thou chang - est not, Thy com - pas - sions, they fail not,
Join with all na - ture in man - i - fold wit-ness,
Strength for to - day and bright hope for to - mor-row,

As Thou has been Thou for ev - er wilt be.
To Thy great faith - ful-ness, mer - cy and love.
Bless - ings all mine, with ten thou - sand be - side!

Text: Thomas O. Chisholm, 1866–1960
Tune: FAITHFULNESS, 11 10 11 10 with refrain; William M. Runyan, 1870–1957
© 1923, renewed 1951, Hope Publishing Company

155 Through the Years You Safely Guide Us

For this God is our God for ever and ever; he will be our guide even to the end.
Psalm 48:14

1. Through the years You safe - ly guide us,
2. On the path we join with oth - ers
3. Cross - ing riv - er, hill, or moun - tain

Awe - some God and ho - ly friend.
In the jour - ney that we share,
Calls for all our strength and skill,

Stay and trav - el close be - side us;
And we count as sis - ters, broth - ers,
But Your grace flows like a foun - tain;

Lead Your peo - ple till the end. At the font with
All Your chil - dren ev - 'ry - where. We break bread in
We can rest and drink our fill. Through the years You

flow - ing wa - ters You have set us on our way.
deep thanks - giv - ing For the bless - ings You be - stow,
safe - ly guide us, God of jour - ney, faith - ful friend.

Led by winds of Spir - it blow - ing
For the gifts of dai - ly liv - ing
Now and al - ways stay be - side us;

We move on - ward ev - 'ry day.
And Your pres - ence as we go.
Lead Your peo - ple till the end.

Text: Ruth Duck, b.1947, © 2005, GIA Publications, Inc.
Tune: HOLY MANNA, 8 7 8 7 D; William Moore, fl.1830, *Columbian Harmony*, 1825

156

All around Me

He is your God, who performed for you those great and awesome wonders you saw with your own eyes.
Deuteronomy 10:21

1. God is high, God is low, God is wide and He
2. God is here, God is there, God is great and He's
3. God is in, God is out, God's so good that it

loves me so, all a-round me,
ev - 'ry-where, all a-round me,
makes me shout, all a-round me,

oh yes, all a-
oh yes, all a-
oh yes, all a-

round me.
round me.
round me.

So high, so low, so
So here, so there, so
So in, so out, so

wide,   and He loves   me   so.
great, and He's ev - 'ry - where.
good   that it makes me   shout.

Text: Cecilia Olusola Tribble
Tune: Cecilia Olusola Tribble
© 2006, Cecilia Olusola Tribble

157 In the Presence of Jehovah

You show me the path of life. In your presence there is fullness of joy;
in your right hand are pleasures forevermore.
Psalm 16:11

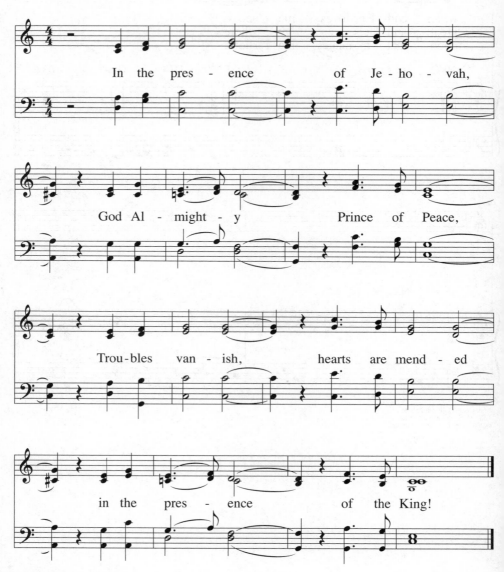

In the pres - ence of Je - ho - vah,
God Al - might - y Prince of Peace,
Trou - bles van - ish, hearts are mend - ed
in the pres - ence of the King!

Text: African American traditional
Tune: African American traditional; arr. by Walter Owens, Jr., © 2000, GIA Publications, Inc.

Yes, God Is Real

158

Then he prays to God, and is accepted by him, he comes into his presence with joy...
Job 33:26

1. There are some things I may not
2. Some folks may doubt, some folks may
3. I can - not tell just how you

know, There are some plac - es I can - not
scorn, All can de - sert and leave me a -
felt When Je - sus took your sins a -

go, But I am sure of this one
lone, But as for me I'll take God's
way, But since that day, yes, since that

thing,   That God is   real for I can feel Him deep with-in.
part,   For God is   real and I can feel Him in my   heart.
hour,   God has been real for I can feel His ho-ly   pow'r.

Solo:

Yes, God is   real,   He's real in my soul;   Yes, God is

Yes, God is yes,   God is real,   real in   my soul;

real   for He has washed   and made me whole;   His love for

real   for He has washed   and made me   whole;

me   is like pure gold.   Yes, God is

His   love for me   is   like pure gold. Yes, God is

Last time

real   for I can feel Him in my soul.

Last time

real   for I can feel Him in my, Him in my soul.

Last time

Text: Kenneth Morris, 1917–1988
Tune: GOD IS REAL, 8 9 8 12 with refrain; Kenneth Morris, 1917–1988; arr. by Evelyn Simpson-Curenton, b.1953
© 1944, (renewed), arr. © 2011, Martin and Morris Inc., admin. by Unichappell Music, Inc.

159 The Glory of the Lord

...the spirit lifted me up, and brought me into the inner court; and the glory of the LORD filled the temple.
Ezekiel 43:5

When the glo-ry of the Lord fills this

ho - ly tem - ple, He will lift us high. And on

an - gels' wings we'll rise to the pure and ho - ly,

when His Spir - it fills this place.

*When His glo - ry, when His glo - ry, when His

glo - ry fills this place. When His glo - ry, when His

glo - ry, when His glo - ry fills this place.

*Alternate text: Let Thy glory… Let Thy glory fill this place…

Text: Gloria Gaither, William Gaither, and Richard Smallwood, b.1948
Tune: Gloria Gaither, William Gaither, and Richard Smallwood, b.1948; arr. by Nolan Williams, Jr., b.1969
© 1988, Hanna Street Music (all rights controlled by Gaither Copyright Mgmt.) and Century Oak/Richwood Music

160

God Is Here

*Take my yoke upon you and learn from me, for I am gentle and humble in heart,
and you will find rest for your souls.*
Matthew 11:29–30

There is a sweet a-noint-ing in this
sanc-tu-ar-y. There is a still-ness in the at-mos-phere.

heal the hope-less heart and bless the bro - ken. Come and lay

down the bur-dens you have car - ried for in this sanc - tu -

ar - y God is here. He is here.

Text: Israel Houghton, Martha Munizzi, and Meleasa Houghton
Tune: Israel Houghton, Martha Munizzi, and Meleasa Houghton; arr. by Jared Haschek
© 2003, arr. © 2010, Integrity's Praise! Music and Say The Name Publishing

161 Siyahamba

Walk while you have the light, so that the darkness may not overtake you.
John 12:35

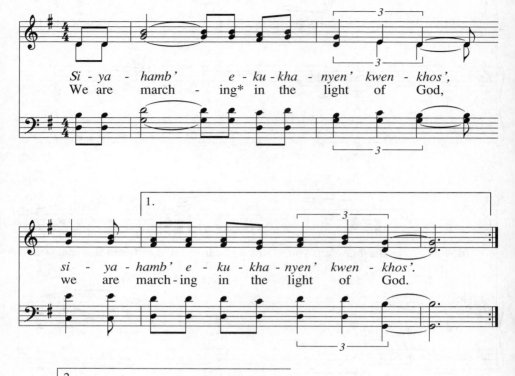

Si - ya - hamb' e - ku - kha - nyen' kwen - khos',
We are march - ing* in the light of God,

1.
si - ya - hamb' e - ku - kha - nyen' kwen - khos'.
we are march - ing in the light of God.

2.
kwen - khos'.
of God.

Si - ya -
We are

hamb' e - ku - kha - nyen' kwen, kha - nyen' kwen - khos'.
march - ing in the light of, the light of God.

Si - ya -
We are

kwen - khos'.
of God.

Alternate text: dancing, singing, praying...

African phonetics:
See-yah-hahmb eh-koo-kah-nyen kwen-kose
See-yah-hahm-bah

Text: South African folksong
Tune: South African folksong
© 1984, Utryck, admin. by Walton Music Corporation

162 Oh, the Glory of Your Presence

...the priests could not stand to minister because of the cloud;
for the glory of the LORD filled the house of God.
2 Chronicles 5:14

Oh, the glo - ry of Your pres - ence;

we, Your tem - ple give You rev - 'rence.

Come and rise to Your rest, and be blest by our

praise as we glo - ry in Your em - brace,

as Your pres - ence now fills this place.

Text: Steve Fry, b.1954
Tune: Steve Fry, b.1954
© 1983, BMG Songs/Birdwing Music, admin. at EMICMGPublishing.com

Over My Head

163

I heard a voice from heaven like the sound of many waters and like the sound of loud thunder...
Revelation 14:2

1. O - ver my head I see trou - ble in the
2. O - ver my head I hear mu - sic in the
3. O - ver my head I hear sing - ing in the
4. O - ver my head I see glo - ry in the

air. O-ver my head I see trou-ble in the
air. O-ver my head I hear mu-sic in the
air. O-ver my head I hear sing-ing in the
air. O-ver my head I see glo-ry in the

air. O-ver my head I see trou-ble in the
air. O-ver my head I hear mu-sic in the
air. O-ver my head I hear sing-ing in the
air. O-ver my head I see glo-ry in the

air;
air;
air;
air;

There must be a God some - where!

Text: Traditional
Tune: OVER MY HEAD, 11 11 11 7; traditional; arr. by Nolan Williams, Jr., b.1969, © 2000, GIA Publications, Inc.

164 O God, Our Help in Ages Past

Lord, you have been our dwelling place in all generations...from everlasting to everlasting you are God.
Psalm 90:1–2

1. O God, our help in a - ges past, Our
2. Un - der the shad - ow of Thy throne Still
3. Be - fore the hills in or - der stood Or
4. Time, like an ev - er - roll - ing stream, Bears
5. O God, our help in a - ges past, Our

hope for years to come, Our shel - ter from the
may we dwell se - cure; Suf - fi - cient is Thine
earth re - ceived her frame, From ev - er - last - ing
all its sons a - way; They fly, for - got - ten,
hope for years to come, Be Thou our guide while

storm - y blast, And our e - ter - nal home!
arm a - lone, And our de - fense is sure.
Thou art God, To end - less years the same.
as a dream Dies at the o - p'ning day.
life shall last, And our e - ter - nal home.

Text: Isaac Watts, 1674–1748
Tune: ST. ANNE, CM; William Croft, 1678–1721

Lord, Be Glorified

165

Who is this King of glory? The LORD of hosts, he is the King of glory.
Psalm 24:10

Verses 1, 2

1. In my life, Lord, be glo-ri-fied,
2. In my home, Lord, be glo-ri-fied,

be glo-ri-fied; In my life, Lord, be glo-ri-fied to-day.
be glo-ri-fied; In my home, Lord, be glo-ri-fied to-

day.

Verses 3, 4

3. In Your Church, Lord, be glo-ri-fied,
4. In my heart, Lord, be glo-ri-fied,

be glo-ri-fied; In Your Church, Lord, be glo-ri-fied to-day.
be glo-ri-fied; In my heart, Lord, be glo-ri-fied to-day.

Text: Bob Kilpatrick, b.1952
Tune: Bob Kilpatrick, b.1952
© 1978, Bob Kilpatrick Music. Assigned 1998 to The Lorenz Corporation.

166 I Just Want to Praise You

Thanks be to God for his indescribable gift!
2 Corinthians 9:15

I just want to praise You for-ev-er, and ev - er, and ev - er, for all You've done for me.

Bless-ings and glo - ry   and hon - or,   they all
be-long   to You.   Thank You, Je - sus   for
bless -   ing me.

Final ending

Text: Arthur Tannous
Tune: Arthur Tannous
© 1996, Thankyou Music, admin. at EMICMGPublishing.com

167 We Have Come into This House

Worship the LORD with gladness; come into his presence with singing.
Psalm 100:2

1. We have come in-to this house to gath-er in His name and wor-ship Him. We have come in-to this house to gath-er in His name and wor-ship Him. We have come in-to this house to

2. So, for - get a - bout your - self, con - cen-trate on Him and wor - ship Him. So, for - get a - bout your - self, con - cen-trate on Him and wor - ship Him. So, for - get a - bout your - self,

3. Let us lift up ho - ly hands, mag - ni - fy His name and wor - ship Him. Let us lift up ho - ly hands, mag - ni - fy His name and wor - ship Him. Let us lift up ho - ly hands,

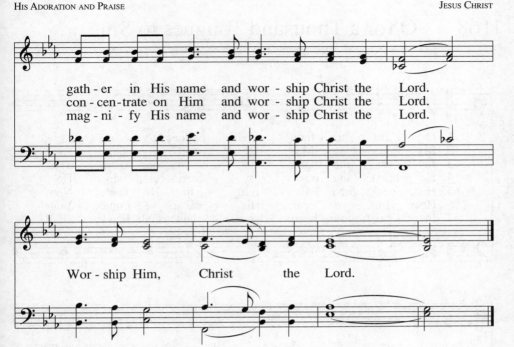

gath - er   in His name   and wor - ship Christ the   Lord.
con - cen-trate on Him   and wor - ship Christ the   Lord.
mag - ni - fy His name   and wor - ship Christ the   Lord.

Wor - ship Him,   Christ   the   Lord.

Text: Bruce Ballinger, b.1945, alt., © 1976, Sound III, Inc.
Tune: WORSHIP HIM, 16 16 18 6; Bruce Ballinger, b.1945, © 1976, Sound III, Inc.; arr. by Stephen Key, © 2000, GIA Publications, Inc.

168 O for a Thousand Tongues to Sing

Then my tongue shall tell of your righteousness and of your praise all day long.
Psalm 35:28

1. O for a thou - sand tongues to sing My great Re - deem - er's praise, The glo - ries of my God and King, The tri - umphs of His grace!
2. My gra - cious Mas - ter and my God, As - sist me to pro - claim, To spread through all the earth a - broad The hon - ors of Thy name.
3. Je - sus! the name that charms our fears, That bids our sor - rows cease, 'Tis mu - sic in the sin - ner's ears, 'Tis life, and health, and peace.
4. He breaks the pow'r of can - celed sin, He sets the pris - 'ner free; His blood can make the foul - est clean; His blood a - vailed for me.
5. He speaks, and lis - t'ning to His voice, New life the dead re - ceive; The mourn - ful, bro - ken hearts re - joice; The hum - ble poor, be - lieve.
*6. Hear Him, ye deaf; His praise, ye dumb, Your loos - ened tongues em - ploy; Ye blind, be - hold your Sav - ior come, And leap, ye lame, for joy.
7. In Christ, your head, you then shall know, Shall feel your sins for - giv'n; An - tic - i - pate your heav'n be - low, And own that love is heav'n.

*May be omitted.

Text: Charles Wesley, 1707–1788
Tune: AZMON, CM; Carl G. Glaser, 1784–1829; arr. by Lowell Mason, 1792–1872

Alpha and Omega

I am Alpha and Omega, the beginning and the end, the first and the last.
Revelation 22:13

You are Al-pha and O-me - ga!

We wor-ship You, our Lord; You are wor-thy to be praised!

We give You all the glo - ry; We

wor-ship You, our Lord; You are wor-thy to be praised!

Text: Erasmus Mutanbira
Tune: Erasmus Mutanbira
© 2005, arr. © 2010, Integrity's Praise! Music and Sound of the New Breed (admin. by Integrity's Praise! Music)

170

Time in Praise

I will praise God's name in song and glorify him with thanksgiving.
Psalm 69:30

Verse

All day long   I've been with Je - sus. All day

long   my lips have ut - tered praise.   All day

long   my heart, my soul's been lift - ed in wor-ship. All day

long   I have been with Him.   All day

Refrain

No   way could I   ev - er   hon-or You e-nough   for

all   You have done   for me.   So I will of - fer

up   thanks-giv-ing from my heart and   praise con-tin - u - al - ly.

No

All day

D.S.

Text: Carlton L. Fellows, b.1954
Tune: Carlton L. Fellows, b.1954
© 1992, Total Praise Music Publishing

171   Praise Him! Praise Him!

Praise the LORD! Praise, O servants of the LORD; praise the name of the LORD.
Psalm 113:1

1. Praise Him! praise Him! Je-sus, our bless-ed Re-deem-er!
2. Praise Him! praise Him! Je-sus, our bless-ed Re-deem-er!
3. Praise Him! praise Him! Je-sus, our bless-ed Re-deem-er!

Sing, O earth— His won-der-ful love pro-claim!
For our sins He suf-fered and bled and died;
Heav'n-ly por-tals loud with ho-san-nas ring!

Hail Him! hail Him! high-est arch-an-gels in glo-ry,
He our Rock, our hope of e-ter-nal sal-va-tion,
Je-sus, Sav-ior, reign-eth for ev-er and ev-er,

Strength and hon-or give to His ho-ly name!
Hail Him! hail Him! Je-sus the Cru-ci-fied.
Crown Him! crown Him! Proph-et and Priest and King!

Like a shep - herd Je - sus will guard His chil - dren—
Sound His prais - es— Je - sus who bore our sor - rows—
Christ is com - ing, o - ver the world vic - to - rious—

In His arms He car - ries them all day long:
Love un - bound - ed, won - der - ful, deep and strong:
Pow'r and glo - ry un - to the Lord be - long:

Praise Him! praise Him! tell of His ex - cel - lent great - ness!

Praise Him! praise Him! ev - er in joy - ful song!

Text: Fanny J. Crosby, 1820–1915
Tune: JOYFUL SONG, 12 10 12 10 11 10 with refrain; Chester G. Allen, 1838–1878

172

Praise Him

Praise the LORD! Praise the LORD, O my soul!
Psalm 146:1

Refrain

Praise Him!   Praise Him!   Praise Him!   Praise Him!
Glo - ry!   Glo - ry!   In   all things   give Him glo - ry.

Je - sus,   bless-ed Sav - ior   He's wor-thy to   be   praised.

Verse 1

1. From the ris - ing of   the   sun   un - til the go - ing down of the

same,   He's wor-thy,   Je-sus is wor-thy,   He's wor-thy to   be   praised.

Verse 2

2. God   is   our   rock,   hope of sal - va   - tion;   A

D.C.

strong de - liv-er - er   in Him will I al-ways trust.

Text: Donnie Harper
Tune: Donnie Harper; arr. by Stephen Key
© 1986, Bud John Tunes, admin. at EMICMGPublishing.com

Jesus

...everyone was awestruck; and the name of the Lord Jesus was praised.
Acts 19:17

173

1. Je -   sus,   Je -   sus,
2. I   wor-ship You,   I   wor-ship You,
3. I   love You, Lord, I   love You, Lord,

Je - sus, Je - sus, Je -   sus.

Coda

Je -   sus,   Je -   sus.

Text: Glen Woodward
Tune: Glen Woodward; arr. by Valeria A. Foster, © 2000, GIA Publications, Inc.

174   We Are Standing on Holy Ground

"Come no closer! Remove the sandals from your feet, for the place on which you are standing is holy ground."
Exodus 3:5

We are stand - ing on Ho - ly Ground,

and I know that there are an - gels all a - round;

Let us praise Je - sus now. We are

stand - ing in His pres - ence on Ho - ly Ground.

Text: Geron Davis, b.1960
Tune: Geron Davis, b.1960, arr. by Nolan Williams, Jr., b.1969
© 1983, Songchannel Music Co./Meadowgreen Music Co., admin. EMICMGPublishing.com

Let's Just Praise the Lord

175

Let everything that breathes praise the LORD! Praise the LORD!
Psalm 150:6

Let's just praise the Lord! Praise the Lord! Let's just
lift our *hands t'ward heav-en and praise the
Lord; Let's just praise the Lord! praise the Lord,
Let's just lift our *hands t'ward heav-en and praise the Lord.

Substitute voice, heart, etc.

Text: Gloria Gaither and William J. Gaither
Tune: William J. Gaither
© 1972, Hanna Street Music (all rights controlled by Gaither Copyright Mgmt.)

176 Majesty, Worship His Majesty

The LORD is king, he is robed in majesty; the LORD is robed, he is girded with strength.
Psalm 93:1

Maj - es - ty, wor-ship His maj - es - ty; un - to

Je - sus be all glo - ry, hon - or, and praise.

Maj - es - ty, king-dom au - thor - i - ty, flow from His

throne un - to His own; His an - them raise. So ex -

Text: Jack Hayford
Tune: MAJESTY, Irregular; Jack Hayford; Eugene Thomas
© 1980, New Spring Publishing (ASCAP)

177 O Come, Let Us Adore Him

Let us rejoice and exult and give him the glory...
Revelation 19:7

1. O come, let us a - dore Him, O come, let us a - dore Him, O come, let us a - dore Him, Christ the Lord.

2. For He alone is worthy,
3. Let's praise His name together,
4. We'll give Him all the glory,

Text: St. 1, John F. Wade, c.1711–1786; tr. by Frederick Oakeley, 1802–1880, alt.
Tune: ADESTE FIDELES, 7 7 7 3; John F. Wade, c.1711–1786; arr. by Stephen Key, © 2000, GIA Publications, Inc.

When Morning Gilds the Skies

178

O LORD, in the morning you hear my voice; in the morning I plead my case to you, and watch.
Psalm 5:3

1. When morn-ing gilds the skies, My heart, a-wak-ing, cries, May Je-sus Christ be praised! A-like at work and prayer To Je-sus I re-pair: May Je-sus Christ be praised!
2. Does sad-ness fill my mind? A sol-ace here I find: May Je-sus Christ be praised! Or fades my earth-ly bliss? My com-fort still is this: May Je-sus Christ be praised!
3. In heav'n's e-ter-nal bliss The love-liest strain is this: May Je-sus Christ be praised! The pow'rs of dark-ness fear When this sweet chant they hear: May Je-sus Christ be praised!
4. Be this, while life is mine, My can-ti-cle di-vine: May Je-sus Christ be praised! Be this the e-ter-nal song, Through all the a-ges long: May Je-sus Christ be praised!

Text: German traditional; trans. by Edward Caswall, 1814–1878
Tune: LAUDES DOMINI, 66 6 66 6; Joseph Barnby, 1838–1896

179 Now Behold the Lamb

In a loud voice they sang: "Worthy is the Lamb, who was slain…"
Revelation 5:12

1. Now be-hold the Lamb, the pre-cious Lamb of God.
2. Ho-ly is the Lamb, the pre-cious Lamb of God.
3. Thank you for the Lamb, the pre-cious Lamb of God.

Bore all my sin, that I may live a-gain: the
Why You love me so, Lord, I shall nev-er know; the
Be-cause of Your grace I can fin-ish the race: the

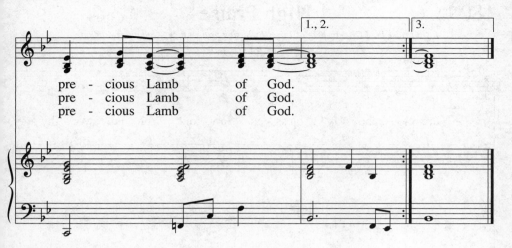

pre - cious Lamb of God.
pre - cious Lamb of God.
pre - cious Lamb of God.

Text: Kirk Franklin, b.1970
Tune: Kirk Franklin, b.1970
© 2007, Lilly Mack Publishing, admin. at EMICMGPublishing.com

180 High Praise

I will praise the LORD as long as I live; I will sing praises to my God all my life long.
Psalm 146:2

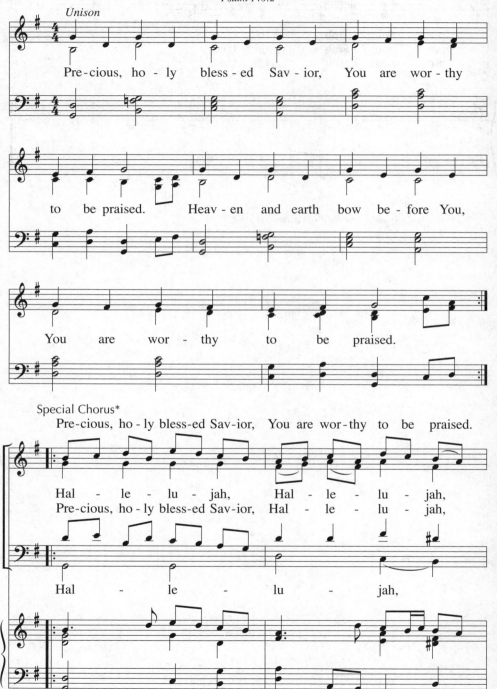

Unison

Pre-cious, ho - ly bless-ed Sav - ior, You are wor - thy

to be praised. Heav - en and earth bow be - fore You,

You are wor - thy to be praised.

Special Chorus*

Pre-cious, ho - ly bless-ed Sav-ior, You are wor-thy to be praised.

Hal - le - lu - jah, Hal - le - lu - jah,
Pre-cious, ho - ly bless-ed Sav-ior, Hal - le - lu - jah,

Hal - le - lu - jah,

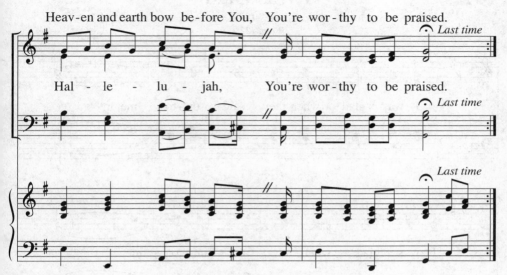

Heav-en and earth bow be-fore You, You're wor-thy to be praised.

Hal - le - lu - jah, You're wor-thy to be praised.

Begin with soprano line, then add each part one at a time.

Text: Margaret Pleasant Douroux, b.1941, © 1989, Rev. Earl Pleasant Publishing
Tune: Margaret Pleasant Douroux, b.1941, © 1989, Rev. Earl Pleasant Publishing; arr. by Nolan Williams, Jr., b.1969, © 2000, GIA Publications, Inc.

181

I Was Glad

I rejoiced with those who said to me, "Let us go to the house of the LORD."
Psalm 122:1

I was glad when they said un-to me,

I was glad when they said un-to me,

"Let us go in-to the house of the Lord."

You'll find peace, joy,

hap-pi-ness   and   rich   re - ward.

Won't you   come,   come,   come?

Text: Robert Wooten, Sr.
Tune: Robert Wooten, Sr.
© Maestro B Music

182 Come, Thou Fount of Every Blessing

Then the angel showed me the river of the water of life...flowing from the throne of God and of the Lamb.
Revelation 22:1

1. Come, thou Fount of ev-'ry bless-ing, Tune my heart to sing Thy grace; Streams of mer-cy, nev-er ceas-ing, Call for songs of loud-est praise: Teach me some me-lo-dious son-net, Sung by flam-ing tongues a-bove; Praise the

2. Here I raise mine *Eb-en-e-zer; Hith-er by Thy help I'm come; And I hope, by Thy good pleas-ure, Safe-ly to ar-rive at home: Je-sus sought me when a stran-ger, Wan-d'ring from the fold of God; He, to

3. O to grace how great a debt-or Dai-ly I'm con-strained to be! Let Thy grace, Lord, like a fet-ter, Bind my wan-d'ring heart to Thee: Prone to wan-der, Lord, I feel it, Prone to leave the God I love; Here's my

*I Samuel 7:12

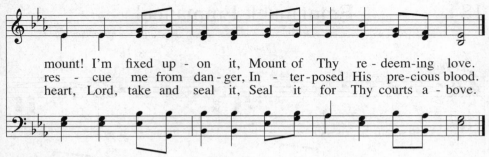

mount! I'm fixed up - on it, Mount of Thy re - deem-ing love.
res - cue me from dan - ger, In - ter-posed His pre-cious blood.
heart, Lord, take and seal it, Seal it for Thy courts a - bove.

Text: Robert Robinson, 1735–1790
Tune: NETTLETON, 8 7 8 7 D; Wyeth's *Repository of Sacred Music*, Pt. II, 1813

While We Are Waiting, Come

183

The one who testifies to these things says, "Surely I am coming soon." Amen. Come, Lord Jesus!
Revelation 22:20

1. While we are wait - ing, come; While we are
2. With pow'r and glo - ry, come; With pow'r and
3. Come, Sav - ior, quick - ly come; Come, Sav - ior,

wait - ing, come.
glo - ry, come. Je - sus, our Lord, Em -
quick - ly come.

man - u - el, While we are wait - ing, come.

Text: Claire Cloninger, b.1942
Tune: Don Cason, b.1954
© 1986, Word Music, LLC

184 Emmanuel, Emmanuel

Look, the young woman is with child and shall bear a Son, and shall name him Immanuel.
Isaiah 7:14

Text: Bob McGee, b.1949
Tune: McGEE, Irregular; Bob McGee, b.1949
© 1976, C. A. Music (div. of C. A. Records, Inc.)

Hail to the Lord's Anointed

The Spirit of the Lord is upon me, because he has anointed me to bring good news to the poor.
Luke 4:18

1. Hail to the Lord's A - noint - ed, Great Da - vid's great - er Son!
2. He comes with suc - cor speed - y To those who suf - fer wrong;
3. He shall come down like show - ers Up - on the fruit - ful earth,
4. To Him shall prayer un - ceas - ing And dai - ly vows as - cend;

Hail in the time ap - point - ed, His reign on earth be - gun!
To help the poor and need - y, And bid the weak be strong;
Love, joy, and hope, like flow - ers, Spring in His path to birth:
His king - dom still in - creas - ing, A king - dom with - out end:

He comes to break op - pres - sion, To set the cap - tive free;
To give them songs for sigh - ing, Their dark - ness turn to light,
Be - fore Him, on the moun - tains, Shall peace, the her - ald, go,
The tide of time shall nev - er His cov - e - nant re - move,

To take a - way trans - gres - sion, And rule in eq - ui - ty.
Whose souls, con - demned and dy - ing, Are pre - cious in His sight.
And right - eous - ness, in foun - tains, From hill to val - ley flow.
His name shall stand for - ev - er; That Name to us is Love.

Text: James Montgomery, 1771–1854
Tune: SHEFFIELD, 7 6 7 6 D; English melody

186 Behold Your God

While I am in the world, I am the light of the world.
John 9:5

Oh, thou that tell - est good tid-ings to Zi - on, oh,

thou that tell - est good tid-ings to Je - ru - sa-lem;

Lift up your voice with strength. Lift it up, don't be a - fraid. Be -

hold your God. A - rise and shine, for the

light of the world is come. Be - hold your God!

Text: Isaiah 40:9
Tune: Kenneth W. Louis, b.1956, © 1985, Kenneth W. Louis

Prepare Ye the Way of the Lord

A voice of one calling: "In the desert prepare the way for the LORD."
Isaiah 40:3

Verse

Text: Kenneth W. Louis, b.1956
Tune: Kenneth W. Louis, b.1956
© 2007, World Library Publications

188 Jesus Came

Christ Jesus came into the world to save sinners—of whom I am the worst.
1 Timothy 1:15

1. Je - sus came, a ten - der shoot;
2. Je - sus came, good news to tell;
3. Je - sus came, a cross to bear;
4. Je - sus came, the lame to heal;

As a stem from Jes - se's root.
God with us, Em - man - u - el.
King - ly robe and thorns to wear.
Lost and dis - card - ed souls to seal.

Je - sus came, a ten - der reed In
Je - sus came, that we might see The
Je - sus came, a path to blaze; The
Je - sus came to set us free; To

cov - e - nant with A - bram's seed.
heart of God trans - par - ent - ly.
way for sin - ners to be saved.
bring new life a - bun - dant - ly.

Text: Nathan Burbank and Sheri Smith
Tune: Nathan Burbank and Sheri Smith
© 1996, See & Say Songs and From Dust Music. Administered by See & Say Songs

189   O Come, O Come, Emmanuel

"...the virgin shall conceive and bear a son, and they shall name him Emmanuel," which means "God is with us."
Matthew 1:23

1. O come, O come, Em - man - u - el, And ran - som cap - tive Is - ra - el, That mourns in lone - ly ex - ile here, Un - til the Son of God ap - pear.

2. O come, thou Wis - dom from on high, And or - der all things, far and nigh; To us the path of knowl - edge show, And cause us in her ways to go.

3. O come, De - sire of na - tions, bind All peo - ples in one heart and mind; Bid en - vy, strife, and quar - rels cease; Fill the whole world with heav - en's peace.

4. O come, thou Day - spring, come and cheer Our spir - its by Thine ad - vent here; Dis - perse the gloom - y clouds of night, And death's dark shad - ows put to flight.

Harmony

Re - joice! Re - joice! Em - man - u - el

Shall come to thee, O Is - ra - el!

Text: Latin 9th C., tr. st. 1, 4, by John Mason Neale, 1818–1866; st. 2, 3, by Henry Sloane Coffin, 1877–1954
Tune: VENI EMMANUEL, LM with refrain; adapt. by Thomas Helmore, 1811–1890

190 Soon and Very Soon

...for he is Lord of lords and King of kings, and those with him are called and chosen, and faithful.
Revelation 17:14

1. Soon and ver - y soon   we are goin' to see the King,
2. No more cry - in' there   we are goin' to see the King,
3. No more dy - in' there   we are goin' to see the King,
4. Soon and ver - y soon   we are goin' to see the King,

Soon and ver - y soon   we are goin' to see the King,
No more cry - in' there   we are goin' to see the King,
No more dy - in' there   we are goin' to see the King,
Soon and ver - y soon   we are goin' to see the King,

Soon and ver - y soon   we are goin' to see the King,
No more cry - in' there   we are goin' to see the King,
No more dy - in' there   we are goin' to see the King,
Soon and ver - y soon   we are goin' to see the King,

Hal - le - lu - jah, Hal - le - lu - jah, we're

goin' to see the King! Hal - le - lu - jah,

Hal - le - lu - jah, Hal - le -

lu - jah, Hal - le - lu - jah.

Text: Andraé Crouch, b.1942
Tune: SOON AND VERY SOON, 12 12 12 14; Andraé Crouch, b.1942
© 1976, Crouch Music/Bud John Songs, admin. at EMICMGPublishing.com

191 Where Shall I Be?

The nations raged, but your wrath has come, and the time for judging the dead, for rewarding your servants...
Revelation 11:18

1. When judg-ment day is draw-ing nigh, Where shall I be?
2. When wick-ed men His wrath shall see, Where shall I be?
3. When heav'n and earth as some great scroll, Where shall I be?
4. All trou-ble done, all con-flict past, Where shall I be?

When God the works of men shall try, Where shall I be?
And to the rocks and moun-tains flee, Where shall I be?
Shall from God's an-gry pres-ence roll, Where shall I be?
And old A-pol-yon bound at last, Where shall I be?

When east and west the fire shall roll, Where shall I be?
When hills and moun-tains flee a-way, Where shall I be?
When all the saints re-deemed shall stand, Where shall I be?
When Christ shall reign from shore to shore, Where shall I be?

How will it be with my poor soul; Where shall I be?
When all the works of men de-cay, Where shall I be?
For-ev-er blest at God's right hand, Where shall I be?
And peace a-bide for-ev-er-more, Where shall I be?

O where shall I be when the first trum - pet sounds, O
where shall I be when it sounds so loud? When it sounds so loud as to
wake up the dead? O where shall I be when it sounds?

Text: Charles P. Jones, 1865–1949
Tune: JUDGEMENT DAY, 8 4 8 4 with refrain; Charles P. Jones, 1865–1949

192 Come, Ye Thankful People, Come

Enter his gates with thanksgiving, and his courts with praise. Give thanks to him, bless his name.
Psalm 100:4

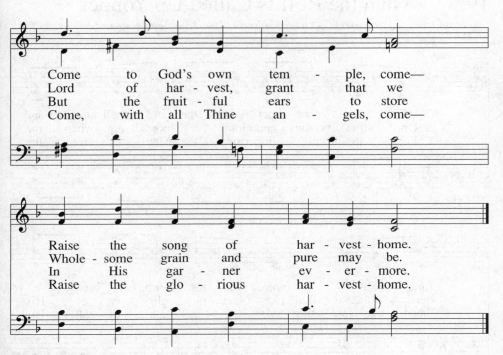

Come   to   God's   own   tem -   ple,   come—
Lord   of   har - vest, grant   that   we
But   the   fruit - ful   ears   to   store
Come,   with all   Thine   an - gels,   come—

Raise   the   song   of   har - vest - home.
Whole - some   grain and   pure   may   be.
In   His   gar - ner   ev - er - more.
Raise   the   glo - rious   har - vest - home.

Text: Henry Alford, 1810–1871
Tune: ST. GEORGE'S WINDSOR, 77 77 D; George J. Elvey, 1816–1893

193 When the Roll Is Called Up Yonder

The Lord himself... with the sound of God's trumpet, will descend from heaven, and the dead in Christ will rise first.
1 Thessalonians 4:16

1. When the trum - pet of the Lord shall sound and
2. On that bright and cloud - less morn - ing when the
3. Let us la - bor for the Mas - ter from the

1. time shall be no more, And the morn - ing breaks e -
2. dead in Christ shall rise And the glo - ry of His
3. dawn till set - ting sun, Let us talk of all His

1. ter - nal, bright and fair— When the saved of earth shall
2. res - ur - rec - tion share— When His cho - sen ones shall
3. won - drous love and care; Then when all of life is

1. gath - er o - ver on the oth - er shore, And the
2. gath - er to their home be - yond the skies, And the
3. o - ver and our work on earth is done, And the

Text: James M. Black, 1856–1938
Tune: ROLL CALL, 15 11 15 11 with refrain; James M. Black, 1856–1938

194 Sign Me Up

And I heard a voice from heaven saying, "Write this: Blessed are the dead who from now on die in the Lord."
Revelation 14:13

Sign me up for the Chris-tian ju-bi-lee,

Write my name on the roll.

I've been changed since the Lord has lift-ed me.

I want to be read-y when Je - sus comes.

When Je - sus comes, oh, the trum-pet will sound

loud, When my Sav - ior comes, all the

saints in Christ shall rise, Oh, I've been

changed since the Lord has lift - ed me, I

Last time

want to be read-y when Je - sus comes.

Last time

Text: Kevin Yancy and Jerome Metcalfe
Tune: Kevin Yancy and Jerome Metcalfe; arr. by James Abbington, b.1960
© 1979, 2000, GIA Publications, Inc.

195   My Lord! What a Morning

Immediately after the suffering of those days the sun will be darkened... and the stars will fall from heaven.
Matthew 24:29

Refrain

My Lord! what a morn-ing, My Lord! what a

morn-ing, Oh, my Lord! what a morn-ing, When the

stars be-gin to fall. When the stars be-gin to fall.

Verses

1. You will hear the trum-pet sound
2. You will hear the sin-ner cry   To wake the
3. You will hear the Chris-tian shout

na-tions un-der-ground, Look-ing to my God's right

D.C.

hand   When the   stars   be - gin   to   fall.

Text: Negro Spiritual
Tune: WHAT A MORNING, 7 8 7 7 with refrain; Negro Spiritual; arr. by Melva Costen, © 1990

196

Are You Ready?

Therefore keep watch, because you do not know the day or the hour.
Matthew 25:12

Read - y,   are you   read-y

for   the com-ing   of   the   Lord?

Be ye al - so read - y;

you know not the day.

Will you be read-y when Je - sus comes?

Text: Larry E. Roberts, Sr.
Tune: Larry E. Roberts, Sr.; arr. by Kenneth W. Louis, b.1956
© 1981, Savgos Music

Jesus Christ Is the Way

Jesus answered, "I am the way and the truth and the life."
John 14:6

Verses

1. When I think a-bout the hour
2. No one knows the day nor the hour,

then I know what I must do,
may be morn, night or noon,

when I think a-bout what God
but just rest as-sured time will be no more,

and say "Je - sus Christ is the

A⁷SUS4   A⁷   Cm⁶   G/D   Gmaj⁷/D   C/D

1.   D.C. ‖ 2.

Way."   Way."

1.
G   C/G   D.C. ‖ 2.
                                            G

Text: Walter Hawkins
Tune: Walter Hawkins
© 1977, Bud John Music, admin. at EMICMGPublishing.com

198

He's Here

You will find a baby wrapped in cloths and lying in a manger.
Luke 2:12

He's here! Je - sus Christ is here! Oh,

Last time to Coda ⊕ 1.

glo - ry, glo - ry, glo - ry to His name. He's

2.

Born of the Vir - gin Mar - y in the

town of Beth - le - hem, the Son of God the Fa - ther, the

D.S. ⊕ Coda

Sav - ior of the world! Oh yeah! He's

Text: Anonymous
Tune: Anonymous

Silent Night, Holy Night

For we observed his star at its rising, and have come to pay him homage.
Matthew 2:2

1. Si - lent night, ho - ly night, All is calm,
2. Si - lent night, ho - ly night, Shep-herds quake
3. Si - lent night, ho - ly night, Son of God,

all is bright Round yon Vir - gin Moth - er and Child,
at the sight; Glo - ries stream from heav - en a - far,
love's pure light Ra - diant beams from Thy ho - ly face,

Ho - ly In - fant so ten - der and mild, Sleep in heav - en - ly
Heav'n - ly hosts sing al - le - lu - ia; Christ, the Sav - ior, is
With the dawn of re - deem - ing grace, Je - sus, Lord, at Thy

peace, Sleep in heav - en - ly peace.
born! Christ, the Sav - ior, is born!
birth, Je - sus, Lord, at Thy birth.

Text: *Stille Nacht, heilige Nacht*; Joseph Mohr, 1792–1849; tr. by John F. Young, 1820–1885
Tune: STILLE NACHT, 66 89 66; Franz X. Gruber, 1787–1863

200

Star-Child

For God so loved the world that he gave his one and only Son…
John 3:16

Verses

1. Star - Child,   earth - Child,
2. Street child,   beat child,
3. Grown child,   old child,
4. Spared child,   spoiled child,
5. Hope - for -   peace Child,

1. go - be - tween of God,   love Child,
2. no place left to go,   hurt child,
3. mem - 'ry full of years,   sad child,
4. hav - ing, want - ing more,   wise child,
5. God's stu - pen - dous sign,   down - to -

Christ Child,   heav - en's light - ning rod:
used child   no   one wants to know:
lost child,   sto - ry told in tears:
faith child   know - ing joy in store:
earth Child,   Star   of stars that shine:

Em⁷   A   Em/G   Bm/F♯   F♯⁷

Refrain

This year,   this year   let   the day ar -

Bm   Dmaj⁷/A   G

rive   when Christ - mas comes for ev - 'ry - one,

D/F♯   D⁷   G⁹   Em⁷   F♯m⁷   Bm

Text: Shirley Erena Murray, b.1931, © 1994, Hope Publishing Company
Tune: NOAH'S SONG, 4 5 4 5 with refrain; Ronald F. Krisman, b.1946, © 2003, GIA Publications, Inc.

201   O Come, All Ye Faithful

"Let us go now to Bethlehem and see this thing that has taken place, which the Lord has made known to us."
Luke 2:15, 20

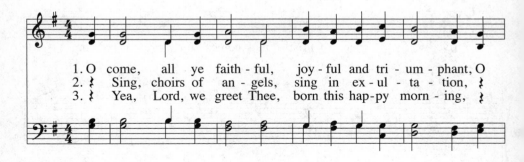

come ye, O come ye to Beth - le - hem;
Sing, all ye cit - i - zens of heav'n a - bove!
Je - sus, to Thee be all glo - ry giv'n;

Come and be - hold Him, born the King of an - gels;
Glo - ry to God, all glo - ry in the high - est;
Word of the Fa - ther, now in flesh ap - pear - ing;

O come, let us a - dore Him, O come, let us a - dore Him,

O come, let us a - dore Him, Christ, the Lord!

Text: *Adeste fideles*; John F. Wade, c.1711–1786; tr. by Frederick Oakeley, 1802–1880, alt.
Tune: ADESTE FIDELES, Irregular with refrain; John F. Wade, c.1711–1786

202

O Holy Night

And she gave birth to her firstborn son and wrapped him in bands of cloth, and laid him in a manger...
Luke 2:7

1. O ho - ly
2. Led by the
3. Tru - ly He

night! the stars are bright - ly shin - ing; It is the
light of faith se - rene - ly beam - ing, With glow - ing
taught us to love one an - oth - er; His law is

night of the dear Sav - ior's birth.
hearts by His cra - dle we stand.
love and His gos - pel is peace.

Long lay the world in sin and er - ror
So led by light of a star sweet - ly
Chains shall He break, for the slave is our

pin - - ing, Till He ap-peared and the soul felt its
gleam - - ing, Here came the Wise Men from O - ri - ent
broth - er, And in His name all op-pres - sion shall

worth.　　　　　　　A thrill of hope— the
land.　　　　　　　The King of kings lay
cease.　　　　　　　Sweet hymns of joy in

wea - ry world re-joic - es, For yon - der breaks a
thus in low - ly man - ger, In all our tri - als
grate - ful cho - rus raise we; Let all with - in us

new and glo - rious morn! Fall on your knees! O
born to be our Friend. He knows our need— to our
praise His ho - ly name. Christ is the Lord! O

hear the an - gel voic - es! O night di -
weak - ness is no stran - ger. Be - hold your
praise His name for - ev - er! His pow'r and

Text: John S. Dwight, 1813–1893
Tune: CANTIQUE DE NOEL, Irregular; Adolphe Adam, 1803–1856

Away in a Manger

While they were there, the time came for her to deliver her child.
Luke 2:6

Unison

1. A - way in a man - ger, no crib for a bed,
2. The cat - tle are low - ing, the ba - by a - wakes,
3. Be near me, Lord Je - sus! I ask You to stay

The lit - tle Lord Je - sus laid down His sweet head.
But lit - tle Lord Je - sus, no cry - ing He makes.
Close by me for ev - er, and love me, I pray.

The stars in the bright sky looked down where He lay,
I love you, Lord Je - sus! look down from the sky,
Bless all the dear chil - dren in Your ten - der care,

The lit - tle Lord Je - sus, a - sleep on the hay.
And stay by my cra - dle till morn - ing is nigh.
And fit us for heav - en, to live with You there.

Text: St. 1, 2, anonymous; st. 3, John T. McFarland, 1851–1913
Tune: CRADLE SONG, 11 11 11 11; William J. Kirkpatrick, 1838–1921

204 Away in a Manger

While they were there, the time came for her to deliver her child.
Luke 2:6

1. A - way in a man - ger, no crib for a bed, The
2. The cat - tle are low - ing, the Ba - by a - wakes, But

lit - tle Lord Je - sus laid down His sweet head; The
lit - tle Lord Je - sus, no cry - ing He makes; I

stars in the sky looked down where He lay,
love Thee, Lord Je - sus! look down from the sky,

The lit - tle Lord Je - sus, a - sleep on the hay.
And stay by my cra - dle till morn - ing is nigh.

3. Be near me, Lord Je - sus, I ask Thee to stay Close

by me for - ev - er, and love me, I pray; Bless

all the dear chil - dren in Thy ten - der care, And

take us to heav - en, to live with Thee there.

Text: St. 1, 2, anonymous, st. 3, John T. McFarland, 1851–1913
Tune: MUELLER, 11 11 11 11; James R. Murray, 1841–1905; arr. by Nolan Williams, Jr., b.1969, © 2000, GIA Publications, Inc.

205 Heaven's Christmas Tree

...they are now justified by his grace as a gift, through the redemption that is in Christ Jesus...
Romans 3:24–25

1. I have heard of a tree, a great Christ-mas tree, It was
2. There is one I be-hold in let-ters of gold, It
3. There is one just a-bove, its ti-tle is love, It is
4. An-oth-er I see, it must be for me, The
5. There are man-y, I'm sure, but just this one more I

stall.
me.
stain.
read.
rest.

fixed in yon Beth-le-hem's, Beth-le-hem's stall. The
hangs on a limb near to, limb near to me. 'Tis
marked by a deep crim-son, deep crim-son stain. For
words "I will help you" I, help you I read. While
speak of a-bove all the, bove all the rest. It

bless-ings of heav-en for you and for me, A
la-beled "sal-va-tion," and Je-sus, I'm told, Has
there it was tied by the Lord when He died, And
hold-ing His hand, by faith I can stand, And
spells "hap-py home" with God near the throne, A

Christ - mas pres - ent for all.
bought that pack - age for me.
glo - ry to His dear name.
this is the pack - age I need.
place where the wea - ry shall rest.

There is a pack-age for me on that tree; A pre - cious

to - ken that some-one loves me. Oh yes, I can see on

Cal - va - ry's Tree, That there is a pack-age for me.

Text: Charles A. Tindley, 1851–1933
Tune: HEAVEN'S CHRISTMAS TREE, 11 9 11 7 with refrain, Charles A. Tindley, 1851–1933; arr. by Charles A. Tindley, Jr.

206 Hark! The Herald Angels Sing

"Glory to God in the highest heaven, and on earth peace among those whom he favors!"
Luke 2:13–14

1. Hark! the her - ald an - gels sing, "Glo - ry to the
2. Christ, by high - est heav'n a - dored, Christ the ev - er -
3. Hail the heav'n - born Prince of Peace! Hail the Sun of

new - born King; Peace on earth, and mer - cy mild
last - ing Lord: Late in time be - hold Him come,
Right - eous - ness! Light and life to all He brings,

God and sin - ners rec - on - ciled!" Joy - ful, all you
Off - spring of the Vir - gin's womb. Veiled in flesh the
Ris'n with heal - ing in His wings. Mild He lays His

na - tions, rise, Join the tri - umph of the skies;
God - head see: Hail the in - car - nate De - i - ty,
glo - ry by, Born that we no more may die,

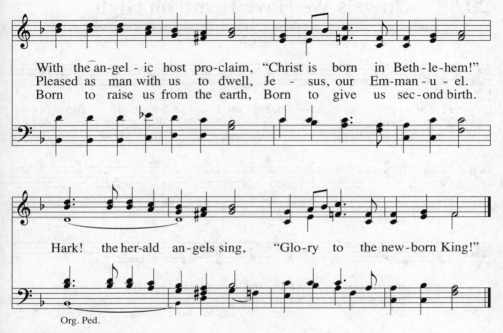

With the an-gel - ic host pro-claim, "Christ is   born   in Beth - le-hem!"
Pleased as man with us   to dwell, Je - sus, our   Em-man - u - el.
Born   to   raise us from the earth, Born   to   give   us sec-ond birth.

Hark!   the her-ald an-gels sing,   "Glo-ry   to   the new-born King!"

Org. Ped.

Text: Charles Wesley, 1707–1788, alt.
Tune: MENDELSSOHN, 77 77 D with refrain; Felix Mendelssohn, 1809–1847

207 Angels We Have Heard on High

And suddenly there was with the angel a multitude of the heavenly host, praising God...
Luke 2:14

1. An - gels we have heard on high Sweet - ly sing - ing
2. Shep - herds, why this ju - bi - lee? Why your joy - ous
3. Come to Beth - le - hem and see Him whose birth the

o'er the plains, And the moun - tains in re - ply
strains pro - long? What the glad - some tid - ings be,
an - gels sing; Come a - dore, on bend - ed knee,

Ech - o - ing their joy - ous strains. Glo -
Which in - spire your heav'n - ly song.
Christ, the Lord, the new - born King.

ri - a

in ex - cel - sis De - o, Glo -

- - - ri - a

in ex - cel - sis De - o.

Text: *Les anges dans nos campagnes*, French c.18th C.; tr. from *Crown of Jesus Music*, London, 1862
Tune: GLORIA, 7 7 7 7 with refrain; French traditional

208 Joy to the World

He will reign over the house of Jacob forever, and of his kingdom there will be no end.
Luke 1:33

1. Joy to the world! the Lord is come: Let earth re-
2. Joy to the world! the Sav-ior reigns: Let us, our
3. No more let sins and sor-rows grow, Nor thorns in-
4. He rules the world with truth and grace, And makes the

ceive her King; Let ev - 'ry heart pre -
songs em - ploy; While fields and floods, rocks,
fest the ground; He comes to make His
na - tions prove The glo - ries of His

pare Him room, And heav'n and na - ture
hills, and plains; Re - peat the sound - ing
bless - ings flow Far as the curse is
right - eous - ness, And won - ders of His

And
Re -
Far
And

sing,   And heav'n and na - ture sing,   And
joy,   Re - peat the sound-ing joy,   Re -
found,   Far as the curse is found,   Far
love,   And won - ders of His love,   And

heav'n and na - ture sing,   And heav'n and na - ture
peat the sound-ing joy,   Re - peat the sound-ing
as the curse is found,   Far as the curse is
won - ders of His love,   And won - ders of His

heav'n,   and heav'n and na - ture sing.
peat,   re - peat the sound - ing joy.
as,   far as the curse is found.
won - ders, won - ders of His love,

sing,   And heav'n and na - ture sing.
joy,   Re - peat the sound - ing joy.
found,   Far as the curse is found.
love,   And won - ders of His love.

Text: Psalm 98; Isaac Watts, 1674–1748
Tune: ANTIOCH, CM; arr. from George F. Handel, 1685–1759, in T. Hawkes' *Collection of Tunes*, 1833

209 Angels, from the Realms of Glory

The angel said, "Do not be afraid... to you is born this day in the city of David a Savior,
who is the Messiah, the Lord."
Luke 2:10–11

1. An - gels, from the realms of glo - ry, Wing your flight o'er
2. Shep - herds, in the fields a - bid - ing, Watch - ing o'er your
3. Sag - es, leave your con - tem - pla-tions, Bright - er vi - sions
4. Saints be - fore the al - tar bend-ing, Watch - ing long in

all the earth; You who sang cre - a - tion's sto - ry,
flocks by night, God with man is now re - sid - ing,
beam a - far; Seek the great De - sire of na - tions,
hope and fear, Sud - den - ly the Lord, de - scend - ing,

Now pro - claim Mes - si - ah's birth:
Yon - der shines the in - fant Light:
You have seen His na - tal star: Come and wor-ship,
In His tem - ple shall ap - pear:

come and wor - ship, Wor-ship Christ, the new-born King.

Text: James Montgomery, 1771–1854
Tune: REGENT SQUARE, 8 7 8 7 8 7; Henry Smart, 1813–1879

Wonderful Counselor

For a child has been born for us... authority rests upon his shoulders; and he is named Wonderful Counselor.
Isaiah 9:6

1. Oh, who do you call the won-der-ful coun-sel-or?
2. Oh, I call Je-sus the won-der-ful coun-sel-or.

Oh, glo-ry hal-le-lu-jah! Oh,

glo-ry hal-le-lu-jah! Glo-ry hal-le-lu-jah to the new-born King!

3. Oh, He's my Savior, the wonderful counselor...
4. He's Mary's baby, the wonderful counselor...
5. He's the Prince of Peace, the wonderful counselor...
6. He's the Mighty God, the wonderful counselor...
7. He's the Light of the World, the wonderful counselor...

Text: Negro Spiritual
Tune: Negro Spiritual; arr. by Evelyn Simpson-Curenton, b.1953, © 2000, GIA Publications, Inc.

211 O Little Town of Bethlehem

O Bethlehem... from you shall come forth for me one who is to rule in Israel, whose origin is from of old...
Micah 5:2

Light;	The	hopes	and	fears	of	all	the	years	Are	met	in	thee	to - night.
birth!	And	prais - es		sing	to	God	the	King,	And	peace	to	all	on earth.
sin,	Where	meek	souls	will	re -	ceive	Him,	still	The	dear	Christ	en - ters	in.
tell;	O	come	to	us,	a -	bide	with	us,	Our	Lord	Em - man - u - el!

Text: Phillips Brooks, 1835–1893
Tune: ST. LOUIS, 8 6 8 6 7 6 8 6; Lewis H. Redner, 1831–1908

212   Rise Up, Shepherd, and Follow

"Let us go now to Bethlehem and see this thing that has taken place, which the Lord has made known to us."
Luke 2:15

1. There's a star in the East on Christ - mas morn,
2. If you take good heed to the an - gel's words,

Rise up, shep - herd, and fol - low, It will
Rise up, shep - herd, and fol - low, You'll for -

lead to the place where the Christ was born,
get your flocks, you'll for - get your herds,

Rise up, shep - herd, and fol - low.
Rise up, shep - herd, and fol - low.

Follow, fol - low, Rise up, shep - herd, and fol - low, Follow the Star of Beth - le - hem, Rise up, shep - herd, and fol - low.

Text: Negro Spiritual
Tune: Negro Spiritual; arr. by Joseph Joubert, b.1958, © 2000, GIA Publications, Inc.

213 It Came upon the Midnight Clear

"Glory to God in the highest, and on earth peace to men on whom his favor rests."
Luke 2:14

1. It came up-on the mid - night clear, That glo - rious song of old, From an - gels bend - ing near the earth To touch their harps of gold: "Peace

2. Still through the clo - ven skies they come, With peace - ful wings un - furled, And still their heav'n - ly mu - sic floats O'er all the wea - ry world: A -

3. Yet with the woes of sin and strife, The world has suf - fered long; Be - neath the heav'n - ly hymn have rolled Two thou - sand years of wrong; And

4. For, lo, the days are has - t'ning on, By proph - ets seen of old, When with the ev - er - cir - cling years Shall come the time fore - told, When

on the earth, good will to all From
bove its sad and low - ly plains They
war - ring hu - man - kind hears not The
peace shall o - ver all the earth Its

heav'n's all gra - cious King"; The
bend on hov - 'ring wing, And
tid - ings which they bring; O
an - cient splen - dors fling, And

world in sol - emn still - ness lay, To
ev - er o'er its Ba - bel sounds The
hush the noise and cease your strife And
all the world give back the song Which

hear the an - gels sing.
bless - ed an - gels sing.
hear the an - gels sing.
now the an - gels sing.

Text: Edmund H. Sears, 1810–1876, alt.
Tune: CAROL, CMD; Richard S. Willis, 1819–1900

214 Go Tell It on the Mountain

So they went with haste and found Mary and Joseph, and the child lying in the manger.
Luke 2:16

Text: Negro Spiritual; adapt. by John W. Work, Jr., 1871–1925
Tune: GO TELL IT ON THE MOUNTAIN, 7 6 7 6 with refrain; Negro Spiritual; arr. by Valeria A. Foster, © 2000, GIA Publications, Inc.

What Child Is This

This child is destined for the falling and the rising of many in Israel...
Luke 2:34

1. What Child is this, who, laid to rest, On
2. Why lies He in such low es - tate Where
3. So bring Him in - cense, gold and myrrh, Come

Mar - y's lap is sleep - ing? Whom an - gels greet with
ox and ass are feed - ing? Good Chris - tian, fear; for
peas - ant, king to own Him; The King of kings sal -

an - thems sweet, While shep - herds watch are keep - ing?
sin - ners here The si - lent Word is plead - ing.
va - tion brings, Let lov - ing hearts en - throne Him.

This, this is Christ the King, Whom shep - herds guard and an - gels sing;

Haste, haste to bring Him laud, The Babe, the Son of Mar - y.

Text: William C. Dix, 1827–1898
Tune: GREENSLEEVES, 8 7 8 7 with refrain; English melody, 16th C.; harm. by John Stainer, 1840–1901

216   Jesus, the Light of the World

I have come as light into the world, so that everyone who believes in me should not remain in the darkness.
John 12:46

1. Hark the her - ald an - gels sing.
2. Joy - ful, all ye na - tions, rise.
3. Christ, by high - est heav'n a - dored.
4. Hail, the heav'n - born Prince of Peace.

Je - sus, the light of the world.

Glo - ry to the new - born King,
Join the tri - umph of the skies.
Christ, the ev - er - last - ing Lord,
Hail, the Sun of right - eous - ness!

Je - sus, the light of the world.

We'll walk in the light, beau - ti - ful light.

Come where the dew-drops of mer - cy shine bright. Oh,

shine all a - round us by day and by night.

Je - sus, the light of the world.

Text: George D. Elderkin; verses by Charles Wesley, 1707–1788
Tune: WE'LL WALK IN THE LIGHT, 7 7 7 7 with refrain; George D. Elderkin; arr. by Evelyn Simpson-Curenton, b.1953, © 2000,
   GIA Publications, Inc.

217 We Three Kings of Orient Are

...they saw the child with Mary his mother; and they knelt down and paid him homage.
Matthew 2:11

1. We three kings of O - ri - ent are,
2. Born a babe on Beth - le - hem's plain,
3. Frank - in - cense to of - fer have I;
4. Myrrh is mine: its bit - ter per - fume
5. Glo - rious now be - hold Him rise,

Bear - ing gifts we tra - verse a - far
Gold we bring to crown Him a - gain;
In - cense owns a De - i - ty nigh,
Breathes a life of gath - 'ring gloom;
King and God and sac - ri - fice:

Field and foun - tain, Moor and
King for ev - er, Ceas - ing
Prayer and prais - ing Glad - ly
Sor - rowing, sigh - ing, Bleed - ing,
Heav'n sings, "Hal - le - lu - jah!"

moun - tain, Fol - low - ing yon - der star.
nev - er, O - ver us all to reign.
rais - ing, Wor - ship - ing God on high.
dy - ing, Sealed in the stone cold tomb.
"Hal - le - lu - jah!" earth re - plies.

O star of won - der, star of night, Star with

roy - al beau - ty bright, West - ward lead - ing,

still pro - ceed - ing, Guide us to Thy per - fect Light.

Text: Matthew 2:1–11; John H. Hopkins, Jr., 1820–1891
Tune: KINGS OF ORIENT, 88 44 6 with refrain; John H. Hopkins, Jr., 1820–1891

218 Behold the Star

When they saw that the star had stopped, they were overwhelmed with joy... they saw the child with Mary...
Matthew 2:10–11

Be-hold the star! Be-hold the star up yon-der!

Be-hold the star! It is the star of Beth-le-hem.

Beth-le-hem. (ooh)

1. There was no room found in the inn,
2. The wise men came from the East
3. A song broke forth up-on the night.

For Him who was born
To wor-ship Him, the
Peace on earth, good-

It is the star of Beth-le-hem. (ooh)

free from sin.
"Prince of Peace."
will to men.

Oh,

It is the star of Beth - le - hem.

Text: Negro Spiritual
Tune: BEHOLD THE STAR, LM with refrain; Negro Spiritual, arr. by Nolan Williams, Jr., b. 1969, © 2000, GIA Publications, Inc.

219 Brightest and Best

...there went the star that they had seen at its rising, until it stopped over the place where the child was.
Matthew 2:9

1. Bright - est and best of the sons of the morn - ing,
2. Say, shall we yield Him in cost - ly de - vo - tion,
3. Vain - ly we of - fer each am - ple ob - la - tion,
4. Cold on His cra - dle the dew - drops are shin - ing,

Dawn on our dark - ness and lend us Thine aid,
O - dors of E - dom and of - f'rings di - vine,
Vain - ly with gifts would His fa - vor se - cure;
Low lies His head with the beasts of the stall;

Star of the east, the ho - ri - zon a - dorn - ing,
Gems of the moun - tain and pearls of the o - cean,
Rich - er by far is the heart's ad - o - ra - tion,
An - gels a - dore Him in slum - ber re - clin - ing,

Guide where our in - fant Re - deem - er is laid.
Myrrh from the for - est, or gold from the mine?
Dear - er to God are the prayers of the poor.
Mak - er and Mon - arch and Sav - ior of all.

Text: Reginald Heber, 1783–1826
Tune: MORNING STAR, 11 10 11 10; James P. Harding, 1850–1911

Peace! Be Still!

220

He said to the sea, "Peace! Be still!" Then the wind ceased, and there was a dead calm.
Mark 4:39

Mas - ter, the tem - pest is rag - ing! The
bil - lows are toss - ing high! The
sky is o'er-shad - owed with black-ness, No
shel - ter or help is nigh: "Car - est Thou
not that we per - ish?" How canst Thou lie a -

storm - tossed sea, Or de - mons, or men, or what-

ev - er it be, No wa - ter can swal - low the

ship where lies the Mas - ter of o - cean and

earth and skies; They all shall sweet - ly o - bey Thy

will! Peace! Peace, be still!

Text: Mary A. Baker
Tune: Horatio R. Palmer, 1834–1907; arr. Nolan Williams, Jr., b.1969, from a version by Rev. James Cleveland, 1931–1991, © 2000,
    GIA Publications, Inc.

221 He Calmed the Ocean

...He made the storm be still, and the waves of the sea were hushed.
Psalm 107:29

o - cean,

He calmed the o - cean, my Lord. Oh! He

o - cean,

said He would, said He would calm the rag-ing sea,

said He would, said He would, He calmed the

o - cean,

o - cean, my Lord. Oh! He said He would,

o - cean,

said He would calm the rag-ing sea, said He would,

said He would. 1. Down by the sea of Gal - li - lee,
2. If you don't be - lieve I've been re - deemed

Said He would calm the rag-ing sea, Said He would,

said He would, Drop your nets and fol - low me
Fol-low me down to the Jor - dan's stream

Said He would calm the rag - ing sea,

Said He would, said He would.

Text: Prof. L. S. Boswell
Tune: Kenneth Morris, 1917–1988
© 1937, First Church of Deliverance

222 Jesus Is a Rock in a Weary Land

The stone that the builders rejected has become the very head of the corner.
1 Peter 2:7

Refrain

Je - sus is a Rock in a wea - ry land, a

wea - ry land, a wea - ry land.

Je - sus is a Rock in a wea - ry land, a

1. shel-ter in a time of storm.   2. shel-ter in a time of storm.   *Last time*

1. I
2. I

Verses

would not be a sin - ner. I'll tell you the rea - son
would not be a back - slid - er. I'll tell you the rea - son

why: I'm a - fraid my Lord might call my name, and I

D.S.

would-n't be read-y to die. Je - sus is Rock.

D.S.

Text: Traditional
Tune: WEARY LAND, 6 6 8 6 with refrain; traditional, arr. by Glenn E. Burleigh, 1949–2007, © 1993, GIA Publications, Inc.

223 The Glory of These Forty Days

She never left the temple but worshiped night and day, fasting and praying.
Luke 2:37

1. The glory of these forty days
2. A - lone and fast - ing Mo - ses saw
3. So Dan - iel trained his mys - tic sight,
4. Then grant that we like them be true,

We cel - e - brate with songs of praise;
The lov - ing God who gave the law;
De - liv - ered from the li - on's might;
Con - sumed in fast and prayer with You;

For Christ, by whom all things were made,
And to E - li - jah, fast - ing, came
And John, the Bride - groom's friend, be - came
Our spir - its strength - en with Your grace,

Him - self has fast - ed and has prayed.
The steeds and char - i - ots of flame.
The her - ald of Mes - si - ah's name.
And give us joy to see Your face.

Text: *Clarum decus jejunii*; Gregory the Great, c.540–604; tr. by Maurice F. Bell, 1862–1947
Tune: OLD HUNDREDTH, LM; Louis Bourgeois, c.1510–1561

All Hail, King Jesus

So they took branches of palm trees and went out to meet him, shouting,
"Hosanna! Blessed is the one who comes in the name of the Lord—the King of Israel!"
John 12:13

224

All hail, King Je - sus, All hail, Em - man - u - el:
King of kings, Lord of lords, Bright Morn - ing
Star. And through - out e - ter - ni -
ty I'm goin' to praise Him, And for -
ev - er - more I will reign with Him.

Text: Dave Moody, b.1948
Tune: Dave Moody, b.1948
© 1978, Dayspring Music, LLC (BMI)

225 All Glory, Laud, and Honor

To the King of the ages, immortal, invisible, the only God, be honor and glory forever and ever. Amen.
1 Timothy 1:17

All glo-ry, laud, and hon - or To

You, Re-deem-er, King! To whom the lips of

chil - dren Made sweet ho-san-nas ring.

1. You are the King of Is - ra - el, And
2. The com - pa - ny of an - gels Are
3. The peo - ple of the He - brews With
4. To You be - fore Your pas - sion They
5. Their prais - es You ac - cept - ed, Ac -

Da - vid's roy - al Son, Now in the Lord's Name
prais - ing You on high; And mor - tals, joined with
palms be - fore You went: Our praise and prayers and
sang their hymns of praise: To You, now high ex -
cept the prayers we bring, Great source of love and

D.C.

com - ing, Our King and Bless - ed One.
all things Cre - a - ted, make re - ply.
an - thems Be - fore You we pre - sent.
alt - ed, Our mel - o - dy we raise.
good - ness, Our Sav - ior and our King.

Text: *Gloria, laus et honor*; Theodulph of Orleans, c. 760–821; tr. by John M. Neale, 1818–1866, alt.
Tune: ST. THEODULPH, 7 6 7 6 D; Melchior Teschner, 1584–1635

226 Ride On, King Jesus

In your majesty ride on victoriously for the cause of truth and to defend the right.
Psalm 45:4

Ride on, King Je - sus, no man can a - hin - der me.

Ride on, King Je - sus, ride on. No man can a - hin - der me, no

1.
man can a - hin - der me.
2.
man can a - hin - der me, no

man can a - hin - der me, no man can a - hin - der me. In that

great get - tin' up morn - ing, fare ye well, fare ye well. In that

Repeat ad lib.

great get-tin' up morn-ing, fare ye well, fare ye well. In that

Last time

well, fare ye well. No man can a-hin-der me, no

man can a-hin-der me, no man can a-hin-der me, no

man can a-hin-der me. Ride on, King Je-sus.

Text: Traditional
Tune: Negro Spiritual; arr. by Stephen Key, from a version by Ernest Davis, © 2000, GIA Publications, Inc.

227

One Day

The sun shall be turned to darkness and the moon to blood, before the coming of the Lord's great and glorious day.
Acts 2:20

Chorus

Liv - ing He loved me, dy - ing He saved me,

bur - ied He car - ried my sins far a - way.

Ris - ing He jus - ti - fied, freed me for heav - en.

One day He's com-ing back, glo - ri-ous day.

Text: J. Wilbur Chapman, 1859–1918
Tune: Charles H. Marsh, 1886–1956; arr. by Evelyn Simpson-Curenton, b.1953, © 2000, GIA Publications, Inc.

I Love Him

228

Rejoice in the Lord always; again I will say, Rejoice.
Philippians 4:4

I love Him, I love Him, Be - cause He first loved me; And

pur - chased my sal - va - tion on Cal - v'ry's tree.

Text: African American folk song
Tune: African American folk song

229

I'm So Glad

If my father and mother forsake me, the LORD will take me up.
Psalm 27:10

1. I'm so glad Je-sus lift-ed me. I'm so glad
Je-sus lift-ed me. I'm so glad Je-sus lift-ed me,
I'm glad that
sing-in' Glo - ry, Hal - le-lu - jah, Je - sus lift-ed me!

2. Satan had me bound; Jesus lifted me…
3. When I was in trouble, Jesus lifted me…

Text: African American Traditional
Tune: African American Traditional; arr. by Evelyn Simpson-Curenton, b.1953, © 2000, GIA Publications, Inc.

Oh, How He Loves You and Me

God proves his love for us in that while we still were sinners Christ died for us.
Romans 5:8

230

1. Oh, how He loves you and me, O, how He loves you and me, He gave His life, what more could He give; O, how He loves me, O, how He loves me, O, how He loves you and me.

2. Je - sus to Cal - v'ry did go, His love for all He did show; What He did there brought hope from de - spair: O, how He loves me, O, how He loves me, O, how He loves you and me.

Text: Kurt Kaiser, b.1934
Tune: PATRICIA, 77 4 5 5 5 7; Kurt Kaiser, b.1934; arr. by Nolan Williams, Jr., b.1969, Evelyn Simpson-Curenton, b.1953, and Robert J. Fryson, 1944–1994
© 1975, Word Music, LLC

231 He Lifted Me

I will extol you, O LORD, for you have drawn me up, and did not let my foes rejoice over me.
Psalm 30:1

1. In loving-kind - ness Je - sus came My
2. He called me long be - fore I heard, Be -
3. His brow was pierced with man - y a thorn, His
4. Now on a high - er plane I dwell, And

soul in mer - cy to re - claim, And from the depths of
fore my sin - ful heart was stirred, But when I took Him
hands by cru - el nails were torn, When from my guilt and
with my soul I know 'tis well; Yet how or why, I

me.

sin and shame Thru grace He lift - ed me.
at His word, For - giv'n He lift - ed me.
grief, for - lorn, In love He lift - ed me. He lift - ed me.
can - not tell, He should have lift - ed me.

me.

From sink - ing sand He lift - ed me, With

ten - der hand   He lift - ed me;   From shades of night   to

plains of light,   O praise His name,   He lift - ed me!

Text: Charles H. Gabriel, 1856–1932
Tune: HE LIFTED ME, 888 6 with refrain; Charles H. Gabriel, 1856–1932

232

Jesus, Remember Me

Then he said, "Jesus, remember me when you come into your kingdom."
Luke 23:42

Ostinato Refrain

Je-sus, re-mem-ber me when You come in-to Your King-dom.

Je-sus, re-mem-ber me when You come in-to Your King-dom.

Flute

(Je-sus, re-mem-ber me)

Text: Luke 23:42; Taizé Community, 1981
Tune: Jacques Berthier, 1923–1994
© 1981, Les Presses de Taizé, GIA Publications, Inc., agent

233

Just for Me

For this is my blood of the covenant, which is poured out for many for the forgiveness of sins.
Matthew 26:28

Just for   me,   just for me,   just for

me,   just   for   me.   They

pierced Him in   His   side.   He   hung   His   head   and

died.   He did all   that   just for me.

Optional Solo:

Oh, what a shame to kill Him, as He hung on that rug - ged

cross. His death was sure - ly need - ed to

save this world from be - ing lost. My blind - ed eyes were

o - pen so that I might see. *Choir:* He did all

that just for me.

Text: Kenneth W. Louis, b.1956
Tune: Kenneth W. Louis, b.1956
© 1986, Kenneth W. Louis

234

You Are God

Simon Peter answered, "You are the Christ, the Son of the living God."
Matthew 16:16

You are   God,   the on - ly   sov - 'reign

God,   the on - ly   liv - ing   God,

ev - er - last - ing,   ev - er   lov - ing,

Text: Kurt Carr
Tune: Kurt Carr
© 2008, Kcartunes/Lilly Mack Publishing, admin. at EMICMGPublishing.com

235   I Gave My Life for Thee

I am the good shepherd. The good shepherd lays down his life for the sheep.
John 10:11

1. I gave My life for thee, My pre-cious blood I
2. My Fa-ther's house of light, My glo-ry-cir-cled
3. I suf-fered much for thee, More than thy tongue can
4. And I have brought to thee, Down from My home a-

shed, That thou might'st ran - somed be, And
throne I left, for earth - ly night, For
tell, Of bit - t'rest ag - o - ny, To
bove, Sal - va - tion full and free, My

quick - ened from the dead; I gave, I gave My
wan - d'rings sad and lone; I left, I left it
res - cue thee from hell; I've borne, I've borne it
par - don and My love; I bring, I bring rich

life for thee— What hast thou giv'n for Me?
all for thee— Hast thou left aught for Me?
all for thee— What hast thou borne for Me?
gifts to thee— What hast thou brought to Me?

Text: Frances R. Havergal, 1836–1879
Tune: KENOSIS, 6 6 6 6 8 6; Philip P. Bliss, 1838–1876

When I Survey the Wondrous Cross 236

May I never boast of anything except the cross of our Lord Jesus Christ...
Galatians 6:14

1. When I sur - vey the won - drous cross
2. For - bid it, Lord, that I should boast,
3. See, from His head, His hands, His feet,
4. Were the whole realm of na - ture mine,

On which the Prince of glo - ry died,
Save in the death of Christ, my God;
Sor - row and love flow min - gled down;
That were a pres - ent far too small:

My rich - est gain I count but loss,
All the vain things that charm me most—
Did e'er such love and sor - row meet,
Love so a - maz - ing, so di - vine,

And pour con - tempt on all my pride.
I sac - ri - fice them to His blood.
Or thorns com - pose so rich a crown?
De - mands my soul, my life, my all.

Text: Isaac Watts, 1674–1748
Tune: HAMBURG, LM; Gregorian Chant; arr. Lowell Mason, 1792–1872

237 Kneel at the Cross

...the cross is foolishness to those who are perishing, but to us who are being saved it is the power of God.
1 Corinthians 1:18

1. Kneel at the cross, Christ will meet you there,
2. Kneel at the cross, There is room for all
3. Kneel at the cross, Give your i-dols up,

Come while He waits for you; List to His voice,
Who would His glo-ry share; Bliss there a-waits,
Look un-to realms a-bove; Turn not a-way

Leave with Him your care And be-gin life a-new.
Harm can ne'er be-fall Those who are an-chored there.
To life's spark-ling cup; Trust on-ly in His love.

Kneel at the cross, Leave ev-'ry

Kneel at the cross, Kneel at the cross, Leave ev-'ry care,

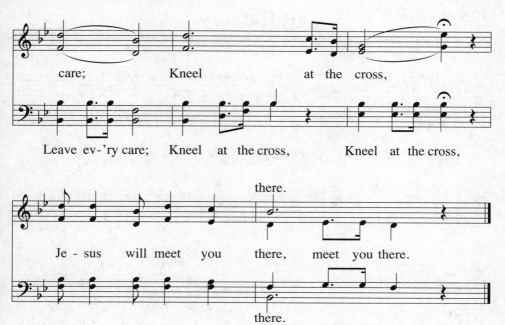

care;   Kneel   at the cross,

Leave ev-'ry care; Kneel   at the cross,   Kneel at the cross,

there.

Je - sus will meet   you   there, meet you there.

there.

Text: Charles E. Moody, fl.1924
Tune: KNEEL AT THE CROSS, 4 5 6 D with refrain; Charles E. Moody, fl.1924
© 1950, Bridge Building Music (BMI)

238

At Calvary

When they came to the place that is called The Skull, they crucified Jesus there with the criminals.
Luke 23:33

1. Years I spent in van - i - ty and pride,
2. By God's Word at last my sin I learned—
3. Now I've giv'n to Je - sus ev - 'ry - thing,
4. O the love that drew sal - va - tion's plan!

Car - ing not my Lord was cru - ci - fied, Know - ing
Then I trem - bled at the Law I'd spurned, Till my
Now I glad - ly own Him as my King, Now my
O the grace that brought it down to man! O the

not it was for me He died on Cal - va - ry.
guilt - y soul im - plor - ing turned to Cal - va - ry.
rap - tured soul can on - ly sing of Cal - va - ry.
might - y gulf that God did span at Cal - va - ry.

Mer - cy there was great and grace was free, Par - don

there was mul-ti-plied to me, There my bur-dened soul found

lib - er - ty— At Cal - va - ry.

Text: William R. Newell, 1868–1956
Tune: AT CALVARY, 99 13 with refrain; Daniel B. Towner, 1850–1919; arr. by Evelyn Simpson-Curenton, b.1953, © 2000, GIA Publications, Inc.

239   He Will Remember Me

Then an angel from heaven appeared to him and gave him strength.
Luke 22:43

1. When on the cross of Cal-v'ry The Lord was cru-ci-
2. O, what a shame to kill Him There on that rug-ged
3. At His dear feet I'm kneel-ing, My sins I now con-

fied; The mob stood 'round a-bout Him And mocked un-til He
cross; But such a death was need-ed To res-cue all the
fess; I bow in deep re-pen-tance, My soul He'll sure-ly

died. Two thieves were nailed be-side Him To share the ag-o-
lost. His blood was made a ran-som To set the cap-tives
bless. My blind-ed eyes He o-pens So that the light I

ny, But one of them cried out to Him, "O Lord re-mem-ber me."
free, I know that I'm in-clud-ed, and He will re-mem-ber me.
see, And when I reach the pearl-y gates, He will re-mem-ber me.

Will the Lord re-mem-ber me When I am called to

Will the Lord re - mem - ber me

go? When I have crossed death's chill - y sea, will

When I have crossed death's

He His love there show? Oh, yes, He heard my

Yes, He heard my

fee - ble cries, from bond - age set me free. And

when I reach the pearl - y gates, He will re-mem-ber me.

Text: Eugene M. Bartlett, 1885–1941
Tune: REMEMBER ME, 7 6 7 6 7 6 8 6 with refrain; Eugene M. Bartlett, 1885–1941; arr. by Nolan Williams, Jr., b.1969
© 1976, renewed 2004, Albert E. Brumley & Sons/SESAC (admin. by ClearBox Rights)

240   Beneath the Cross of Jesus

When the centurion saw what had taken place, he praised God and said, "Certainly this man was innocent."
Luke 23:47

1. Be-neath the cross of Je-sus I glad-ly take my stand: The shad-ow of a might-y rock With-in a wea-ry land, A rest up-on the way, From the wil-der-ness,

2. Up-on that cross of Je-sus My eyes at times can see The ver-y dy-ing form of One Who suf-fered there for me; And from my smit-ten heart, with tears, Two won-ders I con-fess—The

3. I take, O cross, thy shad-ow For my a-bid-ing place; I ask no oth-er sun-shine than The sun-shine of His face, Con-tent to let the world go by, To know no gain or loss, My

burn - ing of the noon-tide heat And the bur - den of the day.
won - ders of His glo - rious love And my un-wor - thi - ness.
sin - ful self my on - ly shame, My glo - ry all the cross.

Text: Elizabeth C. Clephane, 1830–1869
Tune: ST. CHRISTOPHER, 7 6 8 6 8 6 8 6; Frederick C. Maker, 1844–1927

241
The Old Rugged Cross

For many live as enemies of the cross of Christ...
Philippians 3:18

1. On a hill far a - way stood an old rug - ged cross,
2. O that old rug - ged cross, so de - spised by the world,
3. In the old rug - ged cross, stained with blood so di - vine,
4. To the old rug - ged cross I will ev - er be true,

The em - blem of suf - f'ring and shame;
Has a won - drous at - trac - tion for me;
A won - drous beau - ty I see;
Its shame and re - proach glad - ly bear;

And I love that old cross where the dear - est and best
For the dear Lamb of God left His glo - ry a - bove
For 'twas on that old cross Je - sus suf - fered and died
Then He'll call me some day to my home far a - way,

For a world of lost sin - ners was slain.
To bear it to dark Cal - va - ry.
To par - don and sanc - ti - fy me.
Where His glo - ry for ev - er I'll share.

old rug - ged cross,

So I'll cher - ish the cross, the old rug - ged cross, Till my

old rug - ged

tro - phies at last I lay down; I will cling to the cross, the

cross,

old rug - ged cross, And ex-change it some day for a crown.

Text: George Bennard, 1873–1958
Tune: OLD RUGGED CROSS, 12 8 12 8 with refrain; George Bennard, 1873–1958

242 O Sacred Head, Now Wounded

There they crucified him, and with him two others, one on either side, with Jesus between them.
John 19:18

1. O sa - cred Head, now wound - ed, With
2. What Thou, my Lord, hast suf - fered Was
3. The joy can ne'er be spo - ken, A -
4. What lan - guage shall I bor - row, To

grief and shame weighed down, Now scorn - ful - ly sur -
all for sin - ners' gain; Mine, mine was the trans -
bove all joys be - side, When in Thy bod - y
thank Thee, dear - est Friend, For this Thy dy - ing

round - ed, With thorns, Thine on - ly crown; O
gres - sion, But Thine the dead - ly pain. Lo,
bro - ken I thus with safe - ty hide. My
sor - row, Thy pit - y with - out end? Oh,

sa - cred Head, what glo - ry, What
here I fall, my Sav - ior! 'Tis
Lord of life, de - sir - ing Thy
make me Thine for - ev - er; And

bliss till now, was Thine! Yet, though de - spised and
I de - serve Thy place; Look on me with Thy
glo - ry now to see, Be - side the cross ex -
should I faint - ing be, Lord, let me nev - er,

go - ry, I joy to call Thee mine!
fa - vor, Vouch - safe to me Thy grace.
pir - ing, I'd breathe my soul to Thee.
nev - er Out - live my love to Thee.

Text: *Salve caput cruentatum*; ascr. to Bernard of Clairvaux, 1091–1153; tr. by Paul Gerhardt, 1607–1676; English adaptation by James W. Alexander, 1804–1859
Tune: PASSION CHORALE, 7 6 7 6 D; Hans Leo Hassler, 1564–1612; harm. by J. S. Bach, 1685–1750

243 There's Room at the Cross for You

Everything that the Father gives me will come to me, and anyone who comes to me I will never drive away.
John 6:37

1. The cross up-on which Je-sus died Is a shel-ter in which we can hide; And its grace so free Is suf-fi-cient for me, And deep is its foun-tain— as wide as the sea.

2. Tho mil-lions have found Him a friend And have turned from the sins they have sinned, The Sav-ior still waits To o-pen the gates And wel-come a sin-ner be-fore it's too late.

3. The hand of my Sav-ior is strong, And the love of my Sav-ior is long; Through sun-shine or rain, Through loss or in gain, The blood flows from Cal-v'ry to cleanse ev-'ry stain.

There's room at the cross for you, There's room at the cross for you; Tho' mil-lions have come, There's still room for one— Yes, there's room at the cross for you.

Text: Ira Stanphill, 1914–1993
Tune: STANPHILL, 88 45 11 with refrain; Ira Stanphill, 1914–1993
© 1946, New Spring Publishing (ASCAP)

244 Down at the Cross

He said to them, "This is my blood of the covenant, which is poured out for many."
Mark 14:24

1. Down at the cross where my Sav - ior died,
2. I am so won - drous - ly saved from sin,
3. Oh, pre - cious foun - tain that saves from sin,
4. Come to this foun - tain so rich and sweet,

Down where for cleans - ing from sin I cried,
Je - sus so sweet - ly a - bides with - in;
I am so glad I have en - tered in;
Cast thy poor soul at the Sav - ior's feet;

There to my heart was the blood ap - plied; Sing-in',
There at the cross where He took me in; Sing-in',
There Je-sus saves me and keeps me clean; Sing-in',
Plunge in to - day, and be made com - plete; Sing-in',

name! I'm sing-in'

Glo - ry to His name, His name!

name! I'm sing-in'

Glo - ry to His name, Pre-cious name.

I'm sing-in'

Glo - ry to His name, Pre-cious name.

His name.

There to my heart was the blood ap - plied; sing-in'

name.

Glo - ry to His name, His name.

name.

Text: Elisha A. Hoffman, 1839–1929
Tune: GLORY TO HIS NAME, 999 7 with refrain; John H. Stockton, 1813–1877; arr. by Evelyn Simpson-Curenton, b.1953,
© 2000, GIA Publications, Inc.

245

Calvary

... they crucified Jesus there with the criminals, one on his right and one on his left.
Luke 23:33

Refrain

Cal - va - ry, Cal - va - ry, Cal - va -

ry, Cal - va - ry, Cal - va - ry,

Cal - va - ry, Sure - ly He died on Cal - va - ry.

Verses

1. Ev - 'ry time I think a - bout Je - sus, Ev - 'ry
2. Sin - ner, do you love my Je - sus? Sin - ner,
3. We are climb - ing Ja - cob's lad - der, We are
4. Ev - 'ry round goes high - er and high - er, Ev - 'ry

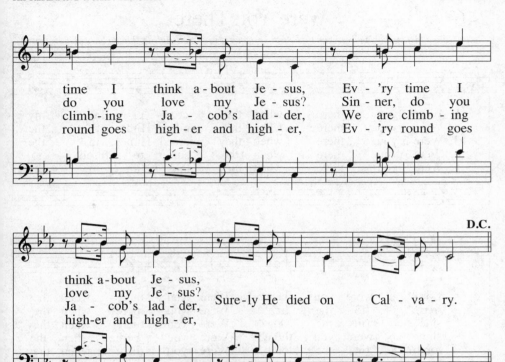

time   I   think a - bout   Je - sus,   Ev - 'ry time   I
do   you   love   my   Je - sus?   Sin - ner, do   you
climb - ing   Ja - cob's   lad - der,   We   are climb - ing
round goes   high - er and   high - er,   Ev - 'ry round goes

D.C.

think a - bout   Je - sus,
love   my   Je - sus?
Ja - cob's   lad - der,   Sure - ly He died on   Cal - va - ry.
high-er and   high - er,

May be sung as a unison a cappella piece.

Text: Negro Spiritual
Tune: CALVARY, LM with refrain; Negro Spiritual

246 Were You There

...God raised him up, having freed him from death, because it was impossible for him to be held in its power.
Acts 2:23–24

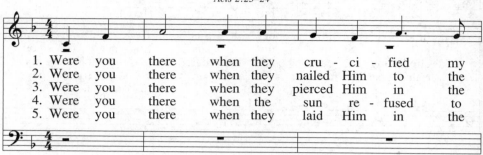

1. Were you there when they cru - ci - fied my
2. Were you there when they nailed Him to the
3. Were you there when they pierced Him in the
4. Were you there when the sun re - fused to
5. Were you there when they laid Him in the

Lord?   (were you there?)   Were you there when they
tree?   (to the tree?)   Were you there when they
side?   (in the side?)   Were you there when they
shine?   (were you there?)   Were you there when they
tomb?   (in the tomb?)   Were you there when the

cru - ci - fied my Lord?
nailed Him to the tree?
pierced Him in the side?   Oh!   Some - times it
sun re - fused to shine?
laid Him in the tomb?

caus - es me to trem - ble, trem - ble, trem - ble,

Were	you	there	when	they	cru - ci - fied	my	Lord?
Were	you	there	when	they	nailed Him	to	the	tree?
Were	you	there	when	they	pierced Him	in	the	side?
Were	you	there	when	the	sun re - fused	to	shine?
Were	you	there	when	they	laid Him	in	the	tomb?

Text: Negro Spiritual
Tune: WERE YOU THERE, 10 10 with refrain; Negro Spiritual; arr. by John Work and Frederick Work

247 He Looked beyond My Fault

When he went ashore, he saw a great crowd; and he had compassion for them and cured their sick.
Matthew 14:14

A - maz - ing   grace   shall   al - ways be   my   song   of   praise,

For it was grace   that bought my lib - er - ty;

I do not know   just why Christ came   to   love me   so,

He looked be - yond   my   fault and saw my   need.

I shall for - ev - er   lift mine eyes to   Cal - va - ry,

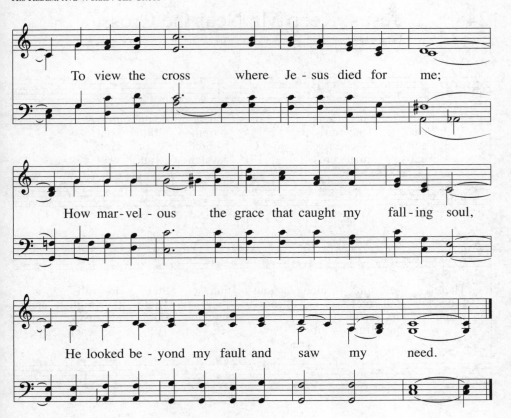

To view the cross where Je - sus died for me;

How mar - vel - ous the grace that caught my fall - ing soul,

He looked be - yond my fault and saw my need.

Text: Dottie Rambo, b.1934, © 1968, New Spring Publishing (ASCAP)
Tune: LONDONDERRY AIRE, 11 10 11 10 D; traditional

248 Jesus, Keep Me Near the Cross

And I, when I am lifted up from the earth, will draw all people to myself.
John 12:32

1. Je - sus, keep me near the cross;
2. Near the cross, a trem - bling soul,
3. Near the cross! O Lamb of God,
4. Near the cross I'll watch and wait,

There's a pre - cious foun - tain, Free to all, a
Love and mer - cy found me; There the bright and
Bring its scenes be - fore me; Help me walk from
Hop - ing, trust - ing ev - er, Till I reach the

heal - ing stream, Flows from Cal - v'ry's moun - tain.
morn - ing star Sheds its beams a - round me.
day to day With its shad - ows o'er me.
gold - en strand Just be - yond the riv - er.

In the cross, in the cross, Be my glo - ry ev - er,

Till my rap - tured soul shall find Rest be-yond the riv - er.

Text: Fanny J. Crosby, 1820–1915
Tune: NEAR THE CROSS, 7 6 7 6 with refrain; William H. Doane, 1832–1915; harm. by J. Jefferson Cleveland, 1937–1988, and Verolga Nix-Allen,
    b.1933, © 1981, Abingdon Press

249 Lift High the Cross

...so must the Son of Man be lifted up, that whoever believes in him may have eternal life.
John 3:14–15

Refrain
Unison

Lift high the cross, the love of Christ pro - claim till

all the world a - dore His sa - cred name.

Verses
Harmony

1. Come, Chris - tians, fol - low where the Mas - ter trod, Our
2. Led on their way by this tri - um - phant sign, The
3. Each new - born fol - l'wer of the Cru - ci - fied Bears
4. O Lord, once lift - ed on the glo - rious tree, Your
5. So shall our song of tri - umph ev - er be: Praise

D.C.

King vic - to - rious, Christ, the Son of God.
hosts of God in con - quering ranks com - bine.
on the brow the seal of Him who died.
death has bought us life e - ter - nal - ly.
to the Cru - ci - fied for vic - to - ry!

Text: 1 Corinthians 1:18; George W. Kitchin, 1827–1912, and Michael R. Newbolt, 1874–1956, alt.
Tune: CRUCIFER, 10 10 with refrain; Sydney H. Nicholson, 1875–1947
© 1974, Hope Publishing Co.

Lead Me to Calvary

250

Then they brought Jesus to the place called Golgotha (which means the place of a skull).
Mark 15:22

1. King of my life I crown Thee now— Thine shall the
2. Show me the tomb where Thou wast laid, Ten - der - ly
3. Let me like Mar - y, thru the gloom, Come with a
4. May I be will - ing, Lord, to bear Dai - ly my

glo - ry be; Lest I for - get Thy thorn-crowned brow,
mourned and wept; An - gels in robes of light ar - rayed
gift to Thee; Show to me now the emp - ty tomb—
cross for Thee; E - ven Thy cup of grief to share—

Lead me to Cal - va - ry.
Guard - ed Thee whilst Thou slept. Lest I for - get Geth -
Lead me to Cal - va - ry.
Thou hast borne all for me.

sem - a - ne, Lest I for - get Thine ag - o - ny,

Lest I for - get Thy love for me, Lead me to Cal - va - ry.

Text: Jennie E. Hussey, 1874–1958
Tune: DUNCANNON, CM with refrain; William J. Kirkpatrick, 1838–1921

251 Only Love

...we have been made holy through the sacrifice of the body of Jesus Christ once for all.
Hebrews 10:10

He could have called ten thou - sand an - gels to

come to His res - cue. On - ly love held Him there

Last time

on the cross.

1. On a

Last time

Last time

Verses

hill   far a - way   stood an   old   rug - ged
(2.) cross,   at the cross   where I   first   saw the

cross,   the em - blem of   suf - f'ring   and
light,   and the bur - den   of   my   heart   rolled a -

Text: Patrick D. Bradley, © 1998; verse 1 by George Bennard, 1873–1960, verse 2 by Ralph Hudson, 1843–1901
Tune: Patrick D. Bradley, © 1998; arr. by Kenneth W. Louis, b.1956, © 2006, GIA Publications, Inc.

252 · I Know It Was the Blood

...we have redemption through his blood, the forgiveness of our trespasses, according to the riches of his grace...
Ephesians 1:7–8

1. I know it was the blood, I
2. They whipped Him all night long, They
3. They pierced Him in His side, They
4. He nev-er said a mum - blin' word, He nev-er
5. He hung His head and died, He
6. He's com - ing back a - gain, He's

know it was the blood, I
whipped Him all night long, They
pierced Him in His side, They
said a mum - blin' word, He nev-er
hung His head and died, He
com - ing back a - gain, He's

know it was the blood for me.
whipped Him all night long for me.
pierced Him in His side for me.
said a mum - blin' word for me.
hung His head and died for me.
com - ing back a - gain for me.

One day when I was lost   He died up-on the cross.

I know it was the blood for me.

Text: African American traditional
Tune: IT WAS THE BLOOD, 66 8 with refrain; African American traditional; arr. by Evelyn Simpson-Curenton, b.1953, © 2000, GIA Publications, Inc.

253   The Blood Will Never Lose Its Power

...now that we have been justified by his blood, will we be saved through him from the wrath of God.
Romans 5:9

1. The blood that Je - sus shed for me,
2. It soothes my doubts and calms my fears,

Way back on Cal - va - ry,
And it dries all my tears;

The
The

blood that gives me strength from day to day, It will

nev - er lose its pow'r.

It reach-es   from the high - est   moun - tain.

(moun - tain) And it flows   to the low - est   val - ley.

(val - ley) The blood   that gives me strength from   day   to

day,   It will nev - er   lose   its   pow'r.

Text: Andraé Crouch, b.1942
Tune: THE BLOOD, 86 10 7 with refrain; Andraé Crouch, b.1942; arr. by Nolan Williams, Jr., b.1969
© 1966, renewed 1994, Manna Music, Inc./ASCAP (admin. by ClearBox Rights)

254

Oh, It Is Jesus

"If I but touch his clothes, I will be made well."
Mark 5:27–28

Chorus

Oh, it is Je - sus. Yes, it is Je - sus. It's

Je - sus in my soul. For I have touched the hem of His

gar - ment and His blood has made me whole.

Text: Andraé Crouch, b.1942
Tune: Andraé Crouch, b.1942; arr. by Stephen Key
© 1985, Crouch Music Corp. (ASCAP)

Alas! And Did My Savior Bleed   255

...God proves his love for us in that while we still were sinners Christ died for us.
Romans 5:8

1. A - las!   And   did   my   Sav - ior   bleed,   And
2. Was   it   for   sins   that   I   have   done   He
3. Well might   the   sun   in   dark - ness   hide,   And
4. But   drops   of   grief   can   ne'er   re - pay   The

did   my   Sov - 'reign   die!   Would   He   de - vote   that
suf - fered   on   the   tree?   A - maz - ing   pit - y!
shut   its   glo - ries   in,   When   Christ,   the   great   Re -
debt   of   love   I   owe;   Here,   Lord,   I   give   my -

sa - cred   head   For   sin - ners   such   as   I!
Grace   un - known!   And   love   be - yond   de - gree!
deem - er,   died   For   hu - man   crea - tures'   sin.
self   a - way;   'Tis   all   that   I   can   do.

Text: Isaac Watts, 1674–1748
Tune: MARTYRDOM, CM; Hugh Wilson, 1766–1824; arr. by Ralph Vaughan Williams, 1872–1958

256

Oh, the Blood of Jesus

You know that you were ransomed from the futile ways... with the precious blood of Christ...
1 Peter 1:18–19

1. Oh, the blood of Je - sus,   Oh, the blood of
2. Oh, the word of Je - sus,   Oh, the word of
3. Oh, the love of Je - sus,   Oh, the love of

Je - sus,   Oh, the blood of Je - sus, it must not suf - fer
Je - sus,   Oh, the word of Je - sus, it cleans - es white as
Je - sus,   Oh, the love of Je - sus, it makes His bod - y

loss.
snow.
whole.

loss.
snow.
whole.

There is pow-er, pow-er, pow-er, pow-er,

Won-der work-ing pow'r, In the blood, in the blood, of the Lamb,

of the Lamb. There is pow-er, pow-er, pow-er, pow-er,

Won-der work-ing pow'r, In the pre-cious blood of the Lamb.

Text: Anonymous
Tune: Anonymous; arr. by James Abbington, b.1960, © 2000, GIA Publications, Inc.

257   There Is a Fountain

...for this is my blood of the covenant, which is poured out for many for the forgiveness of sin.
Matthew 26:28

1. There is a foun-tain filled with blood Drawn from Im-
2. The dy-ing thief re-joiced to see That foun-tain
3. Dear dy-ing Lamb, Thy pre-cious blood Shall nev-er
4. E'er since by faith I saw the stream Thy flow-ing

man-uel's veins, And sin-ners plunged be-neath that flood
in his day, And there may I, though vile as he,
lose its pow'r, Till all the ran-somed Church of God
wounds sup-ply, Re-deem-ing love has been my theme

Lose all their guilt-y stains: Lose all their guilt-y stains,
Wash all my sins a-way: Wash all my sins a-way,
Be saved to sin no more: Be saved to sin no more,
And shall be till I die: And shall be till I die,

Lose all their guilt-y stains; And sin-ners plunged be-
Wash all my sins a-way; And there may I, though
Be saved to sin no more; Till all the ran-somed
And shall be till I die; Re-deem-ing love has

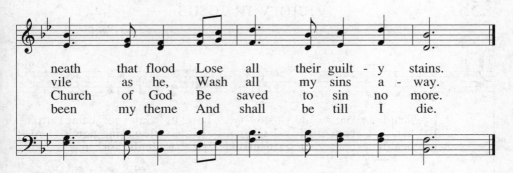

neath	that	flood	Lose	all	their	guilt - y	stains.
vile	as	he,	Wash	all	my	sins a -	way.
Church	of	God	Be	saved	to	sin no	more.
been	my	theme	And	shall	be	till I	die.

Text: William Cowper, 1731–1800
Tune: CLEANSING FOUNTAIN, 8 6 8 66 6 8 6; Early American melody

258   Victory in Jesus

But thanks be to God, who gives us the victory through our Lord Jesus Christ.
1 Corinthians 15:57

1. I heard an old, old sto - ry, how a Sav - ior came from glo - ry, How He gave His life on Cal - va - ry to save a wretch like me; I heard a - bout His groan - ing, of His pre - cious blood's a - ton - ing, Then

2. I heard a - bout His heal - ing, of His cleans - ing pow'r re - veal - ing, How He made the lame to walk a - gain and caused the blind to see; And then I cried, "Dear Je - sus, come and heal my bro - ken spir - it," And

3. I heard a - bout a man - sion He has built for me in glo - ry, And I heard a - bout the streets of gold be - yond the crys - tal sea; A - bout the an - gels sing - ing and the old re - demp - tion sto - ry, And

I re-pent-ed of my sins and won the vic-to-ry.
some-how Je-sus came and brought to me the vic-to-ry.
some sweet day I'll sing up there the song of vic-to-ry.

O vic-to-ry in Je-sus, my Sav-ior for-ev-er! He

sought me and bought me with His re-deem-ing blood; He

loved me ere I knew Him, and all my love is due Him; He

plunged me to vic-to-ry be-neath the cleans-ing flood.

Text: Eugene M. Bartlett, 1885–1941
Tune: HARTFORD, 15 15 15 14 with refrain; Eugene M. Bartlett, 1885–1941
© 1939, E. M. Bartlett, renewed 1967 by Mrs. E. M. Bartlett. Assigned to Albert E. Brumley & Sons/SESAC (admin. by ClearBox Rights).

259 I See a Crimson Stream

He said to them, "This is my blood of the covenant, which is poured out for many."
Mark 14:24

1. On Cal - v'ry's hill of sor - row Where
2. To - day no con - dem - na - tion A -
3. When gloom and sad - ness whis - per You've
4. And when we reach the por - tal Where

sin's de - mands were paid, And rays of hope for to -
bides to turn a - way My soul from His sal -
sinned, no use to pray, I look a - way to
life for - ev - er reigns, The ran - somed hosts grand

mor - row A - cross our path were laid.
va - tion, He's in my heart to stay.
Je - sus, And He tells me to say:
fi - nal, Will be this glad re - frain.

blood.

I see a crim - son stream of blood, stream of blood. It

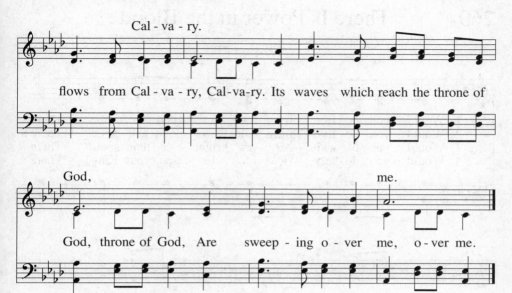

Cal - va - ry.

flows from Cal - va - ry, Cal-va-ry. Its waves which reach the throne of

God,

me.

God, throne of God, Are sweep - ing o - ver me, o - ver me.

Text: G. T. Haywood
Tune: CRIMSON STREAM, 7 6 7 6 with refrain; G. T. Haywood

260 There Is Power in the Blood

In him we have redemption through his blood... according to the riches of his grace.
Ephesians 1:7

1. Would you be free from the bur - den of sin? There's
2. Would you be free from your pas - sion and pride? There's
3. Would you be whit - er, yes bright - er than snow? There's
4. Would you do serv - ice for Je - sus, your King? There's

pow'r in the blood, pow'r in the blood;
pow'r in the blood, pow'r in the blood;
pow'r in the blood, pow'r in the blood;
pow'r in the blood, pow'r in the blood;

Would you o'er e - vil a vic - to - ry win? There's
Come for a cleans - ing to Cal - va - ry's tide— There's
Sin - stains are lost in its life - giv - ing flow— There's
Would you live dai - ly His prais - es to sing? There's

won - der - ful pow'r in the blood.

There is pow'r, pow'r, won-der-work-ing pow'r In the
there is pow'r,

blood of the Lamb; There is
In the blood of the Lamb; There is

pow'r, pow'r, won-der-work-ing pow'r In the
pow'r, there is pow'r,

pre - cious blood of the Lamb.

Text: Lewis E. Jones, 1865–1936
Tune: POWER IN THE BLOOD, 10 9 10 8 with refrain; Lewis E. Jones, 1865–1936

261
At the Cross

...the cross is foolishness to those who are perishing, but to us who are being saved it is the power of God.
1 Corinthians 1:18

1. A - las! And did my Sav - ior bleed? And
2. Was it for crimes that I have done He
3. Well might the sun in dark - ness hide And
4. But drops of grief can ne'er re - pay The

did my Sov - 'reign die? Would He de - vote that
groaned up - on the tree? A - maz - ing pit - y!
shut His glo - ries in, When Christ, the might - y
debt of love I owe: Here, Lord, I give my -

sa - cred head For such a one as I?
grace un-known! And love be - yond de - gree!
Mak - er, died For man the crea - ture's sin.
self a - way— 'Tis all that I can do!

At the cross, at the cross where I first saw the light, And the

bur - den   of   my   heart   rolled   a - way—   It was

rolled a - way—

there   by   faith   I   re - ceived   my   sight,   And

now   I   am   hap - py   all   the   day!

Text: Isaac Watts, 1674–1748; refrain, Ralph E. Hudson, 1843–1901
Tune: HUDSON, CM with refrain; Ralph E. Hudson, 1843–1901

262

Lamb of God

...he saw Jesus coming toward him and declared, "Here is the Lamb of God who takes away the sin of the world!"
John 1:29

1. Your on - ly Son, no sin to hide, But You have
2. Your gift of love they cru - ci - fied, They laughed and
3. I was so lost, I should have died, But You have

sent Him from Your side To walk up - on this guilt - y
scorned Him as He died: The hum - ble King they named a
brought me to Your side To be led by Your staff and

sod, And to be - come the Lamb of God. *(To verse 2)*
fraud, And sac - ri - ficed the Lamb of God. *(To refrain)*
rod, And to be called a lamb of God. *(To refrain)*

O Lamb of God, sweet Lamb of God, I love the

ho - ly Lamb of God! O wash me in His pre-cious

blood, My Je-sus Christ, the Lamb of God. God.

Text: Twila Paris, b.1958
Tune: LAMB OF GOD, LM with refrain; Twila Paris, b.1958
© 1985, Mountain Spring Music/Straightway Music, admin. at EMICMGPublishing.com

263 Nothing but the Blood of Jesus

Indeed, under the law almost everything is purified with blood,
and without the shedding of blood there is no forgiveness of sins.
Hebrews 9:22

1. What can wash a - way my sin? Noth-ing but the blood of Je-sus;
2. For my par-don this I see— Noth-ing but the blood of Je-sus;
3. Noth-ing can for sin a - tone— Noth-ing but the blood of Je-sus;
4. This is all my hope and peace— Noth-ing but the blood of Je-sus;

What can make me whole a - gain? Noth-ing but the blood of Je-sus.
For my cleans-ing, this my plea— Noth-ing but the blood of Je-sus.
Naught of good that I have done— Noth-ing but the blood of Je-sus.
This is all my right-eous-ness— Noth-ing but the blood of Je-sus.

Oh! pre-cious is the flow That makes me white as snow;

No oth-er fount I know, Noth-ing but the blood of Je - sus.

Text: Robert Lowry, 1826–1899
Tune: PLAINFIELD, 7 8 7 8 with refrain; Robert Lowry, 1826–1899; arr. by Nolan Williams, Jr., b.1969. © 2000, GIA Publications, Inc.

Amazing Grace

264

For by grace you have been saved through faith, and this is not your own doing; it is the gift of God.
Ephesians 2:8

1. A - maz - ing grace! how sweet the
2. 'Twas grace that taught my heart to
3. The Lord has prom - ised good to
4. Through man - y dan - gers, toils and
5. When we've been there ten thou - sand

sound That saved a wretch like me!
fear, And grace my fears re - lieved;
me, His word my hope se - cures;
snares, I have al - read - y come;
years, Bright shin - ing as the sun,

I once was lost but now I'm
How pre - cious did that grace ap -
He will my shield and por - tion
'Twas grace hath brought me safe thus
We've no less days to sing God's

found, Was blind but now I see.
pear The hour I first be - lieved.
be As long as life en - dures.
far, And grace will lead me home.
praise Than when we'd first be - gun.

Text: St. 1–3, John Newton, 1725–1807, st. 4, attr. to John Rees, fl.1859
Tune: NEW BRITAIN, CM; *Virginia Harmony,* 1831; arr. by Evelyn Simpson-Curenton, b.1953, © 2000, GIA Publications, Inc.

265 Your Grace and Mercy

"...My grace is sufficient for you, for power is made perfect in weakness."
2 Corinthians 12:9

Your grace and mer - cy brought me through, I'm liv-ing this mo - ment be-cause of You; I want to thank You,

Last time to Coda ⊕   D.C.

and praise You too: Your grace and mer - cy   brought me through.

Last time to Coda ⊕   D.C.

⊕ Coda

mer - cy,   Your grace   and mer - cy   brought me through.

Text: Franklin D. Williams
Tune: Franklin D. Williams; arr. by Nolan Williams, Jr., b.1969
© 1993, Malaco, Inc.

266
Touch Me, Lord Jesus

I will not leave you orphaned; I am coming to you.
John 14:18

1. Touch, touch me, Lord Je - sus,
2. Mold, mold me, dear Sav - ior;
3. Feed, feed me, dear Je - sus,
4. Guide, guide me, Je - ho - vah,

With Thy hand of mer - cy,
As I bow be - fore Thee,
From Thy ho - ly ta - ble,
Thro' this vale of sor - row,

Make each throb-bing heart-beat
Pros-trate, pros - trate and help-less,
Rain, rain bread from heav - en,
I am safe for - ev - er,

Feel Thy pow'r di - vine. O
Make my heart Thy throne. O
Let my cup o'er - flow. O
Trust-ing in Thy love. O

take my will for-ev-er,
purge my dross with his-sop;
na-ked, sick and hun-gry;
bear me thro' the cur-rent;

I will doubt Thee nev-er, O Lord, please
Burn me with Thy fire; O Lord, please
Poor and weak and lone-ly, O Lord, please
O'er the chil-ly Jor-dan, O Lord, please

cleanse me, my dear Sav-ior,
make, make me and use me;
feed feed me, Lord Je-sus
lead me, my dear Sav-ior

Make me whol-ly Thine.
Ev-er all Thine own.
Till I want no more.
To my home a-bove.

Text: Lucie E. Campbell, 1885–1963
Tune: TOUCH ME, 6 6 6 5 D; Lucie E. Campbell, 1885–1963; arr. Evelyn Simpson-Curenton, b.1953, © 2000, GIA Publications, Inc.

267   Think of His Goodness to You

O how abundant is your goodness that you have laid up for those who fear you...
Psalm 31:19

1. When waves of af - flic - tion sweep o - ver the soul,
2. The world may for - sake you, and those whom you trust
3. Mis - for - tune's dark cloud may hang o - ver the way,
4. When dear ones are tak - en a - way from you here,

And sun - light is hid - den from view,
May prove to be false and un - true;
De - spite your best ef - forts to do;
You loved with af - fec - tion so true,

If ev - er you're tempt - ed to fret or com-plain,
There's One you can trust e - ven un - to the end;
The Sav - ior is guard - ing your treas - ures up there;
Look un - to the Sav - ior for strength to en - dure,

Just think of His good - ness to you.
Just think of His good - ness to you.
Just think of His good - ness to you.
And think of His good - ness to you.

Text: R. C. Ward
Tune: GOODNESS, 11 8 11 8 with refrain; R. C. Ward

268   He Touched Me

He stretched out his hand and touched him, saying, "I do choose. Be made clean!"
Matthew 8:3

1. Shack - led by a heav - y bur - den,
2. Since I met this bless - ed Sav - ior,

'Neath a load of guilt and shame;
Since He cleansed and made me whole;

Then the hand of Je - sus touched me, And
I will nev - er cease to praise Him, I'll

now I am no long - er the same.
shout it while e - ter - ni - ty rolls.

Text: William J. Gaither
Tune: HE TOUCHED ME, 8 7 8 9 with refrain; William J. Gaither,
© 1963, Hanna Street Music (all rights controlled by Gaither Copyright Mgmt.)

269

He Lives

The women were terrified and bowed their faces to the ground, but the men said to them,
"Why do you look for the living among the dead?"
Luke 24:5

1. I serve a ris - en Sav - ior, He's in the world to - day;
2. In all the world a - round me I see His lov - ing care,
3. Re - joice, re - joice, O Chris - tian, lift up your voice and sing

I know that He is liv - ing, what - ev - er oth - ers say;
And though my heart grows wea - ry I nev - er will de - spair;
E - ter - nal hal - le - lu - jahs to Je - sus Christ, the King!

I see His hand of mer - cy, I hear His voice of cheer,
I know that He is lead - ing through all the storm - y blast,
The hope of all who seek Him, the help of all who find,

And just the time I need Him He's al - ways near.
The day of His ap - pear - ing will come at last.
None oth - er is so lov - ing, so good and kind.

He lives, He lives, Christ Je - sus lives to -
He lives, He lives,

day! He walks with me and talks with me a -

long life's nar - row way. He lives, He
He lives,

lives, sal - va - tion to im - part! You
He lives,

ask me how I know He lives? He lives with-in my heart.

Text: Alfred H. Ackley, 1887–1960
Tune: ACKLEY, 13 13 13 11 with refrain; Alfred H. Ackley, 1887–1960
© 1933, Word Music, LLC

270 The Strife Is O'er

Jesus said to her, "I am the resurrection and the life. Those who believe in me, even though they die, will live..."
John 11:25

Refrain

Al-le-lu - ia! Al-le-lu - ia! Al-le-lu - ia!

Verses

1. The strife is o'er, the bat - tle done; Now is the
2. Death's might-iest pow'rs have done their worst, And Je - sus
3. He closed the yawn - ing gates of hell; The bars from
4. On the third morn He rose a - gain, Glo - rious in

Vic - tor's tri - umph won; Now be the song of
has His foes dis - persed; Let shouts of praise and
heav'n's high por - tals fell; Let hymns of praise His
maj - es - ty to reign; O let us swell the

praise be - gun: Al - le - lu - ia!
joy out - burst: Al - le - lu - ia!
tri - umph tell: Al - le - lu - ia!
joy - ful strain: Al - le - lu - ia!

D.C.

Text: *Finita iam sunt praelia*; Latin, 12th C.; tr. by Francis Pott, 1832–1909, alt.
Tune: VICTORY, 888 with alleluias; Giovanni da Palestrina, 1525–1594; adapt. by William H. Monk, 1823–1889

I Know That My Redeemer Lives 271

...the Son of Man must be handed over to sinners, and be crucified, and on the third day rise again.
Luke 24:6–7

1. I know that my Re - deem - er lives;
2. He lives, to bless me with His love;
3. He lives, and grants me dai - ly breath;
4. He lives, all glo - ry to His name;

What joy the blest as - sur - ance gives!
He lives, to plead for me a - bove;
He lives, and I shall con - quer death;
He lives, my Sav - ior still the same;

He lives, He lives, who once was dead;
He lives, my hun - gry soul to feed;
He lives, my man - sion to pre - pare;
What joy the blest as - sur - ance gives;

He lives, my ev - er - last - ing Head!
He lives, to help in time of need.
He lives, to bring me safe - ly there.
I know that my Re - deem - er lives!

Text: Samuel Medley, 1738–1799
Tune: DUKE STREET, LM; John Hatton, c.1710–1793

272 On the Third Day Morning

On the third day he will rise again.
Luke 13:33

Verses

1. On the third day morn-ing the Son of God a - rose.
2. On the third day morn-ing the Son of God a - rose.

On the third day morn - ing, as proph - e-cy fore - told.
Vic - to - ry and pow - er the grave could not hold.

Mar - y was the first to see God's
The stone was rolled a - way so that

mir - a - cle   un - fold   when on the third day morn-ing
all the world would know   that on the third day morn-ing

Christ a - rose.
Christ a - rose.   He a -

Refrain

rose,   Je - sus Christ a - rose.   He a - rose,

Je - sus Christ a - rose.   Be - cause He lives   and reigns

for - ev - er,   there's joy* in   my   soul.   'Cause

*peace, hope...

on the third day morn-ing

Christ a-

rose.

D.S.

Last time

D.S.

Text: Harold Wheat, Jr.
Tune: Harold Wheat, Jr.
© 2004, Wheat Music (ASCAP)

273   Christ the Lord Is Risen Today

He has been raised from the dead, and indeed he is going ahead of you to Galilee; there you will see him.
Matthew 28:7

1. Christ the Lord is ris'n to-day, Al - le - lu - ia!
2. Lives a - gain our glo-rious King, Al - le - lu - ia!
3. Love's re - deem - ing work is done, Al - le - lu - ia!
4. Sing we to our God a - bove, Al - le - lu - ia!

Praise e - ter - nal as His love; Al - le - lu - ia!

Sons of men and an - gels say: Al - le - lu - ia!
Where, O death, is now thy sting? Al - le - lu - ia!
Fought the fight, the bat - tle won, Al - le - lu - ia!
Praise e - ter - nal as His love; Al - le - lu - ia!

Praise, ye heav'n - ly host, Al - le - lu - ia!

Raise your joys and tri-umphs high, Al - le - lu - ia!
Dy - ing once, He all doth save, Al - le - lu - ia!
Death in vain for - bids Him rise, Al - le - lu - ia!
Praise Him, all ye heav'n - ly host, Al - le - lu - ia!

Fa - ther, Son, and Ho - ly Ghost. Al - le - lu - ia!

Sing, ye heav'ns, and earth re - ply: Al - le - lu - ia!
Where thy vic - to - ry, O grave? Al - le - lu - ia!
Christ has o - pened par - a - dise, Al - le - lu - ia!
Fa - ther, Son, and Ho - ly Ghost. Al - le - lu - ia!

Text: Charles Wesley, 1707–1788
Tune: EASTER HYMN, 77 77 with alleluias, *Lyra Davidica*, 1708; descant by Nolan Williams, Jr., b.1969, © 2000, GIA Publications, Inc.

274 He Arose

Do not be alarmed; you are looking for Jesus of Nazareth who was crucified. He has been raised; he is not here.
Mark 16:6

1. They cru - ci - fied my Sav - ior And nailed Him to the cross. They
2. Jo - seph begged His bod - y And laid it in the tomb.
3. Mar - y, she came run - ning, A - look - ing for my Lord.
4. An an - gel came from heav - en And rolled the stone a - way. An
cru - ci - fied my Sav - ior And nailed Him to the cross. They
Jo - seph begged His bod - y And laid it in the tomb.
Mar - y, she came run - ning, A - look - ing for my Lord.
an - gel came from heav - en And rolled the stone a - way. An
cru - ci - fied my Sav - ior And nailed Him to the cross.
Jo - seph begged His bod - y And laid it in the tomb.
Mar - y, she came run - ning, A - look - ing for my Lord.
an - gel came from heav - en And rolled the stone a - way.
And the Lord will bear my spir - it home.

He 'rose, He 'rose, He 'rose from the dead, He

He 'rose, He 'rose, He

'rose, He 'rose, He 'rose from the dead. He

He 'rose, He 'rose, He

'rose, He 'rose, He 'rose from the dead, And the

He 'rose, He 'rose, He

Lord will bear my spir - it home.

Text: Negro Spiritual
Tune: HE AROSE, 7 6 7 6 7 6 9 with refrain; Negro Spiritual; arr. by Valeria A. Foster, © 2000, GIA Publications, Inc.

275 Christ Arose

But he said to them, "Do not be alarmed; you are looking for Jesus of Nazareth,
who was crucified. He has been raised..."
Mark 16:6

1. Low in the grave He lay, Je - sus, my Sav - ior!
2. Vain - ly they watched His bed, Je - sus, my Sav - ior!
3. Death could not keep his prey, Je - sus, my Sav - ior!

Wait - ing the com - ing day, Je - sus, my Lord!
Vain - ly they sealed the dead, Je - sus, my Lord!
He tore the bars a - way, Je - sus, my Lord!

Up from the grave He a-rose, With a might - y tri-umph o'er His

He a-rose,

foes; He a-rose a vic-tor from the dark do-main, And He

He a-rose;

lives for-ev-er with His saints to reign; He a-rose! He a-

He a-rose!

rose! Hal - le - lu - jah! Christ a - rose!

He a-rose!

Text: Robert Lowry, 1826–1899
Tune: CHRIST AROSE, 6 5 6 4 with refrain; Robert Lowry, 1826–1899

276 Because He Lives

In a little while the world will no longer see me, but you will see me; because I live, you also will live.
John 14:19

1. God sent His Son, they called Him Je - sus,
2. How sweet to hold a new - born ba - by,
3. And then one day I'll cross the riv - er,

He came to love, heal, and for - give;
And feel the pride, and joy He gives;
I'll fight life's fi - nal war with pain;

He lived and died to buy my par - don, An
But great - er still the calm as - sur - ance, This
And then as death gives way to vic - t'ry, I'll

emp - ty grave is there to prove my Sav - ior lives.
child can face un - cer - tain days be - cause He lives.
see the lights of glo - ry and I'll know He lives.

Be - cause He lives I can face to - mor - row,

Be - cause He lives all fear is gone;

Be - cause I know He holds the fu - ture.

Last time to Coda ⊕

D.C.

And life is worth the liv-ing just be-cause He lives.

know   He holds the fu-ture;   And life is

know   He holds the fu-ture;   And life is

worth   the liv-ing   just be-cause He lives!

worth   the liv-ing   just be-cause He lives!

A - men!

Text: Gloria Gaither and William J. Gaither
Tune: RESURRECTION, 9 8 9 12 with refrain; William J. Gaither; arr. by Nolan Williams, Jr., b.1969
© 1971, Hanna Street Music (all rights controlled by Gaither Copyright Mgmt.)

277

He Is Lord

And every tongue should confess that Jesus Christ is Lord, to the glory of God the Father.
Philippians 2:11

He is Lord, He is Lord! He is ris-en from the

dead and He is Lord! Ev-'ry knee shall bow, ev-'ry

tongue con - fess That Je - sus Christ is Lord.

Text: Based on Philippians 2:11
Tune: HE IS LORD, 6 11 10 6; traditional

278

Jesus Shall Reign

When the Son of Man comes in his glory, and all the angels with him, then he will sit on the throne of his glory.
Matthew 25:31

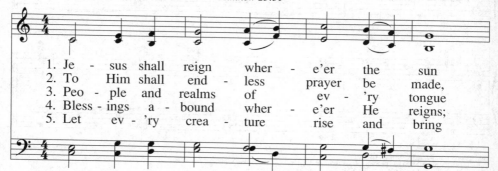

1. Je - sus shall reign wher - e'er the sun
2. To Him shall end - less prayer be made,
3. Peo - ple and realms of ev - 'ry tongue
4. Bless - ings a - bound wher - e'er He reigns;
5. Let ev - 'ry crea - ture rise and bring

Does His suc - ces - sive jour - neys run;
And prais - es throng to crown His head;
Dwell on His love with sweet - est song;
The pris - 'ner leaps to lose his chains;
Bless - ing and hon - or to our King;

His king - dom stretch from shore to shore,
His Name like sweet per - fume shall rise
And in - fant voic - es shall pro - claim
The wea - ry find e - ter - nal rest,
An - gels de - scend with songs a - gain,

Till moons shall wax and wane no more.
With ev - 'ry morn - ing sac - ri - fice.
Their ear - ly bless - ings on His Name.
And all who suf - fer want are blest.
And earth re - peat the loud A - men.

Text: Isaac Watts, 1674–1748, alt.
Tune: DUKE STREET, LM; John Hatton, c.1710–1793

279 Crown Him with Many Crowns

...there was a white cloud, and seated on the cloud was one like the Son of Man, with a golden crown on his head...
Revelation 14:14

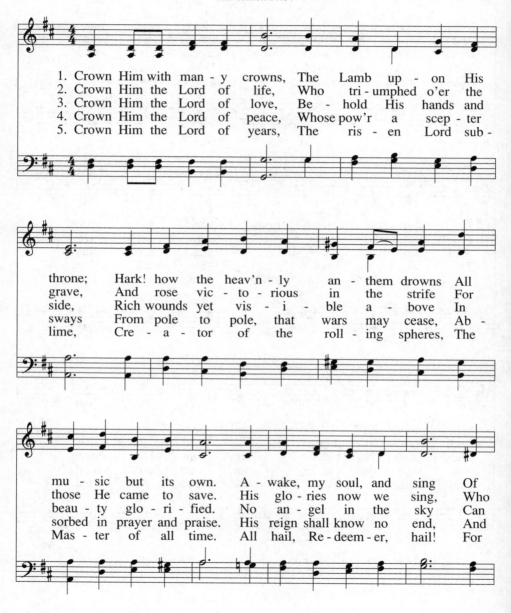

1. Crown Him with man - y crowns, The Lamb up - on His
2. Crown Him the Lord of life, Who tri - umphed o'er the
3. Crown Him the Lord of love, Be - hold His hands and
4. Crown Him the Lord of peace, Whose pow'r a scep - ter
5. Crown Him the Lord of years, The ris - en Lord sub -

throne; Hark! how the heav'n - ly an - them drowns All
grave, And rose vic - to - rious in the strife For
side, Rich wounds yet vis - i - ble a - bove In
sways From pole to pole, that wars may cease, Ab -
lime, Cre - a - tor of the roll - ing spheres, The

mu - sic but its own. A - wake, my soul, and sing Of
those He came to save. His glo - ries now we sing, Who
beau - ty glo - ri - fied. No an - gel in the sky Can
sorbed in prayer and praise. His reign shall know no end, And
Mas - ter of all time. All hail, Re - deem - er, hail! For

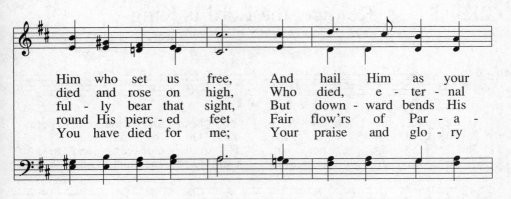

Him who set us free, And hail Him as your
died and rose on high, Who died, e - ter - nal
ful - ly bear that sight, But down - ward bends His
round His pierc - ed feet Fair flow'rs of Par - a -
You have died for me; Your praise and glo - ry

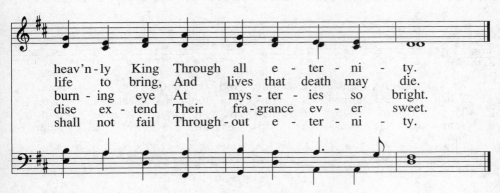

heav'n - ly King Through all e - ter - ni - ty.
life to bring, And lives that death may die.
burn - ing eye At mys - ter - ies so bright.
dise ex - tend Their fra - grance ev - er sweet.
shall not fail Through - out e - ter - ni - ty.

Text: Revelation 19:12; st. 1, 3–5, Matthew Bridges, 1800–1894; st. 2, Godfrey Thring, 1823–1903
Tune: DIADEMATA, SMD; George J. Elvey, 1816–1893

280 Rejoice, the Lord Is King

...for the Lord God will give them light. And they will reign for ever and ever.
Revelation 22:5

1. Re - joice, the Lord is King! Your Lord and King a - dore!
2. The Lord, our Sav - ior, reigns, The God of truth and love;
3. His king - dom can - not fail, He rules o'er earth and heav'n;
4. Re - joice in glo - rious hope! Our Lord the judge shall come

Re - joice, give thanks, and sing, And tri - umph ev - er - more:
When He had purged our sins, He took His seat a - bove:
The keys of death and hell Are to our Je - sus giv'n:
And take His ser - vants up To their e - ter - nal home:

Lift up your heart, lift up your voice!

Re - joice, a - gain I say, re - joice!

Text: Charles Wesley, 1707–1788
Tune: DARWALL'S 148TH, 6 6 6 6 88; John Darwall, 1731–1789; harm. from *The Hymnal 1940*

We Will Glorify

281

They cried out... "Salvation belongs to our God who is seated on the throne, and to the Lamb!"
Revelation 7:10

1. We will glo - ri - fy the King of kings, We will
2. Lord Je - ho - vah reigns in maj - es - ty, We will
3. He is Lord of heav - en, Lord of earth, He is
4. Hal - le - lu - jah to the King of kings, Hal - le -

glo - ri - fy the Lamb; We will glo - ri - fy the
bow be - fore His throne; We will wor - ship Him in
Lord of all who live; He is Lord a - bove the
lu - jah to the Lamb; Hal - le - lu - jah to the

Last time

Lord of lords, Who is the great I Am.
right - eous - ness, We will wor - ship Him a - lone.
u - ni - verse— All praise to Him we give.
Lord of lords, Who is the great I Am.

Last time

Text: Twila Paris, b.1958
Tune: WE WILL GLORIFY, 9 7 9 6; Twila Paris, b.1958
© 1982, New Spring Publishing (ASCAP)

282 Get All Excited

And they went out and proclaimed the good news everywhere, while the Lord worked with them...
Mark 16:20

Get all ex - cit - ed, go tell ev-'ry-bod - y that Je - sus

Christ is King! Get all ex - cit - ed, go tell ev-'ry-bod - y that

Je - sus Christ is King! Get all ex - cit - ed, go tell

ev-'ry-bod - y that Je - sus Christ is King!

Je-sus Christ is still the King of kings, King of kings!

Text: William J. Gaither
Tune: William J. Gaither
© 1972, Hanna Street Music (all rights controlled by Gaither Copyright Mgmt.)

O How I Love Jesus

We love because he first loved us.
1 John 5:19

1. There is a name I love to hear, I love to sing its
2. It tells me of a Sav-ior's love, Who died to set me
3. It tells me what my Fa-ther has In store for ev-'ry
4. It tells of One whose lov-ing heart Can feel my deep-est

worth; It sounds like mu-sic in my ear, The sweet-est
free; It tells me of His pre-cious blood, The sin-ner's
day, And though I tread a gloom-y path, Yields sun-shine
woe, Who in each sor-row bears a part, That none can

name on earth.
per - fect plea.
all the way.
bear be - low.

O how I love Je - sus, O how I love

Je - sus, O how I love Je - sus, Be - cause He first loved me!

Text: Frederick Whitfield, 1829–1904
Tune: HOW I LOVE JESUS, CM with refrain; American melody

284

Perfect Praise

O LORD, our Sovereign, how majestic is your name in all the earth!
Psalm 8:9

Oh Lord, how ex-cel-lent, how ex-cel-lent, how

ex-cel-lent, how ex-cel-lent is Thy

is Thy

is Thy

name!

Oh

There is

none like You,   none like You,   none like You,

Je - sus,   ex-cel-lent   is   is   Thy

is Thy

name!   1.   There   is

*Special Chorus

*Begin with tenor line, repeat adding alto, soprano and bass lines respectively.

Text: Brenda Moore, ©
Tune: Brenda Moore, ©; arr. by Nolan Williams, Jr., b.1969, © 2000, GIA Publications, Inc.

285 His Name Is Wonderful

...He is named Wonderful Counselor, Mighty God, Everlasting Father, Prince of Peace.
Isaiah 9:6

1. His name is Won-der-ful, His name is Won-der-ful,
2. He is the might-y King, Mas-ter of ev-'ry-thing,

His name is Won-der-ful, Je-sus, my Lord;

Je-sus, my Lord. He's the great Shep-herd, the Rock of all

a-ges, Al-might-y God is He; Bow down be-fore Him,

Love and a-dore Him, His name is Won-der-ful, Je-sus, my Lord.

Text: Audrey Mieir, 1916–1996
Tune: Audrey Mieir, 1916–1996
© 1959, 1987, Manna Music, Inc. (admin. by ClearBox Rights)

Bless That Wonderful Name of Jesus 286

Therefore God also highly exalted him and gave him the name that is above every name.
Philippians 2:9

Refrain: Bless that won-der-ful name of Je - sus.
1. There's pow - er in the name of Je - sus.
2. There's heal - ing in the name of Je - sus.

Bless that won-der-ful name of Je - sus.
Pow - er in the name of Je - sus.
Heal - ing in the name of Je - sus.

Bless that won-der-ful name of Je - sus,
Pow - er in the name of Je - sus,
Heal - ing in the name of Je - sus,

no oth - er name I know.

Text: Congregational Praise Song
Tune: Congregational Praise Song; arr. by Stephen Key, © 2000, GIA Publications, Inc.

287   In the Name of Jesus

...there is no other name under heaven given among mortals by which we must be saved.
Acts 4:12

pre - cious Je - sus, we have the vic - to - ry.

Optional Chorus

Vic - to - ry, oh, vic - to - ry, we have the vic - to -

ry. Vic - to - ry, oh, vic - to - ry,

we have the vic - to - ry.

Text: Congregational Praise Song
Tune: Congregational Praise Song; arr. by Walter Owens, Jr., © 2000, GIA Publications, Inc.

288 Glorious Is the Name of Jesus

Ascribe to the LORD the glory due his name; bring an offering, and come before him.
1 Chronicles 16:29

Glo-rious is the name of Je-sus, prais-es to His name. Oh,

glo - rious and right - eous and ho - ly is His

name, Oh, glo - ri - ous is His name.

I feel His pres-ence in this place, His Spir - it has con -

trol.   Can't you   feel   His warm em - brace and all the

joy with-in your   soul,   Oh,   glo - ri -ous is His

name,   Oh,   glo - ri - ous is His   name.

Text: Dr. Robert J. Fryson, 1944–1994
Tune: Dr. Robert J. Fryson, 1944–1994
© 1982, Bob Jay Music Co.

289 The Name of Jesus

Jesus Christ is the same yesterday and today and forever.
Hebrews 13:8

1. The name of Je - sus is so sweet, I
2. I love the name of Him whose heart Knows
3. That name I fond - ly love to hear, It
4. No word of man can ev - er tell How

love its mu - sic to re - peat; It makes my joys full
all my griefs, and bears a part; Who bids all anx - ious
nev - er fails my heart to cheer; Its mu - sic dries the
sweet the name I love so well; Oh, let its prais - es

and com - plete, The pre - cious name of Je - sus.
fears de - part— I love the name of Je - sus.
fall - en tear: Ex - alt the name of Je - sus.
ev - er swell, Oh, praise the name of Je - sus.

1. The pre - cious name

rubato

"Je-sus," O how sweet the name! "Je-sus," ev-'ry day the same;

"Je-sus," let all saints pro - claim   Its   wor-thy praise for - ev - er.

Text: William C. Martin, 1864–1914
Tune: THE NAME OF JESUS, 8 8 8 7 with refrain; Edmund S. Lorenz, 1854–1942

290 How Majestic Is Your Name

O LORD, our Sovereign, how majestic is your name in all the earth!
Psalm 8:9

O Lord, our Lord, how ma-jes-tic is Your name in all the earth. O earth. O Lord, we praise Your name. O Lord, we mag-ni-fy Your name: Prince of Peace, Might-y God; O Lord God Al-might-y. O y.

Text: Michael W. Smith, b.1957
Tune: HOW MAJESTIC, Irregular; Michael W. Smith, b.1957
© 1981, Meadowgreen Music Co., admin. at EMICMGPublishing.com

So Glad I'm Here

291

And now, our God, we give thanks to you and praise your glorious name.
1 Chronicles 29:13

1. So glad I'm here, So glad I'm here, Lord,
2. Pray* while I'm here, Pray while I'm here, Lord,

So glad I'm here in Je - sus' name. Lawd
Pray while I'm here in Je - sus' name. Lawd

So glad I'm here, Lord, So glad I'm here, Lord,
Pray while I'm here, Lord, Pray while I'm here, Lord,

So glad I'm here in Je - sus' name.
Pray while I'm here in Je - sus' name.

*3. Sing while..., 4. Shout while...

Text: Negro Spiritual
Tune: Negro Spiritual; arr. by Evelyn Simpson-Curenton, b.1953, © 2000, GIA Publications, Inc.

292   All Hail the Power of Jesus' Name

...there was a white cloud, and seated on the cloud was one like the Son of Man, with a golden crown on his head...
Revelation 14:14

1. All hail the pow'r of Je - sus' name!
2. Ye cho - sen seed of Is - rael's race,
3. Let ev - 'ry kin - dred, ev - 'ry tribe,
4. Oh, that with yon - der sa - cred throng

Let an - gels pros - trate fall, Let an - gels pros - trate
Ye ran - somed from the fall, Ye ran - somed from the
On this ter - res - trial ball, On this ter - res - trial
We at His feet may fall, We at His feet may

fall. Bring forth the roy - al di - a - dem,
fall, Hail Him who saves you by His grace,
ball, To Him all maj - es - ty as - cribe,
fall! We'll join the ev - er - last - ing song,

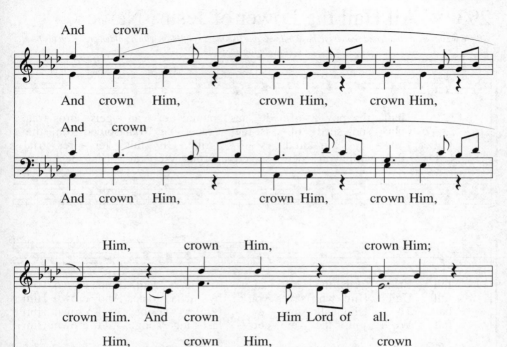

Text: Edward Perronet, 1726–1792
Tune: DIADEM, 8 66 8 with refrain; James Ellor, 1819–1899

293   All Hail the Power of Jesus' Name

...there was a white cloud, and seated on the cloud was one like the Son of Man, with a golden crown on his head...
Revelation 14:14

*Sing this 4th verse if no key change is desired.

Descant:

4. With yon - der

Melody:

4. O that with yon - der

rall.   *a tempo*

sa - cred throng, We all may fall!

sa - cred throng, We at His feet may fall! We'll

Text: Edward Perronet, 1726–1792, alt. by John Rippon, 1751–1836
Tune: CORONATION, 8 6 8 6 8 6; Oliver Holden, 1765–1844; arr. by Nolan Williams, Jr., b.1969, © 2000, GIA Publications, Inc.

All Hail the Power of Jesus' Name 294

...there was a white cloud, and seated on the cloud was one like the Son of Man, with a golden crown on his head...
Revelation 14:14

1. All hail the pow'r of Je - sus' name! Let
2. Ye cho - sen seed of Is - rael's race, Ye
3. Let ev - 'ry kin - dred, ev - 'ry tribe, On
4. O that with yon - der sa - cred throng We

an - gels pros - trate fall; Bring forth the roy - al
ran - somed from the fall, Hail Him who saves you
this ter - res - trial ball, To Him all maj - es -
at His feet may fall! We'll join the ev - er -

di - a - dem,
by His grace, And crown Him, crown Him,
ty as - cribe,
last - ing song,

crown Him, crown Him Lord of all!

Text: Edward Perronet, 1726–1792, alt. by John Rippon, 1751–1836
Tune: MILES LANE, 8 6 8 with refrain; William Shrubsole, 1760–1806

295 Blessed Be the Name

So that at the name of Jesus every knee should bend in heaven and on earth and under the earth.
Philippians 2:10

1. O for a thou - sand tongues to sing,
2. Je - sus, the name that charms our fears,
3. He breaks the pow'r of can - celed sin,

Bless-ed be the name of the Lord! The glo - ries of my
Bless-ed be the name of the Lord! 'Tis mu - sic in the
Bless-ed be the name of the Lord! His blood can make the

God and King, Bless-ed be the name of the Lord!
sin - ner's ears, Bless-ed be the name of the Lord!
foul - est clean, Bless-ed be the name of the Lord!

Bless-ed be the name, Bless-ed be the name,

Bless-ed be the name of the Lord! Bless-ed be the name,

Bless-ed be the name, Bless-ed be the name of the Lord!

Text: Charles Wesley, 1757–1834
Tune: BLESSED NAME, LM with refrain; Ralph E. Hudson, 1843–1901

Psalm 8: O Lord, How Excellent 296

O LORD, our Sovereign, how majestic is your name in all the earth! You have set your glory above the heavens.
Psalm 8:1

Chorus

O Lord, our Lord, how ex-cel-lent is Thy name.

O Lord, our Lord, how ex-cel-lent is Thy name.

Text: Psalm 8:1
Tune: Richard Smallwood, b.1948; arr. by Stephen Key, © 2000, GIA Publications, Inc.

297 Praise the Name of Jesus

From the rising of the sun to its setting the name of the LORD is to be praised.
Psalm 113:3

Praise the name of Je - sus; Praise the name of Je - sus. He's my Rock, He's my For - tress,

He's my De-liv-er - er, in Him will I trust.

Praise the name of Je - sus.

Last time

Text: Psalm 18:1; Roy Hicks, Jr., b.1943
Tune: Roy Hicks, Jr., b.1943; arr. by Joseph Joubert, b.1958
© 1976, Latter Rain Music, admin. at EMICMGPublishing.com

298 There's Something about That Name

...through believing you may have life in his name.
John 20:31

Je - sus, Je - sus, Je - sus! There's just

some-thing a - bout that name!

Mas - ter, Sav - ior, Je - sus! Like the

fra - grance af - ter the rain;

Je - sus, Je - sus, Je - sus! Let all

heav-en　　and earth　pro - claim:

Kings　and　king-doms　will all　pass a - way,　But there's

some-thing　a - bout　that　name!

Text: William J. Gaither and Gloria Gaither
Tune: THAT NAME, 6 8 6 8 6 8 9 8; William J. Gaither
© 1970, Hanna Street Music (all rights controlled by Gaither Copyright Mgmt.)

299 Take the Name of Jesus with You

And whatever you do, in word or deed, do everything in the name of the Lord Jesus.
Colossians 3:17

1. Take the name of Je - sus with you, Child of sor - row and of woe. It will joy and com - fort give you, Take it then wher - e'er you go. Pre - cious name, O how sweet! Hope of

2. Take the name of Je - sus ev - er As pro - tec - tion ev - 'ry - where. If temp - ta - tions 'round you gath - er, Breathe that ho - ly name in prayer.

3. At the name of Je - sus bow - ing, When in heav - en we shall meet, King of kings, we'll glad - ly crown Him When our jour - ney is com - plete.

Pre - cious name, O how sweet! Hope of

pre - cious name, O how sweet!

earth and joy of heav-en; Pre-cious name, O how

pre-cious name,

sweet! Hope of earth and joy of heav-en.

O how sweet!

Text: Lydia Baxter, 1809–1874
Tune: PRECIOUS NAME, 8 7 8 7 with refrain; William H. Doane, 1832–1915

300 Praise Offering

Exalt the LORD our God and worship at his holy mountain, for the LORD our God is holy.
Psalm 99:9

In this praise I of-fer to You, I will glad-ly lift up Your name and ex-alt You with my whole heart and voice. I will mag-ni-fy Your name. You grant me Your mer-cy and grace; I'll for-ev-er give You the praise. I a-dore You, my Sav-ior, my Lord, my God!

Text: Victoria Woodard
Tune: Victoria Woodard
© 1998, Victoria Woodard

I Feel Jesus in This Place

301

...in Christ we speak as persons of sincerity, as persons sent from God and standing in his presence.
2 Corinthians 2:17

Text: Carman Licciardello, b.1956
Tune: Carman Licciardello, b.1956; arr. by Nolan Williams, Jr., b.1969
© 1986, arr. © 2010, MPCA Lehsem Music

302 Never Alone

I will not leave you orphaned; I am coming to you.
John 14:18

1. I've seen the light - ning flash - ing And
2. The world's fierce winds are blow - ing— Temp -
3. When in af - flic - tion's val - ley I
4. He died on Cal - v'ry's moun - tain, For

Refrain: No, nev - er a - lone,

heard the thun - der roll, I've felt sin's break - ers
ta - tion's sharp and keen; I have a peace in
tread the road of care, My Sav - ior helps me
me they pierced His side, For me He o - pened that

No, nev - er a - lone— He prom - ised nev - er to

dash - ing, Try - ing to con - quer my soul;
know - ing My Sav - ior stands be - tween;
car - ry The cross so heav - y to bear;
foun - tain, The crim - son, cleans - ing tide;

leave me, Nev - er to leave me a - lone;

I've   heard   the   voice   of   Je   -   sus
He   stands   to   shield   me   from   dan   -   ger   When
Though   all   a - round   me   is   dark   -   ness   And
For   me   He's   wait - ing   in   glo   -   ry   Up -

No,   *nev - er   a - lone,*

Tell - ing   me   still   to   fight   on: He   prom - ised   nev - er   to
all   my   friends   are   gone: He   prom - ised   nev - er   to
earth - ly   joys   are   flown,   My   Sav - ior   whis - pers   His
on   His   heav - en - ly   throne: He   prom - ised   nev - er   to

No,   *nev - er   a - lone;   He   prom - ised   nev - er   to*

leave   me,   Nev - er   to   leave   me   a - lone.
leave   me,   Nev - er   to   leave   me   a - lone.
prom - ise: Nev - er   to   leave   me   a - lone.
leave   me,   Nev - er   to   leave   me   a - lone.

leave   me,   Nev - er   to   leave   me   a - lone.

Text: Anonymous
Tune: NEVER ALONE, 7 6 7 6 7 6 8 7; anonymous, arr. by Nolan Williams, Jr., b.1969, © 2000, GIA Publications, Inc.

303

No, Not One

...I have called you friends, because I have made known to you everything that I have heard from my Father.
John 15:15

1. There's not a friend like the low - ly Je - sus—
2. No friend like Him is so high and ho - ly—
3. There's not an hour that He is not near us—
4. Was e'er a gift like the Sav - ior giv - en?

No, not one! no, not one! None else could heal all our
No, not one! no, not one! And yet no friend is so
No, not one! no, not one! No night so dark but His
No, not one! no, not one! Will He re - fuse us a

soul's dis - eas - es— No, not one! no, not one!
meek and low - ly— No, not one! no, not one!
love can cheer us— No, not one! no, not one!
home in heav - en? No, not one! no, not one!

Je - sus knows all a - bout our strug - gles, He will guide till the

day   is   done;   There's   not   a   friend   like   the

low - ly   Je - sus—   No,   not   one!   no,   not   one!

Text: Johnson Oatman, Jr., 1856–1922
Tune: HARPER MEMORIAL, 10 6 10 6 with refrain; George C. Hugg, 1848–1907

304   In Times like These

We have this hope, a sure and steadfast anchor of the soul.
Hebrews 6:19

1. In times like these you need a Sav - ior, In times like
2. In times like these you need the Bi - ble, In times like
3. In times like these I have a Sav - ior, In times like

these you need an an - chor; Be ver - y sure, be ver - y
these O be not i - dle; Be ver - y sure, be ver - y
these I have an an - chor, I'm ver - y sure, I'm ver - y

sure Your an-chor holds and grips the Sol-id Rock!
sure Your an-chor holds and grips the Sol-id Rock!
sure My an-chor holds and grips the Sol-id Rock!

This Rock is Je - sus, yes, He's the One; This Rock is
This Rock is Je - sus, yes, He's the One; This Rock is
This Rock is Je - sus, yes, He's the One; This Rock is

Je - sus, the on - ly One! Be ver - y sure, be ver - y
Je - sus, the on - ly One! Be ver - y sure, be ver - y
Je - sus, the on - ly One! I'm ver - y sure, I'm ver - y

sure Your an-chor holds and grips the Sol-id Rock!
sure Your an-chor holds and grips the Sol-id Rock!
sure My an-chor holds and grips the Sol-id Rock!

Text: Ruth Caye Jones, 1902–1972
Tune: IN TIMES LIKE THESE, 9 9 8 10 D; Ruth Caye Jones, 1902–1972
© 1944, New Spring Publishing (ASCAP)

305

I've Got a Feelin'

...do not worry about your life, what you will eat or what you will drink, or about your body, what you will wear.
Matthew 6:25

Verse 1

1. I've got a feel-in' ev-'ry-thing's gon-na be al-right.

I've got a feel-in' ev-'ry-thing's gon-na be al-right.
Oh,

I've got a feel-in' ev-'ry-thing's gon-na be al-right,

be al-right, be al-right, be al-right.

Verse 2

2. The Ho-ly Ghost done told me ev-'ry-thing's gon-na be al-right.

The Ho-ly Ghost done told me ev-'ry-
Oh,

thing's gon-na be al - right. The Ho-ly Ghost done

told me ev-'ry-thing's gon-na be al - right, be al - right,

be al - right, be al - right.

Text: Congregational Praise Song
Tune: Congregational Praise Song; arr. by Kenneth W. Louis, b.1956, and Nolan Williams, Jr., b.1969, © 2000, GIA Publications, Inc.

306   Unbounded Spirit, Breath of God

And with that he breathed on them and said, "Receive the Holy Spirit."
John 20:22

1. Un - bound - ed Spir - it, breath of God, Re - fresh - ing
2. Re - ceive and o - pen for re - view The work we
3. Un - cov - er gen - tly all the ways We run, re -
4. As - sem - ble, leav - en, mix, and knead Our clash - ing
5. In - scribe on ev - 'ry grow - ing skill, On ev - 'ry

wa - ter, cleans - ing flame, We give al - le - giance, by
do, the word we preach, And school us, as we teach
sist, re - bel, or hide. Un - wrap with love and bathe
norms, op - pos - ing views, And bake a loaf of joy
ac - tion, ev - 'ry vow, The liv - ing name of Je -

Your call, To Christ, and to no oth - er name.
and learn, In care - ful thought and truth - ful speech.
in light Our pain, our sad - ness, and our pride.
and peace That hun - gry hearts will not re - fuse.
sus Christ, Be - gin - ning here, be - gin - ning now.

Text: Brian Wren, b.1936, © 2004, Hope Publishing Company
Tune: ROCKINGHAM, LM; adapted by Edward Miller, 1735–1807

Spirit of God, Descend upon My Heart 307

Do not cast me away from your presence, and do not take your holy spirit from me.
Psalm 51:11

1. Spir - it of God, de - scend up - on my heart;
2. I ask no dream, no proph - et ec - sta - sies,
3. Teach me to feel that Thou art al - ways nigh;
4. Teach me to love Thee as Thine an - gels love,

Wean it from earth; through all its puls - es move;
No sud - den rend - ing of the veil of clay,
Teach me the strug - gles of the soul to bear,
One ho - ly pas - sion fill - ing all my frame;

Stoop to my weak - ness, might - y as Thou art,
No an - gel vis - i - tant, no o - p'ning skies;
To check the ris - ing doubt, the reb - el sigh;
The kin - dling of the heav'n - de - scend - ed Dove,

And make me love Thee as I ought to love.
But take the dim - ness of my soul a - way.
Teach me the pa - tience of un - an - swered prayer.
My heart an al - tar, and Thy love the flame.

Text: George Croly, 1780–1860
Tune: MORECAMBE, 10 10 10 10; Frederick C. Atkinson, 1841–1897

308   Holy Ghost, with Light Divine

If you then, who are evil, know how to give good gifts to your children,
how much more will the heavenly Father give the Holy Spirit to those who ask him!
Luke 11:13

1. Ho - ly Ghost, with light di - vine,
2. Ho - ly Ghost, with pow'r di - vine,
3. Ho - ly Ghost, with joy di - vine,
4. Ho - ly Spir - it, all di - vine,

Shine up - on this heart of mine;
Cleanse this guilt - y heart of mine;
Cheer this sad - dened heart of mine;
Dwell with - in this heart of mine;

Chase the shades of night a - way,
Long hath sin with - out con - trol,
Bid my man - y woes de - part,
Cast down ev - 'ry i - dol throne,

Turn my dark - ness in - to day.
Held do - min - ion o'er my soul.
Heal my wound - ed, bleed - ing heart.
Reign su - preme, and reign a - lone.

Text: Andrew Reed, 1787–1862
Tune: MERCY, 77 77; Louis M. Gottschalk, 1829–1869

Come, Holy Spirit, Heavenly Dove   309

But the Advocate, the Holy Spirit, whom the Father will send in my name, will teach you everything…
John 14:26

1. Come, Ho - ly Spir - it, Heav'n - ly Dove, With
2. Look, how we grov - el here be - low, Fond
3. In vain we tune our for - mal songs, In
4. Fa - ther, and shall we ev - er live At
5. Come, Ho - ly Spir - it, Heav'n - ly Dove, With

all Thy quick - 'ning pow'rs; Kin - dle a flame of
of these earth - ly toys; Our souls, how heav - i -
vain we strive to rise; Ho - san - nas lan - guish
this poor dy - ing rate, Our love so faint, so
all Thy quick - 'ning pow'rs; Come, shed a - broad a

sa - cred love In these cold hearts of ours.
ly they go, To reach e - ter - nal joys.
on our tongues, And our de - vo - tion dies.
cold to Thee, And Thine to us so great?
Sav - ior's love, And that shall kin - dle ours.

Text: Isaac Watts, 1674–1748
Tune: ST. MARTIN'S, CM; William Tansur, 1700–1783

310 Spirit, Bear Fruit in My Life

Repent, then, and turn to God, so that your sins may be wiped out...
Acts 3:18

Lord, I pray once a-gain, I re-pent of my sins, Let Your
works, lest I boast, Not by strength of my own, Let Your

Spir - it con-trol, Change my bod-y, mind and soul so You can
Spir - it con-trol, Change my sin-ful heart of stone so You can

fill me. Let Your Spir - it bear fruit in my life. Not by

1.

life. Let Your Spir - it bear fruit in my

2.

life.   Let Your Spir - it bear fruit   in my

life.   Fix my heart   with the char - ac - ter of

Christ.   Let Your Spir - it bear fruit   in my   life.

Text: Gale Jones Murphy, b.1954
Tune: Gale Jones Murphy, b.1954
© Gale Jones Murphy

311 Let It Breathe on Me

...He breathed on them and said to them, "Receive the Holy Spirit."
John 20:22

Refrain

Let it breathe on me, Let it breathe on me, Let the breath of the Lord, now, breathe on me, Let it breathe on me, Let it breathe on me, Let the breath of the Lord, now, breathe on me.

Verses

1. While I'm work - ing Lord, in Your vine - yard here, I can do naught if Thou aren't near, Oh, come, bless - ed Lord, just so close to me That I may feel You breathe on me.

2. When the path - way Lord, I can not see, When the way is dark, if Lord, breathe on me, Give me grace to know when Thou art near Oh, I pray Thee, Lord, please breathe on me.

D.C.

Text: Magnolia Lewis-Butts, c.1880–1949
Tune: Magnolia Lewis-Butts, c.1880–1949; arr. by Joseph Joubert, b.1958
© Benson Music Group

312

Anointing

...the anointing that you received from him abides in you, and so you do not need anyone to teach you.
1 John 2:27

A - noint - ing   fall   on   me.

A - noint - ing   fall   on   me.

Let the pow-er of   the Ho - ly Ghost   fall   on   me.

A - noint - ing   fall   on   me.

Text: Donn C. Thomas, © 1992, New Spring Publishing (ASCAP).
Tune: Donn C. Thomas, © 1992, New Spring Publishing (ASCAP); arr. by Evelyn Simpson-Curenton, b.1953, © 2000, GIA Publications, Inc.

Holy Spirit

313

May God fill you with all joy and hope... so that you may abound in hope by the power of the Holy Spirit.
Romans 15:13

Chorus

We need the pow-er of the Ho-ly Spir-it,

Ho-ly Spir-it. Send Your a-noint-ing. Let it

fall down, fall down,

fall down, down on me!

Text: Richard Smallwood, b.1948
Tune: Richard Smallwood, b.1948; arr. by Nolan Williams, Jr., b.1969
© Century Oak Publishing Group/Richwood Music (BMI), admin. by Conexion Media Group, Inc.

314 Breathe on Me, Breath of God

...He himself gives to all mortals life and breath and all things.
Acts 17:25

1. Breathe on me, Breath of God, Fill me with life a-new, That I may love what Thou dost love And do what Thou wouldst do.
2. Breathe on me, Breath of God, Un-til my heart is pure, Un-til with Thee I will one will, To do and to en-dure.
3. Breathe on me, Breath of God, Till I am whol-ly Thine, Till all this earth-ly part of me Glows with Thy fire di-vine.
4. Breathe on me, Breath of God, So shall I nev-er die, But live with Thee the per-fect life Of Thine e-ter-ni-ty.

Text: Edwin Hatch, 1835–1889
Tune: TRENTHAM, SM; Robert Jackson, 1840–1914

Spirit of the Living God

And John testified, "I saw the Spirit descending from heaven like a dove, and it remained on him."
John 1:32

Rubato

Spir - it of the Liv - ing God, Fall fresh on me,

Spir - it of the Liv - ing God, Fall fresh on me.

accelerando

rall.

Break me, melt me, mold me, fill me.

Spir - it of the Liv - ing God, Fall fresh on me.

Text: Daniel Iverson, 1890–1977
Tune: IVERSON, Irregular; Daniel Iverson, 1890–1977
© 1935, Birdwing Music (ASCAP)

316 Spirit Holy

Do not cast me away from your presence, and do not take your Holy Spirit from me.
Psalm 51:11

1. Spir - it ho - ly in me dwell - ing, Ev - er
2. O how sweet is Thy a - bid - ing! O how
3. Thou hast cleansed me for Thy tem - ple, Gar - nished
4. In me now re - veal Thy glo - ry, Let Thy

work as Thou shalt choose; All my ran - somed pow'rs and
ten - der is the love Thou dost shed a - broad with-
with Thy grac - es rare; All my soul Thou art en -
might be ev - er shown; Keep me from the world's de -

tal - ents For Thy pur - pose Thou shalt use.
in me From the Fa - ther-heart a - bove!
rich - ing By Thy full - ness dwell - ing there.
file - ment, Sa - cred for Thy-self a - lone.

All my

Spir - it ho - ly, Spir - it ho - ly,

Spir - it ho - ly, Spir - it ho - ly,

Text: Charles W. Naylor, 1874–1950
Tune: SPIRIT HOLY, 8 7 8 7 with refrain; Andrew L. Byers, 1869–1952

317 Sweet, Sweet Spirit

... agree with one another, live in peace; and the God of love and peace will be with you.
2 Corinthians 13:11

1. There's a sweet, sweet Spir - it in this
   sweet ex - pres - sions on each
2. There are bless - ings you can - not re -
   one to pro - fit when you
3. If you say He saved you from your
   make it right if you will

place, And I know that it's the
face, And I know they feel the
ceive Till you know Him in His
say, "I am going to walk with
sin, Now you're weak, you're bound, and
yield; You'll en - joy the Ho - ly

Spir - it of the Lord. There are
pres - ence of the Lord. You're the
full - ness, and be - lieve.
Je - sus all the way."
can - not en - ter in, you can
Spir - it that we feel.

Sweet Ho-ly Spir-it, Sweet Heav'n-ly Dove,

Stay right here with us Fill-ing us with Your

love. And for those bless-ings We lift our hearts with

praise; With-out a doubt we'll know that we have

been re-vived, when we shall leave this place.

Text: Doris Akers, 1922–1995
Tune: MANNA, Irregular; Doris Akers, 1922–1995
© 1962, 1990, Manna Music, Inc. (admin. by ClearBox Rights)

318 Spirit Song

Now may our Lord Jesus Christ himself... comfort your hearts and strengthen them in every good work...
2 Thessalonians 2:16, 17

1. Oh, let the Son of God en-fold you, with His Spir-it and His love, Let Him fill your heart and sat-is-fy your soul. Oh, let Him have the things that hold you, and His Spir-it like a

2. Oh, come and sing this song with glad-ness, as your hearts are filled with joy, Lift your hands in sweet sur-ren-der to His name. Oh, give Him all your tears and sad-ness, give Him all your years of

dove,   Will de - scend up - on your life, and make you
pain,   And you'll en - ter in - to life in Je - sus'

whole.
name.   Je - sus.   Oh,

Je - sus,   come and fill your lambs.

Je - sus,   Oh, Je - sus,

come   and   fill   your   lambs.

Text: John Wimber, b.1934
Tune: John Wimber, b.1934; arr. by James Abbington, b.1960
© 1979, Mercy/Vineyard Publishing, admin. by Music Services

319 Every Time I Feel the Spirit

God is spirit, and those who worship him must worship in spirit and truth.
John 4:24

Refrain

Ev - 'ry time I feel the Spir - it mov - ing

in my heart, I will pray. Ev - 'ry time I feel the

Spir - it mov - ing in my heart, I will pray.

Verses

1. Up - on the moun - tain when my God spoke,
   All a - round me, it looked so shine,
2. 'Ol Jor - dan Riv - er, chill - y and cold,
   There ain't but one train that's on this track,

D.C.

Out of God's mouth came   fire and   smoke.
I asked my Lord if   all was   mine.
It chills the bod - y,   but not the   soul.
It runs to heav - en   and runs right   back.

Text: Negro Spiritual
Tune: FEEL THE SPIRIT, 98 98 with refrain; Negro Spiritual; arr. by Nolan Williams, Jr., b.1969, © 2000, GIA Publications, Inc.

We Are One

320

...maintain the unity of the Spirit in the bond of peace.
Ephesians 4:3

We are one,   we are   one.   We are one   in the

Spir-it, we are one.   Hal-le-lu - jah, Hal-le -

lu - jah, we are one in the Spir-it, we are one.

Text: Timothy Wright, 1948–2009, ©
Tune: Congregational Praise Song, arr. Valeria A. Foster, © 2000, GIA Publications, Inc.

321 How Great Is Our God

How great is God—beyond our understanding! The number of his years is past finding out.
Job 36:26

Verses

1. The splen-dor of the King,
(2. And) age to age He stands, and

clothed in maj - es - ty; Let all the earth re - joice,
time is in His hands; Be - gin - ning and the End,

all the earth re - joice. He wraps
Be - gin - ning and the End. The God -

Him - self in light, and
head, three - in - one,

dark - ness tries to hide, and trem - bles at His voice,
Fa - ther, Spir - it, Son, the Li - on and the Lamb,

and trem - bles at His voice.
the Li - on and the Lamb.

How great

Refrain

Descant: Name a - bove all names,

Melody: is our God! Sing with me: How

wor - thy of all praise. My

great is our God! And all will see how

heart will sing: how great is our God!

great, how great is our God!

Eᵇmaj⁷   F   Bᵇ

1.   2.   **D.S.** 3.

2. And   How great How great,

D.S.

how great is our God!

Eᵇmaj⁷   F   Bᵇ

Text: Chris Tomlin, b.1972, Jesse Reeves, and Ed Cash
Tune: Chris Tomlin, b.1972, Jesse Reeves, and Ed Cash
© 2004, worshiptogether.com Songs and sixsteps Music, admin. by EMI CMG; Alletrope Music, admin. by Music Services

322 Come, Thou Almighty King

Moses and Aaron... came out and blessed the people; and the glory of the LORD appeared to all the people.
Leviticus 9:23

1. Come, Thou Al - might - y King, Help us Thy
2. Come, Thou In - car - nate Word, Gird on Thy
3. Come, Ho - ly Com - fort - er, Thy sa - cred
4. To the great One - in - Three E - ter - nal

name to sing, Help us to praise:
might - y sword, Our prayer at - tend:
wit - ness bear, In this glad hour:
prais - es be, Hence ev - er - more:

Fa - ther, all - glo - ri - ous, O'er all vic - to - ri - ous,
Come and Thy peo - ple bless, And give Thy word suc - cess—
Thou who al - might - y art, Now rule in ev - 'ry heart,
His sov - 'reign maj - es - ty May we in glo - ry see,

Come and reign o - ver us, An - cient of Days.
Spir - it of ho - li - ness, On us de - scend.
And ne'er from us de - part, Spir - it of pow'r.
And to e - ter - ni - ty Love and a - dore.

Text: Anonymous, c.1757
Tune: ITALIAN HYMN, 66 4 666 4; Felice de Giardini, 1716–1796

Holy, Holy

323

...without ceasing they sing, "Holy, holy, holy, the Lord God the Almighty, who was and is and is to come."
Revelation 4:8

Unison

1. Ho - ly, ho - ly, ho - ly, ho - ly, Ho - ly,
2. Gra - cious Fa - ther, gra - cious Fa - ther, We're so
3. Pre - cious Je - sus, pre - cious Je - sus, We're so
4. Ho - ly Spir - it, Ho - ly Spir - it, Come and
5. Hal - le - lu - jah, hal - le - lu - jah, Hal - le -

ho - ly, Lord God Al - might - y:
blest to be Your chil - dren, gra - cious Fa - ther;
glad that You've re - deemed us, pre - cious Je - sus;
fill our hearts a - new, Ho - ly Spir - it;
lu - jah, hal - le - lu - jah;

And we lift our hands be - fore You as a to - ken of our love,

Ho - ly, ho - ly, ho - ly, ho - ly.
Gra - cious Fa - ther, gra - cious Fa - ther.
Pre - cious Je - sus, pre - cious Je - sus.
Ho - ly Spir - it, Ho - ly Spir - it.
Hal - le - lu - jah, hal - le - lu - jah.

Text: Jimmy Owens, b.1930
Tune: HOLY, Irregular; Jimmy Owens, b.1930
© 1972, Bud John Songs, Inc. (ASCAP)

324 Holy, Holy, Holy! Lord God Almighty

Let the heavens praise your wonders, O LORD, your faithfulness in the assembly of the holy ones.
Psalm 89:5

1. Ho - ly, Ho - ly, Ho - ly! Lord God Al - might - y!
2. Ho - ly, Ho - ly, Ho - ly! all the saints a - dore Thee,
3. Ho - ly, Ho - ly, Ho - ly! though the dark - ness hide Thee,

Ear - ly in the morn - ing our song shall rise to Thee:
Cast - ing down their gold - en crowns a - round the glass - y sea;
Though the eye made blind by sin Thy glo - ry may not see,

Ho - ly, Ho - ly, Ho - ly! mer - ci - ful and might - y,
Cher - u - bim and ser - a - phim fall - ing down be - fore Thee,
On - ly Thou art ho - ly; there is none be - side Thee,

God in three Per - sons, bless - ed Trin - i - ty.
God ev - er - last - ing through e - ter - ni - ty.
Per - fect in pow'r, in love, and pu - ri - ty.

rall.

Descant:

4. Ho - ly,   Ho - ly!   Lord, God Al - might - y!

4. Ho - ly, Ho - ly,   Ho - ly!   Lord   God Al - might - y!

All   Thy works shall   praise Thy Name in   earth, and sky, and   sea;

All   Thy works shall   praise Thy Name in   earth, and sky, and   sea;

Ho - ly,   Ho - ly,   mer - ci - ful and might - y,

Ho - ly, Ho - ly,   Ho - ly!   mer - ci - ful and might - y,

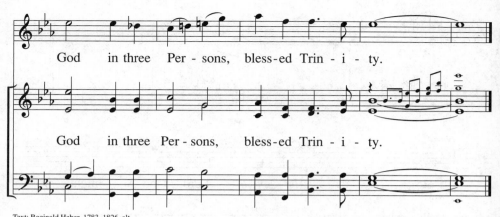

God in three Per - sons, bless-ed Trin - i - ty.

God in three Per - sons, bless-ed Trin - i - ty.

Text: Reginald Heber, 1783–1826, alt.
Tune: NICAEA, 11 12 12 10; John Bacchus Dykes, 1823–1876; arr. by Nolan Williams, Jr., b.1969, © 2000, GIA Publications, Inc.

325 Father, I Adore You

Because your steadfast love is better than life, my lips will praise you.
Psalm 63:2–3

1. Fa - ther, I a-dore You, Lay my life be-
2. Je - sus, I a-dore You, Lay my life be-
3. Spir - it, I a-dore You, Lay my life be-

fore You, How I love You.
fore You, How I love You.
fore You, How I love You.

May be sung as a 3-part round.

Text: Terrye Coelho-Strom, b.1952
Tune: MARANATHA, 6 6 4; Terrye Coelho-Strom, b.1952
© 1972, Universal Music - Brentwood Benson Publishing (ASCAP) / CCCM Music (ASCAP)

Tell Me the Stories of Jesus

326

Then Philip began to speak, and starting with this scripture, he proclaimed to him the good news about Jesus.
Acts 8:35

1. Tell me the sto - ries of Je - sus I love to hear;
2. First let me hear how the chil - dren stood 'round His knee,
3. In - to the cit - y I'd fol - low the chil - dren's band,

Things I would ask Him to tell me if He were here:
And I shall fan - cy His bless - ing rest - ing on me;
Wav - ing a branch of the palm tree high in my hand;

Scenes by the way - side, tales of the sea,
Words full of kind - ness, deeds full of grace,
One of His her - alds, yes, I would sing

Sto - ries of Je - sus, tell them to me.
All in the love - light of Je - sus' face.
Loud - est ho - san - nas, "Je - sus is King!"

Text: William H. Parker, 1845–1929
Tune: STORIES OF JESUS, 12 12 9 9; Frederic A. Challinor, 1866–1952

327 Deeper, Deeper

I pray that you may have the power to comprehend... what is the breadth and length and height and depth...
Ephesians 3:18–19

1. Deep - er, deep - er in the love of Je - sus Dai - ly let me
2. Deep - er, deep - er! bless - ed Ho - ly Spir - it, Take me deep - er
3. Deep - er, deep - er! tho' it cost hard tri - als, Deep - er let me
4. Deep - er, high - er, ev - 'ry day in Je - sus, Till all con - flict

go; High - er, high - er in the school of wis - dom,
still, Till my life is whol - ly lost in Je - sus,
go! Root - ed in the ho - ly love of Je - sus,
past, Finds me con - qu'ror, and in His own im - age

O deep - er yet, I

More of grace to know.
And His per - fect will.
Let me fruit - ful grow. O deep - er yet, I pray,
Per - fect - ed at last.

pray, And high - er ev - 'ry

deep - er yet, I pray, And high - er ev - 'ry day,

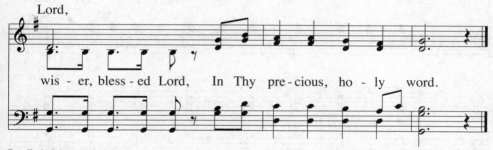

Text: Charles P. Jones, 1865–1949
Tune: DEEPER, 10 5 10 5 with refrain; Charles P. Jones, 1865–1949

328 Order My Steps

Our steps are made firm by the LORD, when he delights in our way.
Psalm 37:23

1. Or - der my steps in Your word, dear Lord,
2. Hum-bly I ask Thee, teach me Your will.
3. Bri - dle my tongue, let my words ed - i - fy, Let the

Lead me, guide me, ev - er - y day.
While You are work - ing, help me be still. Though
words of my mouth be ac - cept - a - ble in Thy sight. Take

Send Your a - noint - ing, Fa - ther, I pray.
Sa - tan is bus - y, God is real!
charge of my thoughts, both day and night.

Or - der my steps in Your word. Please,

or-der my steps in Your word. word. I want to walk

1.

2. *piano, ad lib.*

wor - thy.   My call - ing to ful - fill.

Please or - der my steps, Lord,   And I'll

do Your bless - ed will,   The world is ev - er

chang - ing,   but You are still the same.

If You or-der my steps,   I'll praise Your

name.   I want to walk

Text: Psalm 119:133, Glenn E. Burleigh
Tune: IN YOUR WORD, Irregular; Glenn E. Burleigh
© 1991, Glenn Burleigh (Burleigh Inspirations Music)

329 Is There a Word from the Lord?

*So the word of God spread. The number of disciples in Jerusalem increased rapidly,
and a large number of priests became obedient to the faith.*
Acts 6:7

Is there a word from the Lord? Send Your Word, send Your Word.

We need a word from the Lord. Send Your Word, send Your Word.

There is heal - ing in Your Word, de - liv-er-ance in Your Word, sal -

Text: Based on Jeremiah 37:17 and Psalm 107:20; Glenn E. Burleigh, 1949–2007
Tune: Glenn E. Burleigh, 1949–2007
© 1998, GIA Publications, Inc.

330 Wonderful Words of Life

How sweet are your words to my taste, sweeter than honey to my mouth!
Psalm 119:103

1. Sing them o - ver a - gain to me— Won-der - ful words of
2. Christ, the bless-ed One, gives to all Won-der - ful words of
3. Sweet - ly ech - o the gos - pel call— Won-der - ful words of

Life;   Let   me more of their beau - ty see—
Life;   Lis - ten well to the lov - ing call—
Life;   Of - fer par - don and peace to all—

Won-der - ful words of Life.   Words of life and
Won-der - ful words of Life.   All the won - drous
Won-der - ful words of Life.   Je - sus, on - ly

beau - ty,   Teach me faith and du - ty:
sto - ry,   Show - ing us His glo - ry:
Sav - ior,   Sanc - ti - fy for - ev - er:

Beau - ti - ful words, won - der - ful words,

Won - der - ful words of Life; Life.

1.

2.

Text: Philip P. Bliss, 1838–1876
Tune: WORDS OF LIFE, 8 6 8 6 66 with refrain, Philip P. Bliss, 1838–1876

331 Jesus Loves Me

As the Father has loved me, so I have loved you; abide in my love.
John 15:9

1. Je - sus loves me! this I know, For the Bi - ble
2. Je - sus loves me! He who died Heav-en's gates to
3. Je - sus loves me! loves me still, Tho' I'm ver - y
4. Je - sus loves me! He will stay Close be - side me

tells me so; Lit - tle ones to Him be - long,
o - pen wide! He will wash a - way my sin,
weak and ill; From His shin - ing throne on high,
all the way; If I love Him when I die,

They are weak, but He is strong.
Let His lit - tle child come in.
Comes to watch me where I lie. Yes, Je - sus loves me.
He will take me home on high.

Yes, Je-sus loves me. Yes, Je-sus loves me, for the Bi-ble tells me so.

Text: Anna B. Warner, 1820–1915
Tune: CHINA, 77 77 with refrain; William B. Bradbury, 1816–1868

Break Thou the Bread of Life 332

But he said, "Blessed rather are those who hear the word of God and obey it!"
Luke 11:28

1. Break Thou the bread of life, Dear Lord, to me,
2. Bless Thou the truth, dear Lord, To me, to me,
3. Teach me to live, dear Lord, On - ly for Thee,

As Thou did break the loaves Be - side the sea;
As Thou did bless the bread By Gal - i - lee;
As Thy dis - ci - ples lived In Gal - i - lee;

Be - yond the sa - cred page I seek Thee, Lord;
Then shall all bond - age cease, All fet - ters fall,
Then, all my strug - gles o'er, Then, vic - t'ry won,

My spir - it pants for Thee, O liv - ing word!
And I shall find my peace, My all in all.
I shall be - hold Thee, Lord, The liv - ing One.

Text: Mary A. Lathbury, 1841–1913
Tune: BREAD OF LIFE, 6 4 6 4 D; William F. Sherwin, 1826–1888

333 I Need You to Survive

...so in Christ we who are many form one body, and each member belongs to all the others.
Romans 12:5

I won't harm you with words from my mouth,

I love you, I need you to sur-vive.

D.S.

D.S.

Text: David Frazier
Tune: David Frazier
© God's Music, Inc.

The Church of Christ Cannot Be Bound 334

To him be glory in the church and in Christ Jesus throughout all generations, for ever and ever! Amen.
Ephesians 3:21

1. The Church of Christ can - not be bound By
2. True faith will o - pen up the door And
3. True love will not sit i - dly by When
4. If what we have we free - ly share To
5. The Church of Christ can - not be bound By

walls of wood or stone. Where char - i - ty and
step in - to the street. True serv - ice will seek
jus - tice is de - nied. True mer - cy hears the
meet our neigh - bor's need, Then we ex - tend the
walls of wood or stone. Where char - i - ty and

love are found, There can the Church be known.
out the poor And ask to wash their feet.
home - less cry And wel - comes them in - side.
Spir - it's care Through ev - 'ry self - less deed.
love are found, There can the Church be known.

Text: Adam M. L. Tice, b.1979, © 2009, GIA Publications, Inc.
Tune: McKEE, CM; African American; adapt. by Harry T. Burleigh, 1866–1949

335 Unity (Psalm 133:1)

How very good and pleasant it is when kindred live together in unity!
Psalm 133:1

Be - hold   how good   and how pleas - ant it is   for

kin - dred to dwell   to-geth-er in   u - ni-ty.   Be -

hold   how good and how pleas - ant it is   for kin - dred to

dwell to-geth-er in u – ni-ty. u –ni-ty.

U – ni-ty, u – ni-ty, Lord, we pray for

u – ni-ty. U – ni-ty,

u – ni-ty, Lord, we pray for u – ni-ty.

Text: Psalm 133:1, Glorraine Moone, © 1989. Published by Professionals for Christ Publications (BMI)
Tune: Glorraine Moone, © 1989; arr. by Dr. Daniel Mario Cason II. Published by Professionals for Christ Publications (BMI); adapt. by Valeria A. Foster,
© 2000, GIA Publications, Inc.

336 Renew Thy Church, Her Ministries Restore

No one after lighting a lamp puts it under the bushel basket, but on the lampstand, and it gives light to all in the house.
Matthew 5:15

1. Re - new Thy church, her min - is - tries re - store:
2. Teach us Thy Word, re - veal its truth di - vine;
3. Teach us to pray, for Thou art ev - er near;
4. Teach us to love, with strength of heart and mind,

Both to serve and a - dore. Make her a - gain as
On our path let it shine. Tell of Thy works, Thy
Thy still voice let us hear. Our souls are rest - less
Ev - 'ry - one, all man - kind. Break down old walls of

salt through-out the land, And as light from a stand.
might - y acts of grace; From each page show Thy face.
till they rest in Thee: This our glad des - ti - ny.
prej - u - dice and hate; Leave us not to our fate.

'Mid som - ber shad - ows of the night Where
As Thou hast loved us, sent Thy Son, And
Be - fore Thy pres - ence keep us still, That
As Thou hast loved and giv'n Thy life To

greed and ha - tred spread their blight, O send us forth with
our sal - va - tion now is won, O let our hearts with
we may find for us Thy will And seek Thy guid - ance
end hos - til - i - ty and strife, O share Thy grace from

pow'r en - dued: Help us, Lord, be re - newed!
love be stirred: Help us, Lord, know Thy Word!
ev - 'ry day: Teach us, Lord, how to pray!
heav'n a - bove: Teach us, Lord, how to love!

Text: Kenneth L. Cober, 1902–1993, © 1960, Kenneth Cober, renewed 1985, Judson Press
Tune: ALL IS WELL, 10 6 10 6 88 86; J. T. White's *Sacred Harp*

337 Blest Be the Tie that Binds

Above all, clothe yourselves with love, which binds everything together in perfect harmony.
Colossians 3:14

1. Blest be the tie that binds Our hearts in
2. Be - fore our Fa - ther's throne We pour our
3. We share each oth - er's woes, Each oth - er's
4. From sor - row, toil, and pain, And sin we

Chris - tian love; The fel - low - ship of
ar - dent prayers; Our fears, our hopes, our
bur - dens bear; And of - ten for each
shall be free; And per - fect love and

kin - dred minds Is like to that a - bove.
aims are one, Our com - forts and our cares.
oth - er flows The sym - pa - thiz - ing tear.
joy shall reign Through all e - ter - ni - ty.

Text: John Fawcett, 1740–1817
Tune: DENNIS, SM; John G. Nägeli, 1773–1836; arr. by Lowell Mason, 1792–1872

Enter In

Let us go to his dwelling place; let us worship at his footstool.
Psalm 132:6

En - ter in, en - ter in,

all God's peo - ple en - ter in.

En - ter in, en - ter in,

all God's peo - ple en - ter in. Let us

wor - ship in this ho - ly place;

En - ter in, en - ter in. Let us

bow be - fore His throne of grace. Oh,

en - ter in, en - ter in. Oh,

en - ter in, en - ter in,

en - ter in, en - ter in. Oh,

Last time

Text: Joseph Pace II
Tune: Joseph Pace II
© 2004, arr. © 2010, Integrity's Praise! Music and Pace's Vision Music (admin. by Integrity's Praise! Music)

339

For All the Saints

Remember your leaders,... consider the outcome of their way of life, and imitate their faith.
Hebrews 13:7

1. For all the saints who from their la-bors rest, All
2. You were their rock, their for - tress and their might;
3. O may Your sol - diers, faith - ful, true and bold,
4. O blest com - mun - ion, fam - i - ly di - vine!
5. And when the strife is fierce, the war-fare long,
6. The gold - en eve - ning bright-ens in the west;
7. But then there breaks a yet more glo-rious day: The
8. From earth's wide bounds, from o - cean's far-thest coast, Through

who by faith be - fore the world con - fessed, Your
You, Lord, their Cap - tain in the well-fought fight;
Fight as the saints who no - bly fought of old, And
We fee - bly strug - gle, they in glo - ry shine; Yet
Steals on the ear the dis - tant tri - umph song, And
Soon, soon to faith - ful war - riors comes their rest;
saints tri - um - phant rise in bright ar - ray; The
gates of pearl streams in the count - less host,

Text: William W. How, 1823–1897
Tune: SINE NOMINE, 10 10 10 with alleluias; Ralph Vaughan Williams, 1872–1958

340 The Church's One Foundation

...you are Peter, and on this rock I will build my church, and the gates of Hades will not prevail against it.
Matthew 16:18

1. The Church-'s one foun - da - tion Is Je - sus Christ her Lord, She is His new cre - a - tion By wa - ter and the word; From heav'n He came and sought her To be His ho - ly bride; With His own blood He
2. E - lect from ev - 'ry na - tion, Yet one o'er all the earth, Her char - ter of sal - va - tion, One Lord, one faith, one birth; One ho - ly name she bless - es, Par - takes one ho - ly food, And to one hope she
3. 'Mid toil and trib - u - la - tion, And tu - mult of her war, She waits the con - sum - ma - tion Of peace for ev - er - more; Till with the vi - sion glo - rious, Her long - ing eyes are blest, And the great Church vic -
4. Yet she on earth hath un - ion With God, the Three in One, And mys - tic sweet com - mun - ion With those whose rest is won; O hap - py ones and ho - ly! Lord, give us grace that we Like them, the meek and

bought	her,	And	for	her	life	He	died.
press -	es,	With	ev -	'ry	grace	en -	dued.
to -	rious	Shall	be	the	Church	at	rest.
low -	ly,	On	high	may	dwell	with	Thee.

Text: Samuel J. Stone, 1839–1900
Tune: AURELIA, 7 6 7 6 D; Samuel S. Wesley, 1810–1876

The Church's One Foundation   341

Alternate text:

1. The Church's one foundation is Christ, God's own true Child
   In whom the whole creation is freed and reconciled
   To bring the Church together, Christ lived and freely died;
   Raised up by God, forever, Christ lives to be our Guide.

2. The world and all the nations, created to be one
   Can live in sweet communion with God and God's own Son
   When we who say we love Him begin to live and BE
   A people with great freedom to gain through harmony.

3. Where are the gifts we're seeking if not in our own hearts?
   To share, to offer others so they may know their parts
   In working as the chosen, whose heritage and hopes
   Are in the great Creator, our Christ, our Lord who knows.

4. Let's offer all our talents and wants for setting free
   The homeless and the hungry, the hurting you and me
   Remembering tomorrow, the Son will rise and shine
   To give us Light and helpers to serve Him while there's time.

Text: Rev. Pamela June Anderson, D. Min., © 1991

342

As We Enter

My house shall be called a house of prayer for all the nations.
Mark 11:17

Lord, we come in-to Your pres - ence leav-ing

world - ly cares be-hind. Lift-ing hands in ho - ly rev-

'rence for Your pre - cious joy di - vine. You have

giv - en us the strength we need to face an - oth - er day,

1.
and we praise You as we en-ter in-to this place.

2.
Lord, we en-ter in-to this place.

We praise You as we

en-ter in-to this place.

Text: Stephen F. Key
Tune: Stephen F. Key
© 1998, StepKey Music

343   We Gather Together

We your people...will give thanks to you forever; from generation to generation we will recount your praise.
Psalm 79:13

1. We gath - er to - geth - er to ask the Lord's bless - ing;
2. Be - side us to guide us, our God with us join - ing,
3. We all do ex - tol You our lead - er tri - um - phant,

He chas - tens and has - tens His will to make known;
Whose king - dom calls all to the love which en - dures.
And pray that You still our de - fend - er will be.

The wick - ed op - press - ing now cease from dis - tress - ing:
So from the be - gin - ning the fight we were win - ning:
Let Your con - gre - ga - tion es - cape trib - u - la - tion:

Sing prais - es to His name; He for - gets not His own.
You, Lord, were at our side; all glo - ry be Yours!
Your name be ev - er praised! O Lord, make us free!

Text: *Wilt heden nu treden*, Netherlands folk hymn; tr. by Theodore Baker, 1851–1934, alt.
Tune: KREMSER, 12 11 12 11; *Neder-landtsch Gedenckclanck*, 1626; harm. by Edward Kremser, 1838–1914

Living in the Imagination of God   344

So we fix our eyes not on what is unseen. For what is seen is temporary, but what is unseen is eternal.
2 Corinthians 4:18

Come where God gives us hope. We must stand and tell the good - ness of His love.

Share in God's dream, where we show grace to all peo - ple. We are

living in the im- ag- i- na- tion of God.

Eyes have not seen, nor

ears have heard what God has pre- pared for you and

me. Jour- ney in - to wor- ship and

then you'll see we are liv - ing in the im -

1.

ag - i - na - tion of God.

2.

Repeat as desired

God, of God.

Repeat as desired

Text: Cecilia Olusola Tribble
Tune: Cecilia Olusola Tribble
© 2007, Cecilia Olusola Tribble

345

Just as I Am

He cried out, "Let anyone who is thirsty come to me, and let the one who believes in me drink."
John 7:37–38

1. Just as I am, with - out one plea,
2. Just as I am, and wait - ing not
3. Just as I am, though tossed a - bout,
4. Just as I am, Thou wilt re - ceive,

But that Thy blood was shed for me,
To rid my soul of one dark blot;
With man - y a con - flict, man - y a doubt;
Wilt wel - come, par - don, cleanse, re - lieve;

And that Thou bidst me come to Thee, O
To Thee, whose blood can cleanse each spot, O
Fight - ings with - in and fears with - out, O
Be - cause Thy prom - ise I be - lieve, O

Lamb of God, I come.

Just as I am, Just as I am,
Just as I am, Just as I
Just as I am, Just as I am,

Just as I am, I come.
am, as I am, I come.
Just as I am, I come.

Text: Charlotte Elliott, 1789–1871
Tune: JUST AS I AM, 888 6 with refrain; adapt. from Gaul's *The Holy City* by Evelyn Simpson-Curenton, b.1953, © 2000, GIA Publications, Inc.

346

Just as I Am

He cried out, "Let anyone who is thirsty come to me, and let the one who believes in me drink."
John 7:37–38

1. Just as I am, with-out one plea,
2. Just as I am, and wait-ing not
3. Just as I am, though tossed a-bout
4. Just as I am— poor, wretch-ed, blind;
5. Just as I am— Thou wilt re-ceive,

But that Thy blood was shed for me,
To rid my soul of one deep blot,
With man-y a con-flict, man-y a doubt,
Sight, rich-es, heal-ing of the mind,
Wilt wel-come, par-don, cleanse, re-lieve,

And that Thou bidd'st me come to Thee,
To Thee whose blood can cleanse each spot,
Fight-ings and fears with-in, with-out,
Yea, all I need in Thee to find,
Be-cause Thy prom-ise I be-lieve,

O Lamb of God, I come! I come!

Text: Charlotte Elliott, 1789–1871
Tune: WOODWORTH, LM; William B. Bradbury, 1816–1868

Come to Jesus

347

The Lord is... patient with you, not wanting any to perish, but all to come to repentance.
2 Peter 3:9

1. Come to Je - sus, Come to Je - sus, Come to
2. He will save you, He will save you, He will

Je - sus just now, just now. Come to
save you just now, just now. He will

Je - sus, Come to Je - sus just now!
save you, He will save you just now!

3. He is able,...
4. He is willing,...
5. Come, confess Him,...

6. Come, obey Him,...
7. He will hear you,...
8. He'll forgive you,...

9. He will cleanse you,...
10. Jesus loves you,...
11. Only trust Him,...

Text: Traditional
Tune: COME TO JESUS, 4 4 8 4 6; traditional; arr. by Evelyn Simpson-Curenton, b.1953, © 2000, GIA Publications, Inc.

348 Jesus Is Calling

The Teacher is here and is calling for you.
John 11:28

1. Je - sus is ten - der - ly call - ing thee home—
2. Je - sus is call - ing the wea - ry to rest—
3. Je - sus is wait - ing, O come to Him now—
4. Je - sus is plead-ing, O list to His voice—

Call - ing to - day, call - ing to - day;
Call - ing to - day, call - ing to - day;
Wait - ing to - day, wait - ing to - day;
Hear Him to - day, hear Him to - day;

Why from the sun - shine of love wilt thou roam
Bring Him thy bur - den and thou shalt be blest—
Come with thy sins, at His feet low - ly bow—
They who be - lieve on His name shall re - joice—

Far - ther and far - ther a - way?
He will not turn thee a - way.
Come, and no long - er de - lay.
Quick - ly a - rise and a - way.

Call - ing to - day, Call - ing to -

Call - ing, call-ing to - day, to - day, Call - ing, call - ing to -

day, Je - sus is call - ing, Is

day, to - day; Je - sus is ten - der - ly call - ing to - day, Is

ten - der - ly call - ing to - day.

Text: Fanny J. Crosby, 1820–1915
Tune: CALLING TODAY, 10 8 10 7 with refrain; George C. Stebbins, 1846–1945

349 I Am Praying for You

I am asking... on behalf of those whom you gave me, because they are yours.
John 17:9

1. I have a Savior, He's pleading in glory, A dear, loving Savior, though earth-friends be few; And now He is watching in tenderness o'er me, But, oh, that my Savior were your Savior, too.

2. I have a Father; to me He has given A hope for eternity, blessed and true; And soon will He call me to meet Him in heaven, But, oh, that He'd let me bring you with me, too!

3. I have a robe: 'tis resplendent in whiteness, Awaiting in glory my wondering view; Oh, when I receive it all shining in brightness, Dear friend, could I see you receiving one, too!

4. When Jesus has found you, tell others the story, That my loving Savior is your Savior, too; Then pray that your Savior may bring them to glory And prayer will be answered—'twas answered for you!

For you I am pray - ing, For you I am pray - ing, For
you I am pray - ing, I'm pray - ing for you.

Text: S. O'Malley Cluff
Tune: I AM PRAYING FOR YOU, 11 11 12 11 with refrain; Ira D. Sankey, 1840–1908; arr. by Valeria A. Foster, © 2000, GIA Publications, Inc.

350

We Offer Christ

...we are slaves not under the old written code but in the new life of the Spirit.
Romans 7:6

We of-fer Christ to you, oh, my broth-er, We of-fer Christ to you, oh, my sis-ter. He will give you brand new life Through life a-bun-dant-ly; Oh come, come on to Christ.

Text: Joel Britton, © 1995, Mo'Berries Music (ASCAP) / Y'Shua Publishing (ASCAP)
Tune: Joel Britton, © 1995, Mo'Berries Music (ASCAP) / Y'Shua Publishing (ASCAP); arr. by Valeria A. Foster, © 2000, GIA Publications, Inc.

Give Your Life to Christ

351

For you have died, and your life is hidden with Christ in God.
Colossians 3:3

1. Come to - day, don't de - lay. Make Him your choice.
2. If you come to Him right now, He'll see you through.
3. Cast your cares up - on the Lord. He'll bear them all.

Je - sus wants to save you. Give your life to Christ.
He will nev - er fail you. Give your life to Christ.
Je - sus will pro - tect you. Give your life to Christ.

Give Him all your bur - dens. Give them all to Je - sus.

Je - sus wants to save you; you should give your life to Christ.

Text: Michael Kenneth Ross
Tune: GIVE YOUR LIFE, 6 4 6 5 with refrain; Michael Kenneth Ross
© 1995, MKR Music

352 Plenty Good Room

In my Father's house there are many dwelling places.
John 14:2

Plen - ty good room, plen - ty good room,

plen - ty good room in my Fa - ther's king - dom,

Plen - ty good room, plen - ty good room, just

Last time

choose your seat and sit down. *Last time*

Verses

1. I would not be a sin - ner,
2. I would not be a li - ar, I'll
3. I would not be a back - slid - er,

tell you the rea - son why; cause

if my Lord should call on me I

would-n't be read - y to die.

D.C.

Text: Negro Spiritual
Tune: Negro Spiritual; arr. by Joseph Joubert, b.1958, © 2000, GIA Publications, Inc.

353 Somebody's Knockin'

Listen! I am standing at the door, knocking…
Revelation 3:20

Some - bod - y's knock - in' at your door; Some - bod - y's

knock - in' at your door; O sin - ner, why don't you

an - swer? Some - bod - y's knock - in' at your door.

Solo:

1. Knocks like Je - sus,
2. Can't you hear Him?
3. Je - sus calls you,
4. Can't you trust Him?

All:

Some - bod - y's knock - in' at your

Solo:
All:

door; Knocks like Je - sus, Some-bod - y's knock-in' at your
Can't you hear Him?
Je - sus calls you,
Can't you trust Him?

door. O sin - ner, why don't you

an - swer? Some-bod - y's knock-in' at your door.

Text: Negro Spiritual
Tune: SOMEBODY'S KNOCKIN', Irregular; Negro Spiritual; harm. by Richard Proulx, 1937–2010, alt., © 1986, GIA Publications, Inc.

354 'Tis the Ol' Ship of Zion

Walk about Zion, go all around it... that you may tell the next generation that this is God, our God forever and ever.
Psalm 48:12–14

Verse 1
rubato

1. 'Tis the ol' ship of Zi - on, 'Tis the

ol' ship of Zi - on, 'Tis the ol' ship of

Zi - on; Get on board, get on board!

Verses 2-4

2. It has land-ed man-y a thou-sand, It has
3. King Je - sus is the cap - tain, King
4. Hum

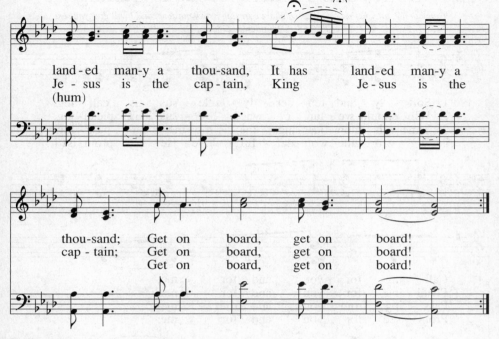

land-ed man-y a thou-sand, It has land-ed man-y a
Je - sus is the cap-tain, King Je - sus is the
(hum)

thou-sand; Get on board, get on board!
cap - tain; Get on board, get on board!
Get on board, get on board!

Text: Negro Spiritual
Tune: OL' SHIP OF ZION, 7 7 7 6; Negro Spiritual; arr. by Stanley Thurston, © 2000, GIA Publications, Inc.

355   Softly and Tenderly Jesus Is Calling

Come to me, all you that are weary and are carrying heavy burdens, and I will give you rest.
Matthew 11:28

Come home, come home, come home, come home, come home, Ye who are
come home, come home, come home,

wea-ry, come home; Ear - nest-ly, ten - der - ly,

Je-sus is call-ing— Call-ing, "O sin-ner, come home!"

Text: Will L. Thompson, 1847–1909
Tune: THOMPSON, 11 7 11 7 with refrain; Will L. Thompson, 1847–1909

356

He's So Real

Many Samaritans from that city believed in him because of the woman's testimony.
John 4:39

Refrain

He's so real, real in my soul to-day! He has

washed all of my sins a-way. Je - sus' love just

bub - bles o - ver in my soul, in my soul.

Verses

1. Some peo - ple doubt the Lord.
2. He's done so much for me.

They   don't be - lieve   in His word;
One   day He   set   me   free.

They   try   to make   you
And,   and now I

think   that God is   dead.
want   the world to   know.

Text: Charles H. Nicks, Jr., 1941–1988, © 1975, Bridgeport Music, Inc.
Tune: Charles H. Nicks, Jr., 1941–1988, © 1975, Bridgeport Music, Inc.; arr. by Kenneth W. Louis, b.1956, © 2006, GIA Publications, Inc.

357   An Evening Prayer

Have mercy on me, O God… Wash me thoroughly from my iniquity, and cleanse me from my sin.
Psalm 51:1–2

1. If I have wound-ed an-y soul to-day,
2. If I have ut-tered i-dle words or vain,
3. If I have been per-verse, or hard, or cold,
4. For-give the sins I have con-fessed to Thee;

If I have caused one foot to go a-stray,
If I have turned a-side from want or pain,
If I have longed for shel-ter in the fold,
For-give the se-cret sins I do not see;

If I have walked in my own will-ful way,
Lest I of-fend some oth-er through the strain,
When Thou hast giv-en me some fort to hold,
O guide me, love me, and my keep-er be.

1. Dear Lord, for-give! (for-give!)
2. A-men. (A-men.)

Text: C. Maude Battersby, 1856–1932
Tune: EVENING, 10 10 10 4; Charles Gabriel, 1856–1932

If You Live Right

358

Blessed are the pure in heart, for they will see God.
Matthew 5:8

1. If you live right, heav-en be-longs to you, If you live right, heav-en be-longs to you, If you live right, heav-en be-longs to you. O, heav-en be-longs to you.

2. If you walk right...
3. If you talk right...
4. If you pray right...
5. Treat your neighbor right...

Text: Congregational Praise Song
Tune: Congregational Praise Song; arr. by James Abbington, b.1960, © 2000, GIA Publications, Inc.

359

O Happy Day

Rejoice in the Lord always; again I will say, Rejoice.
Philippians 4:4

1. O hap - py day that fixed my choice On Thee, my
2. O hap - py bond that seals my vows To Him who
3. 'Tis done, the great trans - ac - tion's done— I am my
4. Now rest, my long - di - vid - ed heart, Fixed on this

Sav - ior and my God! Well may this glow - ing heart re -
mer - its all my love! Let cheer - ful an - thems fill His
Lord's and He is mine; He drew me, and I fol - lowed
bliss - ful cen - ter, rest; Nor ev - er from my Lord de -

joice And tell its rap - tures all a - broad.
house, While to that sa - cred shrine I move.
on, Charmed to con - fess the voice di - vine.
part, With Him of ev - 'ry good pos - sessed.

Hap - py day, hap - py day, When Je - sus

washed my sins a - way! He taught me how to watch and

pray And live re - joic - ing ev - 'ry day; Hap - py

day, hap - py day, When Je - sus washed my sins a - way!

Text: Philip Doddridge, 1702–1751
Tune: HAPPY DAY, LM with refrain; Edward F. Rimbault, 1816–1876

360 I Will Arise

Whoever follows me will never walk in darkness but will have the light of life.
John 8:12

in His arms; In the arms of my dear

Sav - ior, O there are ten thous-sand charms.

Text: Verses, Joseph Hart, 1712–1768, *Hymns Composed on Various Subjects*, 1759, alt.; refrain anonymous
Tune: RESTORATION, 8 7 8 7 with refrain; Walker's *Southern Harmony*, 1835

This tune can also be used for
What a Friend We Have in Jesus *and*
Guide Me, O Thou Great Jehovah.

361

Jesus Paid It All

For the Son of Man came… to give his life a ransom for many.
Mark 10:45

1. I hear the Sav - ior say, "Your strength in - deed is
2. Lord, now in - deed I find Your pow'r, and Yours a -
3. For noth - ing good have I Where - by Your grace to
4. And when be - fore the throne I stand in Him com -

small! Child of weak - ness, watch and pray,
lone, Can change the lep - er's spots
claim— I'll wash my gar - ments white
plete, "Je - sus died my soul to save,"

Find in Me your all in all."
And melt the heart of stone.
In the blood of Cal-v'ry's Lamb. Je - sus paid it
My lips shall still re - peat.

all, All to Him I owe; Sin had left a crim-son

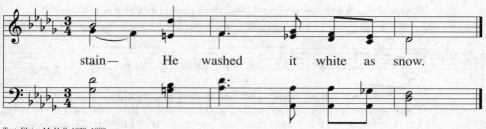

stain— He washed it white as snow.

Text: Elvina M. Hall, 1820–1889
Tune: ALL TO CHRIST, 6 6 7 7 with refrain; John T. Grape, 1835–1915

362 Christ Is All

In that renewal there is no longer Greek and Jew,... slave and free; but Christ is all and in all!
Colossians 3:11

1. I don't pos-sess hous-es or lands, fine clothes or jew'l-ry,
2. There are some folk who look and long for this world's rich-es,
3. Yes Christ is all, means more to me than this world's rich-es,

Sor-rows and cares in this old world my lot seems to
There are some folk who look for pow'r, po-si-tion
He is my sight, my guid-ing light thro' path-less

be, But I have a Christ who paid the price way back on
too, But I have a Christ all in my life, this makes me
seas, Yes it's might-y nice to own a Christ who will my

Cal-v'ry, And Christ is all, all and all this world to
hap-py, For Christ is all, all and all this world to
friend be, Yes Christ is all, all and all this world to

Text: Kenneth Morris, 1917–1988
Tune: CHRIST IS ALL, 13 13 14 11 with refrain; Kenneth Morris, 1917–1988; arr. by Evelyn Simpson-Curenton, b.1953
© 1944 (renewed), arr. © 2011, Unichappell Music, Inc.

363 Come Out the Wilderness

He went into all the region around the Jordan, proclaiming a baptism of repentance for the forgiveness of sins.
Luke 3:3

1. Tell me, how did you feel when you come out the wil-der-ness, come out the wil-der-ness, come out the wil-der-ness. Did you how did you feel when you lean-ing on the Lord. I am lean-ing on the

2. Did you get bap - tized when you come out the wil-der-ness, come out the wil-der-ness, come out the wil-der-ness. Did you get bap - tized when you come out the wil-der-ness, lean-ing on the Lord. I am lean-ing on the

3. Did your soul feel hap-py when you come out the wil-der-ness, come out the wil-der-ness, come out the wil-der-ness. Did your soul feel hap-py when you lean-ing on the Lord. I am lean-ing on the

Lord, I am lean-ing on the Lord. I am lean-ing on the Lord who died on Cal-va-ry.

Text: Negro Spiritual
Tune: Negro Spiritual; arr. by Evelyn Simpson-Curenton, b.1953, © 2000, GIA Publications, Inc.

364

King Jesus Is a-Listenin'

But truly God has listened; he has given heed to the words of my prayer.
Psalm 66:19

Refrain

King Jesus is a-lis-ten-in' all day long, King Jesus is a-lis-ten-in' all day long, King Jesus is a lis-ten-in' all day long, To hear some sin-ner pray.

Verses

1. That Gos-pel train is com-in', A-rum-blin' through the
2. I know I been con-vert-ed, I ain't gon' make no a -

lan',   I   hear them wheels a - hum-min',   Get
larm,   For my soul   is bound for   glo - ry,   And the

D.C.

read   -   y   for   that   train!
dev - il   can't   do   me   no   harm.

Text: Traditional
Tune: KING JESUS, 7 6 7 6 with refrain; Negro Spiritual; arr. by Carl Haywood, b.1949, from *The Haywood Collection of Negro Spirituals*, © 1992

365

New Born Again

Very truly, I tell you, no one can see the kingdom of God without being born from above.
John 3:3

Optional solo:

1. I found free grace and dy - ing love,
2. I know my Lord has set me free, I'm
3. My Sav - ior died for you and me,

new-born a - gain. Been long time talk - ing 'bout my

tri-als here be-low. free grace, free grace,

Oh, there's free grace, free grace,

free grace, sin - ner. free grace,

free grace, sin - ner. Oh, there's free grace,

free grace, I'm new-born a - gain.
yes, I'm   Oh, I'm

so glad, so glad I'm new-born a - gain. Been

long time talk-ing 'bout my tri - als here be - low.

Text: Negro Spiritual
Tune: Negro Spiritual; arr. by Roland M. Carter, b. 1942, © 1999, Mar-Vel

366 I Know the Lord Has Laid His Hands on Me

You hem me in, behind and before, and lay your hand upon me.
Psalm 139:5

Verses

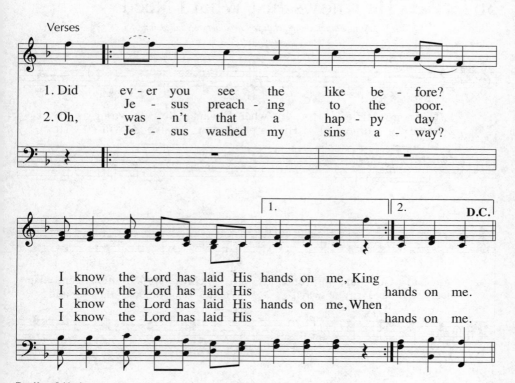

1. Did ev - er you see the like be - fore?
   Je - sus preach - ing to the poor.
2. Oh, was - n't that a hap - py day
   Je - sus washed my sins a - way?

I know the Lord has laid His hands on me, King
I know the Lord has laid His hands on me.
I know the Lord has laid His hands on me, When
I know the Lord has laid His hands on me.

Text: Negro Spiritual
Tune: HANDS ON ME, Irregular with refrain; Negro Spiritual; arr. by Valeria A. Foster, © 2000, GIA Publications, Inc

367 He Knows Just What I Need

... your Father knows what you need before you ask him.
Matthew 6:8

1. There are times when I want to do wrong, so I
2. Some - times in His per - mis - sive will He

go to God in prayer. He com - forts me and He
lets me have my way. When I've fouled up and

guides me a - long. He knows just what I need.
can't re - treat He's there to guard my stay.

He knows just what I need, He a - lone de - cides for

me. Tho' temp-ta - tions come, He is al - ways there, He knows just what I need. He knows just what I need, He knows just what I need.

Text: Dr. Robert J. Fryson, 1944–1994
Tune: HE KNOWS, Irregular with refrain; Dr. Robert J. Fryson, 1944–1994
© 1984, Bob Jay Music Co.

368

Just Let Him In

Listen! I am standing at the door, knocking; if you hear my voice and open the door, I will come in to you...
Revelation 3:20

He'll take a - way all of your heart-aches, He'll take a -

way all of your sins, He'll help you to bear all of your

bur - dens if you will on - ly let Him in. When sin and

grief have filled your soul, just tell my Je - sus, He'll make you

whole. He'll take a - way all, all of your bur - dens, just let Him in.

Text: S. Boddie, ©
Tune: S. Boddie, ©; arr. by Bill Cummings, © 2000, GIA Publications, Inc.

Come, Bring Your Burdens to God/   369
Woza Nomthwalo Wakho

Come to me, all you who are weary and burdened, and I will give you rest.
Matthew 11:28

Come, bring your bur-dens, oh,

Come, bring your bur-dens to God,   come, bring your
Wo - za nom-thwa-lo wa-kho,   wo - za nom-

come, bring your bur - dens,   oh,   come, bring your bur-dens,

bur - dens to God,   come, bring your bur - dens to God   for
thwa - lo wa-kho,   wo - za nom-thwa - lo wa-kho   U-

To repeat   *Last time*

Je-sus will nev-er say no.

Je-sus will nev-er say   no.   Come, bring your   no.
ye-s's-ka-so-za-thi hayi.   Wo - za nom - hayi.

African phonetics: Woh-zah nohm-thwah-loh wah-khoh, U-yehs skah-soh-zah-thee hahyee

Text: South African; tr. by Barbara Clark, Mairi Munro, and Martine Stemerick, © 2008, Iona Community, GIA Publications, Inc., agent
Tune: South African melody; arr. by Welile Sigabi, © 2008, Iona Community, GIA Publications, Inc., agent

370

I Am All I Am

Do not conform any longer to the pattern of this world, but be transformed by the renewing of your mind.
Romans 12:2

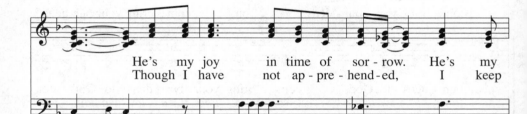

1. I am all I am be-cause of Christ in my
2. Thank God I have changed; noth-ing is the

life. I am all I am be-cause of Him.
same. The Lord helped me make a brand new start.

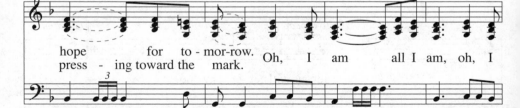

He's my joy in time of sor-row. He's my
Though I have not ap-pre-hend-ed, I keep

hope for to-mor-row. Oh, I am all I am, oh, I
press - ing toward the mark.

am all I am, oh, I am all I am be-cause of Christ.

Text: Margaret Pleasant Douroux, b.1941
Tune: Margaret Pleasant Douroux, b.1941
© 1984, Rev. Earl Pleasant Publishing

He's Blessing Me

371

I do all this for the sake of the gospel, that I may share in its blessings.
1 Corinthians 9:23

Refrain

He's bless-ing me o-ver and o-ver a-gain.

He's bless-ing me right here where I stand.

Ev-'ry time I turn a-round He's

mak-ing a way some-how. O-ver and o-ver a-gain

Last time

He's bless-ing me.

Verses

Solo:

1. The Lord is bless-ing me, bless-ing me right now.
2. He's in my walk, oh yes, the Lord is bless-ing me.

The Lord is bless-ing me,
He's in my talk, oh yes, the

mak-ing a way some-how. You may not be a-ble, be
Lord is bless-ing me. I looked at my hands and

a - ble to see
they looked new.

just what the Lord is
I looked at my feet and

do - ing for me.
they did too.

All:
O - ver and o - ver a - gain
O - ver and o - ver a - gain

He's bless-ing me.
He's bless-ing me.

Solo:
He's bless-ing me.
He's bless-ing me.

D.C.

D.C.

Text: Norris O. Garner
Tune: Norris O. Garner
© 1999, Norris Garner/BMI

372 He's So Freely Passing Out Blessings

From the fullness of his grace we have all received one blessing after another.
John 1:16

1. He's so free - ly pass-ing out bless-ings each day.
2. He's so free - ly pass-ing out bless-ings each day.
3. He's so free - ly pass-ing out bless-ings each day.

Faith - ful - ly He's send-ing a bless-ing my way;
Touch-ing all He sees a - long His way;
An - sw'ring prayers to Him that I have prayed;

More than I have room for, more than I can see.
Al - ways think-ing of me, al - ways bless-ing me.
He knows I'm not wor-thy, yet He bless-es me.

1., 2.

He's so free-ly pass-ing out bless-ings for me.

me. Ev-'ry day He's bless-ing me. He's

bless-ing me. He's bless-ing me. bless-ing me.

He's so free-ly pass-ing out bless-ings for me.

Text: Damian D. Price
Tune: Damian D. Price
© 2002, Damian D. Price and Price-n-Praise Publishing

373 Can't Nobody Do Me like Jesus

But by the grace of God I am what I am, and his grace toward me has not been in vain.
1 Corinthians 15:10

1. Can't no - bod - y
2. Healed my bod - y;
3. Picked me up and

do me like Je - sus. Can't no -
told me to run on. Healed my
turned me a - round. Oh, Picked me

bod - y do me like the Lord.
bod - y; told me to run.
up and turned me a - round.

Can't no - bod - y do me like Je - sus.
Healed my bod - y; told me to run on.
Picked me up and turned me a - round. Oh,

He's my friend!

He's my friend!

Text: Andraé Crouch, b.1942
Tune: HEALING, 9 9 9 3; Andraé Crouch, b.1942; arr. by Nolan Williams, Jr., b.1969
© 1982, Bud John Songs, admin. at EMICMGPublishing.com

374   Satisfied with Jesus

And my God will fully satisfy every need of yours according to his riches in glory in Christ Jesus.
Philippians 4:19

1. I am sat-is-fied with Je - sus,
2. He is with me in my tri - als,
3. I can hear the voice of Je - sus,
4. When my work on earth is end - ed,

He has done so much for me: He has suf-fered to re -
Best of friends of all is He; I can al-ways count on
Call-ing out so plead-ing - ly, "Go and win the lost and
And I cross the mys - tic sea, Oh, that I could hear Him

deem me, He has died to set me free.
Je - sus, Can He al-ways count on me?
stray - ing"; Is He sat - is - fied with me?
say - ing, "I am sat - is - fied with thee."

I am sat - is - fied, I am sat-is-fied, I am sat-is-fied with

Je - sus, But the ques - tion comes to me, As I think of Cal-va-ry, Is my Sav-ior sat - is - fied with me?

Text: B. B. McKinney, 1886–1952
Tune: ROUTH, 8 7 8 7 with refrain; B. B. McKinney, 1886–1952
© 1926, 1953, Broadman Press

375   The Lily of the Valley

It is I, Jesus… I am the root and the descendant of David, the bright morning star.
Revelation 22:16

1. I have found a friend in Je - sus— He's
2. He all my grief has tak - en and
3. He will nev - er, nev - er leave me nor

ev - 'ry - thing to me, He's the fair - est of ten
all my sor - rows borne, In temp - ta - tion He's my
yet for - sake me here, While I live by faith and

thou - sand to my soul; The Lil - y of the
strong and might - y tow'r; I have all for Him for -
do His bless - ed will; A wall of fire a -

Refrain: Lil - y of the

Val - ley— in Him a - lone I see All I
sak - en and all my i - dols torn From my
bout me, I've noth - ing now to fear— With His

Val - ley, the Bright and Morn - ing Star, He's the

need to cleanse and make me ful - ly whole.
heart, and now He keeps me by His pow'r.
man - na He my hun - gry soul shall fill.

great - est of ten thou - sand to my soul.

In sor - row He's my com - fort, in trou - ble He's my stay,
Tho' all the world for - sake me and Sa - tan tempt me sore,
Then sweep - ing up to glo - ry I'll see His bless - ed face,

D.S.

He tells me ev - 'ry care on Him to roll; He's the
Thru Je - sus I shall safe - ly reach the goal; He's the
Where riv - ers of de - light shall ev - er roll; He's the

Hal - le - lu - jah!

Text: Charles W. Fry, 1837–1882
Tune: SALVATIONIST, Irregular; William S. Hays, 1837–1907; adapt. by Charles W. Fry, 1837–1882

376 Just a Little Talk with Jesus

Beloved, pray for us.
1 Thessalonians 5:25

1. I once was lost in sin But Je-sus took me in,
2. Some-times my path seems drear, With-out a ray of cheer,
3. I may have doubts and fears, My eyes be filled with tears,

And then a lit-tle light from heav-en filled my soul;
And then a cloud of doubt may hide the light of day;
But Je-sus is a friend who watch-es day and night;

It bathed my heart in love And wrote my name a-bove,
The mists of sin may rise And hide the star-ry skies,
I go to Him in prayer, He knows my ev-'ry care,

And just a lit-tle talk with Je-sus made me whole.
But just a lit-tle talk with Je-sus clears the way.
And just a lit-tle talk with Je-sus makes it right.

Text: Cleavant Derricks, 1910–1977
Tune: JUST A LITTLE TALK, 66 12 66 12 with refrain; Cleavant Derricks, 1910–1977
© 1937, Bridge Building Music (BMI)

377 The Solid Rock

...For they drank from the spiritual rock that followed them, and the rock was Christ.
1 Corinthians 10:4

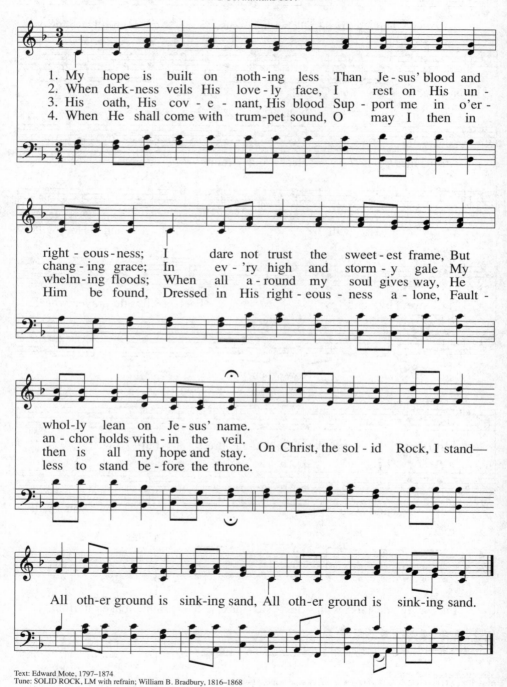

1. My hope is built on noth-ing less Than Je-sus' blood and
2. When dark-ness veils His love-ly face, I rest on His un-
3. His oath, His cov - e - nant, His blood Sup - port me in o'er -
4. When He shall come with trum-pet sound, O may I then in

right - eous-ness; I dare not trust the sweet-est frame, But
chang - ing grace; In ev - 'ry high and storm - y gale My
whelm-ing floods; When all a - round my soul gives way, He
Him be found, Dressed in His right - eous - ness a - lone, Fault -

whol-ly lean on Je - sus' name.
an - chor holds with - in the veil.
then is all my hope and stay.   On Christ, the sol - id Rock, I stand—
less to stand be - fore the throne.

All oth-er ground is sink-ing sand, All oth-er ground is sink-ing sand.

Text: Edward Mote, 1797–1874
Tune: SOLID ROCK, LM with refrain; William B. Bradbury, 1816–1868

Only Trust Him

Trust in the LORD forever, for in the LORD God you have an everlasting rock.
Isaiah 26:4

1. Come, ev-'ry soul by sin op-pressed— There's mer - cy with the Lord, And He will sure - ly give you rest By trust - ing in His word.
2. For Je - sus shed His pre - cious blood Rich bless - ings to be - stow; Plunge now in - to the crim - son flood That wash - es white as snow.
3. Yes, Je - sus is the Truth, the Way, That leads you in - to rest; Be - lieve in Him with - out de - lay And you are ful - ly blest.

Refrain

On - ly trust Him, on - ly trust Him, On - ly trust Him now; He will save you, He will save you, He will save you now.

Text: John H. Stockton, 1813–1877
Tune: ONLY TRUST HIM, CM with refrain; John H. Stockton, 1813–1877

379   I Can Do All Things through Christ

I can do all things through him who strengthens me.
Philippians 4:13

me,   strength - ens   me.

Text: Elbernita "Twinkie" Clark
Tune: Elbernita "Twinkie" Clark
© 1980, Bridgeport Music, Inc.

380   Leaning on the Everlasting Arms

Upon you I have leaned from my birth; it was you who took me from my mother's womb.
Psalm 71:6

1. What a fel-low-ship, what a joy di-vine,
2. O how sweet to walk in this pil-grim way,
3. What have I to dread, what have I to fear,

Lean - ing on the ev - er - last - ing arms;
Lean - ing on the ev - er - last - ing arms;
Lean - ing on the ev - er - last - ing arms?

What a bless - ed - ness, what a peace is mine,
O how bright the path grows from day to day,
I have bless - ed peace with my Lord so near,

Lean - ing on the ev - er - last - ing arms.

Lean - ing, lean - ing,

Lean - ing on Je - sus Christ, my Sav - ior,

Safe and se - cure from all a - larms;

Lean - ing, lean - ing,

Lean - ing on Je - sus Christ, my Sav - ior,

Lean - ing on the ev - er - last - ing arms.

Text: Elisha A. Hoffman, 1839–1929
Tune: SHOWALTER, 10 9 10 9 with refrain; Anthony J. Showalter, 1858–1924; arr. by Nolan Williams, Jr., b.1969, © 2000, GIA Publications, Inc.

381   I Must Tell Jesus

Do not worry about anything, but in everything by prayer... let your requests be made known to God.
Philippians 4:6

1. I must tell Je - sus all of my tri - als,
2. I must tell Je - sus all of my troub - les,
3. Tempt-ed and tried, I need a great Sav - ior,
4. O how the world to e - vil al - lures me!

I can - not bear these bur-dens a - lone;
He is a kind, com - pas-sion-ate Friend;
One who can help my bur-dens to bear;
O how my heart is tempt-ed to sin!

In my dis - tress He kind - ly will help me,
If I but ask Him, He will de - liv - er,
I must tell Je - sus, I must tell Je - sus,
I must tell Je - sus, and He will help me

He ev - er loves and cares for His own.
Make of my troub - les quick - ly an end.
He all my cares and sor - rows will share.
O - ver the world the vic - t'ry to win.

I must tell Je - sus! I must tell Je - sus! I can-not bear my bur-dens a - lone; I must tell Je - sus! I must tell Je - sus! Je-sus can help me, Je-sus a - lone.

Text: Elisha A. Hoffman, 1839–1929
Tune: ORWIGSBURG, 10 9 10 9 with refrain; Elisha A. Hoffman, 1839–1929

382 It Is Well with My Soul

"Are you all right? Is your husband all right? Is the child all right?" She answered, "It is all right."
2 Kings 4:26

1. When peace, like a riv - er, at - tend - eth my
2. Though Sa - tan should buf - fet, though tri - als should
3. My sin— oh, the bliss of this glo - ri - ous
4. And Lord, haste the day when my faith shall be

way, When sor - rows, like sea bil - lows, roll; What-
come, Let this blest as - sur - ance con - trol, That
thought: My sin, not in part but the whole, Is
sight, The clouds be rolled back as a scroll, The

ev - er my lot, Thou hast taught me to say,
Christ has re - gard - ed my help - less es - tate,
nailed to the cross, and I bear it no more,
trump shall re - sound, and the Lord shall de - scend,

It is well, it is well with my soul.
And hath shed His own blood for my soul.
Praise the Lord, praise the Lord, O my soul!
"E - ven so," it is well with my soul.

It is well with my soul,

It is well with my soul,

It is well, it is well with my soul.

Text: Horatio G. Spafford, 1828–1888
Tune: VILLE DU HAVRE, 11 8 11 9 with refrain; Philip P. Bliss, 1838–1876

383 Truly Caring Is Our Savior

He is the Rock, his works are perfect, and all his ways are just.
Deuteronomy 32:4

1. Tru - ly car - ing is our Sav - ior. Great and might - y
2. Though I might not do His will And I might do
3. When we fall short in our do - ings, God is just and

are His works. Awe - some is the king of glo - ry.
things my way, With the morn - ing comes new mer - cies.
God is fair. We, His chil - dren, God will chas - tise

Car - ing is the God we serve.
They are brand new ev - 'ry day.
So that we might know He cares.

Tru - ly car - ing is our Sav - ior. Sin's debt we could

not af - ford.   He paid so that we   might have life.

Tru - ly   car - ing is   our   Lord.

Text: James Anthony Plenty, © 2008
Tune: TRUST IN JESUS, 8 7 8 7 with refrain; William J. Kirkpatrick, 1838–1921

384 Trust and Obey

Blessed rather are those who hear the word of God and obey it!
Luke 11:28

1. When we walk with the Lord In the light of His
2. Not a shad - ow can rise, Not a cloud in the
3. Not a bur - den we bear, Not a sor - row we
4. But we nev - er can prove The de - lights of His
5. Then in fel - low - ship sweet We will sit at His

Word, What a glo - ry He sheds on our way! While we
skies, But His smile quick - ly drives it a - way; Not a
share, But our toil He doth rich - ly re - pay; Not a
love Un - til all on the al - tar we lay; For the
feet, Or we'll walk by His side in the way; What He

do His good will He a - bides with us
doubt nor a fear, Not a sigh nor a
grief nor a loss, Not a frown nor a
fa - vor He shows And the joy He be -
says we will do, Where He sends we will

still, And with all who will trust and o - bey.
tear, Can a - bide while we trust and o - bey.
cross, But is blest if we trust and o - bey.
stows Are for those who will trust and o - bey.
go— Nev - er fear, on - ly trust and o - bey.

Trust and o - bey— For there's no oth - er way To be
hap - py in Je - sus But to trust and o - bey.

Text: John H. Sammis, 1846–1919
Tune: TRUST AND OBEY, 66 9 D with refrain, Daniel B. Towner, 1850–1919

385   Blessed Quietness

...and after the earthquake a fire, but the LORD was not in the fire; and after the fire a sound of sheer silence.
1 Kings 19:12

1. Joys are flow - ing like a riv - er, Since the
2. Bring-ing life and health and glad - ness All a -
3. Like the rain that falls from heav - en, Like the
4. See, a fruit - ful field is grow - ing, Bless - ed
5. What a won - der - ful sal - va - tion, When we

Com - fort - er has come; He a - bides with us for
round this heav'n - ly Guest, Con - quered un - be - lief and
sun - light from the sky, So the Ho - ly Spir - it's
fruit of right - eous - ness; And the streams of life are
al - ways see His face, What a per - fect hab - i -

ev - er, Makes the trust - ing heart His home.
sad - ness, Changed our wea - ri - ness to rest.
giv - en, Com - ing on us from on high.
flow-ing In the lone - ly wil - der - ness.
ta - tion, What a qui - et rest - ing place.

Bless - ed qui - et - ness, Ho - ly qui - et - ness, What as -

sur - ance   in   my   soul;   On the storm-y sea,   Je - sus

speaks to me,   And the bil - lows cease   to   roll.

Text: Marie P. Ferguson, c.1897
Tune: BLESSED QUIETNESS, 8 7 8 7 with refrain; W. S. Marshall, c.1897; arr. by Nolan Williams, Jr., b.1969, © 2000, GIA Publications, Inc.

386   Standing on the Promises

Not one of all the good promises that the LORD had made to the house of Israel had failed; all came to pass.
Joshua 21:45

1. Stand - ing on the prom - is - es of Christ, my King,
2. Stand - ing on the prom - is - es that can - not fail.
3. Stand - ing on the prom - is - es of Christ, the Lord,
4. Stand - ing on the prom - is - es I can - not fall,

Through e - ter - nal a - ges let His prais - es ring;
When the howl - ing storms of doubt and fear as - sail,
Bound to Him e - ter - nal - ly by love's strong cord,
Lis - t'ning ev - 'ry mo - ment to the Spir - it's call,

Glo - ry in the high - est, I will shout and sing,
By the liv - ing word of God I shall pre - vail,
O - ver-com - ing dai - ly with the Spir - it's sword,
Rest - ing in my Sav - ior, as my all in all,

Stand - ing on the prom - is - es of God.

Stand - ing, stand - ing,
Stand - ing on the prom - is - es, Stand - ing on the prom - is - es,
Stand - ing on the prom - is - es of God, my Sav - ior;
Stand - ing, stand - ing,
Stand - ing on the prom - is - es, Stand - ing on the prom - is - es, I'm
stand - ing on the prom - is - es of God.

Text: R. Kelso Carter, 1849–1928
Tune: PROMISES, 11 11 11 9 with refrain; R. Kelso Carter, 1849–1928

387 All My Help Comes from the Lord

My help comes from the LORD, who made heaven and earth.
Psalm 121:2

Verses
1. Fa - ther I stretch
2. When I am weak

1. Fa - ther I stretch, I stretch my hands to Thee.
2. When I am weak, when I'm weak He gives me strength.

I know that You
When I am lone - ly

I know that You, on-ly You, re-mem-ber me. When
When I am lone - ly He com-forts me.

oth - ers for - get, when oth-ers for - get and leave me a - lone,
When I am tired of the load that I am bear - ing,

D.C.

I know that Je - sus, Je - sus, Je - sus will hear my groan.
He gives me cour-age, cour-age, cour-age to bear my share.

Text: Rev. Cleophus Robinson, © 1964, Lion Publishing Co.
Tune: Rev. Cleophus Robinson, © 1964, Lion Publishing Co.; arr. by Evelyn Simpson-Curenton, b.1953, © 2000, GIA Publications, Inc.

388   Farther Along

His disciples did not understand these things at first; but when Jesus was glorified, then they remembered...
John 12:16

1. Tempt - ed and tried we're oft made to won - der,
2. When death has come and tak - en our loved ones,
3. Faith - ful till death said our lov - ing Mas - ter,
4. When we see Je - sus com - ing in glo - ry,

Why it should be thus all the day long;
It leaves our home so lone - ly and drear;
A few more days to la - bor and wait;
When He comes from His home in the sky;

While there are oth - ers liv - ing a - bout us,
Then do we won - der why oth - ers pros - per,
Toils of the road will then seem as noth - ing,
Then we shall meet Him in that bright man - sion,

Nev - er mo - lest - ed though in the wrong.
Liv - ing so wick - ed year af - ter year.
As we sweep through the beau - ti - ful gate.
We'll un - der - stand it all by and by.

Far-ther a - long we'll know all a - bout it, Far-ther a -
long we'll un - der-stand why; Cheer up, don't wor - ry, live in the
sun - shine, We'll un - der - stand it all by and by.

Text: W. B. Stevens, 1862–1940
Tune: FARTHER ALONG, 10 9 10 9 with refrain; W. B. Stevens, 1862–1940; arr. by J. R. Baxter, Jr., 1887–1960

389   Jesus Is All the World to Me

For to me, living is Christ and dying is gain.
Philippians 1:21

1. Je - sus is all the world to me, My life, my joy, my
2. Je - sus is all the world to me, My friend in tri - als
3. Je - sus is all the world to me, And true to Him I'll
4. Je - sus is all the world to me, I want no bet - ter

all; He is my strength from day to day, With -
sore; I go to Him for bless - ings, and He
be; Oh, how could I this friend de - ny, When
friend; I trust Him now, I'll trust Him when Life's

out Him I would fall: When I am sad, to
gives them o'er and o'er: He sends the sun - shine
He's so true to me? Fol - low - ing Him I
fleet - ing days shall end: Beau - ti - ful life with

Him I go, No oth - er one can cheer me so;
and the rain, He sends the har - vest's gold - en grain;
know I'm right, He watch - es o'er me day and night;
such a friend, Beau - ti - ful life that has no end;

When I   am sad,   He makes me glad,   He's my   friend.
Sun - shine and rain,   har - vest of grain,   He's my   friend.
Fol - low - ing Him   by   day and night,   He's my   friend.
E - ter - nal life,   e - ter - nal joy,   He's my   friend.

Text: Will L. Thompson, 1847–1909
Tune: ALL THE WORLD, 8 6 8 6 88 8 3; Will L. Thompson, 1847–1909

390   Just When I Need Him

And my God will fully satisfy every need of yours according to his riches in glory in Christ Jesus.
Philippians 4:19

1. Just when I need Him,   Je - sus is near,
2. Just when I need Him,   Je - sus is true,
3. Just when I need Him,   Je - sus is strong,
4. Just when I need Him,   He is my all,

Just when I fal - ter,   just when I fear;
Nev - er for - sak - ing   all the way thro';
Bear - ing my bur - dens   all the day long;
An - swer - ing when   up - on Him I call;

Read - y to help me,   read - y to cheer,
Giv - ing for bur - dens   pleas - ures a - new,
For all my sor - row   giv - ing a song,
Ten - der - ly watch - ing   lest I should fall,

Just when I need Him most.

Just when I need Him most, Just when I need Him

most; Je - sus is near to com - fort and cheer,

Just when I need Him most.

Text: William C. Poole, 1875–1949
Tune: GABRIEL, 999 6 with refrain; Charles H. Gabriel, 1856–1932

391   'Tis So Sweet to Trust in Jesus

I will put my trust in him.
Hebrews 2:13

1. 'Tis so sweet to trust in Je-sus, Just to take Him at His word, Just to rest up-on His prom-ise, Just to know, "Thus saith the Lord."

2. O how sweet to trust in Je-sus, Just to trust His cleans-ing blood, Just in sim-ple faith to plunge me 'Neath the heal-ing, cleans-ing flood!

3. Yes, 'tis sweet to trust in Je-sus, Just from sin and self to cease, Just from Je-sus sim-ply tak-ing Life and rest and joy and peace.

4. I'm so glad I learned to trust Thee, Pre-cious Je-sus, Sav-ior, Friend; And I know that Thou art with me, Will be with me to the end.

Je-sus, Je-sus, how I trust Him! How I've proved Him o'er and o'er! Je-sus, Je-sus, pre-cious Je-sus! O for grace to trust Him more!

Text: Louisa M. R. Stead, c.1850–1917
Tune: TRUST IN JESUS, 8 7 8 7 with refrain; William J. Kirkpatrick, 1838–1921

We Walk His Way/Ewe, Thina

392

Direct my footsteps according to your word; let no sin rule over me.
Psalm 119:133

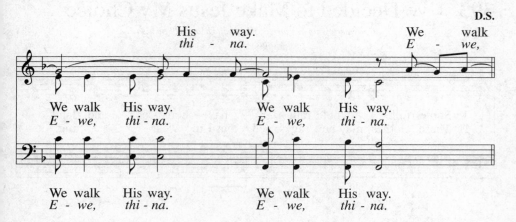

African phonetics: Ay-way thee-nah. See-zoh-wah nyah-thee-lah ah-mah-dee-moh-nee.

Text: South African (Xhosa); tr. by Anders Nyberg and Sven-Bernhard Fast, © 1984, Utryck, Walton Music Corp., agent
Tune: South African melody; arr. by Anders Nyberg, © 1984, Utryck, Walton Music Corp., agent

393 I've Decided to Make Jesus My Choice

For where your treasure is, there your heart will be also.
Matthew 6:21

1. Some folk would rath - er have hous - es and land.
2. These clothes may be rag - ged that I'm wear - ing.

Some folk choose sil - ver and gold.
Heav - y is the load that I'm bear - ing.

These things they treas - ure and for - get a-bout their souls;
These old bur - dens that I'm car - rying

I've de - cid - ed to make Je - sus my choice.

The road is rough; the go-ing gets tough, and the

hills are hard to climb. I've start-ed out a

long time a-go, there's no doubt in my mind; I've de-

cid-ed to make Je-sus my choice.

Text: Harrison Johnson
Tune: Harrison Johnson

394   Nothing Between

The grace of God has appeared, bringing salvation to all, training us to renounce impiety and worldly passions...
Titus 2:11–12

1. Noth - ing be - tween my soul and the Sav - ior,
2. Noth - ing be - tween, like world - ly pleas - ure:
3. Noth - ing be - tween, like pride or sta - tion:
4. Noth - ing be - tween, e'en man - y hard tri - als,

Naught of this world's de - lu - sive dream:
Hab - its of life, though harm - less they seem,
Self or friends shall not in - ter - vene;
Though the whole world a - gainst me con - vene;

I have re - nounced all sin - ful pleas - ure—
Must not my heart from Him ev - er sev - er—
Though it may cost me much trib - u - la - tion,
Watch - ing with prayer and much self - de - ni - al—

Je - sus is mine! There's noth - ing be - tween.
He is my all! There's noth - ing be - tween.
I am re - solved! There's noth - ing be - tween.
Tri - umph at last, with noth - ing be - tween!

Noth-ing be-tween my soul and the Sav-ior, So that His bless-ed

face may be seen; Noth-ing pre-vent-ing the least of His fa-vor:

Keep the way clear! Let noth - ing be - tween.

Text: Charles A. Tindley, 1851–1933
Tune: NOTHING BETWEEN, 10 9 10 9 with refrain; Charles A. Tindley, 1851–1933; arr. by Don Peterman

395 Acceptable to You

Let the words of my mouth and the meditation of my heart be acceptable to you, O LORD, my rock and my redeemer.
Psalm 19:14

Let the words of my mouth and the med-i-ta-tion of my

heart be ac-cept-a-ble in Thy sight. Let the

cept-a-ble Lord, to Thee. Here I am, Lord,

at Your feet, Lord, My soul looks up to

Thee; Make my thoughts, Lord, and my

tongue, Lord, ac - cept - a - ble to Thee.

Text: Eli Wilson, Jr.
Tune: Eli Wilson, Jr.
© 1989, Chenaniah Publications, Inc.

396   Is Your All on the Altar

... present your bodies as a living sacrifice, holy and acceptable to God, which is your spiritual worship.
Romans 12:1

1. You have longed for sweet peace, And for faith to in-
2. Would you walk with the Lord In the light of His
3. O we nev-er can know What the Lord will be-
4. Who can tell all the love He will send from a-

crease, And have ear-nest-ly, fer-vent-ly prayed.
Word, And have peace and con-tent-ment al-way?
stow Of the bless-ings for which we have prayed,
bove, And how hap-py our hearts will be made,

But you can-not have rest, Or be per-fect-ly
You must do His sweet will To be free from all
Till our bod-y and soul He doth ful-ly con-
Of the fel-low-ship sweet We shall share at His

blest, Un-til all on the al-tar is laid.
ill— On the al-tar your all you must lay.
trol, And our all on the al-tar is laid.
feet When our all on the al-tar is laid!

Is your all on the al - tar of sac - ri - fice laid? Your
heart does the Spir - it con - trol? You can
on - ly be blest, And have peace and sweet rest,
As you yield Him your bod - y and soul.

Text: Elisha A. Hoffman, 1839–1929
Tune: YOUR ALL, 66 9 D with refrain; Elisha A. Hoffman, 1839–1929; arr. by Nolan Williams, Jr., b.1969, © 2000, GIA Publications, Inc.

397 I Am Thine

Know that the LORD is God. It is he that made us, and we are his; we are his people, and the sheep of his pasture.
Psalm 100:3

1. I am Thine, O Lord, I have heard Thy voice, And it
2. Con - se - crate me now to Thy serv - ice, Lord, By the
3. O, the pure de - light of a sin - gle hour That be -
4. There are depths of love that I can - not know Till I

told Thy love to me; But I long to rise in the
pow'r of grace di - vine; Let my soul look up with a
fore Thy throne I spend, When I kneel in prayer, and with
cross the nar - row sea; There are heights of joy that I

arms of faith, And be clos - er drawn to Thee.
stead - fast hope, And my will be lost in Thine.
Thee, my God, I com - mune as friend with friend!
may not reach Till I rest in peace with Thee.

near - er,

Draw me near - er, near - er, near - er, bless - ed Lord, To the

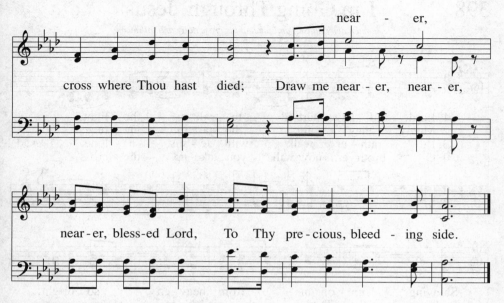

near - er,

cross where Thou hast died; Draw me near - er, near - er,

near - er, bless-ed Lord, To Thy pre - cious, bleed - ing side.

Text: Fanny J. Crosby, 1820–1915
Tune: I AM THINE, 10 7 10 7 with refrain; William H. Doane, 1832–1915

398 I'm Going Through, Jesus

...he must deny himself and take up his cross daily and follow me.
Luke 9:23

1. Lord, I have start-ed to walk in the light,
2. Man-y they are who start in the race;
3. I'd rath-er walk with Je-sus a-lone, And
4. O broth-er, now will you take up the cross?

Shin-ing up-on me from heav-en so bright;
But with the light they re-fuse to keep pace;
have for a pil-low, like Ja-cob, a stone,
Give up the world, and count it as dross;

I bade the world and its fol-lies a-dieu, I've
Oth-ers ac-cept it be-cause it is new, But
Liv-ing each mo-ment with His face in view, Than
Sell all thou hast, and give to the poor, Then

start-ed in Je-sus, and I'm go-ing through.
not ver-y man-y ex-pect to go through.
shrink from my path-way and fail to go through.
go through with Je-sus and those who en-dure.

I'm go - ing through, yes, I'm go-ing through;

I'll pay the price, what - ev - er oth-ers do;

I'll take the way with the Lord's de-spis - ed few,

I'm go - ing through, Je-sus, I'm go-ing through.

Text: Herbert Buffum, 1879–1939
Tune: Herbert Buffum, 1879–1939

399   In Christ There Is No East or West

There is no longer Jew or Greek... male and female; for all of you are one in Christ Jesus.
Galatians 3:28

1. In Christ there is no east or west, In
2. In Him shall true hearts ev - 'ry - where Their
3. Join hands then, broth - ers of the faith, What -
4. In Christ now meet both east and west, In

Him no south or north, But one great fel - low -
high com - mun - ion find; His serv - ice is the
e'er your race may be; Who serves my Fa - ther
Him meet south and north; All Christ - ly souls are

ship of love Through - out the whole wide earth.
gold - en cord Close - bind - ing all man - kind.
as a son Is sure - ly kin to me.
one in Him Through - out the whole wide earth.

Text: Galatians 3:28; William A. Dunkerley, 1852–1941
Tune: ST. PETER, CM; Alexander R. Reinagle, 1799–1877

In Christ There Is No East or West   400

There is no longer Jew or Greek... male and female; for all of you are one in Christ Jesus.
Galatians 3:28

1. In Christ there is no east or west, In Him no south or north, But one great fel - low - ship of love Through - out the whole wide earth.
2. In Him shall true hearts ev - 'ry - where Their high com - mun - ion find; His serv - ice is the gold - en cord Close - bind - ing all man - kind.
3. Join hands then, broth - ers of the faith, What - e'er your race may be! Who serve my Fa - ther as a son Is sure - ly kin to me.
4. In Christ now meet both east and west, In Him meet south and north, All Christ - ly souls are one in Him, Through - out the whole wide earth.

Text: Galatians 3:28; William A. Dunkerley, 1852–1941
Tune: McKEE, CM; African American; adapt. by Harry T. Burleigh, 1866–1949

401   I Have Decided to Follow Jesus

A scribe then approached and said, "Teacher, I will follow you wherever you go."
Matthew 8:19

1. I have de-cid-ed to fol-low Je-sus,
2. Though no one join me, still I will fol-low,
3. The world be-hind me, the cross be-fore me,

I have de-cid-ed to fol-low Je-sus,
Though no one join me, still I will fol-low,
The world be-hind me, the cross be-fore me,

I have de-cid-ed to fol-low Je-sus—
Though no one join me, still I will fol-low—
The world be-hind me, the cross be-fore me—

No turn-ing back, no turn-ing back!
no turn-ing back,

Text: Ascribed to an Indian prince; as sung in Garo, Assam
Tune: ASSAM, 10 10 10 8; Indian Folk melody, Paul B. Smith; harm. by Norman Johnson, 1928–1983
© 1963, New Spring Publishing (ASCAP)

I Surrender All

...there is no one who has left house or wife or brothers... who will not get back very much more in this age.
Luke 18:29–30

1. All to Je - sus I sur - ren - der,
   I will ev - er love and trust Him,
2. All to Je - sus I sur - ren - der,
   World - ly pleas - ures all for - sak - en,
3. All to Je - sus I sur - ren - der,
   Fill me with Thy Ho - ly Spir - it—
4. All to Je - sus I sur - ren - der,
   Fill me with Thy love and pow - er,

All to Him I free - ly give;
In His pres - ence dai - ly live.
Hum - bly at His feet I bow;
Take me, Je - sus, take me now.
Make me, Sav - ior, whol - ly Thine;
Tru - ly know that Thou art mine.
Lord, I give my - self to Thee;
Let Thy bless - ings fall on me.

I sur - ren - der

all, I sur - ren - der all.

I sur - ren - der all, I sur - ren - der all.

All to Thee, my bless - ed Sav - ior, I sur - ren - der all.

Text: Judson W. Van De Venter, 1855–1939
Tune: SURRENDER, 8 7 8 7 with refrain; Winfield S. Weeden, 1847–1908

403

What Shall I Render

What shall I return to the LORD for all his bounty to me?
Psalm 116:12

1. What shall I ren-der un-to God for all His
2. All I can ren-der is my bod-y and my

bless-ings? What shall I ren-der, (Tell me)
soul. That's all I can ren-der. That's

What shall I give?
all I can give.

God has ev-'ry-thing; Ev-'ry-thing be-longs to Him.

God has ev-'ry-thing; Ev-'ry-thing be-longs to Him.

What shall I ren-der, Tell me what shall I give?
All I can ren-der, That's all I can give.

Text: Margaret Pleasant Douroux, b.1941, © 1975, Rev. Earl Pleasant Publishing
Tune: Margaret Pleasant Douroux, b.1941, © 1975, Rev. Earl Pleasant Publishing; arr. by Stephen Key, © 2000, GIA Publications, Inc.

404 Walking Up the King's Highway

Blessed are the pure in heart, for they will see God.
Matthew 5:8

Refrain

It's a high - way to heav - en, none can walk up there but the pure in heart. It's a high - way to heav - en, I am walk - ing up the King's High - way.

Verses

1. My way gets bright - er, my load gets light - er
2. Don't have to wor - ry, don't have to hur - ry
3. If you're not walk - ing, start while I'm talk - ing

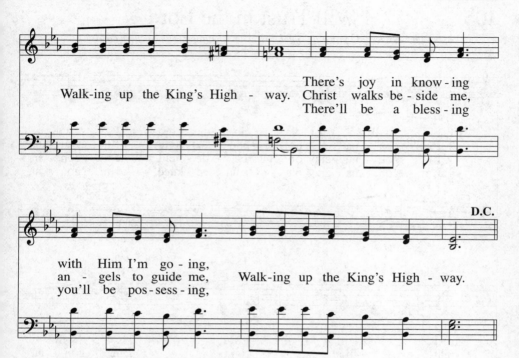

Walk-ing up the King's High - way. There's joy in know-ing
Christ walks be - side me, There'll be a bless - ing

with Him I'm go - ing,
an - gels to guide me, Walk-ing up the King's High - way.
you'll be pos - sess - ing,

D.C.

Text: Mary Gardner and Thomas A. Dorsey, 1899–1993
Tune: KING'S HIGHWAY, 55 7 55 7 with refrain; arr. by Mary Gardner and Thomas A. Dorsey, 1899–1993
© 1940 (renewed), arr. © 2011, Warner-Tamerlane Publishing Corp. and Unichappell Music Inc.

405 I Will Trust in the Lord

In God, whose word I praise, in God I trust; I am not afraid; what can flesh do to me?
Psalm 56:4

1. I will trust in the Lord, I will
2. I'm gon - na treat ev - 'ry-bod - y right, I'm gon - na
3. I'm gon - na stay on the bat - tle - field, I'm gon - na
4. I'm gon - na stay on ⅄ bend - ed knee, I'm gon - na

trust in the Lord, I will
treat ev - 'ry-bod - y right, I'm gon - na
stay on the bat - tle - field, I'm gon - na
stay on bend - ed knee, I'm gon - na

trust in the Lord till I die.
treat ev - 'ry-bod - y right till I die.
stay on the bat - tle - field till I die.
stay on ⅄ bend - ed knee till I die.

I will trust in the Lord, I will
I'm gon - na treat ev - 'ry - bod - y right, I'm gon - na
I'm gon - na stay on the bat - tle - field, I'm gon - na
I'm gon - na stay on ɣ bend - ed knee, I'm gon - na

trust in the Lord, I will
treat ev - 'ry - bod - y right, I'm gon - na
stay on the bat - tle - field, I'm gon - na
stay on ɣ bend - ed knee, I'm gon - na

trust in the Lord till I die.
treat ev - 'ry - bod - y right till I die.
stay on the bat - tle - field till I die.
stay on bend - ed knee till I die.

Alternate lyrics:
Father, I stretch my hands to Thee;
No other help I know.
If Thou withdraw Thyself from me,
O whither shall I go?

Text: Negro Spiritual
Tune: TRUST IN THE LORD, Irregular; Negro Spiritual; arr. by Jeffrey Radford, 1953–2002, and Nolan Williams, Jr., b.1969, © 2000,
   GIA Publications, Inc.

406 I'd Rather Have Jesus

I regard everything as loss because of the surpassing value of knowing Christ Jesus my Lord.
Philippians 3:8

1. I'd rath-er have Je-sus than sil - ver or gold, I'd
2. I'd rath-er have Je-sus than your ap - plause, I'd
3. He's fair-er than lil - ies of rar - est bloom, He's

rath - er be His than have rich - es un - told; I'd
rath - er be faith - ful to His dear cause; I'd
sweet - er than hon - ey from out the comb; He's

rath - er have Je - sus than hous - es or lands, I'd
rath - er have Je - sus than world - wide fame, I'd
all that my hun - ger - ing spir - it needs, I'd

rath - er be led by His nail - pierced hand.
rath - er be true to His ho - ly name.
rath - er have Je - sus and let Him lead.

Than to be the king of a vast do-main Or be held in sin's dread sway; I'd rath-er have Je-sus than an-y-thing This world af-fords to-day.

Text: Rhea Miller, 1894–1966
Tune: I'D RATHER HAVE JESUS, 11 11 11 10 with refrain; George Beverly Shea, b.1909
© 1939, Word Music, LLC

407

Here I Am

Then I said, "Here I am—it is written about me in the scroll— I have come to do your will, O God."
Hebrews 10:7

♩ = 66

Verses

1. Wash me, O God, re - new me.

2. Right now, God, I sub - mit to You.

Cre - ate in me a clean heart, O God.

Here's my life, Lord; use it as You please.

Wash me, O God, re - new me.

Right now, God, I sub - mit to You.

Cre - ate in me a clean heart, O God.

Here's my life, Lord; use it as You please.

To verse 2

To refrain

Refrain

Here I am, here I am,

here I am here I am, O God.

Here I am, here I am,

here I am   here I am, O God.

Here I am,   here I am,

here I am   here I am, O God.

Text: Roderick Vester
Tune: Roderick Vester
© 2004, Simply Cameron Publishing (BMI)

408 I Love the Lord, He Heard My Cry

Hear my cry, O God; listen to my prayer. From the end of the earth I call to you...
Psalm 61:1–2

I love the Lord, He heard my cry; And pit-ied ev - 'ry groan. Long as I

live,   while trou-bles rise,   I'll has-ten   to

His throne.   I love the

throne.   I'll has - ten to His

throne.   I'll has - ten to His throne.

Text: Richard Smallwood, b.1948
Tune: Richard Smallwood, b.1948; arr. by Nolan Williams, Jr., b.1969
© 1990, Century Oak Publishing Group/Richwood Music (BMI), admin. by Conexion Media Group, Inc.

I've Been 'Buked

My friends scorn me; my eye pours out tears to God.
Job 16:20

409

1. I've been 'buked an' I've been scorned,
2. Dere is trou-ble all o-ver dis worl',
3. Ain' gwine lay my 'li-gion down,

I've been 'buked an' I've been scorned, chil-dren;
Dere is trou-ble all o-ver dis worl', chil-dren;
Ain' gwine lay my 'li-gion down, chil-dren;

I've been 'buked an' I've been scorned,
Dere is trou-ble all o-ver dis worl',
Ain' gwine lay my 'li-gion down,

I've been talked a-bout sho's you' born.
Dere is trou-ble all o-ver dis worl'.
Ain' gwine lay my 'li-gion down.

Text: Traditional
Tune: I'VE BEEN 'BUKED, 7 9 7 8; Negro Spiritual; arr. by Carl Haywood, b.1949, from *The Haywood Collection of Negro Spirituals*, © 1992

410

Come unto Jesus

...I have set before you life and death, blessings and curses. Choose life...
Deuteronomy 30:19

Come un - to Je - sus while you have

time. Come un - to Je - sus. Make up your

mind. He will make your life brand new. Oh, He

will take care of you. Come to Je - sus

while you have time.

Just know-ing Je - sus sure has paid off in my life. Come to Je - sus while you have time. Though you may not have a friend, He'll go with you till the end. Come to Je - sus while you have time.

Text: Charles H. Nicks, Jr., 1941–1988,
Tune: Charles H. Nicks, Jr., 1941–1988; arr. by Brandon Waddles
© 2006, Bridgeport Music, Inc. (BMI)

411 My Faith Has Found a Resting Place

...for the LORD will be your everlasting light, and your God will be your glory.
Isaiah 60:19

1. My faith has found a rest-ing place— Not in de-vice nor creed: I trust the Ev - er - liv - ing One— His wounds for me shall plead.
2. E - nough for me that Je - sus saves— This ends my fear and doubt; A sin-ful soul I come to Him— He'll nev - er cast me out.
3. My heart is lean - ing on the Word— The writ-ten Word of God: Sal - va - tion by my Sav - ior's name— Sal - va - tion through His blood.
4. My great Phy - si - cian heals the sick, The lost He came to save; For me His pre - cious blood he shed, For me His life He gave.

I need no oth - er ar - gu-ment, I need no oth - er plea;

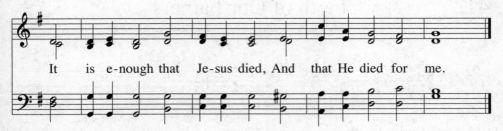

It   is e-nough that   Je-sus died, And   that He died for   me.

Text: Eliza Edmunds Hewitt, 1851–1920
Tune: LANDÅS, CM with refrain; attr. André Grétry, 1741–1813; arr. William J. Kirkpatrick, 1838–1921

412 Faith of Our Fathers

...contend for the faith that was once for all entrusted to the saints.
Jude 3

1. Faith of our fa - thers! liv - ing still
2. Our fa - thers, chained in pris - ons dark,
3. Faith of our fa - thers! we will love

In spite of dun - geon, fire and sword:
Were still in heart and con - science free:
Both friend and foe in all our strife:

O how our hearts beat high with joy
How sweet would be their chil - dren's fate,
And preach thee, too, as love knows how,

When - e'er we hear that glo - rious word!
If they, like them, could die for thee!
By kind - ly words and vir - tuous life:

Faith of our fa - thers, ho - ly faith!

We will be true to thee till death!

Text: Frederick William Faber, 1814–1863
Tune: ST. CATHERINE, 8 8 8 8 8 8; Henri Frederick Hemy, 1818–1888

413   Faith of Our Mothers

I am reminded of your sincere faith, a faith that lived first in your grandmother Lois and your mother Eunice...
2 Timothy 1:5

1. Faith of our moth - ers, liv - ing yet
2. Faith of our moth - ers, lav - ish faith,
3. Faith of our moth - ers, guid - ing faith,
4. Faith of our moth - ers, Chris - tian faith,

In cra - dle song and bed - time prayer,
The fount of child - hood's trust and grace,
For youth - ful long - ing— youth - ful doubt,
In truth be - yond our man - made creeds,

In nur - s'ry love and fire - side love,
O may thy con - se - cra - tion prove
How blurred our vi - sion, blind our way,
Still serve the home and save the church,

Thy pres - ence still per - vades the air:
The well - spring of a no - bler race:
Thy prov - i - den - tial care with - out:
And breathe thy spir - it through our deeds:

Faith of our moth - ers, liv - ing faith,
Faith of our moth - ers, lav - ish faith,
Faith of our moth - ers, guid - ing faith,
Faith of our moth - ers, Chris - tian faith,

We will be true to thee till death.
We will be true to thee till death.
We will be true to thee till death.
We will be true to thee till death.

Text: A. B. Patten, 1864–1952
Tune: ST. CATHERINE, 8 8 8 8 8 8; Henri Frederick Hemy, 1818–1888

414 We've Come This Far by Faith

For we walk by faith, not by sight.
2 Corinthians 5:7

Verse 1

1. Don't be dis-cour-aged when trou-ble's in your

life, He'll bear your bur - dens and

move all mis-er-y and strife. That's why we've

D.S.

2. Just the other day I heard someone say
   He didn't believe in God's word;
   But I can truly say that God had made a way,
   And He's never failed me yet.
   That's why we've...

Text: Albert A. Goodson, b.1933
Tune: Albert A. Goodson, b.1933; arr. by James Abbington, b.1960
© 1965, renewed 1993, Manna Music, Inc./ASCAP (admin. by ClearBox Rights)

415   There's a Bright Side Somewhere

The city has no need of sun or moon to shine on it, for the glory of God is its light, and its lamp is the Lamb.
Revelation 21:23

Chorus

There's a bright side some - where, there's a

bright side some - where. Don't you

rest un - til you find it. There's a

bright side some - where.

Special Chorus

When your way seems dark and dreer, don't have to wor-ry cause

God is near. If in your heart there is no song,

just keep the faith and keep hold-ing on.

Turn your plate down, fast and pray. Je-sus will al-ways make a

way. There's a bright side some-where.

Text: Margaret Jenkins, ©
Tune: Margaret Jenkins, ©; arr. by Joseph Joubert, b.1958, © 2000, GIA Publications, Inc.

416   It's in My Heart

...be filled with the Spirit, as you sing psalms and hymns... singing and making melody to the Lord in your hearts.
Ephesians 5:18–19

1. Tho' some may sing to pass the wea - ry night a -
2. You ask me why I know His blood can cleanse a -
3. You ask me how I find the time to read and
4. I may not know the skill - ful use of tongue or

long, Tho' some may sing to en - ter - tain a world - ly
lone, You ask me why I know He sits up - on the
pray, You ask me how I smile when things are far from
pen, To prove my Lord's re - turn to un - be - liev - ing

throng, (a world - ly throng,) I sing be - cause I wor - ship
throne, (up - on the throne,) And why I know He chose me
gay, (are far from gay,) And how I sing His prais - es,
men, (un - b'liev - ing men,) But this I know, He's com - ing

God in song,
for His own,
come what may,   It's in my heart,   It's in my heart.
back a - gain,

It's in my heart, this mel - o - dy of love di -
it's in my heart,

It's in my heart, this mel - o - dy of love di -

vine, It's in my heart, since I am His and He is
it's in my heart,

vine, It's in my heart, since I am His and He is

mine. It's in my heart, how can I help but sing and
yes, He is mine, it's in my heart,

mine. It's in my heart, how can I help but sing and

heart.

shine, It's in my heart, It's in my
it's in my heart, heart, it's in my heart.

shine, It's in my heart, It's in my heart.

Text: Arthur Slater, b.1941
Tune: IT'S IN MY HEART, 12 12 10 8 with refrain; Arthur Slater, b.1941; arr. by J. G. Boersma
© 1941, renewed 1968, Gospel Publishing House. Assigned 1997 to The Lorenz Corporation.

417   We'll Understand It Better By and By

For now we see in a mirror, dimly, but then we will see face to face. Now I know only in part; then I will know fully...
1 Corinthians 13:12

1. We are of-ten tossed and driv'n
2. We are of-ten des-ti-tute
3. Tri-als dark on ev-'ry hand,
4. Temp-ta-tions, hid-den snares

On the rest-less
Of the things that
And we can-not
Of-ten take us

sea of time. Som-ber skies and howl-ing tem-pests oft suc-
life de-mands. Want of food and want of shel-ter, thirst-y
un-der-stand, All the ways that God would lead us to that
un-a-wares. And our hearts are made to bleed for some

ceed a bright sun-shine. In that land of per-fect day, When the
hills and bar-ren lands. We are trust-ing in the Lord, And ac-
bless-ed Prom-ised Land. But He guides us with His eye And we'll
thought-less word or deed. And we won-der why the test When we

mists have rolled a-way, We will un-der-stand it bet-ter by and
cord-ing to His Word, We will un-der-stand it bet-ter by and
fol-low till we die. For we'll un-der-stand it bet-ter by and
try to do our best, But we'll un-der-stand it bet-ter by and

by. By and by when the morn-ing comes,
When the saints of God are gath-ered home, We will
tell the sto-ry how we've o-ver-come; For we'll
un-der-stand it bet-ter by and by.

Text: Charles A. Tindley, 1851–1933
Tune: BY AND BY, 7 7 15 7 7 11 with refrain; Charles A. Tindley, 1851–1933; arr. by Nolan Williams, Jr., b.1969, © 2000, GIA Publications, Inc.

418   I Don't Feel No Ways Tired

We are afflicted in every way, but not crushed... persecuted, but not forsaken; struck down, but not destroyed.
2 Corinthians 4:8–9

I don't feel no ways tired;

I've come too far from where I've start - ed from.

No - bod - y told me that the road would be eas - y. I

1.

don't be - lieve He brought me this far to leave me.

don't be-lieve He brought me this far, I

don't be-lieve He brought me this far to leave me.

Text: Curtis Burrell
Tune: Curtis Burrell; arr. by Stephen Key and Nolan Williams, Jr., b.1969
© 1978, 1984, Savgos Music, Inc.

419

It's Real

Have you believed because you have seen me? Blessed are those who have not seen and yet have come to believe.
John 20:29

1. O how well do I re-mem-ber how I
2. When the truth came close and search-ing, all my
3. But at last I tired of liv-ing such a
4. So I prayed to God in ear-nest, and not

doubt-ed day by day, For I did not know for
joy would dis-ap-pear. For I did not have the
life of fear and doubt. For I want-ed God to
car-ing what folks said. I was hun-gry for the

cer-tain that my sins were washed a-way; When the
wit-ness of the Spir-it bright and clear; If at
give me some-thing I would know a-bout; So the
bless-ing; my poor soul it must be fed; When at

Spir-it tried to tell me, I would
times the com-ing judg-ment would ap-
truth would make me hap-py, and the
last by faith I touched Him, and, like

not the truth re - ceive. I en - deav - ored to be
pear be - fore my mind, O it made me so un -
light would clear - ly shine, And the Spir - it gave as -
sparks from smit - ten steel, Just so quick sal - va - tion

hap - py, and to make my - self be - lieve.
eas - y, for God's smile I could not find.
sur - ance that I'm His and He is mine.
reached me; O bless God, I know it's real!

But it's real, it's real, O I know it's real; Praise
it's real, I know

God, the doubts are set - tled, For I know, I know it's real.

Text: H. L. Cox, b.1907
Tune: IT'S REAL, 15 15 15 15 with refrain; H. L. Cox, b.1907

420   I Know Who Holds Tomorrow

...I know the one in whom I have put my trust, and I am sure that he is able to guard... what I have entrusted to him.
2 Timothy 1:12

1. I don't know a-bout to-mor-row, I just live from day to day; I don't bor-row from its sun - shine, For its skies may turn to gray. I don't wor - ry o'er the fu - ture, For I

2. Ev - 'ry step is get - ting bright-er As the gold - en stairs I climb; Ev - 'ry bur - den's get - ting light - er, Ev - 'ry cloud is sil - ver lined. There the sun is al - ways shin - ing, There no

3. I don't know a-bout to-mor-row, It may bring me pov - er - ty; But the One who feeds the spar - row, Is the One who stands by me. And the path that is my por - tion, May be

know   what Je - sus said;   And to - day   I'll walk be -
tear   will dim   the eye,   At   the   end - ing   of   the
through   the flame   or flood;   But His   pres - ence goes be -

side Him,   For   He   knows   what is   a - head.
rain - bow,   Where the   moun - tains touch   the sky.
fore me,   And   I'm   cov - ered with   His blood.

Man - y   things   a - bout   to - mor - row   I   don't

seem   to un - der-stand;   But I   know   who holds   to -

mor - row,   And   I   know   who holds   my   hand.

Text: Ira F. Stanphill, 1914–1993
Tune: TOMORROW, 8 7 8 7 D with refrain; Ira F. Stanphill, 1914–1993
© 1950, New Spring Publishing (ASCAP)

421 Hold to God's Unchanging Hand

Jesus Christ is the same yesterday and today and forever.
Hebrews 13:8

1. Time is filled with swift tran - si - tion.
2. Trust in Him who will not leave you.
3. Cov - et not this world's vain rich - es
4. When your jour - ney is com - plet - ed,

Naught of earth un - moved can stand.
What - so - ev - er years may bring.
That so rap - id - ly de - cay.
If to God you have been true,

Build your hopes on things e - ter - nal.
If by earth - ly friends for - sak - en,
Seek to gain the heav'n - ly treas - ures.
Fair and bright the home in Glo - ry

Hold to God's un - chang - ing hand.
Still more close - ly to Him cling.
They will nev - er pass a - way.
Your en - rap - tured soul will view.

Hold to His hand, God's un - chang - ing hand.

Hold to His hand, God's un - chang - ing hand.

Build your hopes on things e - ter - nal.

Hold to God's un - chang - ing hand.

Text: Jennie Wilson
Tune: UNCHANGING HAND, 8 7 8 7 with refrain; Franklin L. Eiland, 1860–1909; arr. by Stephen Key, © 2000, GIA Publications, Inc.

422
Higher Ground

I press on toward the goal for the prize of the heavenly call of God in Christ Jesus.
Philippians 3:14

1. I'm press-ing on the up-ward way, New heights I'm
2. My heart has no de-sire to stay Where doubts a -
3. I want to live a-bove the world, Though Sa-tan's
4. I want to scale the ut-most height, And catch a

gain - ing ev - 'ry day; Still pray-ing as I'm on - ward
rise and fears dis - may; Though some may dwell where these a -
darts at me are hurled; For faith has caught a joy - ful
gleam of glo - ry bright; But still I'll pray till heav'n I've

bound, "Lord, plant my feet on high - er ground."
bound, My prayer, my aim, is high - er ground.
sound, The song of saints on high - er ground.
found, "Lord, lead me on to high - er ground."

Lord, lift me up, and let me stand By faith, on

heav - en's ta - ble - land; A high-er plane than I have found, Lord, plant my feet on high - er ground.

Text: Johnson Oatman, Jr., 1860–1948
Tune: HIGHER GROUND, LM with refrain; Charles H. Gabriel, 1856–1932

423 He'll Understand and Say "Well Done"

I have fought the good fight... I have kept the faith. From now on there is reserved for me the crown of righteousness...
2 Timothy 4:7–8

1. If when you give the best of your serv - ice,
2. Mis - un - der - stood, the Sav - ior of sin - ners,
3. If when this life of la - bor is end - ed,
4. But if you try and fail in your try - ing,

Tell - ing the world that the Sav - ior is come;
Hung on the cross; He was God's on - ly Son;
And the re - ward of the race you have run;
Hands sore and scarred from the work you've be - gun;

Be not dis - mayed when men don't be - lieve you;
Oh! hear Him call - ing His Fa - ther in Heav'n,
Oh! the sweet rest pre - pared for the faith - ful
Take up your cross, run quick - ly to meet Him;

He'll un - der - stand; and say, "Well done."
"Not my will, but Thine be done."
Will be His blest and fi - nal "Well done."
He'll un - der - stand, and say, "Well done."

Oh, when I come to the end of my jour - ney,
Wea - ry of life and the bat-tle is won; Car - ry ing the staff and the
cross of re-demp-tion, He'll un-der-stand and say, "Well done."

Text: Lucie E. Campbell, 1885–1963
Tune: WELL DONE, 10 10 10 8 with refrain; Lucie E. Campbell, 1885–1963; arr. by Evelyn Simpson-Curenton, b.1953, © 2000, GIA Publications, Inc.

424 We Won't Leave Here Like We Came

You who have made me see many troubles and calamities will revive me again...
Psalm 71:20

*We won't leave here like *we came, in Je - sus' name.

Bound, op-pressed, af - flict-ed, sick or lame.

For the Spir - it of the Lord is still the same.

We won't leave here like we came, in Je-sus' name.

*You, I

Text: Rev. Maceo Woods, ©
Tune: Rev. Maceo Woods, ©; arr. by Nolan Williams, Jr., b.1969, © 2000, GIA Publications, Inc.
Administered by GIA Publications, Inc.

O Thou, in Whose Presence

425

Even though I walk through the darkest valley, I fear no evil; for you are with me...
Psalm 23:4

1. O Thou, in whose pres - ence my soul takes de -
2. Where dost Thou, dear Shep - herd, re - sort with Thy
3. O why should I wan - der, an a - lien from
4. Re - store, my dear Sav - ior, the light of Thy
5. He looks! and ten thou - sands of an - gels re -

light, On whom in af - flic - tion I call, My
sheep, To feed them in pas - tures of love? Say,
Thee, Or cry in the des - ert for bread? Thy
face, Thy soul - cheer - ing com - fort im - part; And
joice, And myr - i - ads wait for His word. He

com - fort by day and my song in the
why in the val - ley of death should I
foes will re - joice when my sor - rows they
let the sweet to - kens of par - don - ing
speaks! and e - ter - ni - ty, filled with His

night, My hope, my sal - va - tion, my all!
weep, Or a - lone in this wil - der - ness rove?
see, And smile at the tears I have shed.
grace Bring joy to my des - o - late heart.
voice, Re - ech - oes the praise of the Lord.

Text: Joseph Swain, 1761–1796
Tune: DAVIS, 11 8 11 8; Wyeth's *Repository of Sacred Music, Part II,* 1813; harm. by Austin C. Lovelace, 1919–2010, alt., © 1964, Abingdon Press

426 Somebody Here Needs a Blessing

Blessed are you who are poor, for yours is the kingdom of God.
Luke 6:20

1. Some-bod-y came to this serv-ice read-y to give up. Some-bod-y came to this serv-ice, say-ing, "Lord, I've had e-nough. Some-bod-y in the build-ing wants to be free.

2. Some-bod-y came to this serv-ice with trou-ble on their mind. Fi-nan-ces low, no place to go and their bills are all be-hind.

Some-bod-y in the build-ing needs the vic-to-ry.

Some-bod-y here needs a touch, some-bod-y here needs a

mir-a-cle. Some-bod-y here needs a bless-ing,

Last time

right now, right now, right now.

Last time

Touch, Lord, touch, Lord, touch, Lord, touch, Lord!

D.S.

Touch, Lord, touch, Lord, touch, Lord, touch, Lord!

Text: Eddie A. Robinson
Tune: Eddie A. Robinson
© 2006, Eddie A. Robinson

427 Leave It There

Cast your burden on the LORD and he will sustain you; he will never permit the righteous to be moved.
Psalm 55:22

1. If the world from you with-hold of its sil - ver and its gold,
2. If your bod - y suf-fers pain and your health you can't re-gain,
3. When your en - e - mies as - sail and your heart be - gins to fail,
4. When your youth-ful days are gone and old age is steal-ing on,

And you have to get a long with mea - ger fare,
And your soul is al - most sink - ing in de - spair,
Don't for - get that God in heav - en an - swers prayer;
And your bod - y bends be - neath the weight of care,

Just re - mem-ber, in His Word, how He feeds the lit - tle bird—
Je - sus knows the pain you feel, He can save and He can heal—
He will make a way for you and will lead you safe-ly through—
He will nev - er leave you then, He'll go with you to the end—

Take your bur - den to the Lord and leave it there.

Leave it there, leave it there, Take your

Leave it there, leave it there, leave it there, leave it there, Take your

bur - den to the Lord and leave it there; If you

leave it there;

trust and nev - er doubt, He will sure - ly bring you out. Take your

bur - den to the Lord and leave it there.

Text: Charles A. Tindley, 1851–1933
Tune: LEAVE IT THERE, 14 11 14 11 with refrain; Charles A. Tindley, 1851–1933; arr. by Nolan Williams, Jr., b.1969, © 2000, GIA Publications, Inc.

428 The Storm Is Passing Over

...and the sea ceased from its raging. Then the men feared the LORD even more.
Jonah 1:15–16

Take cour-age my soul and let us jour-ney on, tho' the night is dark and I am far from home. Thanks be to God, the morn-ing light ap-pears. The storm is pass-ing o - ver, the storm is pass-ing o -

ver. The storm is pass-ing o - ver. Hal - le - lu.

Hal - le - lu - jah. Hal - le - lu - jah. Hal - le - lu - jah.

Hal - le - lu - jah.

The storm is pass-ing o - ver. The storm is pass-ing o -

ver. The storm is pass-ing o - ver. Hal - le - lu.

Text: Charles A. Tindley, 1851–1933, and Donald Vails, ©
Tune: Donald Vails, ©; arr. by Evelyn Simpson-Curenton, b.1953, © 2000, GIA Publications, Inc.

429 Savior, like a Shepherd Lead Us

If a shepherd has a hundred sheep... does he not leave the ninety-nine... and go in search of the one that went astray?
Matthew 18:12

1. Sav - ior, like a shep - herd lead us,
2. We are Thine; do Thou be - friend us,
3. Thou hast prom-ised to re - ceive us,
4. Ear - ly let us seek Thy fa - vor;

Much we need Thy ten - der care;
Be the Guard - ian of our way;
Poor and sin - ful though we be;
Ear - ly let us do Thy will;

In Thy pleas - ant pas - tures feed us,
Keep Thy flock, from sin de - fend us,
Thou hast mer - cy to re - lieve us,
Bless - ed Lord and on - ly Sav - ior,

For our use Thy folds pre - pare.
Seek us when we go a - stray.
Grace to cleanse, and pow'r to free.
With Thy love our bos - oms fill.

Bless-ed Je - sus, Bless-ed Je - sus, Thou hast bought us, Thine we are; Bless-ed Je - sus, Bless-ed Je - sus, Thou has bought us, Thine we are.

Bless-ed Je - sus, Bless-ed Je - sus, Hear Thy chil - dren when they pray; Bless-ed Je - sus, Bless-ed Je - sus, Hear Thy chil - dren when they pray.

Bless-ed Je - sus, Bless-ed Je - sus, Ear - ly let us turn to Thee; Bless-ed Je - sus, Bless-ed Je - sus, Ear - ly let us turn to Thee.

Bless-ed Je - sus, Bless-ed Je - sus, Thou hast lov'd us, love us still; Bless-ed Je - sus, Bless-ed Je - sus, Thou hast lov'd us, love us still.

Text: Dorothy A. Thrupp, 1779–1847
Tune: BRADBURY, 8 7 8 7 D; William B. Bradbury, 1816–1868

430 The Beautiful Garden of Prayer

He said to his disciples, "Sit here while I go over there and pray."
Matthew 26:36

1. There's a gar-den where Je-sus is wait-ing,
2. There's a gar-den where Je-sus is wait-ing,
3. There's a gar-den where Je-sus is wait-ing,

There's a place that is won-drous-ly fair,
And I go, with my bur-den and care,
And He bids you to come meet Him there,

For it glows with the light of His pres-ence—
Just to learn from His lips words of com-fort—
Just to bow and re-ceive a new bless-ing—

'Tis the beau-ti-ful gar-den of prayer.
In the beau-ti-ful gar-den of prayer.
In the beau-ti-ful gar-den of prayer.

O the beau-ti-ful gar-den, the gar-den of prayer, O the

beau-ti-ful gar-den of prayer! There my Sav-ior a-waits, and He

o-pens the gates To the beau-ti-ful gar-den of prayer.

Text: Eleanor Allen Schroll, 1878–1966
Tune: BEAUTIFUL GARDEN, 10 9 10 9 with refrain; James H. Fillmore, 1849–1936

431 Does Jesus Care?

Cast all your anxiety on him, because he cares for you.
1 Peter 5:7

1. Does Je - sus care when my heart is pained Too deep - ly for mirth and song; As the bur - dens press, and the cares dis - tress, And the way grows wea - ry and long?
2. Does Je - sus care when my way is dark With a name - less dread and fear? As the day - light fades in - to deep night shades, Does He care e - nough to be near?
3. Does Je - sus care when I've tried and failed To re - sist some temp - ta - tion strong; When for my deep grief I find no re - lief, Though my tears flow all the night long?
4. Does Je - sus care when I've said good - bye To the dear - est on earth to me, And my sad heart aches till it near - ly breaks— Is it aught to Him? does He see?

O yes, He cares— I

know   He cares!   His heart   is touched with   my   grief;

When the   days   are wea - ry,   the   long   nights drear - y,   I

cares.

know   my   Sav - ior   cares,   He   cares.

cares.

Text: Frank E. Graeff, 1860–1919
Tune: MY SAVIOR CARES, 9 8 10 8 with refrain; J. Lincoln Hall, 1866–1930

432 Yield Not to Temptation

No testing has overtaken you that is not common to everyone... with the testing he will also provide the way out.
1 Corinthians 10:13

1. Yield not to temp - ta - tion, For yield - ing is sin;
2. Shun e - vil com - pan - ions, Bad lan - guage dis - dain;
3. To him that o'er - com - eth, God giv - eth a crown;

Each vic - t'ry will help you, Some oth - er to win;
God's name hold in rev - 'rence, Nor take it in vain;
Through faith we will con - quer, Though of - ten cast down;

Fight val - iant - ly on - ward, E - vil pas - sions sub - due;
Be thought-ful and ear - nest, Kind - heart - ed and true;
He who is our Sav - ior, Our strength will re - new;

Look ev - er to Je - sus, He will car - ry you through.

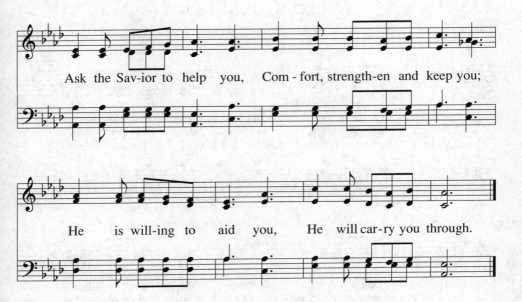

Ask the Sav-ior to help you, Com-fort, strength-en and keep you;

He is will-ing to aid you, He will car-ry you through.

Text: Horatio R. Palmer, 1834–1907
Tune: YIELD NOT, 6 5 6 5 6 6 6 6 with refrain; Horatio R. Palmer, 1834–1907; harm. by Carl Haywood, b.1949, from *Songs of Praise,* © 1992

433 Where Could I Go?

All the ends of the earth shall remember and turn to the LORD...
Psalm 22:27

1. Liv - ing be - low in this old sin - ful world,
2. Neigh - bors are kind, I love them ev - 'ry one,
3. Life here is grand with friends I love so dear,

Hard - ly a com - fort can af - ford; Striv - ing a - lone to
We get a - long in sweet ac - cord; But when my soul needs
Com - fort I get from God's own word; Yet when I face the

face temp - ta - tion sore,
man - na from a - bove, where could I go but to the Lord?
chill - ing hand of death,

Where could I go? Oh, where could I go

Seek - ing a ref-uge for my soul? Need - ing a friend to

save me in the end, Where could I go but to the Lord?

Text: James B. Coats, 1901–1961
Tune: WHERE COULD I GO, 10 8 10 8 with refrain; James B. Coats, 1901–1961; arr. by Valeria A. Foster, © 2000, GIA Publications, Inc.

434 The Lord Is My Shepherd

The LORD is my shepherd, I shall not want.
Psalm 23:1

1. The Lord is my Shep-herd, no want shall I
2. Through the val-ley and shad-ow of death though I
3. In the midst of af - flic - tion my ta - ble is
4. Let good-ness and mer-cy, my boun - ti - ful

know; I feed in green pas - tures, safe - fold - ed I
stray, Since Thou art my Guard-ian, no e - vil I
spread; With bless-ings un - meas - ured my cup run-neth
God, Still fol - low my steps till I meet Thee a -

rest; He lead-eth my soul where the still wa - ters
fear; Thy rod shall de - fend me, Thy staff be my
o'er; With per - fume and oil Thou a - noint-est my
bove: I seek by the path which my an - ces - tors

flow, Re - stores me when wan - d'ring, re -
stay; No harm can be - fall, with my
head; O what shall I ask of Thy
trod, Through the land of their so - journ, Thy

deems when op - pressed; Re - stores me when
Com - fort - er near; No harm can be -
prov - i - dence more? O what shall I
king - dom of love; Through the land of their

wan - d'ring, re - deems when op - pressed.
fall, with my Com - fort - er near.
ask of Thy prov - i - dence more?
so - journ, Thy king - dom of love.

Text: James Montgomery, 1771–1854
Tune: POLAND, 11 11 11 11 11; Thomas Koschat, 1845–1914

435 What a Friend We Have in Jesus

Rejoice in hope, be patient in suffering, persevere in prayer.
Romans 12:12

1. What a Friend we have in Je-sus, All our
2. Have we tri - als and temp - ta - tions? Is there
3. Are we weak and heav - y - la-den, Cum - bered

sins and griefs to bear! What a
trou - ble an - y - where? We should
with a load of care? Pre - cious

priv - i - lege to car - ry Ev - 'ry-
nev - er be dis - cour-aged— Take it
Sav - ior, still our ref - uge— Take it

thing to God in prayer! Oh what
to the Lord in prayer! Can we
to the Lord in prayer! Do thy

peace we of - ten for - feit, Oh what
find a friend so faith - ful, Who will
friends de - spise, for-sake thee? Take it

need - less pain we bear, All be -
all our sor - rows share? Je - sus
to the Lord in prayer! In His

cause we do not car - ry Ev - 'ry -
knows our ev - 'ry weak-ness— Take it
arms He'll take and shield thee— Thou wilt

thing to God in prayer!
to the Lord in prayer!
find a sol - ace there.

Text: Joseph M. Scriven, 1819–1866
Tune: ANNIE LOWERY, 8 7 8 7 D; traditional Celtic; arr. Valeria A. Foster, © 2000, GIA Publications, Inc.

436 What a Friend We Have in Jesus

For the eyes of the Lord are on the righteous, and his ears are open to their prayer.
1 Peter 3:12

1. What a Friend we have in Je - sus, All our
2. Have we tri - als and temp - ta - tions? Is there
3. Are we weak and heav - y - la - den, Cum - bered

sins and griefs to bear! What a priv - i - lege to
troub - le an - y - where? We should nev - er be dis -
with a load of care? Pre - cious Sav - ior, still our

car - ry Ev - 'ry-thing to God in prayer! O what
cour - aged— Take it to the Lord in prayer. Can we
ref - uge— Take it to the Lord in prayer. Do thy

peace we of - ten for - feit, O what need-less pain we
find a friend so faith - ful Who will all our sor - rows
friends de-spise, for - sake thee? Take it to the Lord in

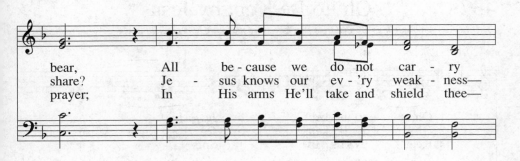

bear,   All   be - cause we   do not   car - ry
share?   Je - sus knows our ev - 'ry weak - ness—
prayer;   In   His arms He'll take and shield thee—

Ev - 'ry - thing to God in   prayer!
Take   it to the Lord in   prayer.
Thou   wilt find a sol - ace there.

Text: Joseph M. Scriven, 1819–1866
Tune: CONVERSE, 8 7 8 7 D; Charles C. Converse, 1832–1918

May also be sung to I Will Arise

437 Oh, to Be Kept by Jesus

O LORD, you brought up my soul from Sheol, restored me to life from among those gone down to the Pit.
Psalm 30:3

1. Oh, to be kept by Je - sus,
2. Oh, to be kept by Je - sus,
3. Kept by His Ho - ly Spir - it,

Kept by the pow - er of God.
Kept by His pow - er di - vine.
To me this is best of all.

Kept from the world un - spot - ted,
Kept through toil and tri - als,
I'm safe in His ho - ly keep - ing,

Tread - ing where Je - sus trod.
Kept by His hand in mine.
He'll ev - er hear my call.

Oh, to be kept by Je - sus;

Lord, at Thy feet I fall;

I would be noth-ing, noth-ing, noth-ing,

Thou shalt be all and all.

Text: Thurston Frazier
Tune: FRAZIER, 7 7 7 6 with refrain; Thurston Frazier; arr. by Kenneth Morris, 1917–1988
© 1966, Frazier-Cleveland Co.

438 Come, Ye Disconsolate

Do not fear, for I am with you, do not be afraid, for I am your God; I will strengthen you, I will help you...
Isaiah 41:10

1. Come, ye dis - con - so-late, wher - e'er ye lan - guish—
2. Joy of the des - o - late, light of the stray - ing,
3. Here see the Bread of Life, see wa - ters flow - ing

Come to the mer - cy-seat, fer - vent-ly kneel;
Hope of the pen - i - tent, fade - less and pure!
Forth from the throne of God, pure from a - bove;

Here bring your wound - ed hearts, here tell your an - guish:
Here speaks the Com - fort-er, ten - der-ly say - ing,
Come to the feast of love— come ev - er know - ing

Earth has no sor - row that heav'n can - not heal.
"Earth has no sor - row that heav'n can - not cure."
Earth has no sor - row but heav'n can re - move.

Text: St. 1, 2, Thomas Moore, 1779–1852; st. 3, Thomas Hastings, 1784–1872
Tune: CONSOLATOR, 11 10 11 10; Samuel Webbe, 1740–1816

Have Thine Own Way, Lord

...yield yourselves to the LORD and come to his sanctuary, which he has sanctified forever...
2 Chronicles 30:8

1. Have Thine own way, Lord! Have Thine own way!
2. Have Thine own way, Lord! Have Thine own way!
3. Have Thine own way, Lord! Have Thine own way!
4. Have Thine own way, Lord! Have Thine own way!

Thou art the pot - ter, I am the clay!
Search me and try me, Mas - ter, to - day!
Wound - ed and wea - ry, Help me, I pray!
Hold o'er my be - ing Ab - so - lute sway!

Mold me and make me Af - ter Thy will,
Bright - er than snow, Lord, Wash me just now,
Pow - er all pow - er Sure - ly is Thine!
Fill with Thy Spir - it 'Til all shall see

While I am wait - ing, Yield - ed and still.
As in Thy pres - ence Hum - bly I bow.
Touch me and heal me, Sav - ior di - vine!
Christ on - ly, al - ways, Liv - ing in me!

Text: Adelaide A. Pollard, 1862–1934
Tune: ADELAIDE, 5 4 5 4 D; George C. Stebbins, 1846–1945

440 Come Here, Jesus, If You Please

Rejoice in hope, be patient in suffering, persevere in prayer.
Romans 12:12

1. No harm have I done You on my knees, on my knees, No harm have I done You on my knees, on my knees, When you see me on my knees, dear Lord, Come here, Jesus, if You please.

2. O Lord, have mer-cy on po' me, on po' me, O Lord, have mer-cy on po' me, on po' me,

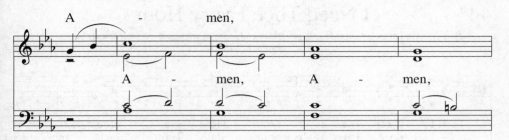

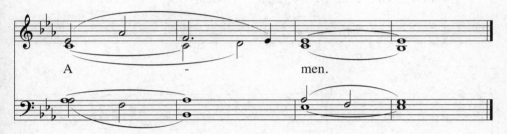

Text: African American traditional; adapt. by Roland M. Carter, b.1942, © 1978, Mar-Vel
Tune: COME HERE JESUS, 9 9 9 7 with amen; African American traditional; arr. by Roland M. Carter, b.1942, © 1978, Mar-Vel

441   I Need Thee Every Hour

With my whole heart I seek you; do not let me stray from your commandments.
Psalm 119:10

1. I need Thee ev-'ry hour, Most gra - cious Lord;
2. I need Thee ev-'ry hour, Stay Thou near - by;
3. I need Thee ev-'ry hour, In joy or pain;
4. I need Thee ev-'ry hour, Teach me Thy will;

No ten - der voice like Thine Can peace af - ford.
Temp - ta - tions lose their pow'r When Thou art nigh.
Come quick - ly and a - bide, Or life is vain.
And Thy rich prom - is - es In me ful - fill.

I need Thee, O I need Thee; Ev - 'ry hour I need Thee;

O bless me now, my Sav - ior, I come to Thee.

Text: Annie S. Hawkes, 1835–1918
Tune: NEED, 6 4 6 4 with refrain; Robert Lowry, 1826–1899

Just a Closer Walk with Thee

442

...but Judah still walks with God, and is faithful to the Holy One.
Hosea 11:12

1. I am weak but Thou art strong;
2. Through this world of toil and snares,
3. When my fee-ble life is o'er,

Refrain: Just a clos-er walk with Thee,

Je - sus, keep me from all wrong;
If I fal - ter, Lord, who cares?
Time for me will be no more;

Grant it, Je - sus, if You please?

I'll be sat - is - fied as long
Who with me my bur - den shares?
Guide me gent - ly, safe - ly o'er

Dai - ly walk-ing close to Thee,

As I walk, let me walk close to Thee.
None but Thee, dear Lord, none but Thee.
To Thy king - dom shore, to Thy shore.

Let it be, dear Lord, let it be.

Text: Anonymous
Tune: CLOSER WALK, 777 8; Anonymous

In Me

443

For I will not venture to speak of anything except what Christ has accomplished through me...
Romans 15:18

1. Thou, O Christ, my Lord and King, Grant in Thine own
2. Thou a won - der work - ing God, Dwell - ing in e -
3. Prince of peace be - yond com - pare, Thou whose pow - er
4. O Thou might - y God of love, Died Thy - self to
5. Je - sus, Thou the life, the way, In Thine im - age
6. Je - sus, Thou the joy un - told, Like a riv - er

name my plea. Take the sac - ri - fice I bring,
ter - ni - ty, As in flesh our plan - et trod,
stilled the sea, Chief a - mong ten thou - sand fair,
set us free. Ho - ly Spir - it, heav'n - ly dove,
let me be; Keep my heart from day to day,
flow - ing free. Be Thou ev - er in my soul,

Be Thou "All Thou art" in me. Be Thou "All Thou
Work Thy might - y work in me. Work Thy might - y
Speak Thy word of peace in me. Speak Thy word of
Mag - ni - fy Thy love in me. Mag - ni - fy Thy
Live Thy ho - ly life in me. Live Thy ho - ly
Let Thy joy a - bound in me. Let Thy joy a -

art" in me. Be Thou "All Thou art" in me. Take the
work in me. Work Thy might - y work in me. As in
peace in me. Speak Thy word of peace in me. Chief a -
love in me. Mag - ni - fy Thy love in me. Ho - ly
life in me. Live Thy ho - ly life in me. Keep my
bound in me. Let Thy joy a - bound in me. Be Thou

sac - ri - fice I bring, Be Thou "All Thou art" in me.
flesh our plan - et trod, Work Thy might - y work in me.
mong ten thou - sand - fair, Speak Thy word of peace in me.
Spir - it, heav'n - ly dove, Mag - ni - fy Thy love in me.
heart from day to day, Live Thy ho - ly life in me.
ev - er in my soul, Let Thy joy a - bound in me.

Text: Charles A. Tindley, 1851–1933
Tune: IN ME, 7 7 7 7 D; Charles A. Tindley, 1851–1933; arr. by Frederick J. Tindley

444 Love Divine, All Love Excelling

We love because he first loved us.
1 John 4:19

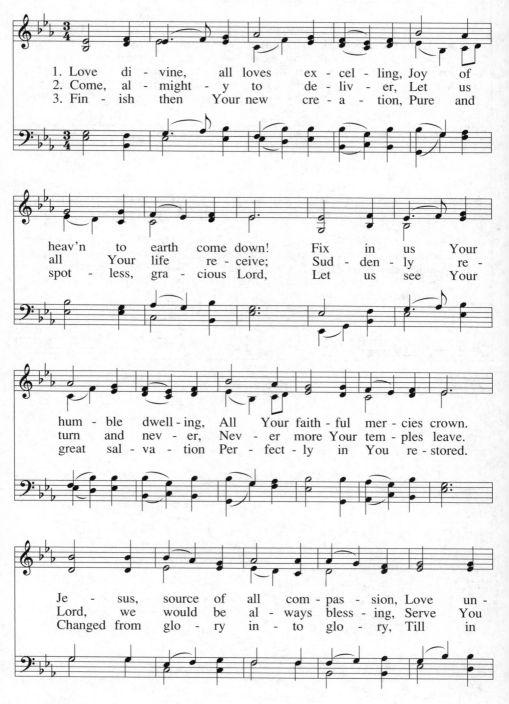

1. Love di - vine, all loves ex - cel - ling, Joy of
2. Come, al - might - y to de - liv - er, Let us
3. Fin - ish then Your new cre - a - tion, Pure and

heav'n to earth come down! Fix in us Your
all Your life re - ceive; Sud - den - ly re -
spot - less, gra - cious Lord, Let us see Your

hum - ble dwell - ing, All Your faith - ful mer - cies crown.
turn and nev - er, Nev - er more Your tem - ples leave.
great sal - va - tion Per - fect - ly in You re - stored.

Je - sus, source of all com - pas - sion, Love un -
Lord, we would be al - ways bless - ing, Serve You
Changed from glo - ry in - to glo - ry, Till in

bound - ed, love all pure; Vis - it us with
as your hosts a - bove, Pray, and praise You
heav'n we take our place, Till we sing be -

Your sal - va - tion, Let Your love in us en - dure.
with - out ceas - ing, Glo - ry in Your pre - cious love.
fore the al - might - y Lost in won - der, love and praise.

Text: Charles Wesley, 1707–1788, alt.
Tune: HYFRYDOL, 8 7 8 7 D; Rowland H. Prichard, 1811–1887

445

Bless This House

The LORD has been mindful of us; he will bless us; he will bless the house of Israel.
Psalm 115:12

Lord, we bow in ad-o-ra-tion, for Thy great-ness and mer-cy.

Lift-ing hearts and hands to Thee as we come to Thee in prayer.

Optional Chant

1. Melt us and mold us, sanctify and make us holy
2. Send Your presence and Your power for the blessing of this hour
3. Bless this house, oh Lord, we pray,
   and all that is within it bless Your holy name.

1., 2.

oh Lord, we pray.

3.

Bless this house, oh

Lord, oh Lord, we pray.

Text: Betty D. Gadling
Tune: Betty D. Gadling
© 1994, Betty D. Gadling. Administered by GIA Publications, Inc.

Jesus, Lover of My Soul

For you are my refuge, a strong tower against the enemy.
Psalm 61:3

446

1. Je - sus, Lov - er of my soul,
   While the near - er wa - ters roll,
2. Oth - er ref - uge have I none;
   Leave, ah, leave me not a - lone,
3. Thou, O Christ, art all I want;
   Raise the fall - en, cheer the faint,
4. Plen - teous grace with Thee is found,
   Let the heal - ing streams a - bound;

Let me to Thy bos - om fly,
While the tem - pest still is
Hangs my help - less soul on Thee;
Still sup - port and com - fort
More than all in Thee I find;
Heal the sick, and lead the
Grace to cov - er all my sin;
Make and keep me pure with -

guide, O re-ceive my soul at last!
head With the shad - ow of Thy wing.
am, Thou art full of truth and grace.
heart, Rise to all e - ter - ni - ty.

Text: Charles Wesley, 1707–1788
Tune: MARTYN, 7 7 7 7 D; Simeon B. Marsh, 1798–1875; arr. by Nolan Williams, Jr., b.1969, © 2000, GIA Publications, Inc.

447 Until I Found the Lord

Pray in the Spirit at all times in every prayer and supplication.
Ephesians 6:18

1. Lord, I prayed and I prayed, prayed all night long,

Oh Lord, I

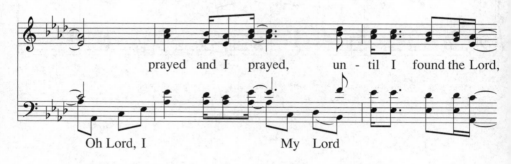

prayed and I prayed, un - til I found the Lord,

Oh Lord, I My Lord

My soul My soul

just could-n't rest con - tent - ed,

My soul

just could-n't rest con - tent - ed,

Lord, I

just could-n't rest con-tent - ed,   un - til I found the Lord.

2. Lord, I cried and I cried,...
3. Lord, I moaned and I moaned,...

Text: Clara Ward, 1924–1973
Tune: Clara Ward, 1924–1973
© 1953, 1981, Clara Ward. Assigned to Gertrude Music. (JJ)

Remember Me   448

Then he said, "Jesus, remember me when you come into your kingdom."
Luke 23:42

1. Re - mem - ber   me,   re - mem - ber
2. Fa - ther I stretch my hands to
3. If Thou with - draw Thy - self from

me, Oh Lord, re - mem - ber me.
Thee, no oth - er help I know.
me, Oh whith - er shall I go?

Text: Congregational Praise Song
Tune: Congregational Praise Song; harm. by Leon C. Roberts, 1950–1999, from *The Mass of St. Augustine*, © 1981, GIA Publications, Inc.

449

Even Me

I will send down the showers in their season; they shall be showers of blessing.
Ezekiel 34:26

1. Lord, I hear of show'rs of bless-ings, Thou art scat - t'ring full and free;
2. Pass me not, O gen - tle Sav - ior, Sin - ful though my heart may be;
3. Bread of heav - en, bread of heav - en, Ev - er let me feed on Thee;

Show'rs the thirst - y souls re - fresh-ing, Let some
I am long - ing for Thy fa - vor, Whilst Thou art
Vine of heav - en, Vine of heav - en, Let Thy

drops now fall on me!
bless - ing, O bless me!
blood a - tone for me!

E - ven me, Lord,

e - ven me.

E - ven me, Lord, e - ven

me.
Let   some   drops   now   fall   on   me!
Whilst Thou art   bless - ing, Lord,   bless   me!
Let   Thy   blood   a - tone   for   me!

Text: Elizabeth H. Codner, 1824–1919
Tune: EVEN ME, 8 7 8 7 777; William B. Bradbury, 1816–1868; arr. by Nolan Williams, Jr., b.1969, © 2000, GIA Publications, Inc.

Jesus, Savior, Pilot Me

450

O afflicted one, storm-tossed, and not comforted...no weapon that is fashioned against you shall prosper.
Isaiah 54:11, 17

1. Je - sus, Sav - ior, pi - lot me, O - ver life's tem - pes - tuous sea: Un - known waves be - fore me roll, Hid - ing rocks and treach-'rous shoal; Chart and com - pass come from Thee— Je - sus, Sav - ior, pi - lot me!

2. As a moth - er stills her child, Thou canst hush the o - cean wild; Bois - t'rous waves o - bey Thy will When Thou say'st to them, "Be still!" Won-drous Sov - 'reign of the sea, Je - sus, Sav - ior, pi - lot me!

3. When at last I near the shore, And the fear - ful break - ers roar 'Twixt me and the peace - ful rest— Then, while lean - ing on Thy breast, May I hear Thee say to me, "Fear not— I will pi - lot thee!"

Text: Edward Hopper, 1816–1888
Tune: PILOT, 77 77 77; John E. Gould, 1822–1875

451

This Day

Give us this day our daily bread.
Matthew 6:11

Give us this day our dai-ly bread. You said You

would sup-ply all my needs ac-cord-ing to Your

rich - es. I have but to ask and I shall re - ceive.

To go from here and share this love You gave to

me, to show some-one who's lost and help them find their

way, the way to truth and faith so they can be free like

me, free like me. Lord, we need Your love.

Lord, we need Your peace. Lord, we need Your joy this

day. this

Thank You for this day. Lord, we thank You for this day.

day.

Text: Edwin Hawkins, b.1943
Tune: Edwin Hawkins, b.1943; arr. by Stephen Key, © 2000, GIA Publications, Inc.

452

A Praying Spirit

Pray in the Spirit at all times in every prayer and supplication.
Ephesians 6:18

Lord, give me a pray - ing spir - it, a

pray - ing spir - it. Lord, help me to say yes,

yes, yes, Lord; yes,

yes, Lord. Lord, when I'm pray - ing tell me

what   to   say!   what   to   say!   Yes!   Yes!

Yes!   Yes, Lord!   Yes,   yes, Lord!

Text: Elbernita "Twinkie" Clark, © 1980, Bridgeport Music, Inc.
Tune: Elbernita "Twinkie" Clark, © 1980, Bridgeport Music, Inc.; arr. by Nolan Williams, Jr., b.1969, © 2000, GIA Publications, Inc.

453
Keep Me Every Day

Keep my steps steady according to your promise, and never let iniquity have dominion over me.
Psalm 119:133

1. Lord, I want to live for Thee, Ev - 'ry
2. In my weak - ness be my strength; In my
3. Leave me not to walk a - lone, Lest I

day and hour; Let Thy Spir - it be with
tri - als all, Be Thou near me all the
droop and die; Let Thy Spir - it go with

me, In its sav - ing pow'r!
day, Hear my ev - 'ry call!
me, And at - tend my cry!

Keep my heart, and keep my hand,

Keep my soul, I pray! Keep my tongue to

speak Thy praise, Keep me all the way!

Text: Franklin L. Eiland, 1860–1909
Tune: EVERY DAY, 7 5 7 5 with refrain; Emmett S. Dean, 1876–1936

454 **Pass Me Not, O Gentle Savior**

See, I am sending my messenger ahead of you, who will prepare your way before you.
Matthew 11:10

1. Pass me not, O gen-tle Sav-ior, Hear my hum-ble
2. Let me at a throne of mer-cy Find a sweet re-
3. Trust-ing on-ly in Thy mer-it, Would I seek Thy
4. Thou the Spring of all my com-fort, More than life to

cry, While on oth-ers Thou art call-ing,
lief; Kneel-ing there in deep con-tri-tion,
face; Heal my wound-ed, bro-ken spir-it,
me, Whom have I on earth be-side Thee?

I'm call-ing

Do not pass me by.
Help my un-be-lief.
Save me by Thy grace.
Whom in heav'n but Thee?

Sav-ior, Sav-ior,

Hear my hum-ble cry; While on oth-ers Thou art

call-ing, Do not pass me by.

Text: Fanny J. Crosby, 1820–1915
Tune: PASS ME NOT, 8 5 8 5 with refrain; William H. Doane, 1832–1915

Abide with Me

455

God abides in those who confess that Jesus is the Son of God, and they abide in God.
1 John 4:15

1. A - bide with me; fast falls the e - ven - tide;
2. Swift to its close ebbs out life's lit - tle day;
3. I need Thy pres - ence ev - 'ry pass - ing hour;
4. I fear no foe, with Thee at hand to bless;
5. Hold Thou Thy cross be - fore my clos - ing eyes;

The dark - ness deep - ens; Lord, with me a - bide
Earth's joys grow dim; its glo - ries pass a - way;
What but Thy grace can foil the tempt - er's pow'r?
Ills have no weight, and tears no bit - ter - ness.
Shine through the gloom and point me to the skies;

When oth - er help - ers fail and com - forts flee,
Change and de - cay in all a - round I see;
Who, like Thy - self, my guide and stay can be?
Where is death's sting? Where, grave, your vic - to - ry?
Heav'n's morn - ing breaks, and earth's vain shad - ows flee;

Help of the help - less, O a - bide with me.
O Thou who chang - est not, a - bide with me.
Through cloud and sun - shine, Lord, a - bide with me.
I tri - umph still, if Thou a - bide with me.
In life, in death, O Lord, a - bide with me.

Text: Henry F. Lyte, 1793–1847
Tune: EVENTIDE, 10 10 10 10; William H. Monk, 1823–1889; arr. by Evelyn Simpson-Curenton, b.1953, © 2000, GIA Publications, Inc.

456   Lord, Help Me to Hold Out

...those who look into the perfect law, the law of liberty, and persevere... they will be blessed in their doing.
James 1:25

Chorus

Lord, help me to hold out,

Lord, help me to hold out,

Lord, help me to hold out, un-til

my change comes.

Text: James Cleveland, 1931–1991, © 1974, Planemar Music Co.
Tune: James Cleveland, 1931–1991, © 1974, Planemar Music Co.; arr. by Evelyn Simpson-Curenton, b.1953, © 2000, GIA Publications, Inc.

My Faith Looks Up to Thee

457

Turn to me and be saved, all the ends of the earth! For I am God, and there is no other.
Isaiah 45:22

1. My faith looks up to Thee, Thou Lamb of
2. May Thy rich grace im - part Strength to my
3. While life's dark maze I tread, And griefs a -
4. When ends life's tran - sient dream, When death's cold,

Cal - va - ry, Sav - ior di - vine! Now hear me
faint - ing heart, My zeal in - spire; As Thou hast
round me spread, Be Thou my guide; Bid dark - ness
sul - len stream Shall o'er me roll; Blest Sav - ior,

while I pray, Take all my guilt a - way,
died for me, O may my love to Thee
turn to day, Wipe sor - row's tears a - way,
then, in love, Fear and dis - trust re - move;

O let me from this day Be whol - ly Thine!
Pure, warm and change - less be, A liv - ing fire!
Nor let me ev - er stray From Thee a - side.
O bear me save a - bove, A ran - somed soul!

Text: Ray Palmer, 1808–1887
Tune: OLIVET, 66 4 666 4; Lowell Mason, 1792–1872

458 Standin' in the Need of Prayer

Hear my prayer, O LORD, and give ear to my cry; do not hold your peace at my tears.
Psalm 39:12

Text: Negro Spiritual
Tune: STANDIN' IN THE NEED; 13 7 13 7 with refrain; Negro Spiritual

459 Thy Way, O Lord

Father, if you are willing, remove this cup from me; yet, not my will but yours be done.
Luke 22:42

1. Thy way, O Lord, not mine, Thy will be done, not mine; Since Thou for me did bleed, And now do inter - cede, Each day I sim - ply plead, Thy will be done.

2. Thy way, O Lord, not mine, Let glo - ry all be Thine; Keep me, lest I may stray, Near Thee from day to day; Teach me to watch and pray, Thy will be done.

3. Hide me from self, O Lord, May I at - tend Thy word; Send pride be - yond re - call, Let each as - sail - er fall, Be Thou my all in all, Thy will be done.

4. Sub - mis - sive - ly I bow; With strength and grace en - dow This wea - ry, sin - ful heart; Shield from each cru - el dart; May I from Thee ne'er part, Thy will be done.

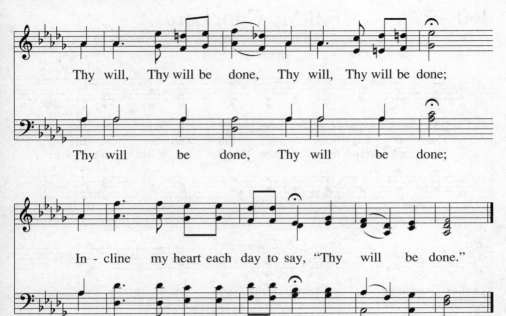

Thy will, Thy will be done, Thy will, Thy will be done;

Thy will be done, Thy will be done;

In - cline my heart each day to say, "Thy will be done."

Text: Nina B. Jackson
Tune: THY WAY, 66 666 4 with refrain; Edward C. Deas

460 Fill My Cup, Lord

I will lift up the cup of salvation and call on the name of the LORD.
Psalm 116:13

1. Like the wom-an at the well I was seek-ing
2. There are mil-lions in this world who are crav-ing
3. So, my friend now, if the things this world gave you

For things that could not sat-is-fy;
The pleas - ure earth-ly things af - ford;
Leave hun - gers that won't pass a - way,

And then I heard my Sav-ior speak-ing:
But none can match the won-drous treas-ure
My bless - ed Lord will come and save you,

"Draw from My well that nev-er shall run dry."
That I find in Je-sus Christ my Lord.
If you kneel to Him and hum-bly pray:

Fill my cup, Lord, I lift it up, Lord! Come and

quench this thirst-ing of my soul; Bread of heav - en, feed me till I

want no more— Fill my cup, fill it up and make me whole!

Text: Richard Blanchard, 1925–2004
Tune: FILL MY CUP, 11 8 9 10 with refrain; Richard Blanchard, 1925–2004
© 1959, Word Music, LLC

461 Fix Me, Jesus

If we confess our sins, he who is faithful and just will forgive us our sins and cleanse us from all unrighteousness.
1 John 1:9

Text: Traditional
Tune: FIX ME, 7 6 7 6 with refrain; Negro Spiritual; arr. by Nolan Williams, Jr., b.1969, © 2000, GIA Publications, Inc.

Oh, Lord, Have Mercy

462

Be merciful to me, O God, be merciful to me, for in you my soul takes refuge…
Psalm 57:1

1. Oh, Lord, have mer - cy. Oh, Lord, have
2. While I am pray - ing, While I am
3. While I am wait - ing, While I am
4. When I'm in trou - ble, When I'm in
5. I am Your child, I am Your

mer - cy. Oh, Lord, have mer - cy,
pray - ing, While I am pray - ing,
wait - ing, While I am wait - ing, Have
trou - ble, When I'm in trou - ble,
child, I am Your child,

mer - cy on me.

Text: Traditional
Tune: HAVE MERCY ON ME, 5 5 5 5; traditional; arr. by Joseph Joubert, b.1958, © 2000, GIA Publications, Inc.

463 Sweet Hour of Prayer

...one of his disciples said to him, "Lord, teach us to pray, as John taught his disciples."
Luke 11:1

1. Sweet hour of prayer, sweet hour of prayer, That calls me from a world of care And bids me at my Fa - ther's throne Make all my wants and wish - es known! In sea - sons of dis - tress and grief My soul has of - ten

2. Sweet hour of prayer, sweet hour of prayer, Thy wings shall my pe - ti - tion bear To Him whose truth and faith - ful - ness En - gage the wait - ing soul to bless; And since He bids me seek His face, Be - lieve His word and

3. Sweet hour of prayer, sweet hour of prayer, May I thy con - so - la - tion share, Till from Mount Pis - gah's loft - y height I view my home and take my flight: This robe of flesh I'll drop, and rise To seize the ev - er -

found   re - lief,   And   oft   es - caped   the   tempt - er's snare
trust   His   grace,   I'll   cast   on   Him   my   ev - 'ry care,
last - ing   prize,   And shout,   while pass - ing through   the   air,

By   thy   re - turn,   sweet   hour   of   prayer.
And   wait   for   thee,   sweet   hour   of   prayer.
"Fare - well,   fare - well,   sweet   hour   of   prayer!"

Text: William W. Walford, 1772–1850
Tune: SWEET HOUR, LMD; William B. Bradbury, 1816–1868

464

Anoint Us

I will sprinkle clean water on you, and you will be clean; I will cleanse you from all your impurities...
Ezekiel 36:25

Cleanse us through the pow - er of Your Name. And we'll be

care - ful to give You all the praise.

And we'll be care - ful to give You all the

1.

2.

praise. Cre - praise. A - noint us!

Text: Glenn E. Burleigh, 1949–2007
Tune: Glenn E. Burleigh, 1949–2007
© 1994, 1997, GIA Publications, Inc.

465   Sanctuary

Who shall ascend the hill of the LORD? Those who have clean hands and pure hearts...
Psalm 24:3–4

Lord, pre - pare me   to be a sanc-tu - ar - y,   pure and

ho - ly,   tried and true;   with thanks-giv - ing,   I'll be a

liv - ing   sanc-tu - ar - y   for   You.

Text: John Thompson, b.1950 and Randy Scruggs
Tune: John Thompson, b.1950 and Randy Scruggs
© 1982, Full Armor Music and Whole Armor Music

Lord, I Want to Be a Christian

For where your treasure is, there your heart will be also.
Matthew 6:21

466

1. Lord, I want to be a Chris-tian In my heart, in my
2. Lord, I want to be more lov-ing In my heart, in my
3. Lord, I want to be more ho-ly In my heart, in my
4. Lord, I want to be like Je-sus In my heart, in my

heart; Lord, I want to be a Chris-tian In my heart,
heart; Lord, I want to be more lov-ing In my heart,
heart; Lord, I want to be more ho-ly In my heart,
heart; Lord, I want to be like Je-sus In my heart,

In my heart, In my heart,

In my heart, In my heart,

Lord, I want to be a Chris-tian In my heart.
Lord, I want to be more lov-ing In my heart.
Lord, I want to be more ho-ly In my heart.
Lord, I want to be like Je-sus In my heart.

Text: Negro Spiritual; adapt. by John W. Work, Jr., 1872–1925, and Frederick J. Work, 1879–1942
Tune: I WANT TO BE A CHRISTIAN, 8 6 8 3 6 8 3; Negro Spiritual; adapt. by Frederick J. Work, 1879–1942

467 Give Me a Clean Heart

Create in me a clean heart O God, and put a new and right spirit within me.
Psalm 51:10

Thee. For I'm not wor - thy of all these bless - ings.

Give me a clean heart, and I'll fol-low Thee.

Last time

Verses

1. I'm   not ask - ing for   the rich - es   of   the   land.
2. Some-times I   am up   and some-times I   am   down.

I'm   not ask - ing for the proud to know my   name.
Some-times I   am al - most lev - el   to   the   ground.

Please   give   me, Lord,   a   clean   heart,   that

I   may fol - low Thee.   Give me a   clean   heart

and I'll fol - low Thee.

Text: Margaret Pleasant Douroux, b.1941, © 1970, Rev. Earl Pleasant Publishing
Tune: Margaret Pleasant Douroux, b.1941, © 1970, Rev. Earl Pleasant Publishing; arr. by Albert Dennis Tessier and Nolan Williams, Jr., b.1969,
© 2000, GIA Publications, Inc.

A Charge to Keep I Have 468

I press on toward the goal for the prize of the heavenly call of God in Christ Jesus.
Philippians 3:14

1. A charge to keep I have, A God to glo - ri - fy,
2. To serve the pres - ent age, My call - ing to ful - fill;
3. Arm me with watch - ful care As in Thy sight to live,
4. Help me to watch and pray, And still on Thee re - ly,

A nev - er - dy - ing soul to save, And fit it for the sky.
O may it all my pow'rs en - gage To do my Mas - ter's will!
And now Thy ser - vant, Lord, pre - pare A strict ac - count to give!
O let me not my trust be - tray, But press to realms on high.

Text: Charles Wesley, 1707–1788
Tune: BOYLSTON, SM; Lowell Mason, 1792–1872

469   Give of Your Best to the Master

We love because he first loved us.
1 John 4:19

1. Give of your best to the Mas - ter,
2. Give of your best to the Mas - ter,
3. Give of your best to the Mas - ter,

Refrain: Give of your best to the Mas - ter,

Give of the strength of your youth;
Give Him first place in your heart;
Naught else is wor - thy His love;

Give of the strength of your youth;

Throw your soul's fresh, glow - ing ar - dor
Give Him first place in your serv - ice,
He gave Him - self for your ran - som,

Clad in sal - va - tion's full ar - mor,

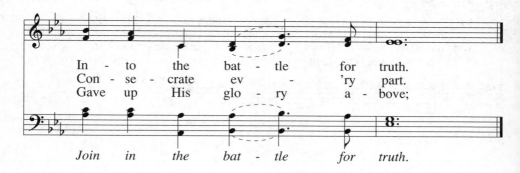

In - to the bat - tle for truth.
Con - se - crate ev - 'ry part.
Gave up His glo - ry a - bove;

Join in the bat - tle for truth.

Je - sus has set the ex - am - ple—
Give, and to you shall be giv - en—
Laid down His life with - out mur - mur,

Daunt - less was He, young and brave;
God His be - lov - ed Son gave;
You from sin's ru - in to save;

Give Him your loy - al de - vo - tion,
Grate - ful - ly seek - ing to serve Him,
Give Him your heart's ad - o - ra - tion,

D.C.

Give Him the best that you have.
Give Him the best that you have.
Give Him the best that you have.

Text: Howard B. Grose, 1851–1939
Tune: BARNARD, 8 7 8 7 D with refrain; Charlotte A. Barnard, 1830–1869

470 Go to the World

So they set out and went from village to village, preaching the gospel and healing people everywhere.
Luke 9:6

1. Go to the world! Go in-to all the earth. Go preach the cross where Christ re-news life's worth, Bap-tiz-ing
2. Go to the world! Go in-to ev-'ry place. Go live the Word of God's re-deem-ing grace. Go seek God's
3. Go to the world! Go strug-gle, bless and pray; The nights of tears give way to joy-ous day, As ser-vant
4. Go to the world! Go as the ones I send, For I am with you till the age shall end, When all the

as the sign of our re - birth.
pres - ence in each time and space.
Church, you fol - low Christ's own way. Al -
hosts of glo - ry cry "A - men!"

le - lu - ia. Al - le - lu - ia.

Text: Sylvia G. Dunstan, 1955–1993, © 1991, GIA Publications, Inc.
Tune: SINE NOMINE, 10 10 10 with alleluias; Ralph Vaughan Williams, 1872–1958

471   We Are Climbing Jacob's Ladder

...he dreamed that there was a ladder... and the angels of God were ascending and descending on it.
Genesis 28:12

1. We are climb-ing Ja-cob's lad-der, We are
2. Ev-'ry round goes high-er, high-er, Ev-'ry
3. Chil-dren, do you love my Je-sus? Chil-dren,
4. If you love Him, why not serve Him? If you
5. Rise, shine, give God glo-ry, Rise,

climb-ing Ja-cob's lad-der, We are climb-ing
round goes high-er, high-er, Ev-'ry round goes
do you love my Je-sus? Chil-dren, do you
love Him, why not serve Him? If you love Him,
shine, give God glo-ry, Rise, shine,

Ja-cob's lad-der, Sol-diers of the cross.
high-er, high-er, Sol-diers of the cross.
love my Je-sus? Sol-diers of the cross.
why not serve Him? Sol-diers of the cross.
give God glo-ry, Sol-diers of the cross.

Text: Negro Spiritual
Tune: JACOB'S LADDER, 8 8 8 5; Negro Spiritual

People Need the Lord

472

Come to me, all you that are weary and are carrying heavy burdens, and I will give you rest.
Matthew 11:28

Peo-ple need the Lord, peo-ple need the Lord;

At the end of bro-ken dreams, He's the o-pen door.
When will we

re - al - ize that peo - ple need the Lord?

Text: Greg Nelson, b.1948, and Phill McHugh, b.1951
Tune: Greg Nelson, b.1948, and Phill McHugh, b.1951
© 1983, Shepherd's Fold Music/River Oaks Music Co., admin. at EMICMGPublishing.com

473 Empower Us, Lord

...the Holy Spirit will teach you all things and will remind you of everything I have said to you.
John 14:25

Verses

1. There's so much work to do, im-pos-si-ble to do, Un-less You
2. The en-e-my is strong, and we won't o-ver-come, Un-less You

show - er us, em - pow - er us; We
show - er us, em - pow - er us; We

know it won't be long be - fore You take us home, So, Lord, please
fol - low Your com-mand to preach in ev - 'ry land, So, Lord, please

show - er us, em - pow - er us.
show - er us, em - pow - er us. Em -

Refrain

pow-er us, Lord, em-pow-er us, Lord, To fin-ish the work till You come back to get us. Em-pow-er us, Lord, em-pow-er us, Lord, Em-pow-er us, Lord, till You come.

Text: Gale Jones Murphy, b.1954
Tune: Gale Jones Murphy, b.1954
© Gale Jones Murphy

474 Lead Me, Guide Me

You are indeed my rock and my fortress; for your name's sake lead me and guide me...
Psalm 31:3

Refrain

Lead me, guide me, a - long the way,

For if You lead me, I can - not stray.

Lord, let me walk each day with Thee.

Lead me, oh Lord, lead me.

Verses

1. I am weak and I need Thy strength and pow'r to help me o-ver my weak-est hour. Help me through the dark-ness Thy face to see, Lead me, oh Lord, lead me.

2. Help me tread in the paths of right-eous-ness, Be my aid when Sa-tan and sin op-press. I am put-ting all my trust in Thee. Lead me, oh Lord, lead me.

3. I am lost if You take your hand from me, I am blind with-out Thy Light to see, Lord, just al-ways let me Thy ser-vant be. Lead me, oh Lord, lead me.

D.C.

Text: Doris M. Akers, 1922–1995
Tune: Doris M. Akers, 1922–1995; harm. by Richard Smallwood, b.1948
© 1953, (renewed), arr. © 2011, Doris M. Akers, admin. by Chappell & Co., Inc.

475 All the Way My Savior Leads Me

My foot has held fast to his steps; I have kept his way and have not turned aside.
Job 23:11

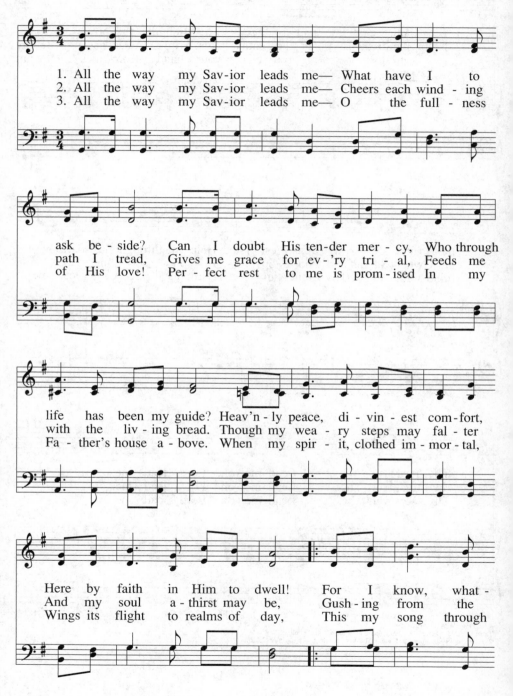

1. All the way my Sav-ior leads me— What have I to
2. All the way my Sav-ior leads me— Cheers each wind - ing
3. All the way my Sav-ior leads me— O the full - ness

ask be - side? Can I doubt His ten-der mer - cy, Who through
path I tread, Gives me grace for ev - 'ry tri - al, Feeds me
of His love! Per - fect rest to me is prom - ised In my

life has been my guide? Heav'n - ly peace, di - vin - est com - fort,
with the liv - ing bread. Though my wea - ry steps may fal - ter
Fa - ther's house a - bove. When my spir - it, clothed im - mor - tal,

Here by faith in Him to dwell! For I know, what -
And my soul a - thirst may be, Gush - ing from the
Wings its flight to realms of day, This my song through

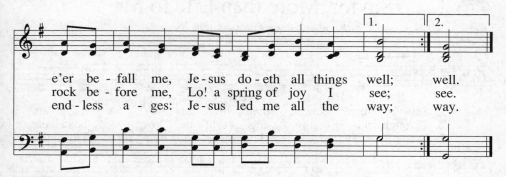

e'er be - fall me, Je - sus do - eth all things well; well.
rock be - fore me, Lo! a spring of joy I see; see.
end - less a - ges: Je - sus led me all the way; way.

Text: Fanny J. Crosby, 1820–1915
Tune: ALL THE WAY, 8 7 8 7 D; Robert Lowry, 1826–1899

476 Savior, More than Life to Me

For to me, living is Christ and dying is gain.
Philippians 1:21

1. Sav - ior, more than life to me, I am
2. Through this chang - ing world be - low, Lead me
3. Let me love Thee more and more, Till this

cling-ing, cling-ing close to Thee; Let Thy pre - cious blood ap-
gen - tly, gen-tly as I go; Trust-ing Thee, I can-not
fleet - ing, fleet-ing life is o'er; Till my soul is lost in

plied, Keep me ev - er, ev - er near Thy side.
stray, I can nev - er, nev - er lose my way.
love, In a bright-er, bright-er world a - bove.

Ev - 'ry day, ev - 'ry hour Let me

Ev - 'ry day and hour, ev - 'ry day and hour

feel   Thy cleans-ing pow'r;   May Thy ten - der love to

me   Bind me clos-er,   clos-er,   Lord,   to   Thee.

Text: Fanny J. Crosby, 1820–1915
Tune: MORE THAN LIFE, 79 79 with refrain; William H. Doane, 1832–1915

477   Savior, Lead Me Lest I Stray

With my whole heart I seek you; do not let me stray from your commandments.
Psalm 119:10

1. Sav - ior, lead me lest I stray, Gen - tly lead me all the way; I am safe when by Thy side,
2. Thou the ref - uge of my soul, When life's storm - y bil - lows roll; I am safe when Thou art nigh,
3. Sav - ior, lead me, then at last, When the storm of life is past; To the land of end - less day,

I would in Thy love a - in Thy love a - bide.
All my hopes on Thee re - hopes on Thee re - ly.
Where all tears are wiped a - tears are wiped a - way.

I would in Thy love a - bide.
All my hopes on Thee re - ly.
Where all tears are wiped a - way.

Lead me, lead me, Sav - ior, lead me, lest I

Sav - ior,

stray; Gen - tly down the stream of

lest I stray; Gen - tly

time, Lead me, Sav - ior, all the way, all the way.

stream of time, way.

Text: Frank M. Davis, 1839–1897
Tune: LEAD ME, 77 77 with refrain; Frank M. Davis, 1839–1897

478 Precious Lord, Take My Hand

Lead me, O LORD, in your righteousness because of my enemies; make your way straight before me.
Psalm 5:8

Verses 1–3

1. Pre - cious Lord, take my hand, Lead me on, help me
2. When my way grows drear, Pre - cious Lord, lin - ger
3. When the dark - ness ap - pears And the night draws

stand; I am tired, I am weak, I am worn;
near; When my life is al - most gone,
near, And the day is past and gone;

Through the storm, through the night, Lead me on to the
Hear my cry, hear my call, Hold my hand lest I
At the riv - er I stand, Guide my feet, hold my

light, Take my hand, pre - cious Lord, lead me home.
fall; Take my hand, pre - cious Lord, lead me home.
hand; Take my hand, pre - cious Lord, lead me home.

Verse 4

4. Pre - cious Lord, I love Your name, When I look

back from whence I came; Some-times stumb-ling, some-times

fall - ing, some-times a - lone. Friends and

loved ones I love so dear, Man-y are gone, but still I'm

here; Take my hand, pre-cious Lord, and lead me on.

Text: Thomas A. Dorsey, 1899–1993
Tune: PRECIOUS LORD, Irregular; George N. Allen, 1812–1877; adapt. by Thomas A. Dorsey, 1899–1993
© 1938, (renewed), arr. © 2011, Warner-Tamerlane Publishing Corp.

479 Jesus, You Brought Me All the Way

Come to me, all you who are weary and burdened, and I will give you rest.
Matthew 11:28

Refrain
♩ = 74

Je-sus, You brought me all the way. You

car-ry my bur-dens ev-er-y day. You are

such a won-der-ful Sav-ior, I've nev-er known You to

fail me yet. 'Cause You brought me, 'cause You brought

yet. 'Cause You brought me, thank God, all of the way,

Some-times I find it so   dif-fi-cult to pray.
My   soul got hap-py   and I   stayed there all day.

Oh, but there's one thing   I can tru-ly say: that You've brought

me,   thank God,   all   the   way.

Text: Kenneth W. Louis, b.1956
Tune: Kenneth W. Louis, b.1956
© 2001, GIA Publications, Inc.

Victory Is Mine

480

The God of peace will shortly crush Satan under your feet.
Romans 16:20

The melody is in the alto part.

1. Vic - to - ry   is mine.   Vic - to - ry   is mine.
2. Joy   is mine.   Joy   is mine.
3. Hap - pi - ness is mine.   Hap - pi - ness is mine.

Vic - to - ry   to - day   is   mine.   I   told Sa - tan
Joy   to - day   is   mine.   I   told Sa - tan
Hap - pi - ness to - day   is   mine.   I   told Sa - tan

get   thee be - hind.   Vic - to - ry   to - day   is   mine.
get   thee be - hind.   Joy   to - day   is   mine.
get   thee be - hind.   Hap - pi - ness to - day   is   mine.

Text: Dorothy Norwood and Alvin Darling
Tune: VICTORY, 5 5 7 8 7; Dorothy Norwood and Alvin Darling; arr. by Stephen Key
© 1994, Malaco Music, Inc.

481 Lead On, O King Eternal

I am the LORD your God, who teaches you for your own good, who leads you in the way you should go.
Isaiah 48:17

1. Lead on, O King E - ter - nal, The day of march has come!
2. Lead on, O King E - ter - nal, Till sin's fierce war shall cease
3. Lead on, O King E - ter - nal, We fol - low — not with fears!

Hence-forth in fields of con - quest Thy tents shall be our home;
And ho - li - ness shall whis - per The sweet A - men of peace;
For glad-ness breaks like morn - ing Wher-e'er Thy face ap-pears;

Thru days of prep - a - ra - tion Thy grace has made us strong,
For not with swords loud clash-ing Nor roll of stir-ring drums—
Thy cross is lift - ed o'er us—We jour-ney in its light:

And now, O King E - ter - nal, We lift our bat - tle song.
With deeds of love and mer - cy The heav'n-ly king-dom comes.
The crown a - waits the con-quest—Lead on, O God of might.

Text: Ernest W. Shurtleff, 1862–1917
Tune: LANCASHIRE, 7 6 7 6 D; Henry T. Smart, 1813–1879; arr. by Jon Drevits, © 1966, New Spring Publishing (ASCAP)

Stand Up for Jesus

482

*Therefore take up the whole armor of God, so that you may be able to withstand on that evil day,
and having done everything, to stand firm.*
Ephesians 6:13

1. Stand up, stand up for Je - sus, Ye sol - diers of the cross!
2. Stand up, stand up for Je - sus, The trum - pet call o - bey;
3. Stand up, stand up for Je - sus, Stand in His strength a - lone;
4. Stand up, stand up for Je - sus, The strife will not be long;

Lift high His roy - al ban - ner— It must not suf - fer loss.
Forth to the might - y con - flict In this His glo - rious day.
The arm of flesh will fail you— Ye dare not trust your own.
This day the noise of bat - tle— The next, the vic - tor's song.

From vic - t'ry un - to vic - t'ry His ar - my shall He lead,
Ye that are men now serve Him A - gainst un - num - bered foes;
Put on the gos - pel ar - mor, Each piece put on with prayer;
To Him that o - ver - com - eth A crown of life shall be:

Till ev - 'ry foe is van - quished And Christ is Lord in - deed.
Let cour - age rise with dan - ger And strength to strength op - pose.
Where du - ty calls or dan - ger, Be nev - er want - ing there.
He with the King of glo - ry Shall reign e - ter - nal - ly.

Text: George Duffield, Jr., 1818–1888
Tune: WEBB, 7 6 7 6 D; George J. Webb, 1803–1887

483 We Are Soldiers

You then, my child, be strong in the grace that is in Christ Jesus...
2 Timothy 2:1

Text: Gospel Hymn
Tune: Gospel Hymn; arr. by Nolan Williams, Jr., b.1969, © 2000, GIA Publications, Inc.

Am I a Soldier of the Cross

484

Keep alert, stand firm in your faith, be courageous, be strong. Let all that you do be done in love.
1 Corinthians 16:13–14

1. Am I a sol - dier of the cross, A fol - l'wer of the Lamb? And shall I fear to own His cause Or blush to speak His name?
2. Must I be car - ried to the skies On flow - 'ry beds of ease, While oth - ers fought to win the prize And sailed through blood - y seas?
3. Are there no foes for me to face? Must I not stem the flood? Is this vile world a friend to grace, To help me on to God?
4. Sure I must fight if I would reign: In - crease my cour - age, Lord; I'll bear the toil, en - dure the pain, Sup - port - ed by Thy word.

Text: Isaac Watts, 1674–1748
Tune: ARLINGTON, CM; Thomas A. Arne, 1710–1778

485 Battle Hymn of the Republic

In your majesty ride on victoriously for the cause of truth and to defend the right...
Psalm 45:4

1. Mine eyes have seen the glo - ry of the
2. I have seen Him in the watch - fires of a
3. He has sound - ed forth the trum - pet that shall
4. In the beau - ty of the lil - ies Christ was

com - ing of the Lord; He is tram - pling out the
hun - dred cir - cling camps; They have build - ed Him an
nev - er call re - treat; He is sift - ing out all
born a - cross the sea, With a glo - ry in His

vin - tage where the grapes of wrath are stored; He hath
al - tar in the eve - ning dews and damps; I can
hu - man hearts be - fore His judg - ment seat; O be
bos - om that trans - fig - ures you and me; As He

loosed the fate - ful light - ning of His ter - ri - ble swift sword;
read the right - eous sen - tence by the dim and flar - ing lamps;
swift, my soul, to an - swer Him; be ju - bi - lant, my feet!
died to make us ho - ly, let us die that all be free!

His truth is march - ing on.
His day is march - ing on.
Our God is march - ing on.
While God is march - ing on.

Glo - ry! Glo - ry! Hal - le - lu - jah! Glo - ry!

Glo - ry! Hal - le - lu - jah! Glo - ry! Glo - ry! Hal - le -

lu - jah! His truth is march - ing on.

Text: Julia W. Howe, 1819–1910
Tune: BATTLE HYMN OF THE REPUBLIC, 15 15 15 6 with refrain; William Steffe, d.1911

486
Ezekiel Saw de Wheel

...when the living creatures rose from the earth, the wheels rose. Wherever the spirit would go, they went...
Ezekiel 1:19–20

Refrain

E - ze-k'el saw de wheel 'Way up in de mid-dle o' de air, E-ze-k'el saw de wheel 'Way in de mid-dle o' de air. De big wheel run by faith, De lit-tle wheel run by de grace o' God, A wheel in a wheel— 'Way in de mid-dle o' de air.

Verses

1. Bet - ter mind, my sis - ter, how you walk on de cross,
2. Let me tell you, broth - er, what a sin - ner will do,

'Way in de mid-dle o' de air,

Your foot might slip an' your
He'll step on you an' he'll

'Way in de mid-dle o' de air.

D.C.

soul be lost.
step on me.

Text: Traditional
Tune: Negro Spiritual; harm. by J. Jefferson Cleveland, 1937–1988, alt., © 1981, Abingdon Press

487 Onward, Christian Soldiers

Share in suffering like a good soldier of Christ Jesus.
2 Timothy 2:3

1. On - ward, Chris - tian sol - diers, March - ing as to war.
2. Like a might - y ar - my Moves the Church of God;
3. Crowns and thrones may per - ish, King - doms rise and wane,
4. On - ward, then, ye peo - ple, Join our hap - py throng;

With the cross of Je - sus Go - ing on be - fore:
Chris - tians, we are tread - ing Where the saints have trod,
But the Church of Je - sus Con - stant will re - main,
Blend with ours your voic - es In the tri - umph song,

Christ, the roy - al Mas - ter, Leads a - gainst the foe;
We are not di - vid - ed, All one bod - y we:
Gates of hell can nev - er 'Gainst that Church pre - vail;
Glo - ry, laud, and hon - or Un - to Christ the King:

For - ward in - to bat - tle, See His ban - ners go.
One in hope and one in faith, One in char - i - ty.
We have Christ's own prom - ise, And that can - not fail.
This through count - less a - ges With the an - gels sing.

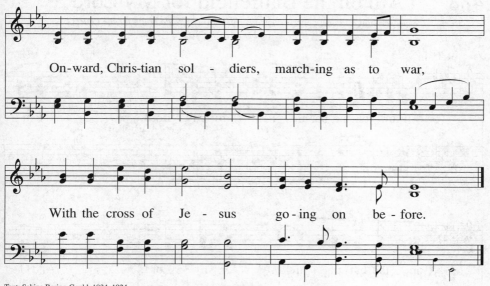

On-ward, Chris-tian sol - diers, march-ing as to war,

With the cross of Je - sus go - ing on be - fore.

Text: Sabine Baring-Gould, 1834–1924
Tune: ST. GERTRUDE, 6 5 6 5 D with refrain; Arthur S. Sullivan, 1842–1900

488 I Am on the Battlefield for My Lord

...your servants will cross over, everyone armed for war, to do battle for the LORD...
Numbers 32:27

Refrain

I am on the bat-tle - field for my Lord, I'm

on the bat-tle - field for my Lord; And I

prom-ised Him that I would serve Him till I die. I am

on the bat-tle - field for my Lord.

Verses

1. I was a - lone and i - dle, I was a sin - ner too, I heard a voice from heav - en Say there is work to do, I took the Mas - ter's hand, And I joined the Chris - tian band, I'm on the bat - tle - field for my Lord.

2. I left my friends and kin - dred Bound for the Prom-ised Land, The grace of God up - on me, The Bi - ble in my hand, In dis - tant lands I trod, Cry - ing sin - ner come to God, I'm on the bat - tle - field for my Lord.

3. Now when I met my Sav - ior, I met Him with a smile, He healed my wound - ed spir - it, And owned me as His child, A - round the throne of grace, He ap - points my soul a place, I'm on the bat - tle - field for my Lord.

D.C.

Text: Sylvana Bell and E. V. Banks
Tune: BATTLEFIELD, 7 6 7 6 67 9 with refrain; Gospel Hymn; arr. by Joseph Joubert, b.1958, © 2000, GIA Publications, Inc.

489   What a Mighty God We Serve

The mighty one, God the LORD, speaks and summons the earth from the rising of the sun to its setting.
Psalm 50:1

What a might - y God we serve.

What a might - y God we serve.

An-gels bow be - fore Him. Heav-en and earth a - dore Him.

1.
Last time

What a might - y God we serve.

Last time

2.

I com-

mand you, Sa-tan, in the name of the Lord to take

up your weap-ons and flee, for the Lord has giv-en me au-

D.C.

thor - i - ty to walk all o - ver thee.

Text: Traditional
Tune: Traditional; arr. by Stephen Key, © 2000, GIA Publications, Inc.

490 Satan, We're Gonna Tear Your Kingdom Down

And the devil who had deceived them was thrown into the lake of fire and sulfur...
Revelation 20:10

1. ⁊ Sa - tan, we're gon - na tear your king-dom
2. The preach-ers are gon - na preach your king-dom
3. The dea - cons are gon - na pray your king-dom
4. The moth - ers are gon - na moan your king-dom

down. ⁊ Sa - tan, we're gon-na tear your king - dom
down. The preach-ers are gon-na preach your king - dom
down. The dea - cons are gon-na pray your king - dom
down. The moth - ers are gon-na moan your king - dom

down. You've been build-ing your king-dom all o - ver this

land. Sa - tan, we're gon-na tear your king-dom down.

Text: Traditional
Tune: KINGDOM DOWN, 10 10 12 10; traditional; arr. by James Abbington, b.1960, © 2000, GIA Publications, Inc.

We Shall Walk through the Valley in Peace 491

Even though I walk through the darkest valley, I fear no evil; for you are with me...
Psalm 23:4

1. We shall walk through the val - ley in peace;
2. There will be no sor - row there;
3. There will be no dy - ing there;

We shall walk through the val - ley in peace;
There will be no sor - row there.
There will be no dy - ing there.

If Je - sus Him - self shall be our Lead - er,

We shall walk through the val - ley in peace.

Text: A. L. Hatter
Tune: PEACEFUL VALLEY, 99 10 9; A. L. Hatter; arr. by Joseph Joubert, b.1958, © 2000, GIA Publications, Inc.

492 # In the Garden

They heard the sound of the LORD walking in the garden…
Genesis 3:8

1. I come to the gar-den a-lone, While the
2. He speaks, and the sound of His voice Is so
3. I'd stay in the gar-den with Him Though the

dew is still on the ros-es; And the voice I hear,
sweet the birds hush their sing-ing; And the mel-o-dy
night a-round me be fall-ing; But He bids me go—

fall-ing on my ear, The Son of God dis-clos-es.
that He gave to me With-in my heart is ring-ing.
through the voice of woe, His voice to me is call-ing.

And He walks with me, and He talks with me,

And He tells me I am His own, And the joy we share as we tar - ry there, None oth - er has ev - er known.

Text: C. Austin Miles, 1868–1946
Tune: GARDEN, 8 9 10 7 with refrain; C. Austin Miles, 1868–1946

493 The Reason Why We Sing

I will give to the LORD the thanks due to his righteousness, and sing praise to the name of the LORD, the Most High.
Psalm 7:17

Verses

1. Some-one asked the ques - tion: why do we sing?
2. Some-one may be won - d'ring: when we sing our song
3. When the song is o - ver, we all say, "A-men."
4. If some-bod - y asks you: was it just a show?
(5.) when we cross the riv - er, we'll stud - y war no more.

When we lift our hands to Je - sus, what
at times we may be cry - ing and
In our heart just keep on sing - ing, and the
Lift your hands and be a wit - ness, and
We will sing our song to Je - sus, the

rea - son why I sing.   Glo - ry, hal - le - lu -

jah!   You're the rea - son why I sing.

1.

2.   D.S.

Last time   5. And   D.S.

Text: Kirk Franklin, b.1970
Tune: Kirk Franklin, b.1970; arr. by Evelyn Simpson-Curenton, b.1953
© 1993, Lilly Mack Publishing, admin. at EMICMGPublishing.com

Something Within

494

Now we have received not the spirit of the world, but the Spirit that is from God...
1 Corinthians 2:12

1. Preach-ers and teach-ers would make their ap-peal,
2. Have you that some-thing, that burn-ing de-sire?
3. I met God one morn', my soul feel-ing bad,

Refrain: Some-thing with-in me that hold-eth the reins,

Fight-ing as sol-diers on great bat-tle-fields;
Have you that some-thing, that nev-er doth tire?
Heart heav-y la-den with a bowed down head.

Some-thing with-in me that ban-ish-es pain;

When to their plead-ings my poor heart did yield,
Oh, if you have it— that Heav-en-ly Fire!
He lift-ed my bur-den, made me so glad,

Some-thing with-in me I can-not ex-plain,

All I can say, there is some-thing with-in.
Then let the world know there is some-thing with-in.
All that I know there is some-thing with-in.

All that I know there is some-thing with-in.

Text: Lucie E. Campbell, 1885–1963
Tune: SOMETHING WITHIN, 10 10 10 10; Lucie E. Campbell, 1885–1963; arr. by James Abbington, b.1960, © 2000, GIA Publications, Inc.

495 Center of My Joy

...I regard everything as loss because of the surpassing value of knowing Christ Jesus my Lord.
Philippians 3:8

Chorus

Je-sus, You're the cen-ter of my joy.

All that's good and per-fect comes from You.

play cues 2nd time only

You're the heart of my con-tent-ment, hope for all I do.

1.
Je-sus, You're the cen-ter of my joy.

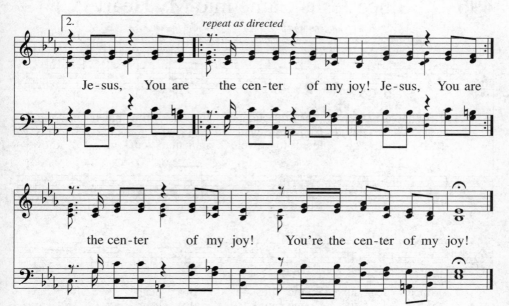

Je-sus, You are the cen-ter of my joy! Je-sus, You are the cen-ter of my joy! You're the cen-ter of my joy!

Text: Richard Smallwood, b.1948, William Gaither and Gloria Gaither
Tune: Richard Smallwood, b. 1948, William Gaither, and Gloria Gaither; arr. by Nolan Williams, Jr.
© 1987, Hanna Street Music (all rights controlled by Gaither Copyright Mgmt.) and Century Oak/Richwood Music

496 Since Jesus Came into My Heart

It is no longer I who live, but it is Christ who lives in me.
Galatians 2:20

1. What a won - der - ful change in my life has been wrought
2. I have ceased from my wan - d'ring and go - ing a - stray,
3. I shall go there to dwell in that cit - y, I know,

Since Je - sus came in - to my heart! I have
Since Je - sus came in - to my heart! And my
Since Je - sus came in - to my heart! And I'm

light in my soul for which long I have sought,
sins, which were man - y, are all washed a - way,
hap - py, so hap - py, as on - ward I go,

Since Je - sus came in - to my heart!
Since Je - sus came in - to my heart!
Since Je - sus came in - to my heart!

Since Je-sus came in-to my in-to my heart, Since Je-sus came in-to my in-to my heart, Floods of joy o'er my soul like the sea bil-lows roll, Since Je-sus came in-to my heart.

Text: Rufus H. McDaniel, 1850–1940
Tune: McDANIEL, 12 8 12 8 with refrain; Charles H. Gabriel, 1856–1932; adapt. by Louis Sykes, © 2000, GIA Publications, Inc.

497 I Love to Tell the Story

I will sing of your steadfast love, O LORD, forever; with my mouth I will proclaim your faithfulness...
Psalm 89:1

sat - is - fies my long-ings   As   noth - ing else would do.
that   is just the rea - son   I   tell   it   now   to thee.
mes - sage of sal - va - tion From God's own ho - ly Word.
be   the old, old sto - ry   That   I   have loved   so long.

I love to tell the sto - ry; 'Twill be my theme in glo - ry—

To   tell   the old, old   sto-ry   Of Je - sus and   His love.

Text: A. Katherine Hankey, 1831–1911
Tune: HANKEY, 7 6 7 6 D with refrain; William G. Fischer, 1835–1912

498   Somebody Prayed for Me

I am asking on their behalf; I am not asking on behalf of the world, but on behalf of those whom you gave me...
John 17:9

1. Some - bod - y prayed for me, had me on their mind,

took the time and prayed for me.

I'm so glad they prayed.   I'm so glad they prayed.

I'm so glad they prayed for me.

2. The preacher prayed for me...
3. My mother prayed for me...
4. Jesus prayed for me...

Text: Dorothy Norwood and Alvin Darling
Tune: Dorothy Norwood and Alvin Darling; arr. by Nolan Williams, Jr., b.1969, and Stephen Key
© 1994, Malaco Music, Inc.

499 Blessed Assurance, Jesus Is Mine

...let us approach (the sanctuary) with a true heart in full assurance of faith, with our hearts sprinkled clean...
Hebrews 10:22

1. Bless-ed as - sur - ance, Je - sus is mine! O what a
2. Per - fect sub - mis - sion, per-fect de - light, Vi-sions of
3. Per - fect sub - mis - sion, all is at rest, I in my

fore - taste of glo - ry di - vine! Heir of sal - va - tion,
rap - ture now burst on my sight; An - gels de - scend - ing
Sav - ior am hap-py and blest; Watch-ing and wait - ing,

pur - chase of God, Born of His Spir - it, washed in His blood.
bring from a - bove Ech - oes of mer - cy, whis-pers of love.
look - ing a - bove, Filled with His good-ness, lost in His love.

This is my sto - ry, this is my song, Prais-ing my

Sav - ior all the day long; This is my sto - ry, this is my song, Prais-ing my Sav - ior all the day long.

Text: Fanny J. Crosby, 1820–1915
Tune: ASSURANCE, 9 10 9 9 with refrain; Phoebe P. Knapp, 1839–1908

500 Jesus Is Real to Me

But thanks be to God, who gives us the victory through our Lord Jesus Christ.
1 Corinthians 15:57

Chorus

Real, real, Je-sus is real to me.

Oh yes, He gives me the vic-to - ry.

So man-y peo-ple doubt Him. I can't live with-out Him.

That is why I love Him so, He's so real to me.

Text: Beatrice Brown, © 1963, Beatrice Brown's Music House
Tune: Beatrice Brown, © 1963, Beatrice Brown's Music House; arr. by Stephen Key, © 2000, GIA Publications, Inc.

The Lord Is Blessing Me Right Now   501

Blessed be the God and Father of our Lord Jesus Christ, who has blessed us in Christ with every spiritual blessing…
Ephesians 1:3

The Lord is

bless-ing me   right   now,   right

now!   The   Lord   is

bless-ing me   right now,   right

now!   He woke   me   up   this

morn - ing,   and start - ed me   on   my

way. The Lord is bless-ing me

right now, right now, right now!

Text: Gospel Song
Tune: Gospel Song; arr. by Glenn L. Jones, b.1949, © 2010, GIA Publications, Inc.

502

Love Lifted Me

...in his love and in his pity he redeemed them; he lifted them up and carried them all the days of old.

Isaiah 63:9

1. I was sink - ing deep in sin, Far from the peace - ful
2. All my heart to Him I give, Ev - er to Him I'll
3. Souls in dan - ger, look a - bove, Je - sus com - plete - ly

shore, Ver - y deep - ly stained with - in,
cling, In His bless - ed pres - ence live,
saves; He will lift you by His love

Sink-ing to rise no more; But the Mas - ter
Ev - er His prais - es sing. Love so might - y
Out of the an - gry waves. He's the Mas - ter

of the sea Heard my de - spair - ing cry,
and so true Mer - its my soul's best songs;
of the sea, Bil - lows His will o - bey;

From the wa - ters lift - ed me— Now safe am I.
Faith - ful, lov - ing serv - ice, too, To Him be - longs.
He your Sav - ior wants to be— Be saved to - day.

Love lift - ed e - ven me, Love lift - ed

me, e - ven me, When noth - ing else could help,

me, Love lift - ed me; Love lift - ed me.

Text: James Rowe, 1865–1933
Tune: SAFETY, 7 6 7 6 7 6 7 4 with refrain; Howard E. Smith, 1863–1918

503 He Has Done Great Things for Me

The LORD has done great things for us, and we rejoiced.
Psalm 126:3

1. He has done great things for me.
2. He has made a way for me.
3. He will give you vic - to - ry.
4. I'm gonna be a wit - ness for Him.
5. I'm gonna let my lit - tle light shine.

Great things, great things.
Made a way, made a way.
Vic - to - ry, vic - to - ry.
Wit - ness, wit - ness.
Shine, shine.

He has done great things for me.
He has made a way for me.
He will give you vic - to - ry.
I'm gonna be a wit - ness for Him.
I'm gonna let my lit - tle light shine.

Text: Shirley M. K. Berkeley, © 1989
Tune: GREAT THINGS, 7 4 7; Shirley M. K. Berkeley, © 1989; arr. by Stephen Key, © 2000, GIA Publications, Inc.

I Am Redeemed

Christ redeemed us from the curse of the law by becoming a curse for us...
Galatians 3:13

504

Chorus

I am re-deemed, bought with a price;

Je - sus has changed my whole life. If

an - y-bod - y asks you just who I am,

Last time

tell them I am re - deemed!

Last time

Last time

Text: Jessy Dixon, b.1938, © Dixon Music, Inc.
Tune: Jessy Dixon, b.1938, © Dixon Music, Inc.; arr. by Nolan Williams, Jr., b.1969, © 2000, GIA Publications, Inc.

505 Glory, Glory, Hallelujah

Cast your burden on the LORD, and he will sustain you; he will never permit the righteous to be moved.
Psalm 55:22

1. Glo - ry, glo - ry, hal - le - lu - jah! Since I laid my bur - dens down.
2. Friends don't treat me like they used to Since I laid my bur - dens down.
3. I'm goin' home to live with Je - sus Since I laid my bur - dens down.

Glo - ry, glo - ry, hal - le - lu - jah!
Friends don't treat me like they used to
I'm goin' home to live with Je - sus

Since I laid my bur - dens down!
Since I laid my bur - dens down!
Since I laid my bur - dens down!

Text: Negro Spiritual
Tune: GLORY, 15 15; Negro Spiritual; arr. by Nolan Williams, Jr., b.1969, © 2000, GIA Publications, Inc.

He's Done So Much for Me

He himself bore our sins in his body on the cross, so that, free from sins, we might live for righteousness...
1 Peter 2:24

1. He's done so much for me, I can-not tell it all,
2. He washed my sins a-way; I can-not tell it all,
3. He walks and talks with me; I can-not tell it all,
4. He gave me vic-to-ry; I can-not tell it all,

I can-not tell it all, I can-not tell it all.
I can-not tell it all, I can-not tell it all.
I can-not tell it all, I can-not tell it all.
I can-not tell it all, I can-not tell it all.

He's done so much for me, I can-not tell it all.
He washed my sins a-way; I can-not tell it all.
He walks and talks with me; I can-not tell it all.
He gave me vic-to-ry; I can-not tell it all.

I can - not tell it all.

Text: Theodore R. Frye and Lillian Bowles, c.1884–1949
Tune: DONE SO MUCH, 12 12 12 6; Theodore R. Frye and Lillian Bowles, c.1884–1949; arr. by Nolan Williams, Jr., b.1969,
© 2000, GIA Publications, Inc.

507 I'll Tell It Wherever I Go

The word of God continued to spread; the number of the disciples increased greatly in Jerusalem...
Acts 6:7

Unison

1. I'll tell of the Sav - ior, I tell of His
2. I know Him, a - dore Him, a good life to
3. If Sa - tan op - press me, His grace will ca -

fa - vor, I'll tell it wher - ev - er I go.
show Him, I'll tell it wher - ev - er I go.
ress me, I'll tell it wher - ev - er I go.

I count ev - 'ry bless-ing, I go on con-
He's near - est, He's clear-est, In my life He's
When trou - bles de - press me, He won't fail to

fess - ing, I'll tell it wher - ev - er I go.
dear - est, I'll tell it wher - ev - er I go.
bless me, I'll tell it wher - ev - er I go.

Text: Thomas A. Dorsey, 1899–1993
Tune: I'LL TELL IT, Irregular; Thomas A. Dorsey, 1899–1993
© 1938 (renewed), arr. © 2011, Unichappel Music, Inc.

508 Look and Live

Blessed are the eyes that see what you see! Many... desired to see what you see, but did not see it.
Luke 10:23–24

1. I've a mes-sage from the Lord, Hal-le-lu-jah! The mes-sage un-to you I'll give. 'Tis re-cord-ed in His Word, Hal-le-lu-jah! It is on-ly that you "look and live."

2. I've a mes-sage full of love, Hal-le-lu-jah! A mes-sage, O my friend, for you. 'Tis a mes-sage from a-bove, Hal-le-lu-jah! Je-sus said it, and I know 'tis true.

3. Life is of-fered un-to you. Hal-le-lu-jah! E-ter-nal life your soul shall have If you'll on-ly look to Him. Hal-le-lu-jah! Look to Je-sus, who a-lone can save.

4. I will tell you how I came, Hal-le-lu-jah! To Je-sus when He made me whole: 'Twas be-liev-ing on His name, Hal-le-lu-jah! I trust-ed and He saved my soul.

"Look and live," my broth-er, live.

"Look and live," my broth-er, live. "Look and live." Look to

Je - sus now and live. 'Tis re - cord - ed in His Word, Hal - le -

lu - jah! It is on - ly that you "look and live."

Text: William A. Ogden, 1841–1897
Tune: LOOK AND LIVE, 11 8 11 9 with refrain; William A. Ogden, 1841–1897

509 He's Sweet I Know

The LORD bless you and keep you; the LORD make his face to shine upon you, and be gracious to you...
Numbers 6:24–25

Refrain: He's sweet, I know. He's sweet, I know.
1. I can't for-get when I was sad.
2. I have my tick-et here in my hand.

Storm clouds may rise, strong winds may blow.
Head hang-ing down, soul feel-ing bad.
I'm go-ing to that beau-ti-ful land.

I'll tell the world wher - ev - er I go.
All I could say was Lord take my heart.
Some - time I weep and some - time I moan.

That I've found a Sav - ior, and He's sweet, I know.
Je - sus heard and saved me, and gave me a start.
But I'm bound for glo - ry, and I'm go - ing on.

Text: Traditional Gospel hymn
Tune: HE'S SWEET, 88 9 11; Traditional Gospel hymn; arr. by Kenneth Louis, b.1956, and Nolan Williams, Jr., b.1969, © 2000, GIA Publications, Inc.

510 We Gather in Memory

Now you are the body of Christ, and each one of you is a part of it.
1 Corinthians 12:27

1. We gath - er in mem - 'ry, in hope, and in praise,
2. We thank You for stead - fast com - pan - ions and friends:
3. To - geth - er in wor - ship, in prayer and in song,
4. We join in the wit - ness of ones gone be - fore

To hon - or the Light that en - light - ens our days:
For neigh - bors and part - ners whose love nev - er ends;
We find in Your house - hold a place to be - long:
Who stand at the thresh - old of Christ's o - pen door:

The dec - ades of serv - ice and e - ons of grace;
For broth - ers and sis - ters, for hus - bands and wives,
In preach - ing that voic - es a truth to be heard,
Your saints, like the stars, who now bril - liant - ly shine

Your faith - ful - ness reach - ing through time and through space.
For par - ents and chil - dren, en - rich - ing our lives.
And calls us to jus - tice and joy in Your Word.
And draw us to full - ness, re - deem - ing the time!

Text: Mary Louise Bringle, b.1953, © 2006, GIA Publications, Inc.
Tune: FOUNDATION, 11 11 11 11; Caldwell's *Unison Harmony*, 1837

The Bond of Love

511

I give you a new commandment... love one another. Just as I have loved you, you also should love one another.
John 13:34

1. We are one in the bond of love, We are
2. Let us sing now, ev - 'ry - one, Let us

one in the bond of love; We have joined our spir - it with the
feel His love be - gun; Let us join our hands that the

Spir - it of God, We are one in the bond of love.
world will know We are one in the bond of love.

Text: Otis Skillings, b.1935
Tune: BOND OF LOVE, 88 12 8; Otis Skillings, b.1935
© 1971, Lillenas Publishing Co.

512

Precious Memories

I will not leave you orphaned; I am coming to you.
John 14:18

Refrain: Pre - cious mem - 'ries
1. Pre - cious mem - 'ries,
2. As I wan - der
3. In sad hours

how they ling - er,
how I prize them
o'er life's jour - ney
when I'm lone - ly

How they ev - er flood my
As the wea - ry years un -
Won - d'ring what the years may
The truth of Je - sus' love is

soul.
fold.
hold.
told.

Last time

In   the   still - ness
Je - sus whis - pers,
As   I   pon - der
In   the si - lence

of   the mid - night
"I'll   be with you."
oh,   sweet won - der!
of   the mid - night

Sa - cred se - crets He'll un -
What   a com - fort to my
Pre - cious mem - 'ries flood my
Pre - cious mem - 'ries flood my

fold.
soul.
soul.
soul.

Text: Roberta Martin, 1912–1969, and Mrs. Georgia Jones, © 1939
Tune: PRECIOUS MEMORIES, 8 7 8 7 with refrain; Roberta Martin, 1912–1969, and Mrs. Georgia Jones, © 1939; arr. by Joseph Joubert, b.1958
© 2000, GIA Publications, Inc.

513

Let Me See!

"Go," said Jesus, "your faith has healed you." Immediately he received his sight and followed Jesus along the road.
Mark 10:52

1. The blind man said to Je - sus, "O
2. Then Je - sus said, "O blind man, Now go
3. Some - times we are that blind man Though

Lord! Son of God! Help me! I am blind and I have been
do just what I have said, And the Heav - en - ly pow'r that
we see with our own eyes There are times we are lost in

since my birth; Let me see this beau - ti - ful earth!"
comes through Me Will heal and make you see!"
a dark place Far a - way from sav - ing grace!

Let me see! Let me see with my own eyes the

beau-ty of the sun, moon and skies; Let me glimpse with my spir - it

me!

what's in store for me, for me! Let me

me!

see how You came to res - cue me. Let me

see how on the cross You set me free. Let me

see! Let me see! O Lord, let me see!

Text: Robert L. Morris, b.1943 (ASCAP)
Tune: Robert L. Morris, b.1943 (ASCAP)
© 2002, Hidden Gems Press

514 There Is a Balm in Gilead

Is there no balm in Gilead? Why then has the health of my poor people not been restored?
Jeremiah 8:22

Refrain

There is a balm   in Gil-e-ad   To make the wound-ed   whole;

There is a balm   in Gil-ead   To heal the sin-sick soul.

Verses

1. Some - times   I   feel   dis - cour - aged   And
2. Don't   ev - er   be   dis - cour - aged,   For
3. If   you   can - not preach   like   Pe - ter,   If you

think   my work's   in   vain,   But   then   the Ho - ly
Je - sus   is   your   friend;   And   if   you lack for
can - not   pray   like   Paul,   You can   tell   the love of

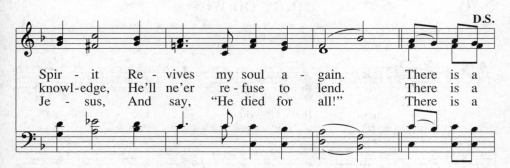

Spir - it Re - vives my soul a - gain. There is a
knowl-edge, He'll ne'er re - fuse to lend. There is a
Je - sus, And say, "He died for all!" There is a

Text: Negro Spiritual
Tune: BALM IN GILEAD, 7 6 7 6 with refrain; Negro Spiritual; arr. by Nolan Williams, Jr., b.1969, © 2000, GIA Publications, Inc.

Come On in My Room 515

"Stay with us, because it is almost evening and the day is now nearly over." So he went in to stay with them.
Luke 24:29

Chorus

1. Come on in my room. Come on in my room. Je - sus is my doc - tor, He writes down all of my 'scrip - tions, He gives me all of my med - i-cines in my room.

2. Joy in my room...
3. Peace in my room...
4. Healing in my room...

Text: Negro Spiritual
Tune: Meter hymn, lined out by Carolyn Bolger-Payne; arr. by Evelyn Simpson-Curenton, b.1953, © 2000, GIA Publications, Inc.

516 Shine on Me

Let your face shine upon your servant; save me in your steadfast love.
Psalm 31:16

1. I heard the voice of Je - sus
2. With pit - y - ing eyes the Prince of

say, "Come un - to me and rest.
Peace Be - held our help - less grief;

Lay down thou wea - ry one, lay
He saw, and O a - maz - ing

down Thy head up - on my breast."
love! He came to our re - lief.

Shine on me, Shine on me. Let the
light from the light-house, Shine on me.
Shine on me. Shine on me. Let the
light from the light-house Shine on me.

Text: Negro Spiritual
Tune: SHINE ON ME, CM with refrain; Negro Spiritual; arr. by James Abbington, b.1960, © 2000, GIA Publications, Inc.

517 It's Alright

It is Christ Jesus, who died, yes, who was raised, who is at the right hand of God, who indeed intercedes for us.
Romans 8:34

Refrain

It's al - right, it's al - right. My Je - sus said He'll fix it and it's al - right. It's al - right, it's al - right. My Je - sus said He'll fix it and it's al - right.

Last time

Verses

1. When it gets dark and I can't see my way,
2. That day when death comes a creep - in' in,
3. Some - times your best friend put you down,

ooh

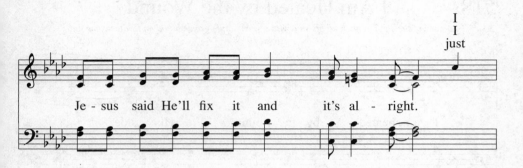

I
I
just

Je - sus said He'll fix it and it's al - right.

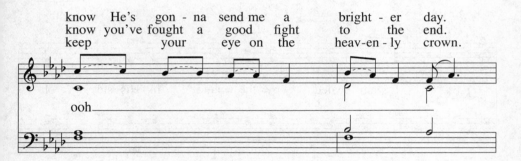

know He's gon - na send me a bright - er day.
know you've fought a good fight to the end.
keep your eye on the heav-en - ly crown.

ooh_____

D.C.

Je - sus said He'll fix it and it's al - right.

Text: Negro Spiritual
Tune: Negro Spiritual; arr. by Bill Cummings, © 2000, GIA Publications, Inc.

518   I Am Healed by the Wound

...one of the soldiers pierced his side with a spear, and at once blood and water came out.
John 19:34

I am healed by the wound in His side.
I am healed by the wound in His side, oh
yes. Oh, they pierced Him in His side, Je-sus hung His head and
died. I am healed by the wound in His side.

Text: Virgin Davis
Tune: Virgin Davis, harm. by Bill Cummings, © 2000, GIA Publications, Inc.

Thank You for the Gifts

519

He appointed some of the Levites to give thanks, and to praise the LORD.
1 Chronicles 16:4

Thank You for the gifts we give back to You to-day.

Thank You for Your love that will nev - er, ev - er sway.

Thank

Thank You for the joy You im - part ev - 'ry day.

You for the joy

Thank You. Thank You.

Text: Robert L. Morris, b.1943 (ASCAP)
Tune: Robert L. Morris, b.1943 (ASCAP)
© Hidden Gems Press

520
Jesus, Jesus, Jesus

But thanks be to God! He gives us the victory through our Lord Jesus Christ.
1 Corinthians 15:57

1. Je - sus, Je - sus, Je - sus. Je - sus, Je - sus, Je - sus,
2. Sav - ior, Sav - ior, Sav - ior, Sav - ior, Sav - ior, Sav - ior,
3. Heal - er, Heal - er, Heal - er, Heal - er, Heal - er, Heal - er,
4. Thank You, thank You, thank You, Thank You, thank You, thank You,

Je - sus, Je - sus, Je - sus, Je - sus,
Sav - ior, Sav - ior, Sav - ior, Sav - ior,
Heal - er, Heal - er, Heal - er, Heal - er,
Thank You, thank You, Thank You, thank You, thank You,

Je - sus, Je - sus, Je - sus.
Sav - ior, Sav - ior, Sav - ior.
Heal - er, Heal - er, Heal - er.
Thank You, thank You, thank You.

Je - sus, Je - sus, Je - sus.

Text: Anonymous
Tune: Anonymous

521 Every Day Is a Day of Thanksgiving

Glorify the LORD with me; let us exalt his name together.
Psalm 34:3

Ev - 'ry day   is a   day   of   thanks-giv-ing.

God's been so   good   to me;   Ev-'ry day He's bless-ing me.

Last time to Coda
Take the time to

Ev - 'ry day   is a   day   of   thanks-giv-ing;

glo - ri-fy   the Lord   to-day.

Verse 1

1. I thank God for the mo-ments when I wor-ship in His name. I thank Him for the sac-ri-fice of praise. It's no mys-ter-y to say how my God is ev-'ry day

o-pens the door that I might see He's bless-ing me. He keeps

bless-ing me, bless-ing me. Take the time to

glo-ri-fy the Lord, glo-ri-fy the Lord to-day.

Verse 2
Yes, there are pressures all around me
When fighting Satan's descending powers
That never cease from trying to bring me down;
But I just lift my hands to glory
Believing in God's redemption story;
Thanking Him for His saving grace
As God gives me power to win this race.

Text: Leonard Burks
Tune: Leonard Burks
© Legré Publishing Co.

522
Thank You, Jesus

...with gratitude in your hearts sing psalms, hymns, and spiritual songs to God.
Colossians 3:16

Sopranos and Altos unison:

Thank You, Je - sus. Thank You, Je - sus for all You've done for

me; Thank You, Je - sus. Thank You, Je - sus for Cal - va - ry.

All:

The pain You bore to set me free. All this and

more You have done for me. Thank You, Je - sus. Thank You

Je - sus, I thank You, Je-sus, my Lord and King.

Text: Bernadette Blount Salley
Tune: Bernadette Blount Salley
© 1984, Bernadette Blount Salley. Administered by GIA Publications, Inc.

One More Day

523

Rejoice in hope, be patient in suffering, persevere in prayer.
Romans 12:12

1. One more day, one more day, I thank God just for
2. One more chance, one more chance, I thank God just for

one more day. One more day, the Lord has made a
one more chance. One more chance to do the best I

way, I thank God just for one more day.
can, I thank God just for one more chance.

Text: Margaret Pleasant Douroux, b.1941, © Rev. Earl Pleasant Publishing
Tune: ONE MORE DAY, 6 8 9 9; Margaret Pleasant Douroux, b.1941, © Rev. Earl Pleasant Publishing; arr. by Nolan Williams, Jr., b.1969,
    © 2000, GIA Publications, Inc.

524 I Will Bless Thee, O Lord

Every day I will bless you, and praise your name forever... Great is the LORD, and greatly to be praised...
Psalm 145:2–3

I will bless Thee, O Lord!
up,
I will bless Thee, O
And my mouth filled with

Lord!
praise,
With a heart of thanks-giv-ing,
With a heart of thanks-giv-ing,
I will bless Thee, O
I will bless Thee, O

Lord! With my hands lift - ed Lord!

Text: Esther Watanabe, © 1970, New Song Music
Tune: Esther Watanabe, © 1970, New Song Music; arr. by Nolan Williams, Jr., b.1969, © 2000, GIA Publications, Inc.

525   Count Your Blessings

Let them thank the LORD for his steadfast love, for his wonderful works to humankind.
Psalm 107:31

1. When up-on life's bil-lows you are tem-pest-tossed,
2. Are you ev-er bur-dened with a load of care?
3. When you look at oth-ers with their lands and gold,
4. So, a-mid the con-flict, wheth-er great or small,

When you are dis-cour-aged think-ing all is lost,
Does the cross seem heav-y you are called to bear?
Think that Christ has prom-ised you His wealth un-told;
Do not be dis-cour-aged, God is o-ver all;

Count your man-y bless-ings, name them one by one,
Count your man-y bless-ings, ev-'ry doubt will fly,
Count your man-y bless-ings, mon-ey can-not buy
Count your man-y bless-ings, an-gels will at-tend,

And it will sur-prise you what the Lord has done.
And you will be sing-ing as the days go by.
Your re-ward in heav-en, nor your home on high.
Help and com-fort give you to your jour-ney's end.

Count your bless-ings, Name them one by one;

Count your bless-ings, See what God has done.

Count your bless-ings, — Name them one by one;

Count your man - y bless-ings, See what God has done.

Text: Johnson Oatman, Jr., 1856–1922
Tune: BLESSINGS, 11 11 11 11 with refrain; Edwin O. Excell, 1851–1921; arr. by Evelyn Simpson-Curenton, b.1953, © 2000, GIA Publications, Inc.

526

I Thank You, Jesus

He prostrated himself at Jesus' feet and thanked him. And he was a Samaritan.
Luke 17:16

1. I thank You, Je - sus. I thank You,
2. You've been my moth - er, You've been my

1. I thank You, Je - sus.
2. You've been my moth - er,

Je - sus. I thank You,
fa - ther, You've been my

I thank You, Je - sus. Je - sus, I thank You,
You've been my fa - ther, sis - ter, my broth - er,

Lord. Oh, You brought me, yes, You brought me from a
too,

might - y, a might - y long way, a might - y long

Text: Kenneth Morris, 1917–1988
Tune: Kenneth Morris, 1917–1988; arr. by Joseph Joubert, b.1958
© 1948, (renewed), arr. © 2011, Martin and Morris Studio, Inc., admin. by Unichappell Music, Inc.

527 We Bring the Sacrifice of Praise

...let us continually offer a sacrifice of praise to God, that is, the fruit of lips that confess his name.
Hebrews 13:15

We bring the sac-ri-fice of praise in-to the house of the Lord. We bring the sac-ri-fice of praise in-to the house of the Lord. And we of-fer up to You the sac-ri-fic-es of thanks-giv-ing, and we of-fer up to You the sac-ri-fic-es of praise.

Text: Kirk Dearman, b.1952
Tune: Kirk Dearman, b.1952; arr. Stephen Key
© 1984, New Spring Publishing (ASCAP)

Rejoice, Ye Pure in Heart

528

Let us rejoice and exult and give him the glory...
Revelation 19:7

1. Re - joice, ye pure in heart, Re - joice, give thanks and sing; Your fes - tal ban - ner wave on high, The cross of Christ your King.
2. Bright youth and snow - crowned age, All those for truth do seek; Raise high your free, ex - ult - ing song, God's won - drous prais - es speak.
3. Yes, on through life's long path, Still chant - ing as ye go; From youth to age, by night and day, In glad - ness and in woe.
4. Then on, ye pure in heart, Re - joice, give thanks and sing; Your glo - rious ban - ner wave on high, The cross of Christ your King.

Re - joice, re - joice, Re - joice, give thanks and sing.

Text: Edward H. Plumptre, 1821–1891
Tune: MARION, SM with refrain; Arthur H. Messiter, 1834–1916

529 Thank You, Lord

I will render thank offerings to you. For you have delivered my soul from death.
Psalm 56:12–13

Chorus

Thank You, Lord, for sav-ing my soul,

Thank You, Lord, for mak-ing me whole;

Thank You, Lord, for giv-ing to me

Thy great sal-va-tion so rich and free.

Text: Seth Sykes, 1892–1950
Tune Seth Sykes, 1892–1950 and Bessie Sykes, 1905–1982
© 1940, New Spring Publishing (ASCAP)

Thank You, Lord

530

I will give thanks to you, O LORD, among the peoples, and I will sing praises to you among the nations.
Psalm 108:3

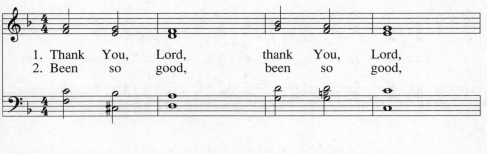

1. Thank You, Lord, thank You, Lord,
2. Been so good, been so good,

thank You, Lord,
been so good,   I just want to thank You, Lord.

Text: Traditional
Tune: Negro Spiritual; arr. by Stephen Key, © 2000, GIA Publications, Inc.

531 Free at Last

In my anguish I cried to the LORD, and he answered by setting me free.
Psalm 118:5

Refrain

Free at last, free at last, I thank God I'm

free at last; Free at last, free at last,

thank God Al-might-y, I'm free at last. O free at last.

Verses

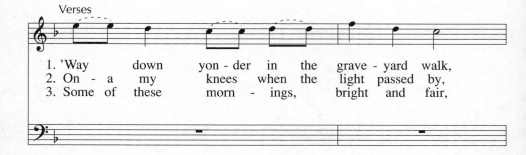

1. 'Way down yon - der in the grave - yard walk,
2. On - a my knees when the light passed by,
3. Some of these morn - ings, bright and fair,

thank God Al-might-y, I'm free at last.
thank God Al-might-y, I'm free at last.
thank God Al-might-y, I'm free at last. Goin'

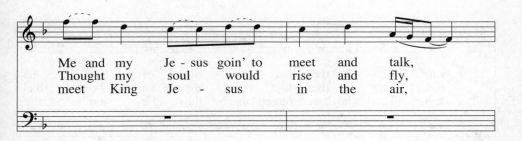

Me and my Je - sus goin' to meet and talk,
Thought my soul would rise and fly,
meet King Je - sus in the air,

D.C.

thank God Al-might-y, I'm free at last. O

Text: Negro Spiritual
Tune: Negro Spiritual; arr. by Kenneth W. Louis, b.1956, © 2006, GIA Publications, Inc.

532 Lift Every Voice and Sing

Let them praise the name of the LORD, for his name alone is exalted; his glory is above earth and heaven.
Psalm 148:13

1. Lift ev - 'ry voice and sing, Till earth and heav - en
2. Ston - y the road we trod, Bit - ter the chas - t'ning
3. God of our wea - ry years, God of our si - lent

ring, Ring with the har - mo - nies of lib - er -
rod, Felt in the days when hope un - born had
tears, Thou who hast brought us thus far on the

ty; Let our re - joic - ing rise High as the lis - t'ning
died; Yet with a stead - y beat, Have not our wea - ry
way; Thou who hast by Thy might, Led us in - to the

skies, Let it re - sound loud as the roll - ing sea.
feet Come to the place for which our peo - ple sighed?
light, Keep us for ev - er in the path, we pray.

Sing a song full of the faith that the dark past has taught us,
We have come o - ver a way that with tears has been wa - tered;
Lest our feet stray from the plac - es, our God, where we met Thee,

Sing a song full of the hope that the pres - ent has
We have come, tread - ing our path through the blood of the
Lest our hearts, drunk with the wine of the world, we for -

brought us; Fac - ing the ris - ing sun Of our new
slaugh - tered; Out from the gloom - y past, Till now we
get Thee; Shad-owed be - neath Thy hand, May we for

day be - gun, Let us march on till vic - to - ry is won.
stand at last Where the bright gleam of our bright star is cast.
ev - er stand, True to our God, true to our na - tive land.

Text: James W. Johnson, 1871–1938
Tune: ANTHEM, 66 10 66 10 14 14 66 10; J. Rosamund Johnson, 1873–1954

533 Go Down, Moses

Then the Lord spoke to Moses, "Go and tell Pharaoh king of Egypt to let the Israelites go out of his land."
Exodus 6:10–11

1. When Is - rael was in E - gypt's land; Let my peo - ple go,
2. Thus saith the Lord, bold Mo - ses said; Let my peo - ple go,
3. No more shall they in bond-age toil; Let my peo - ple go,

Op - pressed so hard they could not stand, Let my peo - ple go.
If not, I'll smite your first - born dead, Let my peo - ple go.
Let them come out with E - gypt's spoil, Let my peo - ple go.

Go down, Mo - ses,
go down, Mo-ses,
'Way down in E-gypt's land.

Go down, go down, Mo - ses,

Tell old Phar - oah, Let my peo - ple go!

Text: Negro Spiritual
Tune: GO DOWN MOSES, 8 5 8 5 with refrain; Negro Spiritual

Steal Away to Jesus

534

For he will hide me in his shelter in the day of trouble; he will conceal me under the cover of his tent...
Psalm 27:5

Refrain

Steal a-way, steal a-way, steal a-way to Je - sus!

Steal a-way, steal a-way home, I ain't got long to stay here.

Verses
Unison

1. My Lord, He calls me, He calls me by the thun - der;
2. Green trees are bend-ing, Poor sin - ners stand a trem-bling;
3. My Lord, He calls me, He calls me by the light - ning;

div.   **D.C.**

The trum-pet sounds with-in my soul; I ain't got long to stay here.

Text: Negro Spiritual
Tune: STEAL AWAY, 5 7 8 7 with refrain; Negro Spiritual

535 Swing Low, Sweet Chariot

...a chariot of fire and horses of fire separated the two of them, and Elijah ascended in a whirlwind into heaven.
2 Kings 2:11

Refrain

Swing low, sweet char - i - ot, Com-ing for to car-ry me home.

Swing low, sweet char - i - ot, Com-ing for to car-ry me home.

Verses

1. I looked o - ver Jor - dan, and what did I see
2. If you get there be - fore I do,
3. The bright - est day that ev - er I saw
4. I'm some - times up and some - times down,

Com-ing for to car-ry me home. A band of an - gels
Com-ing for to car-ry me home. Tell all my friends I'm
Com-ing for to car-ry me home. When Je - sus washed my
Com-ing for to car-ry me home. But still my soul feels

com-ing af-ter me, Coming for to car-ry me home. O,
com - ing too, Coming for to car-ry me home. O,
sins a - way, Coming for to car-ry me home. O,
heav'n - ly bound, Coming for to car-ry me home. O,

Text: Traditional
Tune: SWING LOW, LM with refrain; Negro Spiritual; arr. by Robert Nathaniel Dett, 1882–1943, © 1936 (renewed), Paul A. Schmitt Music Co.,
c/o Belwin-Mills Publishing Corp.

536 Walk Together, Children

I have no greater joy than this, to hear that my children are walking in the truth.
3 John 4

Walk to-geth-er, chil-dren, don't you get wea-ry,

walk to-geth-er, chil-dren, don't you get wea-ry,

walk to-geth-er, chil-dren, don't you get wea-ry,

there's a great camp meet-ing in the prom-ised land.

We're gon-na walk and nev-er tire,

*Sing, Pray, Work

walk and nev - er tire, walk and

nev - er tire, there's a

great camp meet - ing in the prom - ised land.

Text: Traditional
Tune: Negro Spiritual, arr. Evelyn Simpson-Curenton, b.1953, © 2000, GIA Publications, Inc.

537 Oh, Freedom

For freedom Christ has set us free. Stand firm, therefore, and do not submit again to a yoke of slavery.
Galatians 5:1

1. Oh, free-dom, Oh, free-dom,
2. No more moan-ing, no more moan-ing,
3. There'll be sing-ing, there'll be sing-ing,

oh, free-dom o - ver me.
no more moan-ing o - ver me.
there'll be sing-ing o - ver me.

And be-

O - ver me.

fore I'd be a slave I'll be bur-ied in my grave,

and go home to my Lord and be free.

Text: Traditional
Tune: OH FREEDOM, Irregular; Negro Spiritual, arr. by Valeria A. Foster, © 2000, GIA Publications, Inc.

We Shall Overcome

538

For whatever is born of God conquers the world. And this is the victory that conquers the world, our faith.
1 John 5:4–5

1. We shall o - ver - come. We shall o - ver - come. We shall o - ver - come some - day.
2. We'll walk hand in hand. We'll walk hand in hand. We'll walk hand in hand some - day.
3. We shall live in peace. We shall live in peace. We shall live in peace some - day.
4. We are not a - fraid. We are not a - fraid. We are not a - fraid to - day.
5. God will see us through. God will see us through. God will see us through to - day.

Oh, deep in my heart I do be - lieve. We shall o - ver - come some - day.

Text: Negro Spiritual
Tune: WE SHALL OVERCOME, 5 5 7 9 7; Negro Spiritual; arr. by Nolan Williams, Jr., b.1969, © 2000, GIA Publications, Inc.

539
Make Us Disciples

Then the disciples went out and preached everywhere...
Mark 16:20

Lord, we've been cho-sen, to preach in Your
gard - less of cul - ture, gen - der or

name; You are the mes - sage we
creed; Help us to reach those in

bold - ly pro-claim, Re -
dark - ness and in need.

Text: Gale Jones Murphy, b.1954
Tune: Gale Jones Murphy, b.1954
© Gale Jones Murphy

540 Follow Jesus

My sheep listen to my voice; I know them, and they follow me.
John 10:27

1. Fol - low Je - sus,   take no chance get - ting lost. Fol-low
2. Fol - low Je - sus,   He will lead,   He will guide. Fol-low

Je - sus, There'll be des - erts you'll have to cross. Fol - low Je -
Je - sus, Through life's tem-pest He'll let you hide. Fol - low Je -

sus.   He's got a safe   moun - tain plan;   and if
sus.   Reach out and touch,   hold His hand;

He can't take you to the top, there's no-bod-y else who can.

Last time

Don't wor-ry if you can-not see, learn to trust Him and to fol-low His lead. Don't wor-ry if it's day or night. He is bright-er than the bright-est light. And if He can't take you to the top, there's no-bod-y else who can.

Text: Margaret Pleasant Douroux, b.1941, © 1981, Rev. Earl Pleasant Publishing Co.
Tune: Margaret Pleasant Douroux, b.1941, © 1981, Rev. Earl Pleasant Publishing Co.; arr. by Kenneth W. Louis, b.1956, © 2006, GIA Publications, Inc.

541 Get Right with God

In his great mercy he has given us new birth…
1 Peter 1:3

Refrain

Get right with God, and do it now; get right with God, and

hal-le-lu-jah!

He will show you how, Down at the cross, where He shed His

blood, Get right with God, get right, get right with God.

Verses

1. Je - sus Christ my King, He is all to me;
2. He's work - ing now, down in my heart;
3. How great is God, work-ing in the earth;
4. Lord, come the more, me your fa - vors show,

He   blest my heart,   and gives me ev - 'ry-thing;
He   is sweet to   me,   O   what pleas-ure   I   find;
Com-ing un - to   all,   giv - ing us   the   new birth;
Lord,   let me know   which way   to   go;

Liv - ing by His word,   He   is   in   my soul;
He's the liv - ing way,   come, and hear Him say;
Ac - cept the   call,   com - ing un - to   all,
Come   in my heart,   fill - ing ev - 'ry part,

Oh, broth-er,
D.C.

Down   at the cross,   get right, get right with God.

Text: Anonymous
Tune: Anonymous; arr. by Willa A. Townsend, 1880–1947

542

If Jesus Goes with Me

Go...and remember, I am with you always, to the end of the age.
Matthew 28:19–20

1. It may be in the val - ley, Where count - less dan - gers hide; It may be in the sun - shine That I, in peace a - bide; But this one thing I know— If it be dark or fair, If Je - sus is with me, I'll go an - y - where!

2. It may be I must car - ry The bless - ed word of life A - cross the burn - ing des - erts To those in sin - ful strife; And though it be my lot To bear my col - ors there, If Je - sus goes with me, I'll go an - y - where!

3. But if it be my por - tion To bear my cross at home, While oth - ers bear their bur - dens Be - yond the bil - low's foam, I'll prove my faith in Him— Con - fess His judg-ments fair, And, if He stays with me, I'll go an - y - where!

4. It is not mine to ques - tion The judg - ments of my Lord, It is but mine to fol - low The lead - ings of His word; But if to go or stay, Or wheth - er here or there, I'll be, with my Sav - ior, Con - tent an - y - where!

If Je - sus goes with me, I'll go. An - y - where! 'Tis

I'll go.

heav - en to me, Where - e'er I may be, If He is

there! I count it a priv - i - lege here. His cross to

His cross, His cross, His

bear; If Je - sus goes with me, I'll go— An - y - where!

cross to bear;

Text: C. Austin Miles, 1868–1946
Tune: IF JESUS GOES, 7 6 7 6 6 6 6 5 with refrain; C. Austin Miles, 1868–1946
© 1962, Word Music, LLC

543 Rock of Ages

Lead me to the rock that is higher than I; for you are my refuge, a strong tower against the enemy.
Psalm 61:2–3

1. Rock of a - ges, cleft for me, Let me
2. Could my tears for ev - er flow, Could my
3. While I draw this fleet - ing breath, When my

hide my - self in Thee; Let the wa - ter and the
zeal no lan-guish know, These for sin could not a -
eyes shall close in death, When I rise to worlds un -

blood, From Thy wound - ed side which flowed, Be of
tone— Thou must save, and Thou a - lone: In my
known And be - hold Thee on Thy throne, Rock of

sin the dou - ble cure, Save from wrath and make me pure.
hand no price I bring, Sim - ply to Thy cross I cling.
A - ges, cleft for me, Let me hide my - self in Thee.

Text: Augustus M. Toplady, 1740–1778
Tune: TOPLADY, 77 77 77; Thomas Hastings, 1784–1872

Woke Up This Mornin'

544

Those of steadfast mind you keep in peace—in peace because they trust in you.
Isaiah 26:3

1. Woke up this morn - in' with my mind, stayed on
2. No con-dem-na - tion with my mind,
3. Walk-in' and talk - in' with my mind,

mind, my mind was

Woke up this morn - in' with my mind, stayed on
Je - sus. No con-dem-na - tion with my mind,
Walk-in' and talk - in' with my mind,

mind, my mind was

Woke up this morn - in' with my mind, stayed on
Je - sus. No con-dem-na - tion with my mind,
Walk - in' and talk - in' with my mind,

mind, my mind was

Je - sus. Hal - le - lu, hal - le - lu, hal - le - lu - jah.

4. Can't hate your neighbor in your mind...   6. Devil can't catch you in your mind...
5. Love everybody with your mind...   7. Jesus, the captain in your mind...

Text: Congregational Praise Song
Tune: WITH MY MIND, 12 12 12 with hallelujahs; Congregational Praise Song, arr. by Evelyn Simpson-Curenton, b.1953, © 2000,
    GIA Publications, Inc.

545

Here I Am, Lord

Then I heard the voice of the Lord saying, "Whom shall I send, and who will go for us?"
And I said, "Here am I; send me!"
Isaiah 6:8

Verses

Descant:

3. Ah_____ Ah_____

Unison

1. I, the Lord of sea and sky, I have heard my
2. I, the Lord of snow and rain, I have borne my
3. I, the Lord of wind and flame, I will tend the

Ah_____

peo - ple cry.   All who dwell in dark and sin
peo - ple's pain.   I have wept for love of them.
poor and lame.   I will set a feast for them.

My hand will save.   Fin - est bread I

My hand will save.   I, who made the
They turn a - way.   I will break their
My hand will save.   Fin-est bread I

will pro - vide   till their hearts be   sat - is - fied.

stars   of   night,   I will make   their dark - ness bright.
hearts of stone,   Give them hearts   for   love   a - lone.
will   pro - vide   Till their hearts   be   sat - is - fied.

I will give my   life to them.   Whom shall I   send?

Who will bear my light to them?   Whom shall I   send?
I   will speak my word to them.   Whom shall I   send?
I   will give my life to them.   Whom shall I   send?

Refrain

Here I   am,   Lord.   Is   it   I,   Lord?

I have heard You call-ing in the night.

I will go, Lord, if You lead me.

I will hold Your peo - ple in my heart.

1., 2.

3.

heart.

Text: Isaiah 6; Dan Schutte, b.1947
Tune: Dan Schutte, b.1947; arr. by Michael Pope, SJ, and John Weissrock
© 1981, OCP

Where He Leads Me

546

If any want to become my followers, let them deny themselves and take up their cross and follow me.
Matthew 16:24

1. I can hear my Sav - ior call - ing, I can
2. I'll go with Him through the gar - den, I'll go
3. I'll go with Him through the judg - ment, I'll go
4. He will give me grace and glo - ry, He will

Refrain: Where He leads me I will fol - low, Where He

hear my Sav - ior call - ing, I can hear my Sav - ior
with Him through the gar - den, I'll go with Him through the
with Him through the judg - ment, I'll go with Him through the
give me grace and glo - ry, He will give me grace and

leads me I will fol - low, Where He leads me I will

call - ing, "Take thy cross and fol - low, fol - low Me."
gar - den, I'll go with Him, with Him all the way.
judg - ment, I'll go with Him, with Him all the way.
glo - ry, And go with me, with me all the way.

fol - low, I'll go with Him, with Him all the way.

Text: E. W. Blandy, c.1890
Tune: NORRIS, 888 9 with refrain; John S. Norris, 1844–1907

547

Count on Me

Put on the full armor of God...
Ephesians 6:11

1. The Lord has need of work-ers, to till His field to-day,
2. I count on Thee, dear Mas-ter, for cleans-ing in Thy blood,
3. Now gird me for the bat-tle when e-vil pow'rs op-pose,
4. I'll bear an-oth-er's bur-den a-long a lone-ly way,

So kind-ly He has led me to walk in wis-dom's way;
For con-stant streams of bless-ing, a nev-er-fail-ing flood;
And give me faith and cour-age to con-quer o'er Thy foes;
Or teach that bur-den-bear-er with con-fi-dence to pray;

I pray for grace to help me with all my heart to say,
To ev-er-new fru-i-tion I see Thy mer-cies bud,
I pledge Thee my al-le-giance, my soul no oth-er knows,
In serv-ice ev-er loy-al, at home or far a-way,

O bless-ed Sav-ior, count on me.

Count on me, count on me, For lov-ing-heart-ed serv-ice glad and free;

Yes, count on me, count on me, O bless-ed Sav-ior, count on me.

Text: Eliza E. Hewitt, 1851–1920
Tune: COUNT ON ME, 13 13 13 8 with refrain; J. Lincoln Hall, 1866–1930

548 I'll Be Somewhere Listening for My Name

Now the LORD came... calling as before, "Samuel!" And Samuel said, "Speak, for your servant is listening."
1 Samuel 3:10

1. When He calls me I will an - swer, When He calls me I will an - swer, When He calls me I will
2. With a glad heart I will an - swer, With a glad heart I will an - swer, With a glad heart I will
3. When He calls you, will you an - swer? When He calls you, will you an - swer? When He calls you, will you

an - swer; I'll be some-where list-'ning for my name.
an - swer; I'll be some-where list-'ning for my name.
an - swer? Some-where list - 'ning, list-'ning for your name.

1., 2. I'll be some-where list-'ning, I'll be some-where list-'ning,
3. You'll be some-where list-'ning, You'll be some-where list-'ning,

I'll be some-where list-'ning for my name. Oh,
You'll be some-where list-'ning for your name. Oh,

I'll be some-where list-'ning, I'll be some-where
you'll be some-where list-'ning, You'll be some-where

list-'ning, I'll be some-where list-'ning for my name.
list-'ning, You'll be some-where list-'ning for your name.

Text: Eduardo J. Lango
Tune: SOMEWHERE LISTENING, 888 9 66 9 76 9; Eduardo J. Lango; adapt. by Louis Sykes, © 2000, GIA Publications, Inc.

549 More about Jesus

I want to know Christ and the power of his resurrection and the sharing of his sufferings...
Philippians 3:10

1. More a-bout Je - sus would I know, More of His grace to
2. More a-bout Je - sus let me learn, More of His ho - ly
3. More a-bout Je - sus— in His Word Hold-ing com-mun-ion
4. More a-bout Je - sus on His throne, Rich-es in glo - ry

oth - ers show, More of His sav - ing full - ness see,
will dis - cern; Spir - it of God, my Teach - er be,
with my Lord, Hear - ing His voice in ev - 'ry line,
all His own, More of His king - dom's sure in-crease,

More of His love who died for me.
Show - ing the things of Christ to me.
Mak - ing each faith - ful say - ing mine.
More of His com - ing— Prince of Peace.

More, more a-bout Je - sus, More, more a-bout Je - sus; More of His sav - ing full - ness see, More of His love who died for me.

Text: Eliza E. Hewitt, 1851–1920
Tune: SWENEY, LM with refrain; John R. Sweny, 1837–1899

This Little Light of Mine

550

Let your light shine before others, so that they may see your good works and give glory to your Father in heaven.
Matthew 5:16

1. This lit - tle light of mine, I'm gon-na let it shine.
2. Ev - 'ry - where I go, I'm gon-na let it shine.
3. Je - sus gave it to me, I'm gon-na let it shine.

oh

This lit - tle light of mine, I'm gon-na let it shine.
Ev - 'ry - where I go, I'm gon-na let it shine.
Je - sus gave it to me, I'm gon-na let it shine.

oh

This lit - tle light of mine, I'm gon-na let it shine.
Ev - 'ry - where I go, I'm gon-na let it shine.
Je - sus gave it to me, I'm gon-na let it shine.

oh   oh

Let it shine, let it shine, let it shine.

4. Shine, shine, shine, I'm gonna let it shine....
5. All in my home, I'm gonna let it shine....

Text: Harry Dixon Loes, 1895–1965
Tune: LIGHT OF MINE, 12 12 12 9; Harry Dixon Loes, 1895–1965; arr. by Nolan Williams, Jr., b.1969, © 2000, GIA Publications, Inc.

551 Close to Thee

...they began their journey for the sake of Christ.
3 John 7

1. Thou my ev - er - last - ing por - tion, More than
2. Not for ease or world - ly pleas - ure, Nor for
3. Lead me through the vale of shad - ows, Bear me

friend or life to me, All a - long my pil - grim
fame my prayer shall be; Glad - ly will I toil and
o'er life's fit - ful sea; Then the gate of life e -

jour - ney, Sav - ior, let me walk with Thee.
suf - fer, On - ly let me walk with Thee.
ter - nal May I en - ter, Lord, with Thee.

Close to Thee, Close to Thee, Close to Thee, Close to Thee;

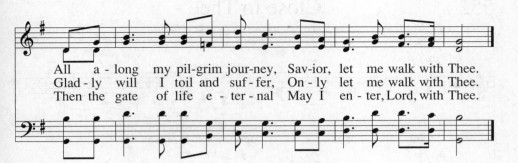

All a-long my pil-grim jour-ney, Sav-ior, let me walk with Thee.
Glad-ly will I toil and suf-fer, On-ly let me walk with Thee.
Then the gate of life e-ter-nal May I en-ter, Lord, with Thee.

Text: Fanny J. Crosby, 1820–1915
Tune: CLOSE TO THEE, 8 7 8 7 with refrain; Silas J. Vail, 1818–1884; arr. by Nolan Williams, Jr., b.1969, © 2000, GIA Publications, Inc.

Close to Thee

552

...they began their journey for the sake of Christ.
3 John 7

1. Thou my ev - er last - ing por - tion,
2. Not for ease or world - ly pleas - ure,

More than friend or life to me,
Nor for fame my prayer shall be;

All a - long my pil - grim jour - ney,
Glad - ly will I toil and suf - fer,

Sav - ior, let me walk with Thee.
On - ly let me walk with Thee.

Text: Fanny J. Crosby, 1820–1915
Tune: CLOSE TO THEE, 8 7 8 7 with refrain; Silas J. Vail, 1818–1884; arr. by Robert E. Wooten, Sr., 1930–2008, © 1981, Mar-Vel

553 Learning to Lean

Trust in the LORD with all your heart, and do not rely on your own insight.
Proverbs 3:5

Learn-ing to lean, learn-ing to lean, I'm learn-ing to lean on Je - sus. Find-ing more pow - er than I've ev - er seen. I'm learn-ing to lean on Je - sus.

Text: John Stallings, b.1938
Tune: John Stallings, b.1938; arr. by Evelyn Simpson-Curenton, b.1953
© 1976, Bridge Building Music, Inc. (BMI)

I Want Jesus to Walk with Me

554

Jesus said to them, "The light is with you for a little longer. Walk while you have the light...
John 12:35

1. I want Je - sus to walk with me,
2. In my tri - als, Lord, walk with me,

I want Je - sus to walk with me,
In my tri - als, Lord, walk with me,

All a - long my pil - grim jour - ney,
When the shades of life are fall - ing,

Lord, I want Je - sus to walk with me.
Lord, I want Je - sus to walk with me.

Text: Negro Spiritual
Tune: WALK WITH ME, 88 8 9; Negro Spiritual; arr. by Nolan Williams, Jr., b.1969, © 2000, GIA Publications, Inc.

555

Lift Him Up

And I, when I am lifted up from the earth, will draw all people to myself.
John 12:32

1. How to reach the mass - es, *men of ev - 'ry birth,
2. Oh! the world is hun - gry for the Liv - ing Bread,
3. Don't ex - alt the preach-er, don't ex - alt the pew,
4. Lift Him up by liv - ing as a Chris - tian ought,

For an an - swer Je - sus gave the key: "And
Lift the Sav - ior up for them to see; Trust
Preach the Gos - pel sim - ple, full and free; Prove
Let the world in you the Sav - ior see; Then

I, if I be lift - ed up from the earth,
Him, and do not doubt the words that He said,
Him and you will find that prom - ise is true,
men will glad - ly fol - low Him who once taught,

Will draw all men un - to Me."
"I'll draw all men un - to Me."
"I'll draw all men un - to Me."
"I'll draw all men un - to Me."

*Saints *can be substituted for* men *throughout this text.*

Lift Him up, Lift Him up,

Lift the pre-cious Sav-ior up, Lift the pre-cious Sav-ior up,

Still He speaks from e-ter-ni-ty: "And I, if I be lift-ed

up from the earth, Will draw all men un-to Me."

Text: Johnson Oatman, Jr., 1856–1922
Tune: LIFT HIM UP, 11 9 11 7 with refrain; B. B. Beall; adapt. by Nolan Williams, Jr., b.1969, Evelyn Simpson-Curenton, b.1953,
   and Robert J. Fryson, 1944–1994, © 2000, GIA Publications, Inc.

556

We Must Work

...pray for us, so that the word of the Lord may spread rapidly and be glorified everywhere...
2 Thessalonians 3:1

We must work while it is day, Spread-ing the

Word of God as we go a-long the way. We must be

will - ing to do God's will, Spread-ing the

Text: Keith C. Laws, 1964–2008, © KCL Music
Tune: Keith C. Laws, 1964–2008, © KCL Music; arr. by Nolan Williams, Jr., b.1969, © 2000, GIA Publications, Inc.

557 Give Me Jesus

They came to Philip, who was from Bethsaida in Galilee, and said to him, "Sir, we wish to see Jesus."
John 12:21

1. I heard my moth-er say, I heard my moth-er say,
2. Dark mid-night was my cry, Dark mid-night was my cry,
3. Oh, when I come to die, Oh, when I come to die,

I heard my moth-er say, Give me Je - sus.
Dark mid-night was my cry, Give me Je - sus.
Oh, when I come to die, Give me Je - sus.

Give me Je - sus. Give me Je - sus,

You may have all this world, Give me Je - sus.

Text: Negro Spiritual
Tune: GIVE ME JESUS, 666 4 with refrain; Negro Spiritual; arr. by Nolan Williams, Jr., b.1969, © 2000, GIA Publications, Inc.

Jesus Saves

558

...the Father has sent his Son as the Savior of the world.
1 John 4:14

1. We have heard the joy-ful sound: Je-sus saves! Je-sus saves!
2. Waft it on the roll-ing tide: Je-sus saves! Je-sus saves!
3. Sing a-bove the bat-tle strife: Je-sus saves! Je-sus saves!
4. Give the winds a might-y voice: Je-sus saves! Je-sus saves!

Spread the tid-ings all a-round: Je-sus saves! Je-sus saves!
Tell to sin-ners far and wide: Je-sus saves! Je-sus saves!
By His death and end-less life: Je-sus saves! Je-sus saves!
Let the na-tions now re-joice: Je-sus saves! Je-sus saves!

Bear the news to ev-'ry land, Climb the steeps and cross the waves;
Sing, ye is-lands of the sea; Ech-o back, ye o-cean caves;
Sing it soft-ly through the gloom, When the heart for mer-cy craves;
Shout sal-va-tion full and free, High-est hills and deep-est caves;

On-ward! 'tis our Lord's com-mand; Je-sus saves! Je-sus saves!
Earth shall keep her ju-bi-lee: Je-sus saves! Je-sus saves!
Sing in tri-umph o'er the tomb: Je-sus saves! Je-sus saves!
This our song of vic-to-ry: Je-sus saves! Je-sus saves!

Text: Priscilla J. Owens, 1829–1907
Tune: JESUS SAVES, 7 6 7 6 7 7 7 6; William J. Kirkpatrick, 1838–1921

559 Only What You Do for Christ Will Last

...store up for yourselves treasures in heaven, where neither moth nor rust consumes...
Matthew 6:19–20

1. You may build great ca - the - drals large or small,
2. You may seek earth - ly pow - er and fame,
3. Though your ar - mies may con - trol each hem - i - sphere,
4. Though your songs and prayers are heard and praised by man,

You can build sky - scrap - ers grand and tall,
The world might be im - pressed by your great name,
And your or - bits out in space cause men to cheer,
They've no mean - ing un - less you've been born a - gain,

You may con - quer all the fail - ures of the past,
Soon the glo - ries of this life will all be past,
Your sci - en - tif - ic knowl - edge may be vast,
Sin - ner, heed these words, don't let this har - vest pass,

But on - ly what you do for Christ will last.
But on - ly what you do for Christ will last.
But on - ly what you do for Christ will last.
For on - ly what you do for Christ will last.

Re-mem-ber on-ly what you do for Christ will last.

Re-mem-ber on-ly what you do for Christ will last.

On-ly what you do for Him will be count-ed at the

end; on-ly what you do for Christ will last!

Text: Raymond Rasberry
Tune: LASTING TREASURES, 10 10 10 10 with refrain; Raymond Rasberry; arr. by Valeria A. Foster
© 1963 (renewed), arr. © 2011, Warner-Tamerlane publishing Corp.

560

Completely Yes

For in him every one of God's promises is a "Yes." For this reason it is through him that we say the "Amen..."
2 Corinthians 1:20

Chorus

1. "Yes, Lord!   Yes, Lord!"   From the
(2.) love you!   I love you!   From the

bot-tom of my heart   to the depths of my soul.
bot-tom of my heart   to the depths of my soul.   I

"Yes, Lord!"   Com-plete-ly yes!   My soul says,
love you!   I real-ly do.   My soul says,

1. "yes!"   2. I "yes!"   *rubato*   3. My soul says, "yes, yes, yes!

Yes, Lord!" From the bot-tom of my heart,

"Yes, Lord!" To the depths of my soul. "Yes, Lord!"

Text: Sandra Crouch, b.1942
Tune: Sandra Crouch, b.1942; arr. by Stephen Key
© 1985, Sanabella Music/Bud John Songs, admin. at EMICMGPublishing.com

561 Thuma Mina

Lead me in your truth, and teach me, for you are the God of my salvation...
Psalm 25:5

African phonetics:
Too-mah mee-nah, So-mahn-dlah

Text: South African Spiritual (Zulu)
Tune: THUMA MINA, 8 7; South African
© 1984, Utryck, Walton Music Corporation, agent

Must Jesus Bear the Cross Alone   562

If any want to become my followers, let them deny themselves and take up their cross daily and follow me.
Luke 9:23

1. Must Je - sus bear the cross a - lone And all the world go free? No, there's a cross for ev - 'ry one, And there's a cross for me.

2. The con - se - crat - ed cross I'll bear Till death shall set me free, And then go home my crown to wear, For there's a crown for me.

3. Up - on the crys - tal pave - ment, down At Je - sus' pierc - ed feet, Joy - ful, I'll cast my gold - en crown And His dear name re - peat.

4. O pre - cious cross! O glo - rious crown! O res - ur - rec - tion day! Ye an - gels, from the stars come down And bear my soul a - way.

Text: Thomas Shepherd, 1665–1739
Tune: MAITLAND, CM; George N. Allen, 1812–1877

563 Hush, Hush, Somebody's Callin' My Name

Do not fear, for I have redeemed you; I have called you by name, you are mine.
Isaiah 43:1

1. Hush.   Hush.   Some - bod - y's
2. Sounds   like   Je - sus.   Some - bod - y's
3. Soon   one   morn - ing,   death come creep - in'
4. I'm   so   glad,   got   me   re -
5. I'm   so   glad   trou - ble don't

call - in'   my   name. Oh,   Hush.
call - in'   my   name. Oh,   Sounds   like
in   my   room. Oh,   Soon   one
lig - ion   on   time. Oh,   I'm   so
last al - ways. Oh,   I'm   so

Hush.   Some - bod - y's call - in' my   name.
Je - sus.   Some - bod - y's call - in' my   name.
morn - ing,   death come creep-in' in   my   room.
glad,   got   me   re - lig - ion on   time.
glad   trou - ble don't last al - ways.

Optional bass accompaniment

Hush. Hush. Some-bod-y's call-in' my
Sounds like Je-sus. Some-bod-y's call-in' my
Soon one morn-ing, death come creep-in' in my
I'm so glad, got me re-lig-ion on
I'm so glad trou-ble don't last al -

name.
name.
room. Oh, my Lord, Oh, my Lord, what shall I do?
time.
ways.

what shall I do?

Text: Traditional
Tune: SOMEBODY'S CALLIN', Irregular; Negro Spiritual; arr. by Nolan Williams, Jr., b.1969, © 2000, GIA Publications, Inc.

564 Something on the Inside

Dear friends, let us love one another, for love comes from God...
1 John 4:7

Some - thing on the in - side, work-ing on the out - side,
Love on the in - side, work-ing on the out - side,
Ho - ly Ghost on the in - side, work-ing on the out - side,

I feel a change in my life!

I feel a change in my life!

Text: African American Prayer and Praise Hymn, c.1900
Tune: African American Prayer and Praise Hymn, c.1900; arr. by Glenn L. Jones, b.1949
© 1987, 1988, 1991, 2011, GIA Publications, Inc.

565 I Will Do a New Thing

I am about to do a new thing; now it springs forth, do you not perceive it? I will make a way in the wilderness...
Isaiah 43:19

"I will do a new thing in you; I will do a new thing in you;

What - ev - er you ask for, what - ev - er you pray for,

noth-ing shall be de-nied," sa-ith the Lord; sa-ith the Lord! Lord!

Text: Audrey Byrd
Tune: Audrey Byrd; arr. by Nolan Williams, Jr., b.1969, © 2000, GIA Publications, Inc.

Revive Us Again

566

Will you not revive us again, so that your people may rejoice in you?
Psalm 85:6

1. We praise Thee, O God, for the Son of Thy love, For
2. We praise Thee, O God, for Thy Spir - it of light, Who has
3. All glo - ry and praise to the Lamb that was slain, Who has
4. Re - vive us a - gain— fill each heart with Thy love; May each

Je - sus who died and is now gone a - bove.
shown us our Sav - ior and scat - tered our night.
borne all our sins and has cleansed ev - 'ry stain.
soul be re - kin - dled with fire from a - bove.

Hal - le - lu - jah, Thine the glo - ry! Hal - le - lu - jah, A -

men! Hal - le - lu - jah, Thine the glo - ry! Re - vive us a - gain.

Text: William P. Mackay, 1837–1885
Tune: REVIVE US AGAIN, 11 11 with refrain; John J. Husband, 1760–1825

567 Showers of Blessing

...I will send down the showers in their season; they shall be showers of blessing.
Ezekiel 34:26

1. "There shall be show-ers of bless - ing"— This is the
2. "There shall be show-ers of bless - ing"— Pre - cious re -
3. "There shall be show-ers of bless - ing"— Send them up -
4. "There shall be show-ers of bless - ing"— O that to -

prom - ise of love; There shall be sea - sons re -
viv - ing a - gain; O - ver the hills and the
on us, O Lord; Grant to us now a re -
day they might fall, Now as to God we're con -

fresh - ing, Sent from the Sav - ior a - bove.
val - leys Sound of a - bun - dance of rain.
fresh - ing, Come and now hon - or Thy Word.
fess - ing, Now as on Je - sus we call!

Show - ers of

Show - ers, show-ers of bless - ing, Show - ers of bless-ing we

need; Mer - cy drops round us are fall - ing,

But for the show - ers we plead.

Text: Daniel W. Whittle, 1840–1901
Tune: SHOWERS OF BLESSING, 8 7 8 7 with refrain; James McGlanahan, 1840–1907

568 Sing a New World into Being

Then I saw a new heaven and a new earth, for the first heaven and the first earth had passed away…
Revelation 21:1

1. Sing a new world in-to be-ing. Sound a bold and hope-ful theme. Find a tune for si-lent yearn-ings. Lend your voice and dare to dream: Dream a church where all who wor-ship Find their lives and loves be-long.

2. Sing a new world in-to be-ing Where each gen-der, class, and race Brings its rain-bow gifts and col-ors To God's lim-it-less em-brace; Where the lines that once di-vid-ed Form in-stead the ties that bind.

3. Sing a new world in-to be-ing Where the home-less find a home, Where no chil-dren ev-er hun-ger But are filled in God's sha-lom; Where all peo-ple work for jus-tice, Where all hate and venge-ance cease.

4. Sing a new world in-to be-ing. Join the an-cient proph-ets' cry For a time of health and plen-ty When all tears have been wiped dry; When com-pas-sion flows like wa-ters, Pour-ing balm for all who grieve.

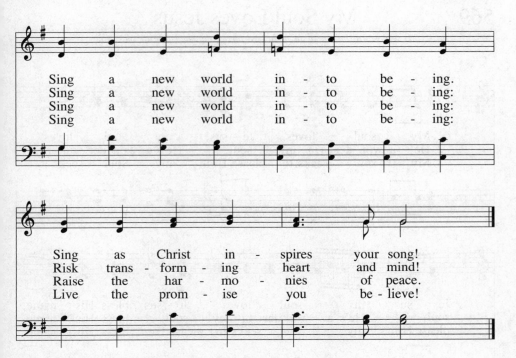

Sing a new world in - to be - ing.
Sing a new world in - to be - ing:
Sing a new world in - to be - ing:
Sing a new world in - to be - ing:

Sing as Christ in - spires your song!
Risk trans - form - ing heart and mind!
Raise the har - mo - nies of peace.
Live the prom - ise you be - lieve!

Text: Mary Louise Bringle, b.1953, © 2006, GIA Publications, Inc.
Tune: HYMN TO JOY, 8 7 8 7 D; arr. from Ludwig van Beethoven, 1770–1827, by Edward Hodges, 1796–1867

569 My Soul Loves Jesus

My soul yearns for you in the night, my spirit within me earnestly seeks you.
Isaiah 26:9

1. My soul loves Je - sus, my soul loves
2. He's a won-der in my soul, He's a won-der in my
3. My soul seeks to please Him, my soul seeks to

Je - sus, my soul loves Je - sus; bless His name.
soul, He's a won-der in my soul; bless His name.
please Him, my soul seeks to please Him; bless His name.

My soul loves Je - sus, my soul loves
He's a won-der in my soul, He's a won-der in my
My soul seeks to please Him, my soul seeks to

Je - sus, my soul loves Je - sus, bless His name.
soul, He's a won-der in my soul, bless His name.
please Him, my soul seeks to please Him, bless His name.

Text: Charles H. Mason
Tune: MY SOUL LOVES JESUS, Irregular; Charles H. Mason; harm. by Iris Stevenson, © 1982, The Church of God in Christ Publishing Board

More Love to Thee

And this is my prayer, that your love may overflow more and more with knowledge and full insight.
Philippians 1:9

1. More love to Thee, O Christ, More love to Thee!
2. Once earth-ly joy I craved, Sought peace and rest;
3. Then shall my lat-est breath Whis - per Thy praise;

Hear Thou the prayer I make On bend - ed knee;
Now Thee a - lone I seek, Give what is best;
This be the part - ing cry My heart shall raise;

This is my ear - nest plea: More love, O Christ, to Thee,
This all my prayer shall be;
This still its prayer shall be;

More love to Thee, More love to Thee!

Text: Elizabeth Prentiss, 1818–1878
Tune: MORE LOVE TO THEE, 6 4 6 4 66 44; William H. Doane, 1832–1915

571 I Really Love the Lord

You shall love the Lord your God with all your heart, and with all your soul, and with all your mind.
Matthew 22:37

I real-ly love the Lord!

I real-ly love the Lord!

You don't know what He's done for

me: Gave me the vic - to - ry! I

love Him! I love Him! I real-ly love the Lord!

Text: Jimmy Dowell, © 1981, Bridgeport Music, Inc. (BMI)
Tune: Jimmy Dowell, © 1981, Bridgeport Music, Inc. (BMI); arr. by Glenn L. Jones, b.1949, © 2011, GIA Publications, Inc.

I Do; Don't You?

Love the brotherhood of believers, fear God, honor the king.
1 Peter 2:17

1. I know a great Sav - ior, I do; don't you? I
2. I need Him to lead me, I do; don't you? Heav'n's
3. I love to be near Him, I do; don't you? He
4. I want Him to use me, I do; don't you? For

live by His fav - or, I do; don't you? For
man - na to feed me, I do; don't you? What -
speaks and I hear Him, I do; don't you? For
serv - ice to choose me, I do; don't you? I

grace I im - plore Him, I wor - ship be - fore Him, I
ev - er be - tide me, I need Him be - side me, In
me He is car - ing, The cross I am bear - ing, I
want Him to bless me, To own and con - fess me, Com -

love and a - dore Him, I do; don't you?
mer - cy to hide me, I do; don't you?
love Him for shar - ing, I do; don't you?
plete - ly pos - sess me, I do; don't you?

Text: Melville W. Miller
Tune: Edwin O. Excell, 1851–1921

573 Is There Anybody Here Who Loves My Jesus?

"Simon son of John, do you love me more than these?" "Yes, Lord; you know that I love you." "Feed my lambs."
John 21:15

Is there an - y - bod - y here who loves my Je - sus? An - y - bod - y here who loves the Lord?

I want to know if you love my Je - sus; I want to know if you love the Lord?

Verses *Unison*

1. Hap - py day, oh, hap - py day.
2. He taught me how to watch and pray.
3. I went to the val - ley but I did-n't go to stay.

div.

I want to know if you love the Lord.

Unison

When Je - sus washed my sins a - way.
And live re - joic - ing ev - 'ry day.
My soul got hap - py and I stayed all day.

div.

D.C.

I want to know if you love the Lord.

Text: Jubilee Song
Tune: ANYBODY HERE, Irregular with refrain; Jubilee Song; arr. by Jeffrey P. Radford, 1953–2002, © 2000, GIA Publications, Inc.

574

I Love You, Lord

May all who seek you rejoice... may those who love your salvation say continually, "Great is the LORD!"
Psalm 40:16

I love You, Lord, and I lift my voice to wor - ship You, O my soul, re - joice! Take

joy, my King, in what You hear: may it be a

sweet, sweet sound in Your ear.

Text: Laurie Klein
Tune: Laurie Klein; arr. by Nolan Williams, Jr., b.1969
© 1978, House of Mercy Music, admin. by Music Services

575 Precious Jesus

...I regard everything as loss because of the surpassing value of knowing Christ Jesus my Lord.
Philippians 3:8

Pre - cious Je - sus, how I love You. How I lift high my

voice with Your praise. Ho - ly Spir - it, I im - plore Thee,

drench my heart as my lips part Your grace. grace.

I am per-suad-ed, Lord, to love You. I have been changed to bless Your name. I am con-strained by this great gos-pel, for ev-er to wor-ship Thee.

Text: Thomas A. Whitfield
Tune: Thomas A. Whitfield; arr. by Thomas W. Jefferson; refrain harm. by Glenn L. Jones, b.1949, © 2011, GIA Publications, Inc.

576 Till We Meet Again

"The LORD turn his face toward you and give you peace."
Numbers 6:26

May His peace be with you till we meet a - gain. May His peace be with you till we meet a - gain. Till we

reach that dis - tant shore,   And we'll shed a tear   no more,

May He give you strength to en - dure   till we meet

a - gain.   Till we meet   a - gain.

Text: Kirk Franklin, b.1970
Tune: Kirk Franklin, b.1970
© 1993, Lilly Mack Publishing, admin. at EMICMGPublishing.com

577 I Love You, Lord, Today

...Yes, Lord; you know that I love you....
John 21:15

1. I love You. I love You. I love You, Lord, to-day
2. My heart, my mind, my soul be-long to You.

be - cause You care for me in
You paid the price for me way

such a spe - cial way.
back on Cal - va - ry. And yes I praise You. I

lift You up. I mag - ni - fy Your name.

That's why my heart is filled with praise.

Text: William F. Hubbard
Tune: William F. Hubbard
© 1985, Chinwah Songs (SESAC)

578 My Jesus, I Love Thee

"...do you love me more than these?" He said to him, "Yes, Lord; you know that I love you."
John 21:15

1. My Je - sus, I love Thee, I know Thou art mine— For
2. I love Thee be - cause Thou hast first lov - ed me And
3. I'll love Thee in life, I will love Thee in death, And
4. In man - sions of glo - ry and end - less de - light, I'll

Thee all the fol - lies of sin I re - sign; My
pur - chased my par - don on Cal - va - ry's tree; I
praise Thee as long as Thou lend - est me breath; And
ev - er a - dore Thee in heav - en so bright; I'll

gra - cious Re - deem - er, my Sav - ior art Thou: If
love Thee for wear - ing the thorns on Thy brow: If
say when the death - dew lies cold on my brow, "If
sing with the glit - ter - ing crown on my brow, "If

ev - er I loved Thee, my Je - sus, 'tis now.
ev - er I loved Thee, my Je - sus, 'tis now.
ev - er I loved Thee, my Je - sus, 'tis now."
ev - er I loved Thee, my Je - sus, 'tis now."

Text: William R. Featherston, 1846–1873
Tune: GORDON, 11 11 11 11; Adoniram J. Gordon, 1836–1895

Zion Is Calling Us

The LORD reigns forever, your God, O Zion, for all generations.
Psalm 146:10

Zi-on is call-ing us to a high-er place of praise.

Stand up-on the moun-tain and mag-ni-fy His name.

Tell all the peo-ple in ev-'ry na-tion that He reigns.

Zi-on is call-ing us to a high-er place of praise.

Text: Stephen Hurd
Tune: Stephen Hurd
© Hurd the Word Music

580 Dwell in the House

I love the house where you live, O LORD, the place where your glory dwells.
Psalm 26:7

One thing have I de-sired of the Lord, one thing

have I de-sired of the Lord, and

that will I seek af - ter, that will I seek af - ter:

that I may dwell in the house,

dwell in the house, that I may dwell in the house *unis.* of the Lord.

One thing

Text: Psalm 27:4; Gale Jones Murphy, b.1954
Tune: Gale Jones Murphy, b.1954
© 2006, GIA Publications, Inc.

581   Will the Circle Be Unbroken

...you are no longer strangers and aliens, but you are citizens with the saints and members of the household of God.
Ephesians 2:19

1. There are loved ones in the glo - ry
2. In the joy - ous days of child - hood,
3. You re - mem - ber songs of heav - en
4. You can pic - ture hap - py gath - 'rings
5. One by one their seats were emp - ty,

Whose dear forms you of - ten miss,
Oft they told of won - drous love,
Which you sang with child - ish voice,
Round the fire - side long a - go,
One by one they went a - way,

When you close your earth - ly sto - ry
Point - ed to the dy - ing Sav - ior,
Do you love the hymns they taught you,
And you think of tear - ful part - ings,
Now the fam - 'ly is part - ed,

Will you join them in their bliss?
Now they dwell with Him a - bove.
Or are songs of earth your choice?
When they left you here be - low.
Will it be com - plete one day?

Will the cir - cle be un - bro - ken by and

by, yes, by and by? In a bet - ter home a -

wait - ing in the sky, in the sky?

Text: Ada R. Habershon, 1861–1918
Tune: UNBROKEN CIRCLE, 8 7 8 7 with refrain; Charles H. Gabriel, 1856–1932; arr. by Evelyn Simpson-Curenton, b.1953, © 2001,
  GIA Publications, Inc.

582   New Name in Glory

To everyone who conquers... I will give a white stone, and on the white stone is written a new name...
Revelation 2:17

I've got a new *name   o-ver in glo-ry,   and it's

mine, mine,   mine.   I've got a new name   o-ver in

glo - ry,   and   it's   mine,   mine,   mine!

Substitute song, shout, etc.

Text: African American traditional
Tune: African American traditional; arr. by Robert J. Fryson, 1944–1994, © 1982, Bob Jay Music Co.

Come and Go with Me

583

For the kingdom of God is not food and drink but righteousness and peace and joy in the Holy Spirit.
Romans 14:17

1. Come and go with me to my Fa-ther's house,
2. Peace and love a - bide in my Fa-ther's house,
3. Peace and hap - pi - ness in my Fa-ther's house,

To my Fa-ther's house, to my Fa-ther's house.
In my Fa-ther's house, in my Fa-ther's house.
In my Fa-ther's house, in my Fa-ther's house.

Come and go with me to my Fa-ther's house;
Peace and love a - bide in my Fa-ther's house;
Peace and hap - pi - ness in my Fa-ther's house;

There is joy, joy, joy!

4. No more dyin' there, in my Father's house...
5. Sweet communion up there, in my Father's house...

Text: Congregational Praise Song
Tune: COME AND GO WITH ME, 10 10 10 5; Congregational Praise Song; arr. by Kenneth W. Louis, b.1956, © 2000, GIA Publications, Inc.

584 I'll Fly Away

O that I had wings like a dove! I would fly away and be at rest.
Psalm 55:6

1. Some glad morn-ing when this life is o'er,
2. When the shad-ows of this life have gone,
3. Just a few more wea-ry days and then,

To that home on
Like a bird from
To a land where

God's ce-les-tial shore,
pris-on bars has flown, I'll fly a-way.
joys shall nev-er end,

Well

I'll fly a-way, O glo-ry, I'll fly a-way;

When I die, Hal - le - lu - jah, by and by, I'll fly a - way.

Text: Albert E. Brumley, 1905–1977
Tune: I'LL FLY AWAY, 9 4 9 4 with refrain; Albert E. Brumley, 1905–1977; arr. by Evelyn Simpson-Curenton, b.1953
© 1932, Hartford Music Co., renewed 1960, Albert E. Brumley & Sons/SESAC (admin. by ClearBox Rights)

585 The Crown

Be faithful until death, and I will give you the crown of life.
Revelation 2:10

1. O what love the Sav-ior for my soul has shown, Glad-ly
2. As re-ward for cross-es that I here may bear, There's a
3. I have loved ones wait-ing for my com-ing there, Soon my

I will la-bor for Him; For a-wait-ing
crown with man-y a gem; It through years un-
Lord will call me to them; We shall sing "Ho-

me I know there is a crown,
end-ing I shall sure-ly wear, In the new Je-ru-sa-lem.
san-na," wear-ing crowns all fair,

bright crown

There's a bright crown wait-ing, wait-ing for me, There's a

bright crown

bright   crown   bright

bright crown wait - ing,   wait-ing for   me,   There's a   bright crown

bright   crown   bright

crown

wait - ing,   wait-ing for   me,   In the new Je - ru-sa - lem.

crown

Text: B. B. Edmiaston, 1882–1955
Tune: THE CROWN, 11 8 11 7 with refrain; Emmett S. Dean, 1876–1936

586   I Call You to My Father's House

I tell you the truth, he who believes has everlasting life.
John 6:47

1. I call you to My Father's house, A love-ly dwell-ing place. He comes to meet you on the road, Arms read-y to em-brace.
2. Lay down your sor-row, calm your fear; The Fa-ther bids you come. With o-pen arms He wel-comes you To your e-ter-nal home.
3. Al-though the way be hard and long In-to the prom-ised land, Be not a-fraid to walk with Me: I hold you by the hand.
4. I have pre-pared a wed-ding feast Of fin-est food and wine. O join us at this ban-quet where My friends, the saints, now dine.
5. I call you to My Father's house, A love-ly dwell-ing place. Be not a-fraid to trav-el there And meet Him face to face.

Text: Delores Dufner, OSB, b.1939, © 1983, 2003, GIA Publications, Inc.
Tune: NEW BRITAIN, CM; *Virginia Harmony,* 1831; arr. by Evelyn Simpson-Curenton, b.1953, © 2000, GIA Publications, Inc.

When the Saints Go Marching In 587

See, the Lord is coming with ten thousands of his holy ones, to execute judgment on all...
Jude 14–15

1. O when the saints go march-ing in,
   O when the saints go march-ing in,
   O Lord, I want to be in that num-ber when the saints go march-ing in.

2. O when the sun re-fused to shine,
   O when the sun re-fused to shine,
   O Lord, I want to be in that when the sun re-fused to shine.

3. O when they crown Him Lord of all,
   O when they crown Him Lord of all,
   when they crown Him Lord of all.

Text: Negro Spiritual
Tune: WHEN THE SAINTS, 88 10 7; Negro Spiritual; arr. by Stephen Key, © 2000, GIA Publications, Inc.

588 Just to Behold His Face

...His servants will worship him; they will see his face, and his name will be on their foreheads.
Revelation 22:3–4

1. Not just to kneel with the an - gels, And
2. Not just to join in the cho - rus, And

not to see loved ones who've gone; And it's not just to
sing with those that are blest; Nor to bathe my

drink at the foun - tain That is un - der the great white
soul that is wea - ry In the sea of heav - en - ly

throne; Not for the crown that He'll give me
rest; But I'll look for the One who has saved me

That I'm try - ing to run this race; I know all that I'll
From a death of sin and dis - grace; I'll have joy when I

Text: Derrick Jackson
Tune: BEHOLD HIS FACE, 8 8 10 8 D with refrain; Derrick Jackson; arr. by Charlene Moore Cooper, © 2000, GIA Publications, Inc.

589 We Shall Behold Him

For the LORD is righteous; he loves righteous deeds; the upright shall behold his face.
Psalm 11:7

1. The sky shall un - fold, pre - par - ing His en - trance;
2. The an - gel shall sound the shout of His com - ing;

The stars shall ap - plaud Him with
The sleep - ing shall rise from their

eyes
main

thun - ders of praise. The sweet light in His eyes,
slum - ber - ing place, And those who re - main,

His eyes shall en - hance those a - wait - ing; And
re - main shall be changed in a mo - ment; And

we shall be - hold Him then face to face.
we shall be - hold Him then face to face.

Text: Dottie Rambo, b.1934
Tune: WE SHALL BEHOLD HIM, 11 11 15 10 wih refrain; Dottie Rambo, b.1934; arr. by Nolan Williams, Jr., b.1969
© 1980, New Spring Publishing (ASCAP)

590 When We All Get to Heaven

In my Father's house there are many dwelling places...
John 14:2

1. Sing the won-drous love of Je - sus, Sing His mer - cy and His grace; In the man - sions bright and bless - ed He'll pre - pare for us a place.
2. While we walk the pil - grim path - way Clouds will o - ver - spread the sky; But when trav - 'ling days are o - ver Not a shad - ow, not a sigh.
3. Let us then be true and faith - ful, Trust - ing, serv - ing ev - 'ry day; Just one glimpse of Him in glo - ry Will the toils of life re - pay.
4. On - ward to the prize be - fore us! Soon His beau - ty we'll be - hold; Soon the pearl - y gates will o - pen— We shall tread the streets of gold.

When we all what a

When we all get to heav - en,

Text: Eliza E. Hewitt, 1851–1920
Tune: HEAVEN, 8 7 8 7 with refrain; Emily D. Wilson, 1865–1942; arr. by Valeria A. Foster, © 2000, GIA Publications, Inc.

591   We're Marching to Zion

And the ransomed of the LORD shall return, and come to Zion with singing; everlasting joy shall be upon their heads; they shall obtain joy and gladness, and sorrow and sighing shall flee away.
Isaiah 35:10

1. Come, we that love the Lord, And let our joys be
2. Let those re - fuse to sing Who nev - er knew our
3. The hill of Zi - on yields A thou - sand sa - cred
4. Then let our songs a - bound, And ev - 'ry tear be

known, Join in a song with sweet ac - cord, Join
God; But chil - dren of the heav'n - ly King, But
sweets Be - fore we reach the heav'n - ly fields, Be -
dry; We're march - ing through Im - man - uel's ground, We're

in a song with sweet ac - cord, And thus sur -
chil - dren of the heav'n - ly King, May speak their
fore we reach the heav'n - ly fields, Or walk the
march - ing through Im - man - uel's ground, To fair - er

1. And thus sur-round the

round the throne, And thus sur-round the throne.
joys a - broad, May speak their joys a - broad.
gold - en streets, Or walk the gold - en streets.
worlds on high, To fair - er worlds on high.

throne, And thus sur - round the throne.

We're march - ing to Zi - on, Beau - ti - ful,

We're march - ing on to Zi - on,

beau - ti - ful Zi - on; We're march - ing up - ward to

Zi - on, The beau - ti - ful cit - y of God.

Zi - on, Zi - on,

Text: Isaac Watts, 1674–1748
Tune: MARCHING TO ZION, 6 6 88 66 with refrain; Robert Lowry, 1826–1899

592

Wear a Crown

And when the chief shepherd appears, you will win the crown of glory that never fades away.
1 Peter 5:4

1. Am I a sol - dier of the cross, A
2. Must I be car - ried to the skies On
3. Are there no foes for me to face? Must
4. Sure I must fight if I would reign; In -

fol - l'wer of the Lamb, And shall I fear to
flow - 'ry beds of ease, While oth - ers fought to
I not stem the flood? Is this vile world a
crease my cour - age, Lord; I'll bear the toil, en -

own His cause, Or blush to speak His name?
win the prize, And sailed thro' blood - y seas?
friend to grace, To help me on to God?
dure the pain, Sup - port - ed by Thy word.

And when the bat - tle's o - ver we shall wear a crown! Yes,

we shall wear a crown! Yes, we shall wear a crown! And when the bat-tle's

o - ver we shall wear a crown In the new Je - ru - sa -

lem. Wear a crown, wear a crown, Wear a

Wear a crown, wear a crown,

bright and shin - ing crown, And when the bat - tle's o - ver

we shall wear a crown In the new Je - ru - sa - lem.

Text: Isaac Watts, 1674–1748
Tune: WEAR A CROWN, CM with refrain; English traditional

593   Where We'll Never Grow Old

...the world and its desire are passing away, but those who do the will of God live forever.
1 John 2:17

1. I have heard of a land On the far - a - way strand,
2. In that beau - ti - ful home Where we'll nev - er - more roam,
3. When our work here is done And the life crown is won,

'Tis a beau - ti - ful home of the soul;
We shall be in the sweet by and by;
And our trou - bles and tri - als are o'er,

Built by Je - sus on high, There we nev - er shall die,
Hap - py praise to the King Through e - ter - ni - ty sing,
All our sor - rows will end, And our voic - es will blend

'Tis a land where we nev - er grow old.
'Tis a land where we nev - er shall die.
With the loved ones who've gone on be - fore.

Text: James C. Moore, 1888–1962
Tune: NEVER GROW OLD, 66 9 D with refrain; James C. Moore, 1888–1962

594 Just Over in the Gloryland

You are no longer strangers... but you are citizens with the saints and also members of the household of God...
Ephesians 2:19

1. I've a home pre - pared where the saints a - bide, Just
2. I am on my way to those man - sions fair, Just
3. What a joy - ful thought that my Lord I'll see, Just
4. With the blood-washed throng I will shout and sing, Just

o - ver in the glo - ry - land; And I long to be
o - ver in the glo - ry - land; There to sing God's praise,
o - ver in the glo - ry - land; And with kin - dred saved,
o - ver in the glo - ry - land; Glad ho - san - nas to

by my Sav - ior's side, Just o - ver in the glo - ry - land.
and His glo - ry share, Just o - ver in the glo - ry - land.
there for - ev - er be, Just o - ver in the glo - ry - land.
Christ, the Lord and King, Just o - ver in the glo - ry - land.

Just o - ver in the glo - ry - land, I'll

Just o - ver, o - ver in the glo - ry - land, I'll

join the hap-py an-gel band, Just
join, yes, join the hap-py an-gel band, Just

o-ver in the glo-ry-land; Just o - ver in the
o-ver in the glo-ry-land; Just o-ver, o-ver in the

glo-ry-land, There with the might-y
glo-ry-land, There with, yes, with the might-y

host I'll stand, Just o-ver in the glo-ry-land.

Text: James W. Acuff, 1864–1937
Tune: IN THE GLORYLAND, 10 8 10 8 with refrain; Emmett S. Dean, 1876–1936

595 Before This Time Another Year

If we live, we live to the Lord, and if we die, we die to the Lord...
Romans 14:8

slow and freely

Leader:

Be - fore this time an-oth-er year...

All:

Be - fore this

time an - oth -

Leader:

er year I may be dead and gone!

All:

I may be

dead and gone! I'll

let you know be-fore I go... I'll let

you   know   be -

fore   I   go   what will be-come of me!

What   will   be -

come   of   me!

Text: Anonymous
Tune: Meter hymn; anonymous; arr. by M. Adams and Louis Sykes, © 2000, GIA Publications, Inc.

596 Ain't-a That Good News

Like cold water to a thirsty soul, so is good news from a far country.
Proverbs 25:25

1. I got a crown up in-a that king-dom,
2. I got a robe up in-a that king-dom, Ain't-a that
3. I got a Sav-ior in-a that king-dom,

good news! I got a crown up in-a that
I got a robe up in-a that
I got a Sav-ior in-a that

king-dom,
king-dom, Ain't-a that good news! I'm-a gon-na lay down this
king-dom,

world, gon-na shoul-der up-a my cross. Gon-na

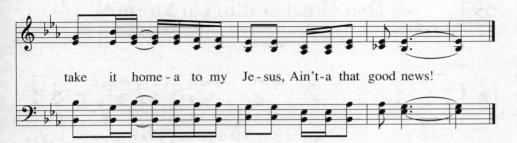

take   it   home-a   to   my   Je-sus, Ain't-a that   good news!

Text: Negro Spiritual
Tune: GOOD NEWS, 10 5 10 5 16 10 5; Negro Spiritual; arr. by Robert J. Fryson, 1944–1994, © 2000, GIA Publications, Inc.

597 In That Great Gittin' Up Mornin'

For the Lord himself... will descend from heaven, and the dead in Christ will rise first.
1 Thessalonians 4:16

Refrain

In that great git-tin' up morn-in', fare ye well, fare ye well, In that

great git-tin' up morn-in', fare ye well, fare ye well. In that

great git-tin' up morn-in', fare ye well, fare ye well. Oh, in a that

great git-tin' up morn-in', fare ye well, fare ye well.

Verses

1. There's a bet - ter day a com-in', fare ye well, fare ye well. There's a
2. There'll be no more dy - in', fare ye well, fare ye well. There'll be
3. Oh, saint's will be a ris - in', fare ye well, fare ye well. Oh,

bet - ter day a com - in', fare ye well, fare ye well. When I
no more dy - in', fare ye well, fare ye well. There'll be
saint's will be a ris - in', fare ye well, fare ye well. There'll be

see King Je - sus, fare ye well, fare ye well. When I
no more cry - in', fare ye well, fare ye well. There'll be
no more striv - in', fare ye well, fare ye well. There'll be

see King Je - sus, fare ye well, fare ye well.
no more cry - in', fare ye well, fare ye well.
no more striv - in', fare ye well, fare ye well.

Text: Negro Spiritual
Tune: FARE YE WELL, 14 14 12 12 with refrain; Negro Spiritual; arr. by Joseph Joubert, b.1958, © 2000, GIA Publications, Inc.

598   I Wanna Be Ready

And I saw the holy city, the new Jerusalem, coming down out of heaven from God, prepared as a bride...
Revelation 21:2

Refrain

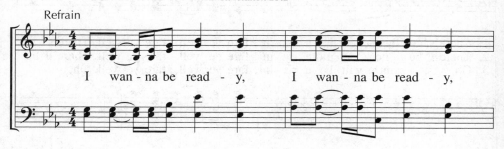

I wan - na be read - y, I wan - na be read - y,

I wan - na be read - y   to walk in Je - ru - sa - lem just like John.

Last time

Verses

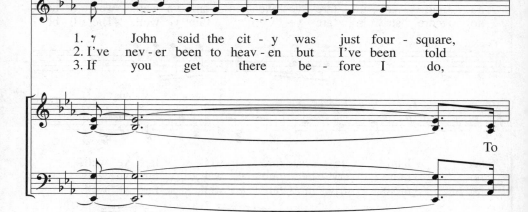

Solo:

1. John said the cit - y was just four - square,
2. I've nev - er been to heav - en but I've been told
3. If you get there be - fore I do,

To

Text: Negro Spiritual
Tune: BE READY, 8 10 8 10 with refrain; Negro Spiritual; arr. by Evelyn Simpson-Curenton, b.1953, © 2000, GIA Publications, Inc.

599   I Bowed on My Knees

...at the name of Jesus every knee should bend... and every tongue should confess that Jesus Christ is Lord...
Philippians 2:10–11

1. I dreamed of a cit-y called glo-ry, so bright and so fair, When I en-tered the gates I cried ho-ly, the an-gels all met me there. They car-ried me from man-sion to man-sion, Oh, the sights I saw. Then I

en-tered the gates of that cit-y, my loved ones all knew me well, They took me down the streets of heav-en, on the scenes too man-y to tell. I saw A-bra-ham, Ja-cob and I-saac; talked with Mark and Tim-o-thy. But I

said I want to see Je-sus, The One who died for me. I bowed on my knees and cried ho-ly, ho-ly, ho-ly, I clapped my hands and sang glo-ry, glo-ry to the

1. Son of God.
2. Then as I God.

Text: Nettie Dudley Washington
Tune: CRIED HOLY, Irregular; E. M. Dudley Cantwell; arr. Louis Sykes
© 1923 (renewed), arr. © 2011, Unichappell Music, Inc.

600   The Uncloudy Day

Death will be no more; mourning and crying and pain will be no more, for the first things have passed away.
Revelation 21:4

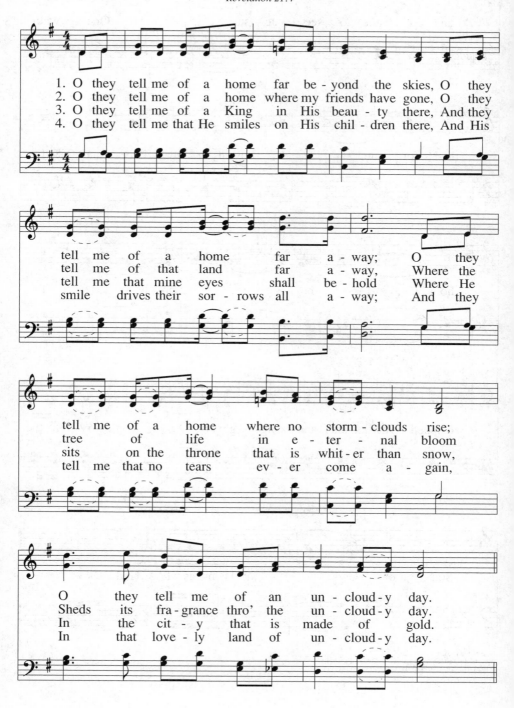

1. O they tell me of a home far be - yond the skies, O they
2. O they tell me of a home where my friends have gone, O they
3. O they tell me of a King in His beau - ty there, And they
4. O they tell me that He smiles on His chil - dren there, And His

tell me of a home far a - way; O they
tell me of that land far a - way, Where the
tell me that mine eyes shall be - hold Where He
smile drives their sor - rows all a - way; And they

tell me of a home where no storm - clouds rise;
tree of life in e - ter - nal bloom
sits on the throne that is whit - er than snow,
tell me that no tears ev - er come a - gain,

O they tell me of an un - cloud - y day.
Sheds its fra - grance thro' the un - cloud - y day.
In the cit - y that is made of gold.
In that love - ly land of un - cloud - y day.

O the land of a cloud-less day, O the land of an

un - cloud-y day. O they tell me of a home where no

storm-clouds rise, O they tell me of an un - cloud-y day.

Text: Rev. J. K. Alwood
Tune: UNCLOUDY DAY, 12 10 12 10 with refrain, Rev. J. K. Alwood; arr. by Valeria A. Foster, © 2000, GIA Publications, Inc.

601   On Jordan's Stormy Banks

Now proceed to cross the Jordan, you and all this people, into the land that I am giving to them.
Joshua 1:2

1. On Jor - dan's storm - y banks I stand, And
2. All o'er those wide - ex - tend - ed plains, Shines
3. No chill - ing winds or poi - s'nous breath Can
4. When shall I reach that hap - py place And

cast a wish - ful eye; To Ca - naan's fair and
one e - ter - nal day; There God the Son for -
reach that health - ful shore; Sick - ness and sor - row,
be for - ev - er blest? When shall I see my

hap - py land, Where my pos - ses - sions lie.
ev - er reigns, And scat - ters night a - way.
pain and death, Are felt and feared no more.
Fa - ther's face, And in God's bo - som rest?

I am bound for the prom - ised land, I am

bound for the prom - ised land; Oh, who will come and

go with me? I am bound for the prom - ised land.

Text: Samuel Stennett, 1727–1795
Tune: STORMY BANKS, CM with refrain; American melody; adapt by Rigdon McCoy McIntosh, 1836–1899; arr. by Norman Johnson, 1928–1983,
© 1965, New Spring Publishing (ASCAP)

602   The Sweet By and By

And the city has no need of sun or moon to shine on it, for the glory of God is its light, and its lamp is the Lamb.
Revelation 21:23

1. There's a land that is fair-er than day, And by
2. We shall sing on that beau-ti-ful shore The me-
3. To our boun-ti-ful Fa-ther a-bove We will

faith we can see it a-far, For the Fa-ther waits o-ver the
lo-di-ous songs of the blest; And our spir-its shall sor-row no
of-fer our trib-ute of praise For the glo-ri-ous gift of His

way To pre-pare us a dwell-ing-place there.
more— Not a sigh for the bless-ing of rest.
love And the bless-ings that hal-low our days.

In the sweet by and by, We shall

In the sweet by and by, by and by,

meet on that beau - ti - ful shore; In the

by and by,

sweet by and by, We shall

In the sweet by and by, by and by,

meet on that beau - ti - ful shore.

Text: Sanford F. Bennett, 1836–1889
Tune: SWEET BY AND BY, 9 9 9 9 with refrain; Joseph P. Webster, 1819–1875

603 Soon-a Will Be Done

When the righteous cry for help, the LORD hears, and rescues them from all their troubles.
Psalm 34:17

Refrain

Soon - a will be done - a with the trou - bles of the world,

Trou - bles of the world, The trou - bles of the world.

Soon - a will be done - a with the trou - bles of the world. Goin'

home to live with God.

Verses

1. No more weep-ing and a - wail - ing, No more weep-ing and a - wail - ing, No more weep-ing and a - wail - ing, I'm goin' to live with God.

2. I want to meet my moth - er, I want to meet my moth - er, I want to meet my moth - er, I'm goin' to live with God.

3. I want to meet my Je - sus, I want to meet my Je - sus, I want to meet my Je - sus, I'm goin' to live with God.

Text: Traditional
Tune: SOON-A WILL BE DONE, 888 6 with refrain; traditional

604 Deep River

Let me cross over to see the good land beyond the Jordan, that good hill country and the Lebanon.
Deuteronomy 3:25

Deep riv-er, my home is o - ver Jor - dan,

Deep riv - er, Lord, I want to cross o - ver in-to

camp - ground. Oh, don't you want to go to that

gos - pel feast, That prom - ised land where

all   is peace?   Oh,   deep

riv - er, Lord,   I want to cross   o - ver in - to camp-ground.

Text: Traditional
Tune: DEEP RIVER, Irregular; Negro spiritual; arr. Carl Haywood, b.1949, © 1992

605 God of Our Fathers

May the LORD, the God of your ancestors, increase you a thousand times more and bless you...
Deuteronomy 1:11

Trumpets before each stanza (optional)

1. God of our fa - thers, whose al - might - y
2. Thy love di - vine hath led us in the
3. From war's a - larms, from dead - ly pes - ti -
4. Re - fresh Thy peo - ple on their toil - some

hand Leads forth in beau - ty all the star - ry
past, In this free land by Thee our lot is
lence, Be Thy strong arm our ev - er - sure de -
way, Lead us from night to nev - er end - ing

band Of shin - ing worlds in splen - dor thru the
cast; Be Thou our rul - er, guard - ian, guide, and
fense; Thy true re - li - gion in our hearts in -
day; Fill all our lives with love and grace di -

skies, Our grate - ful songs be - fore Thy throne a - rise.
stay, Thy word our law, Thy paths our cho - sen way.
crease, Thy boun - teous good - ness nour - ish us in peace.
vine, And glo - ry, laud, and praise be ev - er Thine!

Text: Daniel C. Roberts, 1841–1907
Tune: NATIONAL HYMN, 10 10 10 10; George W. Warren, 1828–1902

The Star-Spangled Banner

606

Some take pride in chariots, and some in horses, but our pride is in the name of the LORD our God.
Psalm 20:7

1. O say can you see by the dawn's ear - ly
2. On the shore, dim - ly seen thro' the mists of the
3. O thus be it ev - er when free - men shall

light, What so proud - ly we hailed at the
deep, Where the foe's haugh - ty host in dead
stand Be - tween their loved homes and the

twi - light's last gleam - ing, Whose broad stripes and bright
si - lence re - pos - es, What is that which the
war's des - o - la - tion! Blest with vic - t'ry and

stars, through the per - il - ous fight, O'er the ram - parts we
breeze, o'er the tow - er - ing steep, As it fit - ful - ly
peace, may the heav'n - res - cued land Praise the Pow'r that hath

Star - Span - gled Ban - ner yet wave O'er the
Ban - ner O long may it wave O'er the
Ban - ner in tri - umph shall wave O'er the

land of the free and the home of the brave?
land of the free and the home of the brave!
land of the free and the home of the brave!

Text: Francis S. Key, 1779–1843
Tune: STAR SPANGLED BANNER, Irregular; John S. Smith, 1750–1836

607 America the Beautiful

...you shall be for me a priestly kingdom and a holy nation.
Exodus 19:6

1. O beau - ti - ful for spa - cious skies, For
2. O beau - ti - ful for pil - grim feet, Whose
3. O beau - ti - ful for he - roes proved In
4. O beau - ti - ful for pa - triot dream That

am - ber waves of grain, For pur - ple moun-tain
stern, im - pas-sioned stress A thor - ough-fare for
lib - er - at - ing strife, Who more than self their
sees be - yond the years Thine al - a - bas - ter

maj - es - ties A - bove the fruit - ed plain!
free - dom beat A - cross the wil - der - ness!
coun - try loved, And mer - cy more than life!
cit - ies gleam, Un - dimmed by hu - man tears!

A - mer - i - ca! A - mer - i - ca! God
A - mer - i - ca! A - mer - i - ca! God
A - mer - i - ca! A - mer - i - ca! May
A - mer - i - ca! A - mer - i - ca! God

shed His grace on thee, And crown thy good with
mend thine ev - 'ry flaw, Con - firm thy soul in
God thy gold re - fine, Till all suc - cess be
shed His grace on thee, And crown thy good with

broth - er - hood From sea to shin - ing sea.
self - con - trol, Thy lib - er - ty in law.
no - ble - ness, And ev - 'ry gain di - vine.
broth - er - hood From sea to shin - ing sea.

Text: Katherine L. Bates, 1859–1929
Tune: MATERNA, CMD; Samuel A. Ward, 1848–1903

608   Eternal Father, Strong to Save

...He got up and rebuked the winds and the sea; and there was a dead calm.
Matthew 8:26

1. E - ter - nal Fa - ther, strong to save, Whose arm has bound the
2. O Sav - ior, whose al - might - y word The wind and waves sub -
3. O Ho - ly Spir - it, who did brood Up - on the cha - os
4. O Trin - i - ty of love and pow'r, All trav - 'lers guard in

rest - less wave, Who bade the might - y o - cean deep Its
mis - sive heard, Who walked up - on the foam - ing deep, And
wild and rude, And bade its an - gry tu - mult cease, And
dan - ger's hour; From rock and tem - pest, fire and foe, Pro -

own ap - point - ed lim - its keep: O hear us when we
calm a - mid its rage did sleep: O hear us when we
gave, for fierce con - fu - sion, peace: O hear us when we
tect them where - so - e'er they go; Thus ev - er - more shall

cry to Thee For those in per - il on the sea.
cry to Thee For those in per - il on the sea.
cry to Thee For those in per - il on the sea.
rise to Thee Glad praise from air and land and sea.

Text: William Whiting, 1825–1878
Tune: MELITA, 88 88 88; John Bacchus Dykes, 1823–1876

Praise Him, All Ye Little Children   609

...have you never read, 'Out of the mouths of infants and nursing babies you have prepared praise for yourself'?
Matthew 21:16

1. Praise Him, praise Him, all ye lit-tle chil-dren,
2. Love Him, love Him, all ye lit-tle chil-dren,
3. Thank Him, thank Him, all ye lit-tle chil-dren,

God is love, God is love;
God is love, God is love;
God is love, God is love;

Praise Him, praise Him, all ye lit-tle chil-dren,
Love Him, love Him, all ye lit-tle chil-dren,
Thank Him, thank Him, all ye lit-tle chil-dren,

God is love, God is love.
God is love, God is love.
God is love, God is love.

Text: Anonymous
Tune: BONNER, 10 6 10 6; Carey Bonner, 1859–1938

610 Children, Go Where I Send Thee

All that you have commanded us we will do, and wherever you send us we will go.
Joshua 1:16

Chil-dren, go where I send thee.

How shall I send thee?

To Coda

I'm gon-na send thee one by one, one is the lit-tle bit-ty

ooh ooh ooh

To Coda

ba - by was born, born,

ooh born, born,

*Three by three, four by four, etc…
**These two measures get repeated in countdown fashion using the following verses.

Verses

3. three   are   the   He - brew   chil - dren,
4. four   are   the   gos - pel   writ - ers,

5. five   are   the   five   that   dressed   so   fine,

6. six   are   the   six   that   could - n't   get   fixed,

7. sev - en   are   the   sev - en   came   down   from   heav - en,

8. eight   are   the   eight   that   stood   at   the   gate,

9. nine   are   the   nine   that   dressed   so   fine,

10. ten   are   the   ten   com - mand - ments,

11. e - lev - en   are   the   'lev - en   came   down   from   heav - en,

12. twelve   are   the   twelve   dis - ci - ples,

Text: African American traditional
Tune: African American traditional; arr. by Evelyn Simpson-Curenton, b.1953, © 2000, GIA Publications, Inc.

Jesus Wants Me for a Sunbeam

611

Depart from evil, and do good; seek peace, and pursue it.
Psalm 34:14

Unison

1. Je-sus wants me for a sun-beam, To shine for Him each day;
2. Je-sus wants me to be lov-ing, And kind to all I see;

In ev-'ry way try to please Him, At home, at school, at play.
Show-ing how pleas-ant and hap-py His lit-tle one can be.

Harmony

A sun-beam, a sun-beam, Je-sus wants me for a sun-beam: A

sun-beam, a sun-beam, I'll be a sun-beam for Him.

Text: Nellie Talbot
Tune: SUNBEAM, CM with refrain; E. O. Excell, 1851–1921

612 The Joy of the Lord

Restore to me the joy of your salvation, and sustain in me a willing spirit.
Psalm 51:12

1. The joy of the Lord is my strength; The
2. If you want joy you must pray for it, If
3. He giv-eth liv-ing wa-ter and I thirst no more, He
4. He heals the bro-ken heart-ed and they cry no more, He

joy of the Lord is my strength; The
you want joy you must pray for it, If
giv-eth liv-ing wa-ter and I thirst no more, He
heals the bro-ken heart-ed and they cry no more, He

joy of the Lord is my strength; The
you want joy you must pray for it, The
giv-eth liv-ing wa-ter and I thirst no more, The
heals the bro-ken heart-ed and they cry no more, The

joy   of   the   Lord   is   my   strength.
joy   of   the   Lord   is   my   strength.
joy   of   the   Lord   is   my   strength.
joy   of   the   Lord   is   my   strength.

Text: Nehemiah 8:10, Alliene G. Vale
Tune: JOY OF THE LORD, Irregular; Alliene G. Vale
© 1971, Multisongs/His Eye Music/Joy of the Lord Publishing, admin. at EMICMGPublishing.com

613

Higher, Higher

For your steadfast love is higher than the heavens, and your faithfulness reaches to the clouds.
Psalm 108:4

1. High-er, high-er, high-er, high-er, high-er, high-er,
2. Low-er, low-er, low-er, low-er, low-er, low-er,
3. Su - per, su - per, su - per, su - per, su - per, su - per,

high-er, high-er. Lift Je - sus high-er!
low-er, low-er. Stomp the dev - il low-er!
su - per, su - per.

Su - per-nat - u-ral pow - er!

Text: Anonymous
Tune: Anonymous; arr. by Nolan Williams, Jr., b.1969, © 2000, GIA Publications, Inc.

Jesus Loves the Little Children   614

Let the little children come to me; do not stop them; for it is to such as these that the kingdom of God belongs.
Mark 10:14

Je - sus loves the lit - tle chil-dren, All the chil-dren of the world; Red and yel-low, black and white, They are pre-cious in His sight, Je - sus loves the lit - tle chil-dren of the world.

Text: C. H. Woolston, 1856–1927
Tune: CHILDREN, 8 7 77 11; George F. Root, 1820–1895

615 My Help Cometh from the Lord

I lift up my eyes to the hills — from where will my help come? My help comes from the LORD...
Psalm 121:1–2

I will look to the hills from whence com-eth my help.

My help com-eth from the Lord. I will look to the hills

from whence com-eth my help. My help com-eth from the

Last time to Coda ⊕

1. | 2.

Lord. My help com-eth from the Lord. Lord.

Optional solo:

He will not suf-fer thy foot to be moved. He that keep-eth thee shall nei-ther

slum-ber nor sleep. The Lord is thy shade up - on thy right hand.

D.S.

He shall pre - serve thy soul for ev - er - more.

help com-eth from the Lord. My help com-eth from the Lord.

Text: Psalm 121; Geraldine Woods, ©
Tune: Geraldine Woods; arr. by Nolan Williams, Jr., b.1969, © 2000, GIA Publications, Inc.

I've Got the Joy, Joy, Joy

616

...and rejoice with an indescribable and glorious joy.
1 Peter 1:8

1. I've got the joy, joy, joy, joy,
2. I've got the peace that pass - eth un - der - stand - ing,
3. I've got the love of Je - sus, love of Je - sus,
4. For there is there - fore now no con - dem - na - tion,

Down in my heart, Down in my heart, Down in my heart;

I've got the joy, joy, joy, joy,
I've got the peace that pass - eth un - der - stand - ing,
I've got the love of Je - sus, love of Je - sus,
For there is there - fore now no con - dem - na - tion,

Down in my heart, Down in my heart to stay.

Text: George W. Cooke, 1848–1923
Tune: I'VE GOT THE JOY, Irregular; George W. Cooke, 1848–1923

617 The Lord Is in His Holy Temple

The LORD is in his holy temple; let all the earth keep silence before him!
Habakkuk 2:20

The Lord is in His ho-ly tem-ple, The
Lord is in His ho-ly tem-ple: Let all the earth keep
si-lence, Let all the earth keep si-lence be-fore
Him— Keep si-lence, keep si-lence be-fore Him.

Text: Habakkuk 2:20
Tune: George F. Root, 1820–1895

Let the Heaven Light Shine on Me 618

Now as he was going along and approaching Damascus, suddenly a light from heaven flashed around him.
Acts 9:3

Let the heav'n light shine on me, Let the heav'n light shine on

me, for low is the way to the up-per bright world, Let the

heav'n light shine on me. Shine on me, Shine on

me. Let the light from heav'n shine on

A - men, A - men.

me. A - men, A - men.

Text: African American traditional; adapt. by Roland M. Carter, b.1942, © 1978, Mar-Vel
Tune: African American traditional; arr. by Roland M. Carter, b.1942, © 1978, Mar-Vel

619

This Is the Day

This is the day that the LORD has made; let us rejoice and be glad in it.
Psalm 118:24

This is the day which the Lord hath made.

Let us re-

rit.

Let us re - joice and be glad in it.

joice! Let us re - joice! A - men.

Text: Psalm 118:24
Music: Everett Williams, Jr., © 1982
Johnny Jordan Co., Washington D.C., sole distributors

A Glorious Introit

620

Say to God, "How awesome are your deeds! Because of your great power, your enemies cringe before you."
Psalm 66:3

All glo - ry be un - to You, Lord. All glo - ry we give to You. All hon - or we give un - to You, Lord. All glo - ry, all hon - or, all praise. We give them un - to You. A - men.

Text: Michael Kenneth Ross
Tune: Michael Kenneth Ross
© 1995, MKR Music

621 Lord, You Are Welcome

...and the temple was filled with smoke from the glory of God and from his power...
Revelation 15:8

Lord, You are wel - come, You're wel - come, You are wel - come, You're wel-come in this place. You are place. Lord, our ho - ly hands we raise to

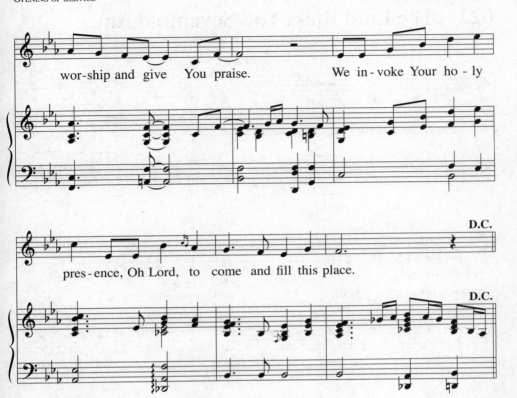

wor-ship and give You praise.   We in-voke Your ho - ly

pres - ence, Oh Lord, to come and fill this place.

Text: Warren Jones, ©
Tune: Warren Jones, ©; arr. by Nolan Williams, Jr., b.1969, © 2000, GIA Publications, Inc.

622 The Lord Bless You/Sevenfold Amen

The LORD bless you and keep you; the LORD make his face to shine upon you, and be gracious to you...
Numbers 6:24–25

The Lord bless you and keep you; The Lord lift His coun-te-nance up-on you, and give you peace, and give you peace, and give you peace; The Lord make His face to shine up-on you, And be gra-cious un-to you, be gra-cious, And be gra-cious, and be gra-cious,

The Lord be gra-cious, gra-cious un - to you.

A - men, A - men, A - men, A - men,
A - men, A - men, A - men, A -
A - men, A - men, A - men, A -

men, A - men, A -
A - men, A - men, A - men,
men, A - men,

men, A - men.
A - men.
A - men, A - men.

men, A - men, A -

men, A - men.

Text: Numbers 6:24–26
Tune: BENEDICTION, Irregular; Peter C. Lutkin, 1858–1931

623   Lord, Make Me More Holy

Pursue peace with everyone, and the holiness without which no one will see the Lord.
Hebrews 12:14

Lord, make me more *ho - ly, Lord, make me more
ho - ly, Lord, make me more ho - ly, un -
til we meet a - gain. Ho - ly, ho - ly,
ho - ly, un - til we meet a - gain.
A - men, a - men, a -

*faithful
**Benediction pronounced here.

men, un-til we meet a-gain. A - men.

Text: African American traditional; adapt. by Roland M. Carter, b.1942, © Mar-Vel
Tune: African American traditional; arr. by Roland M. Carter, b.1942, © Mar-Vel

Always Remember 624

Remember Jesus Christ, raised from the dead, a descendant of David—that is my gospel...
2 Timothy 2:8

Al - ways re - mem - ber Je - sus, Je - sus.

Al - ways re - mem - ber Je - sus, Je - sus.

Al - ways keep Him on your mind.

Text: Andraé Crouch, b.1942
Tune: Andraé Crouch, b.1942; arr. Evelyn Simpson-Curenton, b.1953
© 1985, Crouch Music Corp. (ASCAP)

625 As You Go, Tell the World

As you go, proclaim the good news, 'The kingdom of heaven has come near.'
Matthew 10:7

Text: Anonymous
Tune: Anonymous; arr. by Valeria Foster, © 2000, GIA Publications, Inc.

God Be with You

626

Where can I go from your spirit? Or where can I flee from your presence?
Psalm 139:7

God be with you, God be with you,

God be with you, un-til we meet a - gain;

God be with you, God be with you,

God be with you, un-til we meet a - gain.

Text: Thomas A. Dorsey, 1899–1993
Tune: Thomas A. Dorsey, 1899–1993; arr. by Horace Clarence Boyer, 1935–2009
© 1940 (renewed), arr. © 2011, Warner-Tamerlane Publishing Co., Inc.

627 God Be with You Till We Meet Again

You, O LORD, will protect us; you will guard us from this generation forever.
Psalm 12:7

1. God be with you till we meet a - gain; By God's
2. God be with you till we meet a - gain; 'Neath God's
3. God be with you till we meet a - gain; When life's
4. God be with you till we meet a - gain; Keep love's

coun - sels guide, up - hold you, With God's sheep se - cure - ly
wings pro - tect - ing hide you, Dai - ly man - na still proper - ils thick con - found you, Put God's arms un - fail - ing
ban - ner float - ing o'er you, Smite death's threat-'ning wave be-

fold you: God be with you till we meet a - gain.
vide you: God be with you till we meet a - gain.
round you: God be with you till we meet a - gain.
fore you: God be with you till we meet a - gain.

Till we meet, till we meet, Till we

meet   at Je - sus' feet,   Till we meet,   till we

till we meet,

meet,   God be with you till we meet a - gain.

Text: Jeremiah E. Rankin, 1828–1904
Tune: GOD BE WITH YOU, 9 8 8 9 with refrain; William G. Tomer, 1832–1896

628

Go Ye Now in Peace

The priest replied, "Go in peace. The mission you are on is under the eye of the LORD."
Judges 18:6

Go ye now in peace, and know that the love of God will guide you. Feel His pres-ence here be - side you. He will see you through. Go ye now in peace. Go ye now in peace. Go in peace.

Text: Joyce Eilers Bacak, 1941–2009
Tune: Joyce Eilers Bacak, 1941–2009; arr. by Evelyn Simpson-Curenton, b.1953
© 1981, arr. © 2011, Jenson Publications

Till We Gather Again

629

Peace I leave with you; my peace I give to you.
John 14:27

Till we gath-er a - gain, God be with you. Till we gath-er a - gain, God be with you. May He give you His love, give you His kind - ness, keep you in per - fect peace. God be with you till we meet a - gain.

Text: Stephen F. Key
Tune: Stephen F. Key
© StepKey Music

630 Be with Us All, Lord

...grow in the grace and knowledge of our Lord and Savior Jesus Christ. To him be the glory...
2 Peter 3:18

May the grace of the Lord Je-sus Christ be
with you, and the love of God, and the
fel-low-ship of the Ho-ly Ghost be with us
all. A - men. Grace,

love,   and fel - low - ship   be with us all.

A - men.   A - men!   A -

men!   A - men,   a - men!

Text: Uzee Brown, Jr., b.1950
Tune: Uzee Brown, Jr., b.1950
© 1995, Roger Dean Publishing Co.

631
Halle, Halle, Halle

Hallelujah! Salvation and glory and power to our God...
Revelation 19:1

Hal - le, hal - le, hal - le - lu - jah! Hal - le, hal - le, hal-

Hal - le, hal - le, hal-

lu - jah! le - lu, Hal-le-lu-jah! Hal - le, hal - le, hal - le - lu -

le - lu - jah!

Music: Traditional Caribbean, arr. by John L. Bell, b.1949, © 1990, Iona Community, GIA Publications, Inc., agent; acc. by Marty Haugen, b.1950, © 1993, GIA Publications, Inc.

632 Hallelujah, Amen

Once more they said, Hallelujah!
Revelation 19:3

Hal - le - lu - jah, A - men. Hal - le - lu -
A - men. Hal - le - lu - jah, A -

jah, A - men. Hal - le - lu - jah, A - men.
men. Hal - le - lu - jah, A - men.

Text: Robert L. Morris, b.1942 (ASCAP)
Music: Robert L. Morris, b.1942 (ASCAP)
© Hidden Gems Press

633 Alleluia

He is your praise; he is your God, who has done for you these great and awesome things...
Deuteronomy 10:21

1. Al - le - lu - ia, al - le - lu - ia, al - le - lu - ia, al - le - lu - ia,

al - le - lu - ia, al - le - lu - ia, al - le - lu - ia, al - le - lu - ia.

2. Thank You, Jesus,... 3. Lord, we praise You,... 4. Lord, we love You...

Text: Jerry Sinclair, 1943–1993
Music: Jerry Sinclair, 1943–1993
© 1972, 2000, Manna Music, Inc./ASCAP (admin. by ClearBox Rights)

Threefold Amen

634

...in him every one of God's promises is a "Yes." For this reason it is through him that we say the "Amen,"...
2 Corinthians 1:20

A - men, A - men, A - men.

Music: Danish Amen, anonymous; arr. by Nolan Williams, Jr., b.1969, © 2000, GIA Publications, Inc.

Sevenfold Amen

635

"These are the words of the Amen, the faithful and true witness, the ruler of God's creation."
Revelation 3:14b

A - men, A - men, A -

A-men, A-men, A - men, A - men, A -

A - men, A - men,

men, A - men,

men, A - men, A - men.

A - men, A - men,

Music: John Stainer, 1840–1901

636

Amen

Blessed be the LORD forever. Amen and Amen.
Psalm 89:52

ly - in' in the man - ger on
talk - in' with the eld - ers who
where John was bap - tiz - in' and
talk - in' to the fish - er - men and
o - ver palm branch - es, in
pray - in' to His Fa - ther, in
then they cru - ci - fied Him, but He
He died to save us and He

men, a -

Christ - mas morn - in'.
mar - velled at His wis - dom.
sav - in' all sin - ners.
mak - in' them dis - ci - ples.
pomp and splen - dor.
deep - est sor - row.
rose on East - er.
lives for ev - er.

men, a -

men, a - men, a - men.

Text: Traditional
Music: Negro Spiritual; arr. by Valeria A. Foster, © 2000, GIA Publications, Inc.

637 Praise God from Whom All Blessings Flow

Every generous act of giving, with every perfect gift, is from above, coming down from the Father...
James 1:17

Peo - ple and realms of ev - 'ry tongue
Sing to the Lord with cheer - ful voice,

Dwell on His love with sweet - est song,
Come ye be - fore Him and re - joice,

To Him shall end - less prayer be made,
All peo - ple that on earth do dwell,

And end - less prais - es crown His
Serve Him with mirth, His prais - es

head.
tell. A - men, A - men.

Text: Isaac Watts, 1675–1748, and William Keathe, d.1593; adapt. by Thomas Ken, 1637–1711
Tune: John Hatton, c.1710–1793; adapt. by George Coles, 1792–1858; arr. by Roberta Martin, 1912–1969, © 1968, alt.

638 Doxology

Blessed be the God and Father of our Lord Jesus Christ...
Ephesians 1:3

Praise God, from whom all bless-ings flow; Praise Him, all crea-tures here be-low; Praise Him a-bove, ye heav'n-ly host; Praise Fa-ther, Son, and Ho-ly Ghost.

Text: Thomas Ken, 1637–1711
Tune: OLD HUNDREDTH, LM; *Genevan Psalter*, 1551; attr. to Louis Bourgeois, 1510–1561

639 Gloria Patri

To our God and Father be glory forever and ever. Amen.
Philippians 4:20

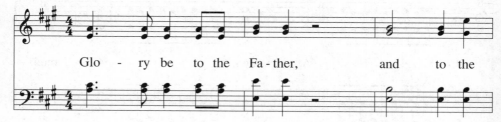

Glo - ry be to the Fa-ther, and to the

Son, and to the Ho - ly Ghost; As it was in the be -

gin-ning, is now, and ev - er shall be,

world with-out end. A - men, A - men.

Text: 2nd Century
Music: Charles Meineke, 1782–1850

Gloria Patri

640

To our God and Father be glory forever and ever. Amen.
Philippians 4:20

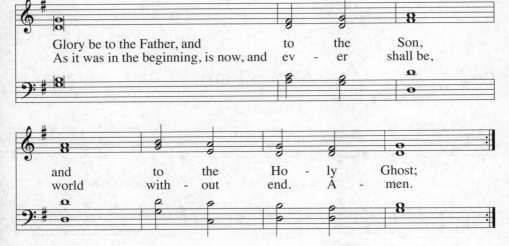

Glory be to the Father, and to the Son,
As it was in the beginning, is now, and ev - er shall be,

and to the Ho - ly Ghost;
world with - out end. A - men.

Text: 2nd Century
Music: Old Scottish Chant

641 Gloria Patri

"I am the Alpha and the Omega," says the Lord God, who is and who was and who is to come, the Almighty.
Revelation 1:8

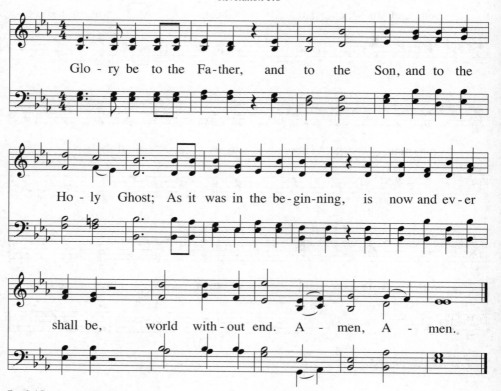

Glo - ry be to the Fa-ther, and to the Son, and to the

Ho - ly Ghost; As it was in the be - gin - ning, is now and ev - er

shall be, world with - out end. A - men, A - men.

Text: 2nd Century
Music: Henry W. Greatorex, 1813–1858

642 Gloria Patri

"I am the Alpha and the Omega, the First and the Last, the Beginning and the End."
Revelation 22:13

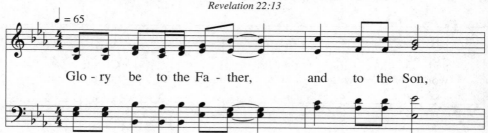

Glo - ry be to the Fa - ther, and to the Son,

and to the Ho - ly Ghost, the Three in One; as it

was in the be - gin - ning, is now and ev - er shall be,

world with-out end. A - men. A - men.

Text: 2nd Century
Music: Glenn L. Jones, b.1949, © 2004, Tehillah International Ministries

Hear Our Prayer 643

Hear my prayer, O LORD; give ear to my supplications in your faithfulness; answer me in your righteousness.
Psalm 143:1

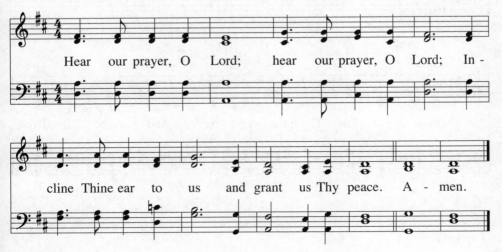

Hear our prayer, O Lord; hear our prayer, O Lord; In -

cline Thine ear to us and grant us Thy peace. A - men.

Text: Psalm 143:1
Tune: George Whelpton, 1847–1930

644   O Lord, Incline Thine Ear to Us

Hear a just cause, O LORD; attend to my cry; give ear to my prayer from lips free of deceit.
Psalm 17:1

peace.* A - men,   A - men, A - men, A - men.

peace.   A - men, A - men, A - men, A - men.

*A separate Amen may begin here.

Text: African American traditional
Tune: African American traditional; arr. by Bernadette Blount Salley, © 1987. Administered by GIA Publications, Inc.

Isaiah 6:3   645

One called to another and said: Holy, holy, holy is the LORD of hosts; the whole earth is full of his glory."
Isaiah 6:3

Ho - ly, ho - ly, ho - ly,   Lord   God   of

Hosts!   Heav'n and earth are full of Thee!

Heav'n and earth are prais - ing Thee, O Lord most high!

Text: Isaiah 6:3, Mary A. Lathbury, 1841–1913
Tune: CHAUTAUQUA, Irregular; William F. Sherwin, 1826–1888

646

Sanctus

...Holy, holy, holy, the Lord God the Almighty, who was and is and is to come.
Revelation 4:8

Slowly ♩ = 72

Ho - ly, ho - ly, ho - ly Lord, God of pow'r and

might. Ho - ly, ho - ly, ho - ly Lord, God of

pow'r and might. Heav - en and earth are full,

full of Your glo - ry. Ho - san - na in the high -

est, ho - san - na in the high - est. Bless-ed is He who

Music: *Deutsche Messe*, Franz Schubert, 1797–1828; adapt. by Richard Proulx, 1937–2010, © 1985, 1989, GIA Publications, Inc.

647 The Lord's Prayer

Pray then in this way: Our Father in heaven, hallowed be your name.
Matthew 6:9

Our Fa - ther, which art in heav - en,

hal-low-ed be Thy name.

Thy king-dom come, Thy will be done on

earth as it is in heav - en. Give us this

Oo

Oo

(Oo)

day our dai - ly bread, and for-give us our debts as

(Oo)

we for-give our debt-ors. And lead us not in-to temp-

ta - tion, but de - liv - er us from e - vil. For Thine is the

king - dom, and the pow - er, and the glo - ry for -

ev - er. A - men.

Music: Albert Hay Malotte, 1895-1964, © 1935, (renewed) G. Schirmer, Inc.; arr. by Evelyn Simpson-Curenton, b.1953, © 2000, G. Schirmer, Inc.

648

The Lord's Prayer

Pray then in this way: Our Father in heaven, hallowed be your name.
Matthew 6:9

slower tempo

Hal - low - ed - a be Thy name.

Verse 4

4. Lead us not in - to temp-ta-tion, Hal-low-ed-a be Thy

name. But de - liv - er us from e - vil,

rall.

Hal - low - ed - a be Thy name.

rall.

Verses 5, 6
brighter tempo

5. Thine is the king - dom, the pow'r and the glo - ry,
6. A - men, a - men, a - men,

(5.) and the glo - ry,
(6.) a - men,

Hal - low - ed - a be Thy name. For ev - er, and
Hal - low - ed - a be Thy name. A - men, a - men, a -

ev - er, Hal - low - ed - a be Thy name.
men, a - men. Hal - low - ed - a be Thy

1.

2. *rall.*

name. Hal - low - ed - a be Thy name.

rall.

Text: The Lord's Prayer
Tune: West Indian traditional; arr. by Nolan Williams, Jr., b.1969, © 2000, GIA Publications, Inc.

Let the Words of My Mouth

Let the words of my mouth and the meditation of my heart be acceptable to you, O LORD...
Psalm 19:14

Let the words of my mouth, let the words of my mouth, and the

med-i-ta-tions of my heart be ac-cept-a-ble in Thy sight; Wilt Thou

teach me how to serve Thee, Wilt Thou teach me how to pray?

Our Father, who art in heaven, hallowed be Thy name.
Give us this day our dai - ly bread.
Lead us not into temptation, but deliver us from evil.

Thy Kingdom come, Thy will be done on earth as it is in heav'n.
And forgive us our trespasses as we forgive those who trespass a - gainst us.
For Thine is the kingdom, and the power and the glory for ever and ever. A - men.

Text: Psalm 19:14 and The Lord's Prayer
Music: C. E. Leslie; adapt. by Nolan Williams, Jr., b.1969, Evelyn Simpson-Curenton, b.1953, and Robert J. Fryson, 1944–1994, © 2000,
  GIA Publications, Inc.

650 Mayenziwe/Your Will Be Done

Your will be done, on earth as it is in heaven.
Matthew 6:10

African phonetics:
My-yen-zee-way tahn-doe yah-koe.

Text: from the Lord's Prayer, South African, (Xhosa)
Music: South African traditional, as taught by George Mxadana; transcribed by John L. Bell, b.1949; © 1990, Iona Community,
   GIA Publications, Inc., agent

All Things Come of Thee

651

But who am I, and what is my people, that we should be able to make this freewill offering?
1 Chronicles 29:14

All things come of Thee, O Lord, and of Thine own have we giv - en Thee.

Text: I Chronicles 29:14
Music: Attr. to Ludwig van Beethoven, 1770–1827

652 You Can't Beat God Giving

God is able to provide you with every blessing in abundance...
2 Corinthians 9:8

You can't beat God giv-ing, no mat-ter how you try. And just as sure as you are liv-ing and the Lord is in heav-en on high, the more you give, the

more He gives to you. Just keep on giv-ing be-

cause it's real - ly true. That You can't beat God

giv-ing no mat-ter how you try.

Text: Doris Akers, 1922–1995
Tune: Doris Akers, 1922–1995; arr. by Evelyn Simpson-Curenton, b.1953
© 1957, 1985, Manna Music, Inc. (admin. by ClearBox Rights)

653 Hallelujah, I've Been Redeemed!

For you have been born again through the living and enduring word of God.
1 Peter 1:23

Refrain

Bap - tized in the name of the Fa - ther.

Bap - tized in the name of the Son.

Bap - tized in the name of the Ho - ly Ghost.

Hal - le - lu - jah, I've been re - deemed!

Text: Glenn L. Jones, b.1949
Tune: Glenn L. Jones, b.1949
© 2006, Tehillah International Ministries

654 Come, Holy Spirit, Dove Divine

...suddenly the heavens were opened to him and he saw the Spirit of God descending like a dove...
Matthew 3:16

1. Come, Ho - ly Spir - it, Dove Di - vine,
2. We love Thy name, we love Thy laws,
3. We sink be - neath Thy mys - tic flood;
4. And as we rise, with Thee to live,

On these bap - tis - mal wa - ters shine,
And joy - ful - ly em - brace Thy cause;
O bathe us in Thy cleans - ing blood;
O let the Ho - ly Spir - it give

And teach our hearts, in high - est strain,
We love Thy cross, the shame, the pain,
We die to sin, and seek a grave,
The seal - ing unc - tion from a - bove,

To praise the Lamb, for sin - ners slain.
O Lamb of God, for sin - ners slain.
With Thee, be - neath the yield - ing wave.
The breath of life, the fire of love.

Text: Adoniram Judson, 1788–1850
Tune: ERNAN, LM, Lowell Mason, 1792–1872

Baptized in Water

Sing to him, sing praise to him; tell of all his wonderful acts.
1 Chronicles 16:8

655

1. Bap-tized in wa - ter, Sealed by the Spir - it, Cleansed by the
2. Bap-tized in wa - ter, Sealed by the Spir - it, Dead in the
3. Bap-tized in wa - ter, Sealed by the Spir - it, Marked with the

blood of Christ our King: Heirs of sal - va - tion, Trust-ing His
tomb with Christ our King: One with His ris - ing, freed and for -
sign of Christ our King: Born of one Fa - ther, We are His

prom - ise, Faith - ful - ly now God's praise we sing.
giv - en, Thank - ful - ly now God's praise we sing.
chil - dren, Joy - ful - ly now God's praise we sing.

Text: Michael Saward, b.1932, © 1982, The Jubilate Group (admin. Hope Publishing Company)
Tune: BUNESSAN, 5 5 8 D; Gaelic melody; acc. by Robert J. Batastini, b.1942, © 1999, GIA Publications, Inc.

656

Take Me to the Water

"Look, here is water! What is to prevent me from being baptized?"
Acts 8:36

Text: Negro Spiritual
Tune: TO THE WATER, Irregular; Negro Spiritual; arr. by Valeria A. Foster, © 2000, GIA Publications, Inc.

Wade in the Water

So those who welcomed his message were baptized, and that day about three thousand persons were added.
Acts 2:41

Refrain

Wade in the wa - ter, wade in the wa - ter, chil - dren,

Wade in the wa - ter, God's gon - na trou - ble the wa - ter.

Verses

1. See that host all dressed in white,
2. See that band all dressed in red, God's gon-na trou-ble the
3. If you don't be-lieve I've been re-deemed,

The lead - er looks like the Is - rael - ite,
wa - ter. Looks like the band that Mo - ses led,
Just fol - low me down to Jor - dan's stream,

D.C.

God's gon - na trou - ble the wa - ter.

Text: Negro Spiritual
Tune: WADE, 7 8 8 8 with refrain; Negro Spiritual; arr. by James Abbington, b.1960, © 2000, GIA Publications, Inc.

658
Certainly, Lord

Let the redeemed of the LORD say so, those he redeemed from trouble.
Psalm 107:2

1. Have you got good re-lig-ion,
2. Do you love ev-'ry-bod-y,
3. Have you been con-vert-ed,
4. Have you been to the wa-ter,
5. Have you been bap-tized,

Have you
Do you
Have you
Have you
Have you

Cert-'n-ly, Lord!

got good re-lig-ion,
love ev-'ry-bod-y,
been con-vert-ed,
been to the wa-ter,
been bap-tized,

Have you got good re-lig-ion?
Do you love ev-'ry-bod-y?
Have you been con-vert-ed?
Have you been to the wa-ter?
Have you been bap-tized?

Cert-'n-ly, Lord!

Last time

Cert-'n-ly, Lord!   Cert-'n-ly, cert-'n-ly, cert-'n-ly, Lord!

Last time

Text: Negro Spiritual
Tune: CERTAINLY LORD, 7 4 7 4 7 4 10; Negro Spiritual; arr. by Evelyn Simpson-Curenton, b.1953, © 2000, GIA Publications, Inc.

Hallelujah, 'Tis Done

...all the people of Jerusalem were going out to him, and were baptized... in the river Jordan, confessing their sins.
Mark 1:5

Hal - le - lu - jah,   'tis   done,   I   be -
lieve   on   the   Son.   I   am saved   by   the
blood   of   the   cru - ci - fied   One.   One.

Note: This is a baptismal hymn taken from the African American worship oral tradition.

Text: Traditional
Tune: African American traditional; arr. by Evelyn Simpson-Curenton, b.1953, © 2000, GIA Publications, Inc.

660 Hallelujah, 'Tis Done

...all the people of Jerusalem were going out to him, and were baptized... in the river Jordan, confessing their sins.
Mark 1:5

1. 'Tis the prom - ise of God full sal - va - tion to
2. Tho' the path - way be lone - ly, and dan - ger - ous
3. There's a part in that cho - rus for you and for

give Un - to Him who on Je - sus, His Son, will be - lieve.
too, Sure - ly Je - sus is a - ble to car - ry me through.
me, And the theme of our prais - es for - ev - er will be:

Hal - le - lu - jah, 'tis done! I be - lieve on the

Son; I am saved by the blood of the

cru – ci - fied One. cru – ci - fied One.

Text: Philip P. Bliss
Tune: TIS DONE, 12 12 with refrain; Philip P. Bliss
© 1954, First Church of Deliverance

661 Wash, O God, Our Sons and Daughters

Baptism...now saves you —not as a removal of dirt from the body, but as an appeal to God for a good conscience...
1 Peter 3:21

1. Wash, O God, our sons and daugh - ters, Where Your
2. We who bring them long for nur - ture; By Your
3. O how deep Your ho - ly wis - dom! Un - i -

cleans - ing wa - ters flow. Num - ber them a - mong Your
milk may we be fed. Let us join Your feast, par -
mag - ined, all Your ways! To Your name be glo - ry,

peo - ple; Bless as Christ blessed long a - go. Weave them
tak - ing Cup of bless - ing, liv - ing bread. God, re -
hon - or! With our lives we wor - ship, praise! We Your

gar - ments bright and spar - kling; Com - pass
new us, guide our foot - steps; Free from
peo - ple stand be - fore You, Wa - ter -

them   with   love   and   light.   Fill, a - noint   them;
sin   and   all   its   snares,   One with Christ   in
washed and   Spir - it -   born.   By   Your grace,   our

send Your Spir - it,   Ho - ly   dove and   heart's de - light.
liv - ing, dy - ing,   By Your Spir - it,   chil - dren, heirs.
lives we   of - fer.   Re - cre - ate us;   God, trans - form!

Text: Ruth Duck, b.1947, © 1989, The United Methodist Publishing House
Tune: BEACH SPRING, 8 7 8 7 D, attr. to B. F. White, 1800–1879; harm. by Ronald A. Nelson, b.1927, © 1978, *Lutheran Book of Worship*

662

Do This in Remembrance of Me

And he took bread, gave thanks and broke it, and gave it to them, saying,
"This is my body given for you; do this in remembrance of me."
Luke 22:18

Do this   in re-mem-brance of   Me.

Do this   in re-mem-brance of Me.   I hung out on a tree

for thee, for thee.   Do this   in re-mem-brance of   Me.

Eat this bread,   drink this cup

to show forth My suf-fer-ing till I come. I hung out on a tree called Cal-va-ry, oh, do this in re-mem-brance of Me. Eat this bread,

Do this in re-mem-brance of Me. Oh,

Do this in re-mem-brance of Me.

Last time to Coda

Coda

Text: Based on 1 Corinthians 11:24–26; Glenn E. Burleigh, 1949–2007
Tune: Glenn E. Burleigh, 1949–2007
© 1995, 1997, GIA Publications, Inc.

663

Taste and See

Taste and see that the LORD is good…
Psalm 34:8

Refrain

Taste and see the good-ness of the Lord.

Taste and see the good-ness of the Lord. He's

o-pened doors for me, doors that I just could-n't see.

Oh, taste and see the good-ness of the Lord.

Verse

I will bless the Lord at all times. His
praise shall al-ways be on my lips. My
soul shall glo-ry in the Lord, for He's been good to me.
Oh, taste and see the good-ness of the Lord.

D.C.

Text: Psalm 34; Kenneth W. Louis, b.1956
Tune: Kenneth W. Louis, b.1956
© 2001, GIA Publications, Inc.

664 Come to the Table

This is my body, which is for you; do this in remembrance of me.
1 Corinthians 11:24

Verses

1. Come to the ta-ble, oh My chil-dren, par-take of Me.

(2.) life that you may live, par-take of Me.
(3.) death un-til I come, par-take of Me.

Come to the ta-ble, oh My

I gave My life that you may live,
Show forth My death un-til I come,

chil-dren, par - take of Me.   This you

par - take of Me.   The crim - son
par - take of Me.   They hung Me

do   in re - mem - brance of   Me   lest you for-

blood   I   shed   for   you,   the price for
high   and   stretched Me   wide,   it pleased My

Come to the ta-ble, oh My chil-dren, par - take of Me.

1.

2., 3.

2. I gave My

3. Show forth My

Last time

D.S.

D.S.

Text: Glenn L. Jones, b.1949
Tune: Glenn L. Jones, b.1949
© 2000, Tehillah International Ministries

665 Risen Lord, We Gather Round You

I am the bread of life.
John 6:48

1. Ris - en Lord, we gath - er round You,
2. Sis - ters, broth - ers stand be - side us,
3. By the loaf and cup You of - fer,
4. "Go where lives are bruised and bro - ken;

Drawn by words for - ev - er new:
Called from ev - 'ry land and race.
Strength - en us to fol - low You.
Go where chil - dren waste and blight.

"Come, My peo - ple, all are wel - come;
One the Bread of Life that feeds us;
By Your bod - y, ris - en, giv - en,
Go a - mong the lost, for - got - ten;

Share the feast pre - pared for you!" Emp - ty hands and
One the Cup of brim - ming grace. Form us, Lord, a
Heal us, Christ, and make us new. Help us hear Your
Be for them My heal - ing Light! Take the Bread of

hearts that hun - ger, Christ, we bring to You to - day.
sin - gle bod - y, Free from en - mi - ty and strife.
ur - gent sum - mons, Cut - ting through our fear of loss:
Life I give you; Share it with a world in pain.

Here You feed us with Your Bod - y,
Je - sus, by Your res - ur - rec - tion,
"Go, My peo - ple! Be My ser - vants!
Go, My peo - ple! I am with you

Gift of love for which we pray.
Fill us with the Spir - it's life!
Bear with Me the wait - ing cross!"
Till on earth My love shall reign!"

Text: Herman G. Stuempfle, Jr., 1923–2007, © 2006, GIA Publications, Inc.
Tune: HOLY MANNA, 8 7 8 7 D; William Moore, fl.1830

666 Lord, I Have Seen Thy Salvation

...now you are dismissing your servant in peace, according to your word; for my eyes have seen your salvation...
Luke 2:29–30

1. Lord, I have seen Thy sal - va - tion, Lord, I have seen
2. Lord, I have heard of Thy king - dom, Lord, I have heard

Thy sal - va - tion, drank of the blood, held the bod - y,
of Thy prom - ise, looked on Thy birth, cried at Cal - v'ry,

Lord, I have seen, seen with my eyes, seen with my heart.
Lord, I have heard, Lord, I have heard, Lord, I have heard.

Fell on my knees, down at the al - tar, bowed down my head, whis-pered a pray-er. Have mer-cy, Lord, I'm not wor-thy, I be-lieve, Yes, I be-lieve, now I am sure.

Text: John D. Cooper, b.1925
Tune: THY SALVATION, 8 8 8 12 with refrain; John D. Cooper, b.1925
© 1980, Dangerfield Music Co.

667 We Remember You

The cup of blessing that we bless, is it not a sharing in the blood of Christ?
1 Corinthians 10:16

As we drink this cup, we wor-ship You; As we

eat this bread, we hon-or You; And we of - fer You our

lives as You have of - fered Yours for us. We re -

mem - ber all You've done for us, We re - mem - ber Your

cov - e - nant with us, We re - mem - ber, and

wor - ship You, O Lord.

Text: Kirk Dearman, b.1952
Tune: Kirk Dearman, b.1952
© 1988, Maranatha Praise, Inc., admin. by Music Services

668   Alleluia! Sing to Jesus

...and the blood of Jesus, his Son, purifies us from all sin.
1 John 1:7

1. Al - le - lu - ia! Sing to Je - sus!
2. Al - le - lu - ia! Not as or - phans
3. Al - le - lu - ia! Bread of an - gels,
4. Al - le - lu - ia! King e - ter - nal,

His the scep - ter, His the throne.
Are we left in sor - row now;
Here on earth our food, our stay!
You the Lord of lords we own;

Al - le - lu - ia! His the tri - umph,
Al - le - lu - ia! He is near us;
Al - le - lu - ia! Here the sin - ful
Al - le - lu - ia! Born of Mar - y,

His the vic - to - ry a - lone.
Faith be - lieves, nor ques - tions how.
Flee to You from day to day.
Earth Your foot - stool, heav'n Your throne.

Hark! The songs of peace - ful Zi - on
Though the cloud from sight re - ceived Him
In - ter - ces - sor, friend of sin - ners,
You with - in the veil have en - tered,

Thun - der like a might - y flood:
When the for - ty days were o'er,
Earth's re - deem - er, plead for me,
Robed in flesh, our great high priest;

"Je - sus out of ev - 'ry na - tion
Shall our hearts for - get His prom - ise:
Where the songs of all the sin - less
Here on earth both priest and vic - tim

Has re - deemed us by His blood."
"I am with you ev - er - more?"
Sweep a - cross the crys - tal sea.
In the eu - cha - ris - tic feast.

Text: Revelation 5:9; William C. Dix, 1837–1898
Tune: HYFRYDOL, 8 7 8 7 D; Rowland H. Prichard, 1811–1887

669 Let Us Break Bread Together

...we who are many are one body, for we all partake of the one bread.
1 Corinthians 10:17

2. Let us drink wine together...
3. Let us praise God together...

Text: Traditional
Tune: BREAK BREAD TOGETHER, 10 10 14 7; traditional; arr. by James Abbington, b.1960, © 2000, GIA Publications, Inc.

670 ACKNOWLEDGMENTS

100 © 1996, T. Autumn Music. This arrangement © 2010 by T. Autumn Music All Rights Administered by Universal Music - Z Songs. International Copyright Secured. All Rights Reserved. Reprinted by permission of Hal Leonard Corporation.

101 © 1971, Bud John Songs (ASCAP), admin. at EMICMG-Publishing.com. All Rights Reserved. Used by Permission.

102 © Gale Jones Murphy

104 © 2008, Kcartunes (BMI)/Lilly Mack Publishing, admin. at EMICMGPublishing.com. All Rights Reserved. Used by Permission.

105 Tune: © 1967, 1980, Universal Music - Brentwood-Benson Publishing (ASCAP), admin. by Music Services. All Rights reserved. International Copyright Secured. Used by Permission.

106 © 1998, Leon Roberts. Published by OCP, 5536 NE Hassalo, Portland, OR 97213. All rights reserved. Used with permission.

108 Arr.: © 2000, GIA Publications, Inc.

109 © 2009, Meaux Hits (ASCAP)/Gospo Music Thang (ASCAP)/216 Music (ASCAP), admin. at EMICMGPublishing.com. All Rights Reserved. Used by Permission.

110 Text and tune: © 1981, Sound III, Inc. Co-owned by MCA Music Publishing, 2440 Sepulveda Blvd., Suite 100, Los Angeles, CA 90064-1712 and The Lorenz Corporation, P.O. Box 802, Dayton, OH 45401-0802. All Rights Reserved. International Copyright Secured. Arr.: © 2000, GIA Publications, Inc.

111 Text and tune: © 1992, Joy Publishing Co. (SESAC). Arr.: © 2000, GIA Publications, Inc.

112 © 1991, CMI-HP Publishing, admin. by Word Music, LLC, Life Spring Music, admin. by Warner/Chappell Music, Inc. All Rights Reserved. Used By Permission.

113 © 1973, Bud John Songs (ASCAP), admin. at EMICMG-Publishing.com. All Rights Reserved. Used by Permission.

114 © 1963, 1965, 1980, Fred Bock Music Company, Inc. All rights reserved. Used by Permission.

115 Arr.: © 1990, Iona Community, GIA Publications, Inc., agent

116 © 1993, StepKey Music

118 Arr.: © 2000, GIA Publications, Inc.

120 Text and tune: © 1988, Universal Music - MGB Songs (ASCAP), admin. by Music Services. All Rights Reserved. Used by Permission. Arr.: © 2000, GIA Publications, Inc.

121 Arr.: © 2000, GIA Publications, Inc.

123 Text and tune: © 1994, Carlton Burgess. Administered by GIA Publications, Inc. Arr.: © 2000, GIA Publications, Inc.

124 Arr.: © 1992, Horace Clarence Boyer

126 Text and tune: © 1976, Bob Jay Music Co.; Arr.: © 2000, GIA Publications, Inc.

127 © 1959 (renewed), Martin and Morris, Inc. All Rights Administered by Unichappell Music, Inc. Used by Permission of Alfred Publishing Co., Inc.

129 Arr.: © 2000, GIA Publications, Inc.

130 Text: © 1989, Bob Jay Music Co. Arr: © 2000, GIA Publications, Inc.

136 Arr.: © 2000, GIA Publications, Inc.

137 Harm.: © Estate of Wendell Whalum

140 Harm.: © 1984, New Spring Publishing (ASCAP), admin. by Music Services. All Rights Reserved. Used by Permission.

142 © 1949, 1953, The Stuart K. Hine Trust. U.S.A. print rights administered by Hope Publishing Company, Carol Stream, IL 60188. Used by permission.

143 Arr.: © 1990, Hezekiah Brinson, Jr.

144 Arr.: © 2008, Iona Community, GIA Publications, Inc., agent

145 Arr.: © 2000, GIA Publications, Inc.

146 © 1982, Lanny Wolfe Music. All rights controlled by Gaither Copyright Management. Used by permission.

147 © Gale Jones Murphy

148 Text and tune: © 1989, Keith Hunter, published by Arrand Publishing Co. Arr.: © 2000, GIA Publications, Inc.

149 Text and tune: © 1973, Arr.: © 2000, Davike Music Co./Fricon Music Co.

151 Text and tune: © 1968, Greater Detroit Music and Record Mart. Arr.: © 2000, GIA Publications, Inc.

152 © 1981 by Peermusic III, Ltd. and Savgos Music, Inc. All Rights Administered by Peermusic III, Ltd. International Copyright Secured All Rights Reserved. Reprinted by permission of Hal Leonard Corporation.

153 Arr.: © 2000, GIA Publications, Inc.

154 © 1923, renewed 1951, Hope Publishing Company, Carol Stream, IL 60188. All rights reserved. Used by permission.

155 Text: © 2005, GIA Publications, Inc.

156 © 2006, Cecilia Olusola Tribble

157 Arr.: © 2000, GIA Publications, Inc.

158 © 1944 (renewed), Martin and Morris. All Rights Administered by Unichappell Music, Inc. This arr. © 2011, Martin and Morris. All Rights Reserved. Used by Permission of Alfred Publishing Co., Inc.

159 © 1988, Hanna Street Music (all rights controlled by Gaither Copyright Management) and Century Oak/Richwood Music. All rights reserved. Used by permission.

160 © 2003, this Arr. © 2010, Integrity's Praise! Music/BMI (c/o Integrity Media, Inc., 1000 Cody Road, Mobile, AL 36695) and Say The Name Pubishing. All Rights Reserved. International Copyright Secured. Used by Permission. Reprinted by permission of Hal Leonard Corporation.

161 © 1984, Utryck, All Rights Administered by Walton Music Corporation. International Copyright Secured. All Rights Reserved.

162 © 1983, Birdwing Music (ASCAP)/BMG Songs (ASCAP), admin. at EMICMGPublishing.com. All Rights Reserved. Used by Permission.

163 Arr.: © 2000, GIA Publications, Inc.

165 © 1978, Bob Kilpatrick Music. Assigned 1998 to The Lorenz Corporation.

166 © 1996, Thankyou Music (PRS), admin. at EMICMGPublishing.com. All Rights Reserved. Used by Permission.

167 Text and tune: © 1976, Sound III, Inc. Co-owned by MCA Music Publishing, 2440 Sepulveda Blvd., Suite 100, Los Angeles, CA 90064-1712 and The Lorenz Corporation, P.O. Box 802, Dayton, OH 45401-0802. All Rights Reserved. International Copyright Secured. Arr.: © 2000, GIA Publications, Inc.

169 © 2005, this Arr. © 2010, Integrity's Praise! Music/BMI and Sound of the New Breed/BMI (admin. by Integrity's Praise! Music), c/o Integrity Media, Inc., 1000 Cody Road, Mobile, AL 36695 All Rights Reserved. International Copyright Secured. Used by Permission. Reprinted by permission of Hal Leonard Corporation.

170 © 1992, Total Praise Music Publishing

172 © 1986, Bud John Tunes (SESAC), admin. at EMICMG-Publishing.com. All Rights Reserved. Used by Permission.

173 Arr.: © 2000, GIA Publications, Inc.

174 © 1983, Songchannel Music Co. (ASCAP)/Meadowgreen Music (ASCAP), admin. at EMICMGPublishing.com. All Rights Reserved. Used by Permission.

175 © 1972, Hanna Street Music. All rights controlled by Gaither Copyright Management. Used by permission.

176 © 1980, New Spring Publishing (ASCAP), admin. by Music Services. All Rights Reserved. Used by Permission.

177 Arr.: © 2000, GIA Publications, Inc.

179 © 2007, Lilly Mack Publishing, admin. at EMICMGPublishing.com. All Rights Reserved. Used by Permission.

180 Text and tune: © 1989, Rev. Earl Pleasant Publishing, Arr.: © 2000, GIA Publications, Inc.

181 © Robert Wooten, Sr.

183 © 1986, Word Music, LLC, admin. by Warner/Chappell Music Services, Inc. All Rights Reserved. Used By Permission.

184 © 1976, C.A. Music (div. of C. A. Records, Inc.) All Rights Reserved. (ASCAP)

186 Tune: © 1985, Kenneth W. Louis

187 © 2007, World Library Publications

188 © 1996, From Dust Music, admin. by See & Say Songs, c/o The Copyright Company, Nashville, TN. All Rights Reserved. International Copyright Secured. Used By Permission.

ACKNOWLEDGMENTS/continued

190 © 1976, Crouch Music (ASCAP)/Bud John Songs (ASCAP), admin. at EMICMGPublishing.com. All Rights Reserved. Used by Permission.

194 © 1979, 2000, GIA Publications, Inc.

195 Arr.: © 1990, Melva Costen

196 © 1981, Savgos Music, Inc., International Copyright Secured. All rights Reserved. Reprinted by permission of Hal Leonard Corporation.

197 © 1977, Bud John Music (BMI), admin. EMICMGPublishing.com. All Rights Reserved. Used by Permission.

200 Text: © 1994, Hope Publishing Company, Carol Stream, IL 60188. All rights reserved. Used by permission. Tune: © 2003, GIA Publications, Inc.

204 Arr.: © 2000, GIA Publications, Inc.

210 Arr.: © 2000, GIA Publications, Inc.

212 Arr.: © 2000, GIA Publications, Inc.

214 Arr.: © 2000, GIA Publications, Inc.

216 Arr.: © 2000, GIA Publications, Inc.

218 Arr.: © 2000, GIA Publications, Inc.

220 Arr.: © 2000, GIA Publications, Inc.

221 © 1937, First Church of Deliverance

222 Arr.: © 1993, GIA Publications, Inc.

224 © 1978 Dayspring Music, LLC (BMI). All Rights Reserved

226 Arr.: © 2000, GIA Publications, Inc.

227 Arr.: © 2000, GIA Publications, Inc.

229 Arr.: © 2000, GIA Publications, Inc.

230 © 1975, Word Music, LLC, admin. by Warner/Chappell Music Services, Inc. All Rights Reserved. Used By Permission.

232 © 1981, Les Presses de Taizé, GIA Publications, Inc., agent

233 © 1986, Kenneth W. Louis

234 © 2008, Kcartunes/Lilly Mack Publishing, admin. at EMICMGPublishing.com. All Rights Reserved. Used by Permission.

237 © 1950, Bridge Building Music (BMI) admin. Music Services. All Rights Reserved. Used By Permission.

238 Arr.: © 2000, GIA Publications, Inc.

239 © 1976, renewed 2004, Albert E. Brumley & Sons/SESAC (admin. by ClearBox Rights). All rights reserved. Used by permission.

243 © 1946, New Spring Publishing (ASCAP), admin. by Music Services. All Rights Reserved. Used by Permission.

244 Arr.: © 2000, GIA Publications, Inc.

247 Text: © 1968, New Spring Publishing (ASCAP), admin. by Music Services. All Rights Reserved. Used by Permission.

248 Harm.: © 1981, Abingdon Press (Administered By The Copyright Company, Nashville, TN) All Rights Reserved. International Copyright Secured. Used By Permission.

249 © 1974, Hope Publishing Company, Carol Stream, IL 60188. All rights reserved. Used by permission.

251 © 1998, Patrick D. Bradley. Arr.: © 2006, GIA Publications, Inc.

252 Arr.: © 2000, GIA Publications, Inc.

253 © 1966, renewed 1994, Manna Music, Inc./ASCAP (admin. by ClearBox Rights). All Rights Reserved. Used by Permission.

254 © 1985, Crouch Music Corp. (ASCAP), admin. by Music Services. All Rights Reserved. Used by Permission.

256 Arr.: © 2000, GIA Publications, Inc.

258 © 1939, E.M. Bartlett, renewed 1966 by Mrs. E.M. Bartlett. Assigned to Albert E. Brumley & Sons/SESAC (admin. by ClearBox Rights). All rights reserved. Used by permission.

262 © 1985, Mountain Spring Music (ASCAP)/Straightway Music (ASCAP), admin. at EMICMGPublishing.com. All Rights Reserved. Used by Permission.

263 Arr.: © 2000, GIA Publications, Inc.

264 Arr.: © 2000, GIA Publications, Inc.

265 © 1993, Malaco Music, Inc. International Copyright Secured. All Rights Reserved. Reprinted by permission of Hal Leonard Corporation.

266 Arr.: © 2000, GIA Publications, Inc.

268 © 1963, Hanna Street Music. All rights controlled by Gaither Copyright Management. Used by permission.

269 © 1933, Word Music, LLC, admin. by Warner/Chappell Music Services, Inc. All Rights Reserved. Used By Permission.

272 © 2004, Wheat Music (ASCAP)

273 Descant: © 2000, GIA Publications, Inc.

274 Arr.: © 2000, GIA Publications, Inc.

276 © 1971, Hanna Street Music. All rights controlled by Gaither Copyright Management. Used by permission.

281 © 1982, New Spring Publishing (ASCAP), admin. by Music Services. All Rights Reserved. Used by Permission.

282 © 1972, Hanna Street Music. All rights controlled by Gaither Copyright Management. Used by permission.

284 Text and tune: © 1989, Brenda Joyce Moore. Arr.: © 2000, GIA Publications, Inc.

285 © 1959, renewed 1987, Manna Music, Inc./ASCAP (admin. by ClearBox Rights). All Rights Reserved. Used by Permission.

286 Arr.: © 2000, GIA Publications, Inc.

287 Arr.: © 2000, GIA Publications, Inc.

288 © 1982, Bob Jay Music Co.

290 © 1981, Meadowgreen Music Co. (ASCAP), admin. at EMICMGPublishing.com. All Rights Reserved. Used by Permission.

291 Arr.: © 2000, GIA Publications, Inc.

293 Arr.: © 2000, GIA Publications, Inc.

296 Arr.: © 2000, GIA Publications, Inc.

297 © 1976, Latter Rain Music (ASCAP), admin. at EMICMGPublishing.com. All Rights Reserved. Used by Permission.

298 © 1970, Hanna Street Music. All rights controlled by Gaither Copyright Management. Used by permission.

300 © 1998, Victoria Woodard

301 © 1986, this Arr. © 2010, MPCA Lehsem Music, admin. by MPCA Music, LLC. International Copyright Secured. All Rights Reserved. Reprinted by permission of Hal Leonard Corporation.

302 Arr.: © 2000, GIA Publications, Inc.

304 © 1944, New Spring Publishing (ASCAP). A div. of Brentwood-Benson Music Publishing, Inc., admin. by Music Services. All Rights Reserved. Used by Permission.

305 Arr.: © 2000, GIA Publications, Inc.

306 Text: © 2004, Hope Publishing Company, Carol Stream, IL 60188. All rights reserved. Used by permission.

310 © Gale Jones Murphy

311 © Benson Music Group. A div. of Brentwood-Benson Music Publishing, Inc., admin. by Music Services. All Rights Reserved. Used by Permission.

312 Text and tune: © 1992, New Spring Publishing (ASCAP), admin. by Music Services. All Rights Reserved. Used by Permission. Arr.: © 2000, GIA Publications, Inc.

313 © Century Oak Publishing Group/Richwood Music (BMI), admin. by Conexion Media Group, Inc.

315 © 1935, Birdwing Music (ASCAP), admin. at EMICMGPublishing.com. All Rights Reserved. Used by Permission.

317 © 1962, renewed 1990, Manna Music, Inc./ASCAP (admin. by ClearBox Rights). All Rights Reserved. Used by Permission.

318 © 1979, Mercy/Vineyard Publishing (ASCAP), admin. in North America by Music Services o/b/o Vineyard Music USA

319 Arr.: © 2000, GIA Publications, Inc.

320 Text: © Timothy Wright. Arr.: © 2000, GIA Publications, Inc.

321 © 2004, worshiptogether.com Songs and sixsteps Music (ASCAP), admin. by EMI CMG Publishing; Alletrop Music (BMI), admin. by Music Services. All Rights Reserved. Used by Permission.

323 © 1972, Bud John Songs (ASCAP), admin. at EMICMGPublishing.com. All Rights Reserved. Used by Permission.

324 Arr.: © 2000, GIA Publications, Inc.

ACKNOWLEDGMENTS/continued

325 © 1972, Universal Music - Brentwood Benson Publishing (ASCAP) / CCCM Music (ASCAP). All rights for the world on behalf of CCCM Music admin. by Universal Music - Brentwood Benson Publishing, admin. by Music Services. All Rights Reserved. Used By Permission.

328 © 1991, Glenn Burleigh (Burleigh Inspirations Music)

329 © 1998, GIA Publications, Inc.

333 © God's Music, Inc.

334 Text: © 2009, GIA Publications, Inc.

335 Text and tune: © 1989, Glorraine Moone. Published by Professionals for Christ Publications (BMI). Adapt.: © 2000, GIA Publications, Inc.

336 Original words by K. L. Cober, © 1960, Kenneth L. Cober, renewed 1985, Judson Press. 1-800-4-JUDSON. www.judsonpress.com.

338 © 2004, this Arr. © 2010, Integrity's Praise! Music/BMI and Pace's Vision Music/BMI (admin. by Integrity's Praise! Music), c/o Integrity Media, Inc., 1000 Cody Road, Mobile, AL 36695 All Rights Reserved. International Copyright Secured. Used by Permission. Reprinted by permission of Hal Leonard Corporation.

341 Alt. text: © 1991, Reverend Pamela June Anderson, D.Min.

342 © 1998, StepKey Music

344 © 2007, Cecilia Olusola Tribble

345 Adapt.: © 2000, GIA Publications, Inc.

347 Arr.: © 2000, GIA Publications, Inc.

349 Arr.: © 2000, GIA Publications, Inc.

350 Text and tune: © 1995, Mo'Berries Music (ASCAP) / Y'Shua Publishing (ASCAP), distributed by the NOAH Company, P.O. Box 11243, Jackson, Mississippi 39283-1243; Arr.: © 2000, GIA Publications, Inc.

351 © 1995, MKR Music, 1421 Rogers Street, Richmond, VA 23223

352 Arr.: © 2000, GIA Publications, Inc.

353 Harm.: © 1986, GIA Publications, Inc.

354 Arr.: © 2000, GIA Publications, Inc.

356 © 1975, Bridgeport Music, Inc. Arr.: © 2006, GIA Publications, Inc.

358 Arr.: © 2000, GIA Publications, Inc.

362 © 1946, (renewed) Unichappell Music, Inc. This arr. © 2011, Unichappell Music, Inc. All Rights Reserved. Used by Permission of Alfred Publishing Co., Inc.

363 Arr.: © 2000, GIA Publications, Inc.

364 Arr.: © 1992, Carl Haywood

365 Tune: Arr. © 1999, Mar-Vel

366 Arr.: © 2000, GIA Publications, Inc.

367 © 1984, Bob Jay Music Co.

368 Text and tune: © S. Boddie. Arr.: © 2000, GIA Publications, Inc.

369 Tr. and Arr.: © 2008, Iona Community, GIA Publications, Inc., agent

370 © 1984, Rev. Earl Pleasant Publishing

371 © 1999, Norris Garner/BMI

372 © 2002, Damian D. Price and Price-n-Praise Publishing

373 © 1982, Bud John Songs (ASCAP), admin. at EMICMG-Publishing.com. All Rights Reserved. Used by Permission.

374 © 1926, 1953, Broadman Press

376 © 1937, Bridge Building Music (BMI), admin. by Music Services. All Rights Reserved. Used by Permission.

379 © 1980, Bridgeport Music, Inc.

380 Arr.: © 2000, GIA Publications, Inc.

383 Text: © 2008, James Anthony Plenty

385 Arr.: © 2000, GIA Publications, Inc.

387 Text and tune: © 1964, Lion Publishing Co. Arr.: © 2000, GIA Publications, Inc.

392 © 1984, Utryck, Walton Music Corp., agent

395 © 1989, Chenaniah Publications, Inc.

396 Arr.: © 2000, GIA Publications, Inc.

401 © 1963, New Spring Publishing (ASCAP), admin. by Music Services. All Rights Reserved. Used by Permission.

403 Text and tune: © 1975, Rev. Earl Pleasant Publishing, Arr.: © 2000, GIA Publications, Inc.

404 © 1940 (renewed), Warner-Tamerlane Publishing Corp. and Unichappell Music Inc. All Rights Reserved. Used by Permission of Alfred Publishing Co., Inc.

405 Arr.: © 2000, GIA Publications, Inc.

406 © 1939, Word Music, LLC, admin. by Warner/Chappell Music Services, Inc. All Rights Reserved. Used By Permission.

407 © 2004, Simply Cameron Publishing (BMI)

408 © 1990, Century Oak Publishing Group/Richwood Music (BMI), admin. by Conexion Media Group, Inc.

409 Arr.: © 1992, Carl Haywood

410 © 2006, Bridgeport Music, Inc. (BMI)

414 © 1965, renewed 1993, Manna Music, Inc./ASCAP (admin. by ClearBox Rights). All Rights Reserved. Used by Permission.

415 Text and tune: © Margaret Jenkins. Arr.: © 2000, GIA Publications, Inc.

416 © 1941, renewed 1968, Gospel Publishing House. Assigned 1997 to The Lorenz Corporation.

417 Arr.: © 2000, GIA Publications, Inc.

418 Text and tune: © 1978, 1984, by Malaco, Inc. d/b/a Savgos Music, Inc., International Copyright Secured. All rights Reserved. Reprinted by permission of Hal Leonard Corporation.

420 © 1950, New Spring Publishing (ASCAP), admin. by Music Services. All Rights Reserved. Used by Permission.

421 Arr.: © 2000, GIA Publications, Inc.

423 Arr.: © 2000, GIA Publications, Inc.

424 © Rev. Maceo Woods. Arr.: © 2000, GIA Publications, Inc. Administered by GIA Publications, Inc.

425 Harm.: © 1964, Abingdon Press (Administered By The Copyright Company, Nashville, TN) All Rights Reserved. International Copyright Secured. Used By Permission.

426 © 2006, Eddie A. Robinson

427 Arr.: © 2000, GIA Publications, Inc.

428 Text: ©, Charles A. Tindley and Donald Vails. Tune: ©, Donald Vails. Arr.: © 2000, GIA Publications, Inc.

432 Harm.: © 1992, Carl Haywood

433 Arr.: © 2000, GIA Publications, Inc.

435 Arr.: © 2000, GIA Publications, Inc.

437 © 1966, Frazier-Cleveland Co.

440 Text adapt. and arr.: © 1978, Mar-Vel.

445 © 1994, Betty Gadling. Administered by GIA Publications, Inc.

446 Arr.: © 2000, GIA Publications, Inc.

447 © 1953, 1981, Clara Ward. Assigned to Gertrude Music (SESAC). This is a new arrangement.

448 Harm.: © 1981, GIA Publications, Inc.

449 Arr.: © 2000, GIA Publications, Inc.

451 Arr.: © 2000, GIA Publications, Inc.

452 Text and tune: © 1980, Bridgeport Music, Inc. Arr.: © 2000, GIA Publications, Inc.

455 Arr.: © 2000, GIA Publications, Inc.

456 Text and tune: © 1974, Planemar Music Co. Arr.: © 2000, GIA Publications, Inc.

460 © 1959, Word Music, LLC, admin. by Warner/Chappell Music Services, Inc. All Rights Reserved. Used By Permission.

461 Arr.: © 2000, GIA Publications, Inc.

462 Arr.: © 2000, GIA Publications, Inc.

464 © 1994, 1997, GIA Publications, Inc.

465 © 1982, Full Armor Music and Whole Armor Music. Admin. by the Kruger Organization, Inc. International Copyright Secured. All rights reserved. Used by Permission.

467 Text and tune: © 1970, Rev. Earl Pleasant Publishing, Arr.: © 2000, GIA Publications, Inc.

470 Text: © 1991, GIA Publications, Inc.

472 © 1983, Shepherd's Fold Music (BMI)/River Oaks Music Co. (BMI), admin. at EMICMGPublishing.com. All Rights Reserved. Used by Permission.

473 © Gale Jones Murphy

474 © 1953 (renewed), Doris M. Akers All Rights Administered by Chappell & Co., Inc. This arr. © 2011, Doris M. Akers. All Rights Reserved. Used by Permission of Alfred Publishing Co., Inc.

ACKNOWLEDGMENTS/continued

478 © 1938 (renewed), Warner-Tamerlane Publishing Corp. All Rights Reserved. Used by Permission of Alfred Publishing Co., Inc.

479 © 2001, GIA Publications, Inc.

480 © 1994, Malaco Music, Inc. International Copyright Secured. All Rights Reserved. Reprinted by permission of Hal Leonard Corporation.

481 Arr.: © 1966, New Spring Publishing (ASCAP), admin. by Music Services. All Rights Reserved. Used by Permission.

483 Arr.: © 2000, GIA Publications, Inc.

486 Harm.: © 1981, Abingdon Press (Administered By The Copyright Company, Nashville, TN) All Rights Reserved. International Copyright Secured. Used By Permission.

488 Arr.: © 2000, GIA Publications, Inc.

489 Arr.: © 2000, GIA Publications, Inc.

490 Arr.: © 2000, GIA Publications, Inc.

491 Arr.: © 2000, GIA Publications, Inc.

493 © 1993, Lilly Mack Publishing, admin. at EMICMGPublishing.com. All Rights Reserved. Used by Permission.

494 Arr.: © 2000, GIA Publications, Inc.

495 © 1987, Hanna Street Music (all rights controlled by Gaither Copyright Management) and Century Oak/Richwood Music. All rights reserved. Used by permission.

496 Adapt.: © 2000, GIA Publications, Inc.

498 © 1994, Malaco Music, Inc. International Copyright Secured. All Rights Reserved. Reprinted by permission of Hal Leonard Corporation.

500 Text and tune: © 1963, Beatrice Brown's Music House. Arr.: © 2000, GIA Publications, Inc.

501 Arr.: © 2010, GIA Publications, Inc.

503 Text and tune: © 1989, Shirley M. K. Berkeley. Arr.: © 2000, GIA Publications, Inc.

504 Text and tune: © Dixon Music, Inc. Arr.: © 2000, GIA Publications, Inc.

505 Arr.: © 2000, GIA Publications, Inc.

506 Arr.: © 2000, GIA Publications, Inc.

507 © 1938 (renewed), Unichappell Music, Inc. All Rights Reserved. Used by Permission of Alfred Publishing Co., Inc.

509 Arr.: © 2000, GIA Publications, Inc.

510 Text: © 2006, GIA Publications, Inc.

511 © 1971, Lillenas Publishing Co., admin. Music Services. All Rights Reserved. International Copyright Secured. Used By Permission.

512 Text and tune: © 1939, Roberta Martin and Mrs. Georgia Jones. Arr.: © 2000, GIA Publications, Inc.

513 © 2002, Hidden Gems Press

514 Arr.: © 2000, GIA Publications, Inc.

515 Arr.: © 2000, GIA Publications, Inc.

516 Arr.: © 2000, GIA Publications, Inc.

517 Arr.: © 2000, GIA Publications, Inc.

518 Arr.: © 2000, GIA Publications, Inc.

519 © Hidden Gems Press

521 © Legré Publishing Co.

522 © 1984, Bernadette B. Salley. Administered by GIA Publications, Inc.

523 Text and tune: © Rev. Earl Pleasant Publishing, Arr.: © 2000, GIA Publications, Inc.

524 Text and tune: © 1970, New Song Music. Arr.: © 2000, GIA Publications, Inc.

525 Arr.: © 2000, GIA Publications, Inc.

526 © 1948 (renewed), Martin and Morris Studio, Inc. All Rights Administered by Unichappell Music, Inc. This arr. © 2011, Martin and Morris Studio, Inc. All Rights Reserved. Used by Permission of Alfred Publishing Co., Inc.

527 © 1984, New Spring Publishing (ASCAP), admin. by Music Services. All Rights Reserved. Used by Permission.

529 © 1940, New Spring Publishing (ASCAP), admin. by Music Services. All Rights Reserved. Used by Permission.

530 Arr.: © 2000, GIA Publications, Inc.

531 Arr.: © 2006, GIA Publications, Inc.

535 Arr.: © 1936 (renewed), Paul A. Schmitt Music Co. Copyright assigned to Belwin-Mills Publishing Corp. All Rights Controlled and Administered by Alfred Publishing Co., Inc. All Rights Reserved. Used by Permission of Alfred Publishing Co., Inc.

536 Arr.: © 2000, GIA Publications, Inc.

537 Arr.: © 2000, GIA Publications, Inc.

538 Arr.: © 2000, GIA Publications, Inc.

539 © Gale Jones Murphy

540 © 1981, Rev. Earl Pleasant Publishing Co. Arr.: © 2006, GIA Publications, Inc.

542 © 1962, Word Music, LLC, admin. by Warner/Chappell Music Services, Inc. All Rights Reserved. Used By Permission.

544 Arr.: © 2000, GIA Publications, Inc.

545 Text and Music © 1981, OCP, Published by OCP. 5536 NE Hassalo, Portland, OR 97213. All rights reserved. Used with permission.

548 Adapt.: © 2000, GIA Publications, Inc.

550 Arr.: © 2000, GIA Publications, Inc.

551 Arr.: © 2000, GIA Publications, Inc.

552 Arr.: © 1981, Mar-Vel

553 © 1976, Bridge Building Music, Inc. (BMI). A div. of Brentwood-Benson Music Publishing, Inc., admin. by Music Services. All Rights Reserved. Used by Permission.

554 Arr.: © 2000, GIA Publications, Inc.

555 Adapt.: © 2000, GIA Publications, Inc.

556 Text and tune: © KCL Music. Arr.: © 2000, GIA Publications, Inc.

557 Arr.: © 2000, GIA Publications, Inc.

559 © 1965 (renewed), Warner-Tamerlane Publishing Corp. This arr. © 2011, Warner-Tamerlane Publishing Corp. All Rights Reserved. Used by Permission of Alfred Publishing Co., Inc.

560 © 1985, Sanabella Music (ASCAP)/Bud John Songs (ASCAP), admin. at EMICMGPublishing.com. All Rights Reserved. Used by Permission.

561 © 1984, Utryck, Walton Music Corporation Sole Selling Agent. International Copyright Secured. All Rights Reserved.

563 Arr.: © 2000, GIA Publications, Inc.

564 © 1987, 1988, 1991, 2011, GIA Publications, Inc.

565 Arr.: © 2000, GIA Publications, Inc.

568 Text: © 2006, GIA Publications, Inc.

569 Harm.: © 1982, The Church of God in Christ Publishing Board. A div. of Brentwood-Benson Music Publishing, Inc., admin. by Music Services. All Rights Reserved. Used by Permission.

571 Text and tune: © 1981, Bridgeport Music, Inc. (BMI). Arr.: © 2011, GIA Publications, Inc.

573 Arr.: © 2000, GIA Publications, Inc.

574 © 1978, House of Mercy Music, admin. by Music Services. All Rights Reserved. International Copyright Secured. Used By Permission.

575 Refrain harm.: © 2011, GIA Publications, Inc.

576 © 1993, Lilly Mack Publishing, admin. at EMICMGPublishing.com. All Rights Reserved. Used by Permission.

577 © 1985, Chinwah Songs (SESAC)

579 Text: Stephen HurdTune: Stephen Hurd© Hurd the Word Music

580 © 2006, GIA Publications, Inc.

581 Arr.: © 2001, GIA Publications, Inc.

582 Arr.: © 1982, Bob Jay Music Co.

583 Arr.: © 2000, GIA Publications, Inc.

584 © 1932 in "Wonderful Message" by Hartford Music Co. Renewed 1960 by Albert E. Brumley & Sons/SESAC (admin. by ClearBox Rights). All rights reserved. Used by permission.

586 © 1983, 2003, GIA Publications, Inc. Arr.: © 2000, GIA Publications, Inc.

587 Arr.: © 2000, GIA Publications, Inc.

588 Arr.: © 2000, GIA Publications, Inc.

589 © 1980, New Spring Publishing (ASCAP), admin. by Music Services. All Rights Reserved. Used by Permission.

590 Arr.: © 2000, GIA Publications, Inc.

595 Arr.: © 2000, GIA Publications, Inc.

ACKNOWLEDGMENTS/continued

596 Arr.: © 2000, GIA Publications, Inc.
597 Arr.: © 2000, GIA Publications, Inc.
598 Arr.: © 2000, GIA Publications, Inc.
599 © 1923 (renewed), Unichappell Music Inc. This arr. © 2011, Unichappell Music, Inc. All Rights Reserved. Used by Permission of Alfred Publishing Co., Inc.
600 Arr.: © 2000, GIA Publications, Inc.
601 Arr.: © 1965, New Spring Publishing (ASCAP), admin. by Music Services. All Rights Reserved. Used by Permission.
604 Arr.: © 1992, Carl Haywood
610 Arr.: © 2000, GIA Publications, Inc.
612 © 1971, Multisongs (SESAC)/His Eye Music (SESAC)/Joy of the Lord Publishing, admin. at EMICMGPublishing.com. All Rights Reserved. Used by Permission.
613 Arr.: © 2000, GIA Publications, Inc.
615 Text and tune: © Geraldine Woods. Arr.: © 2000, GIA Publications, Inc.
618 Text: Adapt. © 1978, Mar-Vel. Tune: Arr. © 1978, Mar-Vel
619 Music: © 1982, Everett Williams, Jr., Johnny Jordan Co., Washington D.C., sole distributors
620 © 1995, MKR Music, 1421 Rogers Street, Richmond, VA 23223
621 Text and tune: © Warren Jones. Arr.: © 2000, GIA Publications, Inc.
623 Text: Adapt. © Mar-Vel. Tune: Arr. © Mar-Vel
624 © 1985, Crouch Music Corp. (ASCAP), admin. by Music Services. All Rights Reserved. Used by Permission.
625 Arr.: © 2000, GIA Publications, Inc.
626 Text and tune: © 1940 (renewed), Warner-Tamerlane Publishing Corp. This arr. © 2011, Warner-Tamerlane Publishing Corp. All Rights Reserved. Used by Permission of Alfred Publishing Co., Inc.
628 © 1981, arr. © 2011, Jenson Publications. International Copyright Secured. All Rights Reserved. Reprinted by permission of Hal Leonard Corporation.
629 © StepKey Music
630 © 1995, Roger Dean Publishing Co., a div. of The Lorenz Corporation.
631 Arr.: © 1990, Iona Community, GIA Publications, Inc., agent. Acc. © 1993, GIA Publications, Inc.
632 © Hidden Gems Press
633 © 1972, renewed 2000, Manna Music, Inc./ASCAP (admin. by ClearBox Rights). All Rights Reserved. Used by Permission.

634 Arr.: © 2000, GIA Publications, Inc.
636 Arr.: © 2000, GIA Publications, Inc.
637 Arr.: © 1968, Roberta Martin
642 Music: © 2004, Tehillah International Ministries
644 Arr.: © 1987, Bernadette B. Salley. Administered by GIA Publications, Inc.
646 Adapt.: © 1985, 1989, GIA Publications, Inc.
647 Tune: © 1935, (renewed) G. Schirmer, Inc.; arr. © 2000, G. Schirmer, Inc. (BMI) International Copyright Secured. All Rights Reserved.
648 Arr. © 2000, GIA Publications, Inc.
649 Adapt.: © 2000, GIA Publications, Inc.
650 Trans.: © 1990, Iona Community, GIA Publications, Inc., agent
652 © 1957, 1985, Manna Music, Inc./ASCAP (admin. by ClearBox Rights). All Rights Reserved. Used by Permission.
653 © 2006, Tehillah International Ministries
655 Text: © 1982, The Jubilate Group (Admin. Hope Publishing Company, Carol Stream, IL 60188). All rights reserved. Used by permission. Acc.: © 1999, GIA Publications, Inc.
656 Arr.: © 2000, GIA Publications, Inc.
657 Arr.: © 2000, GIA Publications, Inc.
658 Arr.: © 2000, GIA Publications, Inc.
659 Arr.: © 2000, GIA Publications, Inc.
660 © 1954, First Church of Deliverance
661 Text: © 1989, The United Methodist Publishing House. (Administered by The Copyright Company, Nashville, TN) All Rights Reserved. International Copyright Secured. Used By Permission. Harm.: © 1978, LUTHERAN BOOK OF WORSHIP. Reprinted by permission of Augsburg Fortress.
662 © 1995, 1997, GIA Publications, Inc.
663 © 2001, GIA Publications, Inc.
664 © 2000, Tehillah International Ministries
665 Text.: © 2006, GIA Publications, Inc.
666 © 1980, Dangerfield Music Co.
667 © 1988, Maranatha Praise, Inc., admin. by Music Services. All Rights reserved. International Copyright Secured. Used by Permission.
669 Arr.: © 2000, GIA Publications, Inc.

Alfred Music Publishing
P.O. Box 10003
Van Nuys, CA 91410-0003
Ph: (818) 891-5999
Fax: (818) 891-4875
www.alfred.com

Arrand Publishing Co.
sarahcatlett@hotmail.com
(248) 398-4061

Augsburg Fortress Publishers
100 S. Fifth Street, Suite 600
Minneapolis, MN 55402
(800) 421-0239
(800) 426-0115
www.augsburgfortress.org

Bob Jay Music Co.
P.O. Box 515
Lincolnton Station
New York, NY 10037-0515
(212) 283-4980

Patrick D. Bradley
dion_27@hotmail.com
Fax: (972) 436-7668

Bridgeport Music, Inc.
18500 W. 10 Mile Rd.
Southfield, MI 48075-2662
(248) 398-4061

Hezekiah Brinson Jr.
c/o Nineveh Baptist Church
1009 Wilker Neal Avenue
Metairie, LA 70003
Ph: (504) 464-9610
Fax: (504) 712-0830

Broadman Press
127 9th Ave.
North Nashville, TN 37234

Burleigh Inspirations Music
5244 Parkview Dr.
Haltom City, TX 76148

Chenaniah Publications, Inc.
Eli Wilson Ministries, Inc.
P.O. Box 680712
Orlando, FL 32868-0712
www.eliwilson.com

Chinwah Songs
10220 Glade
Chatsworth, CA 91311
Ph: (818) 341-2264
Fax: (818) 341-1008

ClearBox Rights, LLC
P.O. Box 1547
Brentwood, TN 37024
Ph: (615) 630-7500
Fax: (615) 630-7501
license@clearboxrights.com
www.clearboxrights.com

Conexion Media Group, Inc.
1301 16th Ave.
South Nashville, TN 37212
Ph: (615) 250-4602
Fax: (615) 691-7140
janices@conexion-media.com

Dangerfield Music Co.
286 Strawberry Hill Rd.
Centerville, MA 02632

Jessy Dixon
c/o Dixon Music, Inc.
P.O. Box 336
Crete, IL 60417
(708) 672-8682

EMI Christian Music Publishing
EMICMGPublishing.com
Ph: (615) 371-4300
Ph: (615) 371-6897

First Church of Deliverance
4301 S. Wabash Ave.
Chicago, IL 60653-3198
Ph: (773) 373-7700
Fax: (773) 451-2663
admin@firstchurchofdeliverance.org

Fred Bock Music Company
P.O. Box 570567
Tarzana, CA 91357
Ph: (818) 996-6181
Fax: (818) 996-2043
www.fredbock.com

Fricon Entertainment Company
134 Bluegrass Circle
Hendersonville, TN 37075
Ph: (615) 826-2288
Fax: (615) 826-0500
fricon@comcast.net

G. Schirmer, Inc.
257 Park Ave. South
New York, NY 10010
Ph: (212) 254-2100
Fax: (212) 254-2013
schirmer@schirmer.com
www.schirmer.com

Gaither Copyright Management
1703 S. Park Ave.
Alexandria, IN 46001
Ph: (765) 724-8233
Fax: (765) 724-8290

Gertrude Music
10220 Glade Ave.
Chatsworth, CA 91311
Ph: (818) 341-2264
Fax: (818) 341-1008

God's Music, Inc.
6 Gramatan Ave. – 5th Floor
Mount Vernon, NY 10550
Ph: (914) 663-9122
Fax: (914) 668-4721
gmjlaw@verizon.net

Hal Leonard Corporation
7777 W. Bluemound Rd.
Milwaukee, WI 53213
Ph: (414) 774-3630
Fax: (414) 774-3259

Dr. Carl Haywood
CWHaywood@nsu.edu
(757) 573-7477

Hidden Gems Music
13329 Hummingbird Lane
Apple Valley, MN 55124
rlmorris@frontiernet.net
(952) 997-4343

Hope Publishing Company
380 S. Main Place
Carol Stream, IL 60188
Ph: (630) 665-3200
Ph: (800) 323-1049
Fax: 630-665-2552
www.hopepublishing.com

Hurd the Word Music
info@hurdthewordmusic.com

Joy Publishing Co.
P.O. Box 26854
Indianapolis, IN 46226-0854
(317) 335-5640

Judson Press
P.O. Box 851
Valley Forge, PA 19482-0851
permissions@judsonpress.com

ADDRESSES OF COPYRIGHT HOLDERS/continued

Kenneth W. Louis
c/o Holy Comforter/St. Cyprian
 Church
1357 E. Capitol Street SW
Washington, DC 20003
Ph: (202) 546-1885 x815
Fax: (202) 544-1385

Mar-Vel Music Co.
P.O. Box 6082
Chattanooga, TN 37401
(423) 266-7728

MKR Music
1421 Rogers St.
Richmond, VA 23223

Brenda Joyce Moore
15241 Chicago Rd., Apt. 2A
Dolton, IL 60419
(773) 785-5483

Gale Jones Murphy
galejones.murphy@gmail.com

Music Services
5409 Maryland Way, #200
Brentwood, TN 37027
(615) 371-1320
www.musicservices.org

Oregon Catholic Press (OCP)
P.O. Box 18030
Portland, OR 97218-0030
Ph: (503) 281-1191
Ph: (800) 548-8749
Fax: (503) 282-3486

Damian D. Price and Price-n-Praise
 Publishing
damiandprice@yahoo.com

Rev. Earl Pleasant Publishing
P.O. Box 3247
Thousand Oaks, CA 91359
Gospelmeg@aol.com

Eddie A. Robinson
earob01@aol.com

Simply Cameron Publishing
Roderick Vester
980 Nesting Wood Cir. W
Cordova, TN 38018-0433

StepKey Music
Stephen F. Key
skmuzic@yahoo.com

Tehillah International Ministries
Glenn L. Jones
4116 Hollister Ln.
Perrysburg, OH 43551-7237

The Copyright Company
P.O. Box 128139
Nashville, TN 37212-8139
Ph: (615) 244-9848
Fax: (615) 244-9850
www.thecopyrightco.com

The Lorenz Corporation
501 East Third St.
Dayton, OH 45402-2280
Ph: (937) 228-6118
Fax: (937) 223-2042
info@lorenz.com

Total Praise Music Publishing
PO Box 93031
Cleveland, OH 44101
(216) 253-5250
godsinger04@yahoo.com

Cecilia Olusola Tribble
ceciliaolusola.tribble@gmail.com

Trust Music Management
P.O. Box 22274
Carmel, CA 93922
Ph: (831) 626-1030
Fax: (831) 626-1026

Walton Music Corporation
935 Broad St., #31D
Bloomfield, NJ 07003
Ph: (973) 743-6444
Fax: (206) 426-6782
kathleenkarcher@hotmail.com

Warner/Chappell Music
20 Music Square
East Nashville, TN 37203

Victoria Woodard
(501) 553-3030
melodiou2003@yahoo.com
FELICIA@vickiewoodard.com

Word Music Group, LLC
20 Music Square
East Nashville, TN 37203

World Library Publications (WLP)
3708 River Road, Ste. 400
Franklin Park, IL 60131
Ph: (800) 621-5197
Fax: (888) 957-3291
www.wlpmusic.com

SCRIPTURE PASSAGES RELATED TO HYMNS   672

Scripture Passages Related to Hymns/continued

Scripture Passages Related to Hymns/continued

SCRIPTURE PASSAGES RELATED TO HYMNS/continued

SCRIPTURE PASSAGES RELATED TO HYMNS/continued

673 RESPONSIVE READING INDEX

RESPONSIVE READING INDEX/continued

RESPONSIVE READING INDEX/continued

TOPICAL INDEX/continued

372 He's So Freely Passing Out Blessings
108 I Will Bless the Lord
181 I Was Glad
524 I Will Bless Thee, O Lord
507 I'll Tell It Wherever I Go
569 My Soul Loves Jesus
637 Praise God from Whom All Blessings Flow
567 Showers of Blessing
426 Somebody Here Needs a Blessing
656 Take Me to the Water
622 The Lord Bless You/Sevenfold Amen
501 The Lord Is Blessing Me Right Now
602 The Sweet By and By
661 Wash, O God, Our Sons and Daughters

BLOOD (See JESUS CHRIST— BLOOD)

BROTHERHOOD AND WORLD PEACE
607 America the Beautiful
337 Blest Be the Tie that Binds
399 In Christ There Is No East or West
400 In Christ There Is No East or West
153 Old Time Religion
498 Somebody Prayed for Me
511 The Bond of Love
451 This Day

BURDENS
119 A Mighty Fortress Is Our God
455 Abide with Me
387 All My Help Comes from the Lord
475 All the Way My Savior Leads Me
264 Amazing Grace
261 At the Cross
121 Be Still, God Will Fight Your Battles
131 Be Still, My Soul
240 Beneath the Cross of Jesus
337 Blest Be the Tie that Binds
362 Christ Is All
369 Come, Bring Your Burdens to God/ Woza Nomthwalo Wakho
309 Come, Holy Spirit, Heavenly Dove
438 Come, Ye Disconsolate
525 Count Your Blessings
327 Deeper, Deeper
431 Does Jesus Care?
351 Give Your Life to Christ
505 Glory, Glory, Hallelujah
627 God Be with You Till We Meet Again
126 God Is
160 God Is Here
151 God Never Fails
138 God Will Take Care of You
439 Have Thine Own Way, Lord
268 He Touched Me
509 He's Sweet I Know
124 His Eye Is on the Sparrow
308 Holy Ghost, with Light Divine
122 How Firm a Foundation
420 I Know Who Holds Tomorrow
408 I Love the Lord, He Heard My Cry
381 I Must Tell Jesus
259 I See a Crimson Stream
554 I Want Jesus to Walk with Me
360 I Will Arise
507 I'll Tell It Wherever I Go
229 I'm So Glad
409 I've Been 'Buked
305 I've Got a Feelin'
542 If Jesus Goes with Me
157 In the Presence of Jehovah
382 It Is Well with My Soul
517 It's Alright
222 Jesus Is a Rock in a Weary Land

389 Jesus Is All the World to Me
348 Jesus Is Calling
446 Jesus, Lover of My Soul
331 Jesus Loves Me
450 Jesus, Savior, Pilot Me
479 Jesus, You Brought Me All the Way
442 Just a Closer Walk with Thee
376 Just a Little Talk with Jesus
345 Just as I Am
346 Just as I Am
368 Just Let Him In
390 Just When I Need Him
453 Keep Me Every Day
474 Lead Me, Guide Me
427 Leave It There
532 Lift Every Voice and Sing
125 My Heavenly Father Watches over Me
302 Never Alone
365 New Born Again
303 No, Not One
394 Nothing Between
202 O Holy Night
283 O How I Love Jesus
242 O Sacred Head, Now Wounded
537 Oh, Freedom
462 Oh, Lord, Have Mercy
437 Oh, to Be Kept by Jesus
145 Oh, What He's Done for Me
163 Over My Head
472 People Need the Lord
109 Praise Him in Advance
171 Praise Him! Praise Him!
478 Precious Lord, Take My Hand
512 Precious Memories
374 Satisfied with Jesus
516 Shine on Me
426 Somebody Here Needs a Blessing
494 Something Within
190 Soon and Very Soon
458 Standin' in the Need of Prayer
463 Sweet Hour of Prayer
430 The Beautiful Garden of Prayer
253 The Blood Will Never Lose Its Power
334 The Church of Christ Cannot Be Bound
375 The Lily of the Valley
152 The Lord Is My Light
434 The Lord Is My Shepherd
377 The Solid Rock
428 The Storm Is Passing Over
260 There Is Power in the Blood
415 There's a Bright Side Somewhere
267 Think of His Goodness to You
100 Total Praise
384 Trust and Obey
306 Unbounded Spirit, Breath of God
447 Until I Found the Lord
258 Victory in Jesus
538 We Shall Overcome
417 We'll Understand It Better By and By
414 We've Come This Far by Faith
246 Were You There
435 What a Friend We Have in Jesus
436 What a Friend We Have in Jesus
178 When Morning Gilds the Skies
593 Where We'll Never Grow Old
158 Yes, God Is Real
265 Your Grace and Mercy

CALLS TO WORSHIP
620 A Glorious Introit
580 Dwell in the House
618 Let the Heaven Light Shine on Me
621 Lord, You Are Welcome
617 The Lord Is in His Holy Temple
619 This Is the Day

CARE AND GUIDANCE (see GOD-CARE AND GUIDANCE)

CHALLENGE (See also LOYALTY AND COURAGE; WARFARE, CHRISTIAN)
196 Are You Ready?
276 Because He Lives
541 Get Right with God
538 We Shall Overcome

CHILDHOOD
413 Faith of Our Mothers
614 Jesus Loves the Little Children
609 Praise Him, All Ye Little Children
200 Star-Child
581 Will the Circle Be Unbroken

CHILDREN OF GOD
118 A Child of the King
128 God Leads Us Along
137 Guide My Feet
323 Holy, Holy
488 I Am on the Battlefield for My Lord
331 Jesus Loves Me
462 Oh, Lord, Have Mercy
171 Praise Him! Praise Him!
429 Savior, like a Shepherd Lead Us
600 The Uncloudy Day
536 Walk Together, Children
661 Wash, O God, Our Sons and Daughters

CHILDREN'S HYMNS
156 All around Me
203 Away in a Manger
204 Away in a Manger
610 Children, Go Where I Send Thee
613 Higher, Higher
616 I've Got the Joy, Joy, Joy
614 Jesus Loves the Little Children
611 Jesus Wants Me for a Sunbeam
615 My Help Cometh from the Lord
609 Praise Him, All Ye Little Children
612 The Joy of the Lord
550 This Little Light of Mine

CHORUSES
495 Center of My Joy
515 Come On in My Room
126 God Is
148 God Is a Good God
313 Holy Spirit
504 I Am Redeemed
571 I Really Love the Lord
500 Jesus Is Real to Me
553 Learning to Lean
456 Lord, Help Me to Hold Out
254 Oh, It Is Jesus
227 One Day
472 People Need the Lord
296 Psalm 8: O Lord, How Excellent
529 Thank You, Lord
415 There's a Bright Side Somewhere
483 We Are Soldiers
265 Your Grace and Mercy

CHRISTMAS
207 Angels We Have Heard on High
209 Angels, from the Realms of Glory
203 Away in a Manger
204 Away in a Manger
214 Go Tell It on the Mountain
206 Hark! The Herald Angels Sing
198 He's Here
205 Heaven's Christmas Tree
213 It Came upon the Midnight Clear
188 Jesus Came
208 Joy to the World
201 O Come, All Ye Faithful

TOPICAL INDEX/continued

TOPICAL INDEX/continued

TOPICAL INDEX/continued

TOPICAL INDEX/continued

TOPICAL INDEX/continued

TOPICAL INDEX/continued

TOPICAL INDEX/continued

675 Index of Composers, Authors, and Sources

INDEX OF COMPOSERS, AUTHORS, AND SOURCES/continued

Index of Composers, Authors, and Sources/continued

INDEX OF COMPOSERS, AUTHORS, AND SOURCES/continued

Index of Composers, Authors, and Sources/continued

INDEX OF COMPOSERS, AUTHORS, AND SOURCES/continued

676 Metrical Index of Tunes

SM (SHORT METER - 6 6 8 6)
468 BOYLSTON
337 DENNIS
314 TRENTHAM

SMD (SHORT METER DOUBLED)
279 DIADEMATA
140 TERRA BEATA

CM (COMMON METER - 8 6 8 6)
208 ANTIOCH
484 ARLINGTON
168 AZMON
562 MAITLAND
129 255 MARTYRDOM
334 400 MCKEE
264 586 NEW BRITAIN
164 ST. ANNE
309 ST. MARTIN'S
399 ST. PETER

CM WITH REFRAIN
250 DUNCANNON
138 GOD CARES
283 HOW I LOVE JESUS
261 HUDSON
411 LANDÅS
378 ONLY TRUST HIM
516 SHINE ON ME
601 STORMY BANKS
611 SUNBEAM
592 WEAR A CROWN

CMD (COMMON METER DOUBLE)
213 CAROL
607 MATERNA

LM (LONG METER - 8 8 8 8)
271 278 DUKE STREET
654 ERNAN
236 HAMBURG
223 638 OLD HUNDREDTH
306 ROCKINGHAM
346 WOODWORTH

LM WITH REFRAIN
218 BEHOLD THE STAR
295 BLESSED NAME
245 CALVARY
359 HAPPY DAY
139 HE LEADETH ME
422 HIGHER GROUND
262 LAMB OF GOD
103 NAZREY
377 SOLID ROCK
549 SWENEY
535 SWING LOW
189 VENI EMMANUEL

66 4 666 4
322 ITALIAN HYMN
457 OLIVET

66 9 D WITH REFRAIN
593 NEVER GROW OLD
396 YOUR ALL
384 TRUST AND OBEY

7 6 7 6 WITH REFRAIN
514 BALM IN GILEAD
259 CRIMSON STREAM
461 FIX ME
214 GO TELL IT ON THE MOUNTAIN
248 NEAR THE CROSS

7 6 7 6 D
340 AURELIA
481 LANCASHIRE
242 PASSION CHORALE
185 SHEFFIELD

225 ST. THEODULPH
482 WEBB

7 7 7 7 D
443 IN ME
446 MARTYN

7 7 7 7 WITH REFRAIN
207 GLORIA
216 WE'LL WALK IN THE LIGHT

77 77 77
543 TOPLADY
450 PILOT

77 77 WITH REFRAIN
331 CHINA
477 LEAD ME

8 5 8 5 WITH REFRAIN
533 GO DOWN MOSES
454 PASS ME NOT

8 7 8 7 D
475 ALL THE WAY
435 ANNIE LOWERY
661 BEACH SPRING
429 BRADBURY
436 CONVERSE
155 665 HOLY MANNA
444 668 HYFRYDOL
107 568 HYMN TO JOY
182 NETTLETON

8 7 8 7 D WITH REFRAIN
469 BARNARD
420 TOMORROW

8 7 8 7 WITH REFRAIN
385 BLESSED QUIETNESS
551 552 CLOSE TO THEE
215 GREENSLEEVES
590 HEAVEN
512 PRECIOUS MEMORIES
299 PRECIOUS NAME
360 RESTORATION
374 ROUTH
567 SHOWERS OF BLESSING
316 SPIRIT HOLY
402 SURRENDER
383 391 TRUST IN JESUS
581 UNBROKEN CIRCLE
421 UNCHANGING HAND

888 6 WITH REFRAIN
231 HE LIFTED ME
345 JUST AS I AM
603 SOON-A WILL BE DONE

10 10 10 10
455 EVENTIDE
307 MORECAMBE
605 NATIONAL HYMN
494 SOMETHING WITHIN

10 10 WITH REFRAIN
249 CRUCIFER
246 WERE YOU THERE

10 8 10 8 WITH REFRAIN
594 IN THE GLORYLAND
433 WHERE COULD I GO

10 9 10 9 WITH REFRAIN
430 BEAUTIFUL GARDEN
388 FARTHER ALONG
394 NOTHING BETWEEN
381 ORWIGSBURG
380 SHOWALTER

METRICAL INDEX OF TUNES/continued

ONE OF A KIND

METRICAL INDEX OF TUNES/continued

METRICAL INDEX OF TUNES/continued

Metrical Index of Tunes/_{continued}

11 7 11 7 WITH REFRAIN
355   THOMPSON

11 8 11 7 WITH REFRAIN
585   THE CROWN

11 8 11 8
425   DAVIS

11 8 9 10 WITH REFRAIN
460   FILL MY CUP

11 10 11 10 D
247   LONDONDERRY AIRE

11 10 11 10 WITH REFRAIN
154   FAITHFULNESS

11 11 WITH REFRAIN
566   REVIVE US AGAIN

11 11 11 7
163   OVER MY HEAD

11 11 11 9 WITH REFRAIN
386   PROMISES

11 11 11 10 WITH REFRAIN
406   I'D RATHER HAVE JESUS

11 11 11 11 11
434   POLAND

11 11 12 11 WITH REFRAIN
349   I AM PRAYING FOR YOU

11 11 15 10 WIH REFRAIN
589   WE SHALL BEHOLD HIM

11 12 12 10
324   NICAEA

12 10 12 10 11 10 WITH REFRAIN
171   JOYFUL SONG

12 10 12 10 WITH REFRAIN
600   UNCLOUDY DAY

12 11 12 11
343   KREMSER

12 12 WITH REFRAIN
660   TIS DONE

12 12 9 9
326   STORIES OF JESUS

12 12 10 8 WITH REFRAIN
416   IT'S IN MY HEART

12 12 12 WITH HALLELUJAHS
544   WITH MY MIND

12 12 12 6
506   DONE SO MUCH

12 12 12 9
550   LIGHT OF MINE

12 12 12 14
190   SOON AND VERY SOON

13 13 13 8 WITH REFRAIN
547   COUNT ON ME

13 13 13 11 WITH REFRAIN
269   ACKLEY

13 13 14 11 WITH REFRAIN
362   CHRIST IS ALL

13 7 13 7 WITH REFRAIN
458   STANDIN' IN THE NEED

14 11 14 11 WITH REFRAIN
427   LEAVE IT THERE

14 14 47 8
117   LOBE DEN HERREN

14 14 12 12 WITH REFRAIN
597   FARE YE WELL

15 11 15 11 WITH REFRAIN
193   ROLL CALL

15 15
505   GLORY

15 15 15 6 WITH REFRAIN
485   BATTLE HYMN OF THE REPUBLIC

15 15 15 14 WITH REFRAIN
258   HARTFORD

15 15 15 15 WITH REFRAIN
419   IT'S REAL

16 16 18 6
167   WORSHIP HIM

TUNE INDEX/continued

INDEX OF FIRST LINES AND COMMON TITLES 678

Index of First Lines and Common Titles/continued

INDEXES

Index of First Lines and Common Titles/continued

555 How to Reach the Masses
563 Hush, Hush, Somebody's Callin' My Name
370 I Am All I Am
518 I Am Healed by the Wound
488 I Am on the Battlefield for My Lord
349 I Am Praying for You
504 I Am Redeemed
374 I Am Satisfied with Jesus
397 I Am Thine
442 I Am Weak but Thou Art Strong
599 I Bowed on My Knees
586 I Call You to My Father's House
379 I Can Do All Things through Christ
546 I Can Hear My Savior Calling
492 I Come to the Garden Alone
572 I Do; Don't You?
418 I Don't Feel No Ways Tired
420 I Don't Know about Tomorrow
362 I Don't Possess Houses or Lands
599 I Dreamed of a City Called Glory
301 I Feel Jesus in This Place
365 I Found Free Grace
235 I Gave My Life for Thee
596 I Got a Crown up in-a That Kingdom
349 I Have a Savior
401 I Have Decided to Follow Jesus
375 I Have Found a Friend in Jesus
593 I Have Heard of a Land
205 I Have Heard of a Tree
361 I Hear the Savior Say
258 I Heard an Old, Old Story
557 I Heard My Mother Say
516 I Heard the Voice of Jesus Say
166 I Just Want to Praise You
572 I Know a Great Savior
252 I Know It Was the Blood
271 I Know That My Redeemer Lives
366 I Know the Lord Has Laid His Hands on Me
420 I Know Who Holds Tomorrow
228 I Love Him
408 I Love the Lord, He Heard My Cry
497 I Love to Tell the Story
574 I Love You, Lord
577 I Love You, Lord, Today
381 I Must Tell Jesus
441 I Need Thee Every Hour
333 I Need You to Survive
376 I Once Was Lost in Sin
571 I Really Love the Lord
259 I See a Crimson Stream
269 I Serve a Risen Savior
402 I Surrender All
526 I Thank You, Jesus
545 I, the Lord of Sea and Sky
125 I Trust in God Wherever I May Be
598 I Wanna Be Ready
554 I Want Jesus to Walk with Me
181 I Was Glad

502 I Was Sinking Deep in Sin
360 I Will Arise
108 I Will Bless the Lord
524 I Will Bless Thee, O Lord
110 I Will Call upon the Lord
565 I Will Do a New Thing
615 I Will Look to the Hills
405 I Will Trust in the Lord
406 I'd Rather Have Jesus
548 I'll Be Somewhere Listening for My Name
584 I'll Fly Away
507 I'll Tell It Wherever I Go
507 I'll Tell of the Savior
398 I'm Going Through, Jesus
422 I'm Pressing on the Upward Way
229 I'm So Glad
594 I've a Home Prepared Where the Saints Abide
508 I've a Message From the Lord
409 I've Been 'Buked
393 I've Decided to Make Jesus My Choice
305 I've Got a Feelin'
582 I've Got a New Name over in Glory
616 I've Got the Joy, Joy, Joy
109 I've Had My Share of Ups and Downs
302 I've Seen the Lightning Flashing
357 If I Have Wounded Any Soul Today
542 If Jesus Goes with Me
427 If the World from You Withhold
423 If When You Give the Best of Your Service
358 If You Live Right
399 In Christ There Is No East or West
400 In Christ There Is No East or West
231 In Loving Kindness Jesus Came
443 In Me
165 In My Life, Lord, Be Glorified
128 In Shady, Green Pastures
597 In That Great Gittin' Up Mornin'
111 In the Beauty of Holiness
492 In the Garden
287 In the Name of Jesus
157 In the Presence of Jehovah
104 In the Sanctuary
300 In This Praise I Offer to You
304 In Times like These
329 Is There a Word from the Lord?
573 Is There Anybody Here Who Loves My Jesus
396 Is Your All on the Altar
645 Isaiah 6:3
213 It Came upon the Midnight Clear
382 It Is Well with My Soul
542 It May Be in the Valley
404 It's a Highway to Heaven
517 It's Alright
416 It's in My Heart
419 It's Real
173 Jesus

INDEX OF FIRST LINES AND COMMON TITLES/continued

INDEX OF FIRST LINES AND COMMON TITLES/continued

INDEX OF FIRST LINES AND COMMON TITLES/continued

INDEX OF FIRST LINES AND COMMON TITLES/continued